FINAL NOTICE

by

BARRY R. SMITH

© Copyright — Barry Smith

Published by Barry Smith Family Evangelism
ISBN 0-908961-02-2

Dennis & Becky Capell with children
Gemma Lee (left) & Saskia

Barry & May Smith

John & Rachel Koutsimanis with
children (from the left) Andrew James,
Stephanie & Christina

Debbie Smith

Andrew & Saskia Smith with children
Daniel and Anneke

CONTENTS

*The information listed on pages 117-119 is published as a result of the investigations of The London Times, Dr. Douglas and Dr. Strecker. This Author cannot, and does not, attempt to favour any of these opinions. What is clear is that AIDS was created by man, probably with population control in mind.

SPECIAL TRIBUTES

Brother Ern. Edwards, a tireless worker amongst the Maori folk; particularly in the Waikato, New Zealand. He taught me the Jesus' way of telling a story, and holding peoples' attention. He also taught me the laid-back Polynesian lifestyle. He taught me my first Samoan words. I now preach in that language. Thousands of souls who have come to Christ through this ministry will not know him, yet will meet him one day, beyond the river.

Brother Fred Mercer, a man of God. Hour after hour, whilst travelling around the shores of Lake Taupo on our way to preach to the prison populations, he taught me the ways and dealings of the Lord.

Brother Maurice Luce, who spent many hours praying with me whilst in Western Samoa. Through his lovely life, I am inspired to try harder 'to be like Jesus'.

Brother Makisua Fatialofa. The man whom God used to lead the revival in Western Samoa. Along with his wife Mau, examples of selflessness, they missed many meals. They fasted, they prayed, they wept, they loved. May and I are proud to call them our dear friends.

After winning over 10,000 souls, the Lord called him home. He still speaks however, as in my meetings, I use his bold, forthright, open invitation to make a public stand for Christ.

AS THESE OLDER MEN WERE LIGHTS IN MY YOUNG LIFE, MAY I BE A LIGHT TO OTHER YOUNG PEOPLE.

'As for me and my house, we will serve the Lord.'

ACKNOWLEDGEMENTS

May, my dear wife who has stood with me through life and on occasions in close brushes with death. Her love and encouragement has helped me to carry on, when occasionally I weep with fatigue and want to stop travelling.

She is also a lovely mother and together we have brought up our four children in the ways of the Lord. As a hostess she is unsurpassed and definitely given to hospitality.

Our children, Dennie and Becky Capell and their family. Dennie, who like a real son, repairs my vehicles often and still smiles. Becky, who typed this manuscript over and over for month after month, until we got it 'right'. Thank you to you both. May and I bless you all.

Our children, Johnie and Rachel Koutsimanis and their family. Johnie, my Greek-born son who helps me with the Greek language translations and other matters. Rachel, our second daughter, who like her mother before her, is a great homemaker, given to hospitality. We love you both along with your little family.

Andrew and Saskia Smith and children.
Andy, my manager son who helps with the other family members to take the burden off Dad. He is a chip off the old block. Saskia, our Dutch born daughter, a great little wife and mother who adapts well to the unusual Smith lifestyle. We love you and thank the Lord for your family.

Deborah Smith, our youngest daughter. She is faithful in her office work, and spends much time sending out our book orders. A Martha-type who works on cleaning up when others have gone to bed and one who looks out for the unloved. She has the Jesus' spirit. We love you Deb.

Susan McGregor, who has become part of our extended family (daughter of our old friends Don and Aileen McGregor.) Special thanks for spending valuable time typing some of the manuscript for this very comprehensive volume.

Our Australian agents and friends, Urs and Kathy Leimgruber and family. For all your loving help and input over the years. Your prayers and faithful support has made our task so much easier — Thank you.

Bob and Ann Brown and family. Our close friends and advisors in Sydney, Australia. You've saved us much heartache with your warm concern and wise counsel.

To Chris and Libby Murphy, our U.K. agents, living on the Isle of Wight. Your enthusiasm for the Lord and His work has endeared you to us. Our grateful thanks to you and yours.

Our U. S. agents Stan Ball and Andy Seirp who run a great office in New Mexico. Two dedicated brothers in the Lord whom we love and thank for their combined dedication.

Mr Peter Woolley of 'Peter Woolley Graphics', Christchurch — for your generous assistance in the production of the art work for this book. Christian greetings.

To the artist, Tony Bond. We marvel at your God-given talent. Your work through this book will travel all over the world. Grateful thanks for your unlimited patience with us, and also for the excellent pictures in this book.

Paul Jones — a young Christian friend who spent hours assisting me with corrections of this manuscript — Thank you Paul.

To James and Christine Bigbee, of Inner Faith Travel, Gold Coast, our love and thanks for taking us to Israel and to your homes in New Mexico and Queensland on many occasions. Great friends indeed.

We dedicate this book therefore, TO THE GREATER GLORY OF GOD.

Footnote.
This book was started on the deck of the inter-island Ferry *Aratika*, on a crossing from the North to the South Island of New Zealand in September 1987.

The book was completed at an altitude of 8,400 feet in a little log cabin situated in the Sangre de Cristo Mountains (the Blood of Christ Mountains), Eagle Nest, New Mexico, U.S.A. in June 1989.

RECAP OF CHAPTERS

Introduction

1. Update 1989.
Noah's Ark found — 666 has arrived — A challenge.

2. Black Monday and Tuesday.
October crash — Where the big crash will start — Japan — Maruyu under threat — 5 day week — The Fed. — Seal on U.S. dollar bill.

3. The Plot Thickens.
N.Z. — Australia links — G7 — I.M.F. — The Fed. — Undermining of nations' sovereignty — Loans equity swap — Corporatisation — Privatisation — Bedfellows — World Govt groups — 10 world regions — Eye on church wall — Chain of suggestion.

4. Global 2000.
Babel — 5 global problems — New Age influence — N.Z. 1990 — Mystery of iniquity — Peace treaty in the M.E. — H. Kissinger's role in peace — Prophecy correct.

5. Australasia's Part in Global 2000.
Why N.Z. and Australia must be first — Wise will understand — Prototype for E.C. 1992 — How to destroy a thriving society — Apparent goodies and baddies — Business Round Table influence — P.W.O. or P.G.A. (in the beehive) — Sovereignty undermined.

6. Beginnings.
Illuminati history — World dominion aim — Main aims — Fabian Socialism — N.Z. a State of Australia — Taxation, a weapon — A nasty shock — N.Z. Fabianism.

7. The Protocols.
Prieure de Sion — Masons — Vatican — Jesuits — Mormons — Link-up Pope John 23rd, R.C. and Protestants — Link-up Pope John 23rd, R.C. and Freemasons — Link-up David Yallop's book, R.C. and Mafia.

20. The Shocking Aids Story.
The Aids cover-up — Various cures.

21. Change, Change, Change.
Efforts to fiddle with Constitution.

22. The Highly Organised Destruction of New Zealand.
Links with Australia — 1.7.90 an important date — Selling off assets
ultimately to yourself.

23. Change of Allegiances.
Why the apparent ANZUS break — Equal opportunity.

24. Overthrow of New Zealand Sovereignty.
Created racial tension — Divide and rule — Commo cliches out-
dated — Peace groups — A set-up.

25. Telecom and Surveillance.
New Zealand and U.S.S.R both test cases — Must link together
for World Government plan.

26. Australian Surveillance.
Deakin Centre — Tax File Numbers — Medicare — N.Z. computer
centre soon — Swedish warning — Prisons — T.V. monitors —
Airports and PASS — E.C. generally behind — Fictitious analysis
for example — Pine Gap's influence.

27. N.Z. Surveillance.
Faxes cheaper than letter — Waihopai -Tax evasion — G.S.T. —
Tax — PAYE — Health computers — PAXUS — Israelis teach
interrogation — I.D. for New Zealand.

28. Surveys.
Phone information — Phones with pictures coming — photo on
license.

29. Bits and Pieces.
EFTPOS changes — 4 banks link — BNZ options open —
Fundamentalist Christians increasing — Trans-Tasman travel
increasing — Noah's Ark found — Computers in the Islands.

30. Others Can Spy Too.
I.D. cards in Europe — Barcodes on cars — Fibre optics in London.

31. The Sinking of the Lermontov.
List of unanswered questions — Lermontov — Wrong specifications

(Lloyd's Register) — Wrong profile — Wrong description — Wrong loading depth — Questions not asked in enquiry.

32. Commos Are Such Nice People.
Spy bases Wellington — Canberra — Listening in to telephone Microwaves — Soviet aims in Pacific.

33. The Soviet Union and Communism.
Soviets and Antarctica — Soviets testing democracy — 4 power groups — Reason for USSR strength — Karl Marx, a fraud — Lenin's aims — Violent and non-violent methods — Socialism and communism, the same — Soviet history = lies — Boredom under socialism — Soviet airlines unsafe — USSR military might, a myth — U.S. feeds USSR — Communism cruel — No standards in communism — Brutality acceptable behaviour — USSR = devious behaviour — USSR and N.Z. = common policies — Come into my parlour.

34. Soviets Link With Religion.
World Government links with World Church.

35. Soviets Future Predicted.
Link U.S. and USSR — Bush, the key man — Nuclear energy for joint space travel — Russia in prophecy — The destruction of Soviet communism.

36. Unionism.
Unionism finished — A demonic spirit controls all unions — A spiritual remedy.

37. The U.S.A. in World Government Plans.
U.S. servicemen in the Pacific war — U.S. Presidency — Curse on Presidents — Skull and Bones Club — The Order — Managed conflict between U.S. and USSR — Soviets and the Order — Presidents and Christianity — Key Trilateralists — Henry Kissinger and his activities — Moscow can work with Bush — U.S. in prophecy? — Trojan horse — Harmonic locations — Freemasonry and its influence — Links with U.S. to Europe in Illuminati — Bad times ahead for U.S.A. — Visions past and present — The selling of America — Japanese influence in the U.S. — Canada for sale — Japan playing hard to get — U.S. food manipulation — Cut in U.S. population — Ways of destroying U.S. freedoms — Spiritual revival — Federal Reserve — OPEC — Methods for destroying world's economy — The secret power, stronger than the Fed. — G10 and G7 — Bank of International Settlements.

38. Computerization Equals Bondage.

The first computers — Thinking computers — Texas banks going broke — Plastic cards a temporary measure — Plastic card expansion — Worldwide — Bye bye tellers — Swiss accounts — Black money — Cashless society will stop this.

39. The E.C. and its Leader in World Government Plans.
Recap on E.C. history — Description of E.C. in prophecy — List of qualifications for leader — Applicants for 13th position — Three nations will be expelled — Lead up to 1992.

40. The Future of the E.C. prophesied.
E.C. must have a strong leader — Strong and weak nations — Details on the leader's popularity — E.C. last world empire — It will last but a short time — Politics and religion link.

41. Subversion of the Children.
Curriculum organizers devilish — Teaching in no absolutes — Strap or police baton — Corporal punishment outlawed — Psychology causes problems — God's wisdom — A choice for parents — Human wisdom or God's wisdom — Humanism teaches self — Christianity teaches 'others first'.

42. Is Education Improving?
Look and say, a tragedy — Back to basics — Taking away landmarks — Results of change — Poor standards — Sex education — Video censorship — Nuclear education — Hinduism in classrooms — Tomorrow's schools.

43. Evolution and Education.
Creation forbidden in N.S.W. schools — 6,000 year history — Evolution or creation, a choice — Atheism, a bad choice — Bunyan's discussion with former atheist, in hell — Atheists downward path — Unisex madness — Differences in the sexes God ordained.

44. Evolution and Atheism.
Agnosticism is foolishness — A true life illustration.

45. Endtime Occult Activity.
Girl levitates — Devil dog — Queen witch — Satan links all world government groups — Politicians need prayer — Master Jesus — False Christ — Communists and capitalists link — Lawless spirits on the increase — 3 leaders to rule soon — Psychic predictions for 1988 — True prophets — List of forbidden practises — The enemy

is working flat out. Why? — Vile games and occult explosion — A false Christ — Gradual occult acceptance — Creeping into the church — Pity the kids — Witchcraft a crime in New Zealand — Strange changes — Demonism.

46. New Age Deception — Planned Lucifer Worship.
Raising of consciousness equals the road to hell — Severe warning — Hinduism, the basis of New Age — Satan in visualization — Witnessing to New Agers — The mark of the Beast — Reincarnation — Their teachings — New Age in the USSR — New Age propaganda man — The Satanic Initiation — Key = Food — Food a bondage — World Leader — 4 stages — Peer pressure — The problem of small communities — Deception — The true way — Is Jesus the only way? — Ivan Panin proofs — the Initiation en masse — Truth versus error.

47. New Age and the Occult.
Error, looking inside one's self — The old lie — Hinduism — Write you own road rules — Self worship — U.F.O.'s — 2 sources a) U.S.A. b) From hell.

48. Israel.
1986 trip to Israel — Strange happenings — God's clock — Prophecies fulfilled — 3 battles in M.E. outlined — Many Jews leaving the Soviet Union — A 2nd exodus — Is Jerusalem the Jewish capital? — Ethiopian Jews' exodus — Raiders of the Lost Ark — Kissinger and M.E. Peace — Bible, miraculous predictions — 4 people to watch — Rumours of Messiah — A generation 50 years — When will Messiah come?

49. Freemasonry and the Occult.
Strange happenings — Freemasonry demon — A challenge — a cancer healing — Masons backtrack — Witchcraft — Curses on Freemasons — Some church leaders involved — Proof, proof, proof — Demonic anger a feature — Freemasonry is blasphemous — 17th degree password — Can a Christian be a mason? — Above the law — Roman Catholics and Freemasonry — Origin of Freemasonry — Church of England's findings apply to New Zealand and Great Britain — 'Harmless old duffers' — Nothing to hide? — Women should be admitted — What to do — Information vindicated — They must be warned — Shouting and raving to be expected — A good substitute fellowship — Other secret groups — A final eyeopener.

55. Hell.
The horrors of scenes in hell — Voices from beyond the grave —
A solemn warning.

56. Heaven.
Scenes in Glory — Not to be missed — Your choice essential.

57. Calvary.
The cost — Salvation provided — God's grace — The sinner's choice.

ADDITIONAL MATERIAL BY THE BARRY SMITH FAMILY EVANGELISM TRUST.

Books:

'Warning' by Barry R. Smith
'Second Warning' by Barry R. Smith
'Final Notice' by Barry R. Smith
'Postscript' by Barry R. Smith

Music Cassettes:

'Trials of Your Faith' by Andrew and Saskia Smith
'Hidden Man of the Heart' by Andrew and Saskia Smith
'Hallelujah One' by Mark Baker and Andrew and Saskia Smith
'If My People' by Andrew and Saskia Smith

Regular new releases.
Video Cassettes:

'Daniel 9 - How Long Have We Got?	(2 hours)
'The Occult and New Age Movement'	(2 hours)
'After Death - WHAT?'	(2 hours)
'Scarlet Woman - One World Church'	(2 hours)
'Chaos of the Cults'	(2 hours)
'Christian Family Series'	(3 videos - total of 6 hours)
'The Eye In The Triangle	(4 video set)

Stock may be limited so please write for current catalogue and price
list.

To order please write to:
International Support Ministries - Pacific
Pelorus Bridge, Rai Valley
Marlborough, NEW ZEALAND
Ph: 3 57 16046
Fax: 3 57 16135
W.A. Buchanan
P.O. Box 206, Geebung, Queensland 4034
AUSTRALIA
Ph. (07) 865 2222

EMMANUEL CHRISTIAN FELLOWSHIP (ISM)

27 - 31 READING ROAD SOUTH
FLEET HAMPSHIRE
RG13 9QP UNITED KINGDOM

FAX/TEL. 01252 812189

International Support Ministries -USA
P.O. Box 2158
Poulsbo, WA 98370
Ph: (206) 437-0418
FAX: (206) 437-0432   write to:

AUSTRALIA
Veritas Publishing Company Pty. Ltd.,
P. O. Box 20, Bullsbrook, Western Australia, 6084.

CANADA
Veritas Publishing Company,
(A Division of Veritas Holdings Limited)
P. O. Box 67555, Station "O", Vancouver B.C., Canada VSW 3V1

NEW ZEALAND
Veritas Publishing Co. Pty. Ltd.,
P. O. Box 4389,
Auckland, New Zealand

BRITAIN
Bloomfield Books,
26 Meadow Lane,
Sudbury, Suffolk, England C010 6TD

SOUTH AFRICA
Dolphin Press (Pty.) Ltd.,
P. O. Box 18223,
Dalbridge, 4014, South Africa.

UNITED STATES OF AMERICA
Concord Books,
P. O. Box 2707,
Seal Beach CA. 90740

PREFACE

This book, I predict will be the hottest of its kind on the market. It will evoke many emotions, some positive, some negative.

Let the reader remember at all times, we are all on the journey of life. We all have a destination. Anger, threats and hatred should be suppressed, while the intellect has opportunity to mull over the information here presented.

Over the years, many have said I was wrong, only to contact me later saying 'I'm sorry, you were correct.' I am not infallible, but I love my fellow man.

RECOMMENDED READING

'Warning' by Barry Smith

'Second Warning' by Barry Smith

'Mystery 666' by Don Stanton

'None Dare Call it Conspiracy' by Gary Allen

'Cosmic Conspiracy' by Stan Deyo

'The Bridge to Infinity' by Bruce Cathie

'Occult Theocracy' by Lady Queenborough (Edith Starr Miller); obtainable at 'Midnight Messenger', P.O. Box 472, Altadena, CA 91001, U.S.A.

'Bible Handbook' by Henry H. Halley; obtainable at Box 774, Chicago 90, Illinois, U.S.A.

'The Unseen Hand' by A. Ralph Epperson; obtainable at 'American Media', Box 4646, Westlake Village, CA 91359, U.S.A.

'The Order' - 4 books by Anthony Sutton.

INTRODUCTION

Country — Australia.

Date — 2nd April 1985.

The guard, a Rambo type figure, armed with gun and fixed bayonet, looked suspiciously as the small group of viewers approached the conference's main exhibit.

There she was, a shop mannequin, smiling (in fact, beaming) showing where on the body, the proposed I.D. mark would be placed.

No prizes for guessing where.

There were fine dotted lines in a rectangular shape setting out the extremes for the two preferred locations on the body for the mark.

1.   FOREHEAD — central, above and between eyes and below hairline.

2.   RIGHT WRIST/HAND — flat part on top of right arm/wrist, just next to hand joint and away from round, bony piece.

A more detailed amputated arm from another mannequin demonstrated light focusing from the laser scanner unit, purporting to read the marks on the model's body.

This display was anonymous with no one group claiming responsibility, yet was arranged in such a manner as to show the natural and logical sequence from the many credit and debit cards (along with I.D. cards) to a single card, thus leading to a world wide system —

a painless,

invisible mark,

on or in the body.

No doubt, the fine print included such catch words as SAFE — SIMPLE — QUICK — INVISIBLE — PAINLESS — FOOLPROOF — UNALTERABLE — IRREMOVABLE — EASY — CONVENIENT — MODERN — LATEST — PERMANENT.

A prominent West Australian politician, during the month of October 1987, was reported by the press as saying that the proposed I.D. card as mooted by the then Australian Government; could finally be identified with the Scriptural reference in Rev. 13:16-18.

'And he causeth all, both small and great, rich and poor, free and bond, to receive a mark in their right hand or in their foreheads.

And that no man might buy or sell, save he that had the mark, or the name of the beast, or the number of his name.
Here is wisdom. Let him that hath understanding count the number of the beast, for it is the number of a man, and his number is Six hundred, threescore and six.'

Predicted 96 A.D.

Fulfilled 2 APRIL 1985 IN AUSTRALIA AT THIS EXHIBITION.

Readers of my previous two books, WARNING and SECOND WARNING will be aware that we have been waiting patiently for these events to be fulfilled.

All Scripture references in this book are taken from the Authorised Version unless otherwise stated.

Words in brackets are the Author's explanations, to enable clear understanding.

'b' after a verse refers to the second half of the verse.

CHAPTER 1

Update '89

Readers of our book 'Second Warning' will be aware of some of this information.

GENESIS CORRECT.

Noah's Ark Found.

1988. I picked up the phone in Australia and spoke to Tom Crotzer, an American living in Scotland.

Self: 'My name is Barry Smith, Tom. I would like to ask you a question. Is it true that you have photographed Noah's Ark?'
   Tom: 'Yes. I photographed half of it during our 1974 expedition. The other half of the ark has broken off and fallen down the glacier.'
   Self: 'Where can I obtain a copy of this photo Tom?'
   Tom: 'On a video film entitled 'In Search of Noah's Ark.'
   I have since procured a copy of this video and can prove to any visitor to our home that Noah's Ark is on Mount Ararat.
   The video also includes a satellite scan of the area, showing something very significant at that very spot.
   Challenge — If that is not Noah's Ark on Ararat, then somebody rowed a boat up there.
   'Why hasn't it been recovered?' you ask.
   The political tension on the border between Armenia and the USSR has, up to this point in history, made this very difficult.
   However, watch this area carefully as in time, this recovery of the two sections of the Ark, will take place.
   What a blow this will be to all unbelievers, not to mention the Soviet Union's atheistic government.
   (Note — Please do not ask us for copies of this video. We do not have any information on where it may be procured.)
   Therefore, THE BOOK OF GENESIS IS CORRECT.

REVELATION CORRECT — Proofs.

Stage 1
Some years ago, most developed western countries had strange marks appearing on their food packages.

Named 'universal product codes', (UPC) or bar codes, these series of thick and thin lines have become familiar to most folk. Please pick up a product and observe the following points.

a. At the beginning of the mark in the middle and at the end, please notice the guard bars i.e. two thin lines, slightly longer than the others.

b. Notice also that although the other lines have a number underneath them, the guard bars do not have a corresponding number.

c. The reason for this is that they don't need them. Their purpose is merely to initially set up the system to read the code on the right hand side of the bar code, hit the guard bar in the middle, change the code, read the left hand side, then hit the left hand guard bar and shut off.

d. However, on side B of the bar code, often times you will notice no.6 is directly beneath two thin lines exactly the same shape as the guard bars.

e. Therefore, very cleverly, and psychologically speaking, each guard bar could be seen as a 6.

Therefore, 3 guard bars equal 666 on every piece of food on your shelf.

UNIVERSAL PRODUCT CODE

0

1 2345 67890

FOREHEAD OR HAND

Stage 2.

Now, many computer firms are adding little bar-codes underneath the bigger bar codes.

Notice on either side of these smaller bar codes the letter F. and H. These letters have a dot after each one, showing that they are abbreviations.

Therefore — F. = forehead
— H. = hand

2

1

2

3

4

Don't leave home
without it.

Stage 3 — 1983

In 1983, Dr Henry Kissinger was in Australia speaking to banking executives and others about Electronic Funds Transfers at the Point of Sale (EFTPOS).

In the same year, the Sydney Morning Herald printed a cartoon showing a bald headed man with a bar code on his head along with the words 'Don't leave home without it.'

Stage 4 — 1984

The Westpac bank in Australia distributed their advertising folder headed up with the words WORLD'S FIRST.

i.e. EFTPOS on a national basis.

During the same year, the Sydney Morning Herald put out an article, once more showing the cartoon picture of the man with the bar code on his head, with an accompanying article which spoke of a plan to 'brand everyone with a number.....IT IS SEEN AS THE ONLY POSSIBLE SOLUTION.' End quote. (Emphasis added.)

Stage 5 — 1985

The laser gun unveiled — the female dummy — the marks on the forehead and right hand.

During the same year, the Sydney Morning Herald published a cartoon showing a customer having his forehead pressed down on a bar code scanner in a shop.

What better way to present an innovation as drastic as this, than to make people laugh.

Therefore, THE BOOK OF REVELATION IS CORRECT.

As we prepare this book for its first printing, some have shown disquiet regarding the laser printing of a mark on the body. It is not the author's aim to prove the type of mark that will be placed on the body, as at this stage, there are various possibilities being presented i.e. In the 'Dominion' newspaper, 21 September 1987, we read 'Human barcode implants made possible.

Implanting barcodes into the necks of sheep, horses, salmon, pet dogs — or even people — to record information or monitor movement, is possible.....' End quote.

During the month of February 1989, references appeared in New Zealand newspapers about a Big Brother style microchip which could be implanted in the flesh.

Through animal rights groups, the suggestion was made that

a chip the size of a grain of rice may be implanted in the body of the animal using a disposable syringe. It is said to be painless, and therefore, no distress would be caused.

Of course, people involved with civil liberties and others with strong Christian beliefs would object to this taking place. The Christians would immediately identify this type of thing as the beginning of the Mark of the Beast era. The mark would be read using scanners.

It has been suggested that laser marking would cause serious skin burning and therefore, other alternatives may well be used.

We can now establish:

a. Genesis is correct
b. Revelation is correct
c. Everything in between is correct
d. We all desperately need the Lord.

Happy reading!

CHAPTER 2

Black
Monday and Tuesday

October 19th and 20th 1987 will go down in economic history as earth-shattering.

Psychologists world-wide had their busiest runs in the history of their professions, as multitudes with dollar signs rapidly fading from bloodshot eyeballs, crashed on to couches, voices trembling with emotion; pleading piteously for help.

One such psychologist told his patients that 'greed' or the expectations of a fast and easy buck had led them to their present position. Now, they had to learn to relax and sway with the punches.

The reader will instantly perceive that advice such as this, is comparable in value to the erstwhile security of all these stocks, bonds and shares. People made in the image of God require much more than this to help in times of stress.

The Australian Treasurer, Paul Keating, says 'There is no need to panic.' He also scoffed at predictions of a depression saying that 'the world economic scene was not geared for a depression along the lines of the Great Depression of the 1930's.' Christchurch Press 22 October 1987.

I agree with him.

THE DEPRESSION THAT IS COMING WILL BE FAR WORSE THAN ANYTHING THAT HAS HAPPENED UP TO THIS POINT.

IT WILL MEAN THE COMPLETE AND UTTER END OF CHEQUES, BANK NOTES AND COINS.

The only reason this crash did not follow through to its conclusion is that the World Government advocates do not have the new substitute system finally set up yet at the time of writing. Therefore, it is not the time to crash the old. (Nov.'87)

At the time of writing, the newspapers are full of reports on the crash. My phone has been running hot with people asking 'Is this the big one?'

The answer to that is 'NO'.

A number of questions are in order here.

Q.1. Was the crash an accident?

A. No.

Q.2. Who organised it?

A. World Government advocates.

Q.3. Why?

(a) To shake loose small investors and stock market dabblers.

(b) To prepare the stage for the Republican George Bush administration so that during his reign, the new system would come in.

(c) To involve the Federal Reserve — a group of private bankers who give the illusion of being the official federal banking group in the U.S.A. These men took over the U.S. debt at that point and bailed out the stock market to keep it afloat, so that when the 'big crash' time arrived, they could withdraw their supporting funds and crash the whole system overnight.

The key piece of information in the news is a small paragraph.

'The U.S. Federal Reserve Board (the Fed) was ready to provide liquidity.' Christchurch Press 22 October 1987.

Here come the cavalry, with the big guns.

THE PLAN

Statement — There are 13 families or groups heading up the World Government plan.

These families are portrayed as the 13 layers of blocks found on the strange seal on the reverse side of the U.S. $1 bill.

Japan First.

The real Wall St crash will start in Japan (yen), on to the U.S.A. (dollar) and then to West Germany (deutschmark). Then down goes the whole world system.

The reasons for this are that with the U.S.A. being the world's greatest debtor nation, and Japan being the world's greatest creditor nation, Japan's economic downfall will set the whole thing off. The Japanese rely so much on their manufacturing output that, as one man suggested to me, what was really needed in that country was a mass of moving belts reaching from each manufacturing establishment to a cliff top. As it is essential to their economy that manufacture never stops, a continual supply of articles would leave each factory; the articles needed for sale or export could be taken from the moving belts and the rest would fall over the cliffs to destruction. This would keep the workers

9

working with full employment, imports and exports moving and prevent stagnation of their economy which is essential to their survival.

Now, because Japan is a 'loner' country, and has been doing so well, the World Government people have turned their attention in their direction.

In order to bring down the world currency system, notice the information coming out from this area.

(a) The Japanese people have always been great savers. This spirit was, until recently, encouraged by the Japanese government.

In the Australian Financial Review (5th April 1988) we read: 'In an important shift of policy, the government of Prime Minister, Mr Takeshita, on Friday began to take a 20 percent slice of interest earned on certain savings accounts, which had been exempt from taxes for 25 years.

Maruyu

The tax free system known as maruyu was a major inducement for the Japanese to save. The maruyu system allowed each person to have up to three tax free accounts of three million yen or $24,000 each.

This led to a proliferation of small accounts, many opened under fictitious names to get around the legal limit. Many Japanese viewed maruyu as an officially sanctioned means of tax evasion.

Many economists expected a good flow of this money to flow into the high flying Tokyo stock market.

Other likely attractions, some analysts said, were investment trusts, gold and possibly U.S. treasury bonds and notes.' End quote.

Again, from Australia's Financial Review — 8th June 1988, we read: 'Japan's Life Insurance Groups lose Billions over U.S. Bonds.....this was due mostly to the continuous purchase of U.S. Government Treasury bonds since the American dollar began to plunge in September 1985.

Japan's Ministry of Finance, which has been attempting to prop up the ailing U.S. currency, pressured the companies into making U.S. treasury bond purchases.' End quote.

In other words, Japan has now been caught out with rapidly failing U.S. bonds. This is not by accident. The men at the top have a long range plan. Japan is now being picked off.

11

Five Day Week

Have a look at this. Late in 1988, we read that the Government of Japan has switched from a six day to a five day working week.....

The shorter week was scheduled to begin in February 1989. Japan, upon U.S. 'advice', is now slowing down the conveyor belt.

Only those with all the facts, many of which are presented in this book will see the result of this.

Sorry Japan — you're next.

CHAPTER 3

The Plot Thickens

One of the most distant countries from the city of Jerusalem is little New Zealand situated out to the east of Australia.

The plan is to use Australia and New Zealand in union, one with the other, as a test case for World Government. Very little is known about this area by people living in the northern hemisphere, and it is this fact that makes the two countries very suitable for this diabolical experiment. We know that New Zealand is the first country in the world to receive the sun each new day, that is apart from Tonga, but Tonga is not widely known as a world economic power. The money computers roll first of all in New Zealand.

New Zealand/Australia Links

In 'The New Zealand Herald', 27th July 1989, we read "easier investing rules bring warning on sovereignty.

New Zealand could be faced with no alternative than to hand over its economy and sovereignty to Australia, the Wilson and Horton Limited chairman warned at the annual meeting in Auckland yesterday . . ." End quote.

Circumstances could be arranged by World Government advocates to assist the New Zealand government into making this final decision to join with Australia, politically as well as economically.

(a) Through their destructive policies, drive New Zealanders to the apparently greener fields of Australia to look for housing and employment, until the New Zealand population declines to such a degree that amalgamation with Australia would be the only way to go.

(b) Destroy the value of the New Zealand dollar.

(c) Sell up New Zealand's corporations to overseas buyers and shareholders or to locals who borrow overseas. They in turn can then state that all future operations will be conducted from Australia. 'Press', 12th July 1988. 'It makes no sense for the Government to sell financially viable businesses in order to retire its debt', says the Public Service Association....' End quote.

'Press', 1st June 1989. 'State Owned Enterprises (S.O.E.s) Should be Privatised.

State-owned enterprises should be privatised to prevent future political interference in their management, the chief executive of the Electricity Corporation.....said last evening....' End quote.

This is obviously the plan in part, behind the rushing through of privatisation plans and the selling up of the family silver (including State Owned Enterprises SOEs) to overseas investors. Poor little New Zealand away down in the South Pacific has been sold out to overseas bidders—'Why?' I hear you cry.

ANSWER: I didn't really know until August 1987 when my wife and I were in Sydney, Australia. At that time I knew that New Zealand had a huge third world debt on its shoulders. Along with most countries in the world, New Zealand could never pay it back.

I also knew that these debts had been inflicted on much of the world by groups of international money lenders i.e.

G7

The World Bank

The International Monetary Fund

The Federal Reserve and others

Travelling by plane to Papua New Guinea some years ago, I picked up a Readers Digest and read an astounding article. It told of a number of young businessmen, who armed with suitcases packed full with bank notes were jetting from country to country around the world, offering this cash to national leaders in the form of loans with very reasonable interest. These young men in their smart business suits, travelled by air, first class of course, stayed at luxury hotels, used limousines, all expenses paid, lent the money, went home, filled their suitcases and started all over again.

I read this to my wife May and then said 'It must be a hoax article. What a magnificent business to be in, if by any chance it were true.'

(New Zealand newspaper readers may remember reading sometime ago that little Niue Island, a mere dot in the South Pacific, was told to borrow 'for dignity'.)

Reader–it was true, and every nation on earth has been systematically undermined financially, thus putting them in the hands of the unscrupulous manipulators of modern business–the International World Government financiers.

15

Who was it again who said 'The rich ruleth over the poor and the borrower is servant to the lender.' *Ref.1.

The chickens came home to roost during the month of August 1987. We were in Sydney, Australia on a lecture tour when about 11:55 a.m. on the 13th August, I called a business firm enquiring as to whether they had a certain product. The lady who answered my call went to look for the article and left the phone receiver down by the radio set. The midday news came on and suddenly I heard the most astounding information. I shouted 'What?' My wife ran over asking if somebody had died, to which I replied 'No, wait and I'll explain.'

The next morning I rushed down to the local newspaper shop, picked up a copy of the Financial Review dated 14.8.88 and read the following article.

Loans Equity Swap
'The U.S. Federal Reserve Board announced yesterday it was granting new authority for U.S. banks to swap loans made in developing countries for direct ownership of property in these countries......to promote new approaches to solving the third world debt crisis including such arrangements as SWAPPING DEBTS HELD BY THE BANKS FOR DIRECT OWNERSHIP of factories, mines and real estate in developing countries.

The Federal Reserve said its new rule, which goes into effect immediately, would allow banks through their subsiduaries TO OWN UP TO 100 PERCENT OF FOREIGN FINANCIAL AND NON-FINANCIAL COMPANIES'. End quote. (Emphasis added.)

Corporatisation
Now New Zealanders will understand why certain Government individuals evolved an ugly word called 'Corporatisation'.

With the power of the Queen's representative to veto bills being taken away, the Corporatisation bill was easily passed.
These people took six Government Departments, paid off many of the staff with redundancy pay, thus shattering the security of thousands, and turned the Departments into Corporations.

Why?

Because you can't sell a Government department to the overseas money lenders to pay off your debts.

16

Privatisation
New step — Privatisation.
Why?
To allow overseas money lenders and their front men to gradually take over the shareholding of these new private corporations.

Now, you the reader, can understand the picture in the Bulletin magazine from Australia dated 12 April 1988, showing the Prime Ministers of New Zealand and Australia in bed together — both in pyjamas, both gripping the top sheet with both hands and underneath in bold type, the statement:
WHY NEW ZEALAND SHOULD BECOME THE 8TH AND 9TH STATES OF AUSTRALIA.

Bedfellows
In the article, it points out...'Nearly a thousand New Zealanders every week enter Australia, taking advantage of immigration laws that assume their nation and Australia are one. Soon there will be a move towards a uniform legal system, taxation and currency. The Australian constitution already provides for the inclusion of New Zealand. Why don't we get on with it?' End quote.

This will also explain why everything that is important for the future of New Zealand's independence as a nation is being sold off.

Once people begin to realise what their 'elected representatives' have done in selling off that which their forefathers worked hard and long to buy, government representatives would naturally need to try and play down the seriousness of the situation to avoid a possible lynching taking place.

'Press', 26th May 1989. 'Privatisation Became Inevitable.... Corporatisation was never intended as a precursor to privatisation, the Minister for State-Owned Enterprises....said last evening. .....While some concern about selling State assets to foreigners (this) sic was really 'something of a bad joke', he said....' End quote.

I read this man's words yet strangely enough, find it difficult to muster up even a hint of a smile at this so-called 'bad joke'. We New Zealanders do not enjoy seeing our assets sold up.

Obviously the plan is that New Zealand very shortly will cease to be a nation but 'gradually' through Closer Economic Relations (C.E.R.) and Closer Political Relations (C.P.R.) both Australia and New Zealand will be forced to merge.

17

With the money collected from the sales in 1988, debts in 1989 can be partially paid off. This is a once only move however. What happens in 1990 and beyond?

Do I hear a cry of outrage?

Whilst in Canberra recently on a lecture tour, we viewed the outstanding new Parliament Buildings, probably some of the most beautiful of such buildings in the world, and it was explained to us that in this building, room will be made for at least two leaders from New Zealand to attend State Premiers' Conferences.

The question may now be asked 'Is this privatisation only affecting Australia and New Zealand?'

Answer—In the study of World Government themes, a number of names appear regularly in the publications one may read on the subject e.g.

1. Council on Foreign Relations (C.F.R.)—A group of approximately 1600 men and women who advise the Presidents of the United States on Foreign Policy. The majority of these persons are Globalists or World Government Advocates. In the C.F.R. study no.7, it states 'The U.S. must strive to build a New International Order.'

2. The Bilderbergers—named after a hotel in Holland where this World Government group in Europe first met. This is the European equivalent of the C.F.R. from the U.S.A and each of their annual meetings is attended by about 3/4 of the C.F.R.

   The press and photographers are forbidden entrance. They discuss such subjects as 'Globalisation' and the 'New International Economic Order'. (N.I.E.O.)

3. The Trilateral Commission—Another World Government group, the brainchild of Mr David Rockefeller.

   Included in their membership list as of March 15, 1985 the following interesting names appear:

(a) Zbigniew Brzezinski—Senior Advisor Georgetown University Centre for Strategic and International Studies; former U.S. Assistant to the President for National Security Affairs.

(b) Alan Greenspan—Who has just taken over the Federal Reserve chairman's job from Paul Volcker. (In the late 1980's.)

(c) Henry A. Kissinger—Former U.S. Secretary of State. Now involved in running a firm called 'Kissinger Associates' advising on strategies in business and political life.

18

(d) Robert S. McNamara—Former President of the World Bank.

(e) David Rockefeller—There is no statement on his qualifications.

(f) Baron Edmund de Rothschild—Chairman Compagnie Financiere Holding—Paris.

4. The Club of Rome—who purport to be a group of environmentalists who have fed their masses of information on world conditions into a giant machine nicknamed the 'Doomsday Computer'. This machine churns out possible future scenarios and tells us that the world cannot continue at its present rate beyond the year 2000.

No wonder the Plan is called 'Global 2000'.

As mentioned on page 49 in my book SECOND WARNING, here are the proposed 10 regions of the Club of Rome.

Region no.1.—North America—Notice that the U.S.A. and Canada have a similar C.E.R. agreement as Australia and New Zealand.

Region no.2.—Western Europe—Whilst in Great Britain lecturing during October 1988 I was able to tell the English people that their number was '2' in this World Government plan.

Region no.3.—Japan—Remember, the greatest creditor nation in the world at time of writing 1988. This nation stands alone, mainly because of cultural differences. Their whole society from ancient times has been very independent. The problem is to teach them to give up sovereignty. This is being done however, as you have already seen. A word used to describe Japan's national characteristic might be 'intolerence' of outside pressure or interference.

Region no.4.—Australia, New Zealand, South Africa, Israel, Oceania-the Pacific Islands. (At time of writing 1988 please notice telecommunications systems are being set up with microwave dishes and fibre optic cables linking the Pacific and New Zealand. Any Pacific Island people reading this book should notice that it is useless to leave New Zealand or Australia for a home in the islands in the hope of dodging this world plan. In like manner, I warn New Zealanders in my public lectures about the folly of fleeing to Australia to dodge the dreadful things happening in New Zealand. 'Out of the frying pan into the fire' is the correct phrase I believe.

Region no.5.—Eastern Europe.

Region no.6. — Latin America

Region no.7. — North Africa and Middle East — This is important as some time after the U.S. and Israeli elections in November 1988, a seven year peace treaty will be ratified with Israel which is region number 4 you will remember. Therefore, regions 4 and 7 will be linked in the future i.e. Israel and Arabs for at least three and a half years.

Region no.8. — Main Africa.

Region no.9. — South and South East Asia.

Region no.10. — Centrally planned Asia.

Included in the foregoing list of names of World Government groups and individuals, the name Rothschilds figures very prominently.

One prominent ancestor of this family, Meyer Amschel Rothschild, is credited with saying 'Give me control over a nations economy and I care not who writes its laws.'

In the 'Weekend Australian' newspaper dated January 2-3 1988, we read of two men i.e. Mr Oliver Letwin and Mr John Whittingdale, both members of Rothschild's International Privatisation Unit.

Quote: 'Since arriving at Rothschild, they have worked on a slew of privatising projects. (Mr Letwin has written a book to be published next year called 'PRIVATISING THE WORLD'.' Emphasis added.

Why?

Key word — Interdependence.

The aim is to destroy each country's INDEPENDENCE to make way for INTERDEPENDENCE.

For example, during the course of our many years on the lecture trail, we have pointed out that each country on the globe will become responsible for certain commodities, upon which the rest of the world will depend to such a degree that wars and other conflicts will hopefully become obsolete as the country you attack in the future may be your benefactor with regard to a certain product.

An illustration of the above statement is given to us by the 'National Business Review', August 23rd 1989. This article by innuendo vindicates the statements we have made, that New Zealand was no longer to be a supplier of primary farm produce. Farmers were to be driven off the land, thus leaving it free to be planted out in trees.

The reason for this being that New Zealand has the second fastest growth rate in the world for forestry.

We now quote an excerpt from the above article — "Rules Changed to Speed up Sale of State Forests.

The Government looks set to reap a multi-billion dollar harvest by selling State Forests in one lot.

The Forestry Corporation has confirmed the 540,000 hectares of forest will go on the market simultaneously rather than region by region as earlier planned.

. . . The spokesman denied the strategy was aimed at filling Treasury coffers this financial year . . ." End quote.

As the World Government plan must move quickly in New Zealand, please take careful note of the continuation of the above quote.

". . . Under the previous strategy, it would have taken up to three years to quit all the forests . . ." End quote.

This makes it clear to us all that speed is all important as we move into the 1990's.

Now, back to the article on the Rothschild family. This passage also includes some art work, with a LARGE EYE very prominently displayed in the centre.

Those who are familiar with THE PLAN also would know about the eye principle. (See Warning and Second Warning for full explanation.)

This eye is found on the reverse side of the U.S. one dollar bill and is actually the Eye of Horus from Egyptian mythology, or the Eye of Lucifer — now called Satan. It is also found on Masonic Lodge walls and is worn by the Grand Master as part of his jewellery.

There is also a religious aspect to all this.

A little story to illustrate.

During 1987, on one of our Middle East tours, we visited a Roman Catholic church in Nazareth. This church was supposedly built over the dwelling place of Joseph, Mary and Jesus.

Just as we were about to go down the steps to visit the house we saw on the wall of the church, directly above this dwelling place, the giant eye in the triangle.

I turned to our guide and asked him what the eye signified. He replied 'The eye of God, sir.' I then said 'You are an Arab aren't you? You should know that that is the eye of Horus from Egyptian mythology, in other words, the eye of Satan.'

With a smile he agreed that this was the case. I then asked him why he told the people lies.

Here was his answer. 'We don't want to upset the tourists, sir.'

As I am invited by the media to take part in interviews, I now notice that my words are being taken very seriously.

Make no mistake about it. Neither New Zealand or Australia are being controlled by the official governments of the day.

There is a chain of 'advice' from overseas and these people send their representatives over from time to time to issue fresh instructions.

In these two countries, a small dedicated group, unknown to the rest of their loyal party as differing in political doctrine, receive the overseas directions (in the form of advice or suggestions of course) through the World Government advocates of big business living in these two countries respectively. This large group then advises the small governmental co-operating groups what to do.

CHAIN OF 'SUGGESTION'

1. World Government Globalists and Money Lenders — many operating out of New York or Basle, Switzerland. The top 13 families.
2. Travelling representatives who fly in to New Zealand and Australia and other countries by night. Shades of black limousines with black curtains.
3. Large business groups who listen to these representatives' advice and hold meetings and offer their own friendly 'advice' to governments.
4. A small group within the Government who listen to this advice, and who make things happen, usually against the wishes of their colleagues or political party base.
5. The rest of the Government who of course don't know or understand what is happening.
6. The political party whose front men make up the Government, (including caucus), who haven't got a clue what these individuals are up to, hold meetings in the background regularly, reshuffling ideas and positions around and thinking all the time 'This is not what our party stands for. Let's hope the man in the street doesn't understand what is happening or we'll all be out of a job'.

I suspect this book will make its way into these peoples' hands and open their eyes.

To these people I say now, 'Don't bother writing to thank me. I know how grateful you must be for this information so clearly outlined.'

CHAPTER 4

Global 2000

They've tried it once and failed.
They'll try it once more only and fail again.
Date 2218-2188 B.C.

Babel

'And the Lord said, behold the people is one, and they have all one language, and this they begin to do, and now nothing will be restrained from them, which they have imagined to do.

Go to, let us go down and there confound their language, that they may not understand on anothers' speech.

So the Lord scattered them abroad from thence upon the face of all the earth, and they left off to build the city.

Therefore is the name of it called Babel, because the Lord did there confound the language of all the earth and from thence did the Lord scatter them abroad, upon the face of all the earth.' *Ref.1.

A Second Attempt

The Global 2000 Report to the President was:
a. commissioned by Carter — May 23rd 1977,
b. disregarded by Reagan,
c. will be picked up again by Bush.

Quote from Report: 'If present trends continue, the world in 2000 will be more crowded, more polluted, less stable ecologically and more vulnerable to disruption.

Serious stresses involving population resources and environment are clearly visible ahead. Despite greater material output, the worlds' people will be poorer in many ways than they are today.

For hundreds of millions of the desperately poor, the outlook for food and other necessities will be no better. For many it will be worse. Barring revolutionary advances in technology, life for most people on earth will be more precarious in 2000 than it is now — unless the nations of the earth act decisively to alter current trends.....' End quote.

5 Problems

The five basic problems initially dealt with were:

a. Population
b. Capital
c. Resources
d. Pollution
e. Food.

The study was to look ahead, primarily to the year 2000, but not much beyond.

Now, as we have already seen, the name of the plan is 'Global 2000'.

During Christmas 1987, my wife and I were invited to lecture in one of the Australian States.

One night, we were invited out to the home of a very gracious couple, who also had other friends around.

A man and his wife who were present, told of a woman who came into their shop near the end of 1987. She said that she represented a group called '2000'. The suggestion was made quite forcibly that should this couple place their business on the register of the '2000' group, then they would continue to trade successfully. If, however, they refused to go along and did not sign on to the register, their business could come to a fairly rapid halt. This couple told us it sounded like the Mafia all over again, and as there was a fee payable to join this group, it sounded a little too much like protection money. They declined the offer and the visiting lady used their phone to tell her superior that they would not join. They went on to explain to my wife and I, that until they heard us speak on 'Global 2000', they did not realise the implications of all that had happened to them.

It should not therefore, surprise any person living in this southern hemisphere of the globe to read the word GLOBAL continually in our newspapers and periodicals, i.e.

a. Global publishing helps expand the international community.
b. Brierley going Global with I.E.P. Industrial Equity Ltd Deal.
c. Private Enterprise Plan for Global optical fibre network.
d. The Global Resource Bank.
e. The Globalisation of Air Cargo.

Travelling one day from Blenheim to Auckland, New Zealand, my bag which held all my suits went missing.

I called at the airline counter to make enquiries and was told to wait a little while as a tracer had gone through to Houston, Texas.

Observing my puzzled expression, the counter-clerk explained that the computer that did baggage traces was situated in Texas.

I replied 'But I've only come from Blenheim, a journey of approximately 400 miles.'

I went on to tell the story of the man who whilst checking in his bags at an airline counter, said 'Would you please send this bag to Hong-Kong, this one to New York and this one to Colombia?' The airline clerk answered and said 'We can't do that sir,' to which the traveller replied 'Why not? You did it last time.'

f. (Ex-New Zealand Prime Minister) Muldoon going Global and will help frame global economic advice to the new President of the United States. (George Bush) — Global Economic Action Institute.

g. Towards a Global Airline. Conference to be held in London.

h. Dr Henry Kissinger has a Global Concept.

i. Companies go Global'.....Sydney 'Morning Herald', 14th November 1988 — Adelaide Steamship, Amatil, Amcor, AWA, Bond Corp., BTR, Nylex, CSR, David Jones, ANL, Arnotts, Boral, Brambles, Burns Philp, Coles Meyer, Elders, IXL, FAI, Goodman Fielder Wattie, James Hardy, Hooker, Leighton, Lend Lease, Mayne Nickless, Nob, News Corp., Northern Star Holdings, Pacific Dunlop, Petersville, Sleigh, Pioneer Concrete, Rothmans Holdings, TNT, Westfield Holdings, Westpac, Woolworths.

I have on my desk a pile of other leaflets that I have collected with the word GLOBAL or '2000' prominently displayed —

1. Global Business Management Diaries for 1989.
2. Global Landrights.
3. Global Sharemarket — Shares going global.
4. Logistics Management Conference. 'Moving towards 2000'.
5. A Global property market
6. Operation Co-operation — Global co-operation for a better world. Patrons include Jimmy Carter, Cory Aquino, Malcolm Frazer, George Negus, Rowena Wallace, Peter Brock.
7. Parliamentarians for Global Action. Want world peace through world law.
8. World Heritage List — 'Green' parties from 20 countries form pact.

9. OPEC 2000 — OPEC is changing the way it sells oil. Going off the U.S. dollar.
10. Global Networks Integrated Systems Digital Network ISDN.
11. A Global Village — Telecommunications.
12. New International Economic Order (or Novus Ordo Seclorum) link with New World Order.
13. 'Vision 2000' New Age Management Technique.

New Age Influence

This latter group promoted by the New Age Movement calls for Telecom staff in Australia to 'build the best enterprise in Australia by the year 2000'. It is introduced to the staff in a pamphlet called 'Excellence Through People' and displays a rainbow and golden pyramid.

This system is a New Age Management Technique or Corporate Change programme designed to restructure an enterprise in preparation for the 'New Age' or 'Age of Aquarius'.

'The Power of Positive Thinking' (Norman Vincent Peale) is counterfeit Christianity. His form of visualisation is given as:

Picturise,

Prayerise,

Actualise, i.e.

Visualise it — pray about it — and then make it happen.

Warning

The Christ these people will receive will not be the real Christ, he will be 'Antichrist'.

With Vision '2000', participants are not offered any views or information showing failures — negative results — or anything contrary to the 'Emerging Corporate Vision'.

They are offered only positives or 'transformed negatives' which can lead to 'mass delusion'. Notice at this point the subtle influence of Satanic religion. The New Age Movement.

Think these terms over also.

a. International Youth Year.

b. International Year for Peace 1986.

c. International Labour Organisation.

d. International Law.

e. International Peace Treaties.

f. United Nations Educational Science Cultural Organisation (UNESCO).

g. World Environment Days.
h. World Decade for Women.
i. World Women's Forum.
j. Human Rights.
k. World Council of Churches.
l. One World Money System.
m. One World Identification Mark.

N.Z. 1990

Finally, on this list remember the year chosen for the first
WORLD GOVERNMENT MEETING TO BE HELD IN
NEW ZEALAND — 1990.
Do we know what the plans are for the decade 1990 — 2000?
We do, and in a lot of detail.

What we will present here will not be discovered through
astrology, the black arts, tea-cup or palm reading, tarot cards or
the occult. The answers come from the Word of the living God.

'The secret things belong unto the Lord our God but these things
which are revealed belong unto us, and to our children forever...'
*Ref.2.

Precis of Global 2000 — Future Plans

a. This plan is well over 200 years old.
b. It is so devious that the average person would get lost very
early on in the piece and sum it up as too way out or as
unmitigated absurdity.
c. It is Luciferian (satanic) in nature and diabolically clever.
d. Many, many groups are involved in it, but a master spiritual
being is pulling all the loose ends together. Notice the New
Age Movement creeping in.
e. Its aim is the complete enslavement of individuals of the
planet earth, leaving them no rights whatsoever.
f. One World Government will control all things political.
g. One World Church will control all things religious.
h. No individuals will own their own properties.
i. A One World Money System will involve:
  1. A number for each individual.
  2. A computer network — using link numbers to make up
  a complete dossier on each person.
  3. A mark on the individuals' bodies, impregnated with
  a laser gun, silicone chip implant, or even some
  identifying substance planted in the blood system.

29

j. Fortunately for us living in these days, their plans are in written form.

k. The official name of the plan is as we have discovered:

GLOBAL 2000

The ancient prophecies spoke of this plan and labelled it the Mystery of Iniquity.

'And now ye know what withholdeth that he might be revealed in his time.

For the MYSTERY OF INIQUITY doth already work, only he who now letteth will let until he be taken out of the way.' (Emphasis added.) *Ref.3.

This means that at the appropriate time in history, the plan will become public. This book reveals the plan before that time.

My writing was interrupted again. This time a telephone call from Sydney, Australia.

Hanging on the wall of my home is a short quotation which may help somebody else.

'I complained because my work was constantly interrupted until I realised, the interruptions were my work.'

I was asked the question on behalf of some Australian news media — 'What is next on the agenda prophetically speaking?'

Answer:

Peace Treaty in Middle East.

1. A peace treaty in the Middle East will be signed for a period of seven years and will be confirmed by a Jewish man, skilled in the art of diplomacy, peace initiatives, world finance and politics.

Since I commenced speaking on these subjects in the year 1969, I have told the people in my meetings that a non-religious Jewish man will arise at the end of this era and will be recognised by his confirmation of a seven year peace treaty in the Middle East and he will also be appointed leader of the European Community (E.C.).

During the months of September and October 1988, my wife and I led a tour consisting of 100 people to Greece, Turkey, Jordan and Israel. I was determined to go at this particular time as 1988 was the end of the 40 year period since the creation of the State of Israel in 1948. I knew that something important must happen at this time, as the number 40 in the Word of God stands for a time of 'testing' or 'probation'. Since 1988 therefore, reality is in store for Israel.

30

On the 2nd of October 1988, we were staying in a hotel in Tiberias, right on the shores of the sea of Galilee. My mother, Vera Smith handed me a copy of the Jerusalem Post and said 'This could be of interest to you son.'

On page 5 of this paper was a full page article dedicated to an interview with Dr Henry Kissinger, speaking about the state of the world. My eyes skimmed rapidly across the page until I found the portion on the Middle East. This excerpt almost blew my mind.

That night, along with a number of guests from the hotel, with the waters of the Sea of Galilee lapping along the shore, our party relaxed under the floodlights on the front lawn as I outlined portions of Bible prophecy about to be fulfilled.

I spoke of the seven year treaty which would need to be fulfilled shortly, as the Arab shopkeepers' strike (which at that time, Oct. 1988, had continued on for ten months), was destroying the economy in that area of the world.

Here is the Kissinger article which I read to my listeners:

Henry Kissinger and Peace.

'In the Middle East, I believe if you attempt to achieve a total solution, it must fail, because as of this moment the differences are too great. But what is achievable in the Middle East is a series of interim arrangements that improve the situation for, say, FIVE TO TEN YEARS (emphasis added), at the end of which the situation will be discussed anew. At this moment, for example, the biggest problem on the West Bank is to get agreement in principle from Israel to withdraw from some Arab territories even if not all. If one could get some self governing structure into Gaza and parts of the West Bank governed by local Arabs, supported perhaps by Jordan, Egypt and Saudi Arabia, and if that group could then coexist with Israel in a concrete manner for say FIVE TO SEVEN YEARS (emphasis added). At the end of that period, one could consider the role of other organizations. This I believe is possible, and after the American and Israeli elections that should be attempted.' End quote.

Prophecy Correct

I continued on with my outdoor message. 'You will shortly get a peace treaty in this area. It will not be for five or ten years, but it will be for SEVEN years and the man who confirms it will be called ANTI-CHRIST.

Israeli Leadership

Readers, please notice that the Israeli elections were concluded on November 1st 1988, with Shamir winning. This man held a very important post with the Israeli Secret Service called the 'Mossad'. Don't forget surveillance is the name of the game as World Government approaches.

U.S.A. Leadership

On November 8th 1988, George Bush was elected the 41st President of the United States. This man held a very important post with the C.I.A. Don't forget surveillance is the name of the game as World Government approaches.

U.S.S.R. Leadership

The man leading Russia at that time was Gorbachev. He also had strong connections with the KGB. Surveillance is the name of the game.

According to Dr Henry Kissinger the stage should now be set sometime in the not too distant future for a five to seven year peace treaty in the Middle East. Unless I had ample reason and authority to make this statement, this could be misconstrued as an act of downright presumption — Believe me, the Word of God does not lie when it narrows this period down to 7 years.

'And he shall confirm the covenant with many for one week' (which is seven years in Jewish reckoning) 'and in the midst of the week he shall cause the sacrifice and the oblation to cease.' *Ref.4. (This implies that after 3 1/2 years, he will break the peace treaty) and interfere with their religious rites.

2. This man will also be appointed a loosely knit leader of the European Community — E.C. (Notice the word 'economic is no longer used by the media as the community is financially embarrassed.) i.e. There is very little economy left.

3. This great world leader will be accepted by the world community at large and the prophecies label him with many names or titles, four of which are:
   (a) Antichrist
   (b) Beast
   (c) Man of Sin
   (d) Son of Perdition

This latter title was previously applied to another man in

32

history—Judas Iscariot—The man dies but the evil spirit lives on. Thus in the latter part of this century, prior to the year 2000, this man will reveal himself, according to the prophecy, 'in his own appointed time.'

If you are seeking to identify this great world leader, please do not look for a man with horns, a forked tail and a pitch fork.

Rather, look for a brilliant diplomat, a man who is skilled in the 'peace' process and also is involved in international finance.

Just as the original bearer of the title 'son of perdition', Judas Iscariot was an acceptable member of the 'Jesus team', (even acting as treasurer for the group), so this man in the latter days will be apparently a very popular character until, like his predecessor, 'Satan will enter into him', and he will take on his final role as 'son of perdition'.

By the way, a Canadian newspaper in the month of January 1989, boldly stated that President George Bush was bringing Dr Henry Kissinger out of mothballs to conduct Middle East peace negotiations. For previous predictions please look up pages 37-44 in my book 'Warning' written in 1980, and pages 57-63 in my book 'Second Warning'.

Born again Christians, committed to our Lord Jesus Christ, have known for some time that there is a book in heaven called the Lamb's Book of Life. All whose names are in that book are heaven-bound. All whose names are not in that book are hell-bound.

My eldest daughter Becky, put it beautifully one day when she said 'God is very precise, isn't He Dad. He doesn't indulge in woolly thinking.'

Some predictions from the ancient prophets may help at this point.

e.g. 'And whosoever was not found written in the book of life was cast into the lake of fire.' *Ref.5.

All who speak English should pick up the meaning of this statement fairly swiftly.

Now, we read 'And they that dwell on the earth shall wonder, whose names were not written in the book of life from the foundation of the world, when they behold the beast that was and is not and yet is.' *Ref.6.

An explanation of the above.

To the committed Bible reading Christian who knows his or

her name is in this heavenly record book, this information is not shocking because they are aware of:

  a. World Government trends.
  b. The imminent rise of the Antichrist World Leader.
  c. The fact that the same devil that was in Judas Iscariot will be in this future world leader soon after he is revealed through confirming a Middle East peace treaty.

The vast majority of people in the world are due for a tremendous shock when all these things become apparent. That is the reason for the scripture saying—they will 'wonder'.

You will not be surprised at all as you are reading about this secret plan now.

The whole world system must continue in its mad plunge into utter chaos and then Lucifer will whisper to his front man—'Now' and he will appear on the world scene for his new role.

Some folk say 'This can't be happening. Prophecy was fulfilled in the past. Prophecy will be fulfilled in the future, but prophecy must not be fulfilled now in the present because I'm here.'

This author predicts that the decade 1990-2000 will have so much change taking place all over the world that books of this nature (and there are others) will be of great assistance in sorting out the reality from the lies and deceit.

Chapter by chapter, we will now establish the reality brought to us by the ancient prophets and provide an answer to it all.

Some years ago, travelling in a plane over the North Island of New Zealand, I struck up a conversation with a neighbour seated alongside me. He was a kiwifruit farmer, who was in the throes of being gradually dispossessed and pauperised by a few politicians who were pulling the political Fabian Socialist strings at the time.

We got so deeply involved in our conversation and he was so fascinated with all the information I was able to present, that we didn't notice, until we felt the jolt of the wheels on the ground, that we had landed.

The pilot put the engines into reverse thrust, kicking up a terrible noise. I heard another noise whining above the sound of the jet engines. No, it was not a union organiser complaining about conditions.

Turning in my seat, I stared into the anguished face of my companion. With palms upraised, I heard him shout, 'What do I have to do?'

I told him.

If you, during the reading of this manuscript, have the same feelings, please turn immediately to the back of the book where I have set out the answer.

Good reading.

CHAPTER 5

Australia and New Zealand in Global 2000

NEW ZEALAND—AO TE AROA—THE LAND OF THE LONG WHITE CLOUD

(Grafitti sign on wall in Wellington—THE LAND OF THE WRONG WHITE CROWD). Obviously written by a disgruntled citizen.

YOU HAVE TO MAKE A START SOMEWHERE.

Much of Biblical prophecy concerns the city of Jerusalem in Israel.

The original gospel message started from there and was to be carried to the uttermost part of the earth—even away down in N.Z. many are turning to the Lord. They realise that there is no other way to beat this wicked system.

'From the ends of the earth will I cry unto thee when my heart is overwhelmed.' *Ref.1.

'And ye shall be witnesses unto me, both in Jerusalem, and in all Judea and in Samaria, and unto the uttermost part of the earth.' *Ref.2.

From Jerusalem, this has to be New Zealand. Having just returned from a second tour of the Holy Land in 1988, this becomes very apparent as one sits in a number of planes for approximately 24 hours. It makes the eight hour jouney from Auckland to Hawaii seem like a Sunday afternoon jaunt.

Sure enough, little old New Zealand has been chosen by the globalists to conduct their nefarious schemes on an originally unsuspecting public. A few are waking up at last to the fact that something untoward is taking place in the two countries of Australia and New Zealand. To those who don't know where these countries are situated, please look towards the southern hemisphere on your map. We are called 'the folk down under'.

Many readers would naturally presume that the U.S. or Europe would be ahead in all this. The reason that they are not is because their people are extremely difficult to manipulate.

Why New Zealand and Australia First

These two countries of Australasia have been chosen for the following reasons:

1. New Zealand starts the day's trading in the world's financial sector.
2. Both groups of people are in the main, very slack in their approach to life and do not react violently, or even passively for that matter, whilst being manipulated.
   (a) New Zealand's motto—'She'll be right'.
   (b) Australia's motto—'She'll be right mate'.
3. These countries are both islands and have relatively small populations. New Zealand—three and a half million and Australia—seventeen million.

As New Zealand is the key country in these World Government negotiations, we were not surprised to read the following in 'The Evening Post', 21st August 1989. "NZ eyed as global data store.

Disarmament Minister . . .says the Government is funding a study to assess costs and benefits of New Zealand becoming a global centre for the storage of information . . .

The study was expected to take a year . . ." End quote.

Now, as we have already seen, the name of the plan is GLOBAL 2000.

Now, in the Australian newspapers, we read of certain politicians being branded Fabian Socialists. In an article entitled 'A Ripple in an Election Teacup' (Sydney Morning Herald—1 July 1987) we read '......the Fabians named symbolically after a victorious Roman general noted for his cautious conduct of war.....There are about 1000 registered Australian members of the Fabian Society and plenty of well-known faces.

Mr U............h may not be a member, although he has addressed the Young Fabian Society, but Mr H.......e is. So are Foreign Affairs Minister, B..l H.........n, and two Premiers, J.....n C....n and J.....n B..........n. G.......h W.........m remains a prominent member of the N.S.W. branch of which N........e W....n is the patron. The N.S.W. Attorney-General, T......y S...........n is the link between the Fabians and the N.S.W. Government. R....e M.............s, the Victorian Minister for Arts and Police, heads the Australian Fabian Society.' End quote.

In New Zealand in the 1980s, there were a group of politicians in parliament who did not in any way claim to be Fabian Socialists, yet like their Australian counterparts, they followed the three major planks to a tee.

(a) Gradualism — Permeation

(b) Dispossession

(c) Pauperisation

The thing that confused the public was that in both countries, they were destroying society as it was, with the aim of building a new society or a New World Order on a socialist foundation, yet on the other hand, the politicians hob-nobbed with the rich and famous.

Note. This is a completely new ball game and only those with a Christian heritage and divine wisdom could catch them out. It was written years ago —

The Wise Will Understand

'The wicked shall do wickedly and none of the wicked shall understand but the wise shall understand.' *Ref.3.

An anecdote will fit in well at this point.

Some years ago, we were standing alongside a river in Auckland, New Zealand, conducting a baptism.

A lady came up to me and asked 'Are you the Mr Smith that speaks on Bible Prophecy?' I replied 'Yes, from time to time.'

She went on to state that her son had heard me speak and went home to explain it all to his unbelieving Dad.

His father, upon hearing what seemed to him to be a way out fable said 'What a lot of nonsense,' to which the boy quickly replied 'It's okay Dad. Mr Smith read to us from the Bible where it said 'none of the wicked would understand'.'

The two countries referred to as New Zealand and Australia will sometimes, from now on, be referred to as 'Australasia'.

Up until ten years ago, i.e. 1978, things were humming along nicely. New Zealand was referred to as 'God's own country' and Australia — 'The lucky country.'

A change of political parties came later and as all honest citizens will agree, the rot set in. By this statement, I am not intending to slight any reader's political persuasion.

In New Zealand, we discovered that a small group within the Labour Party (who traditionally stood up for the working people) brought in some very odd policies in line with their counterparts across the Tasman Sea in Australia.

New Zealand, the Prototype for the E.C. and Rest of the World.

People in other countries, take note — this is how they are

treating the guinea pig nations. This is how they will treat you. The E.C. countries in particular, have been singled out for this form of treatment.

1. In New Zealand their policies led to masses of farmers leaving the land with subsidies being withdrawn.
2. Small businesses being shut down. All small businesses must be destroyed as all major companies must be fully computerised and merged.
3. Farming communities being decimated.
4. Government workers being made redundant, who stood in stunned disbelief as their redundancy money was handed over.
5. Masses moving to the cities looking for work and security.
6. Big business began booming.
7. Former National and Liberal voters voted Labour as their personal bank accounts grew.
8. Yuppies bought new Jaguars and BMW motor cars.
9. Small businesses were bought out by big business. Note — the plan is to destroy all small business initially.
10. Large corporations began merging and centralising. Thus big business takes over, and then they in turn are taken over by World Government groups. Easy isn't it? Who will finally be in control? Got any ideas?
11. The police force of the country was cut down in numbers.
12. The armed forces were also cut back in numbers. This is important as law and order needs to be weakened in case any person or group finds out what is going on regarding World Government plans and tries to use legitimate law enforcement to stop it.
13. The politicians responsible for all this chaos replied using cliches which kept the majority quiet for long enough to completely destroy the Australian and New Zealand quality of life as we knew it.

Cliche no.1. There is some belt tightening to do.

Cliche no.2. We must endure some PAIN. It was highly noticeable that those who talked most about PAIN didn't appear to suffer any themselves.

Cliche no.3. We are restructuring you know. This is code for pauperisation or destruction of each sector.

Restructuring really means 'to make worthless then cancel.' Like Germany in 1948. There must be no other alternative i.e. no 'us' and 'them'. No one left to fight, and no fight left in anyone. This is to be done for our benefit, or thus it must appear to be. Cliche no.4. Things will improve shortly.

No matter which small business enterprise seemed to be successful e.g. deer farming, some method was thought up to wreck it. i.e. Livestock tax etc., which put increasing and sudden pressure on the farmers to pay a tax on each saleable beast in lieu of selling it. This meant that masses of capital had to be found all at once — an impossibility for some, and this sudden change overtaxed the stamina of a dedicated group of accountants who had to readjust all these figures once the animal was actually sold.

Then there was Goods and Services Tax which became a nightmare of book-keeping for small business persons and stock-taking was enough to have a man led away in a strait jacket by a man with a white coat. This can be raised from time to time, gradually of course, to avoid much flak from the voting public e.g. From 10% to 12 and a half% as has happened in New Zealand. The lying politicians initially promise that there will not be any increase in this tax.

While all this was going on, this particular small group of politicians were receiving bountiful advice from various 'business groups', whose men seemed to be doing 'quite well thank you' while others suffered — in the lower income brackets.

None of the foregoing information is designed to be a criticism. Just a simple record written without any emotion by one who felt the heart of the average citizen.

Goodies or Baddies

This record will go down in written history once the author has moved on and future generations will be called upon to rise up and in the light of future developments, call this small group of politicians 'blessed' for the splendid results that they achieved on behalf of the citizens of Australasia or, on the other hand, the 'most miserable wretches' who ever strode the halls of power, for the bondage they imposed upon their trusting voters.

Let history decide

One of New Zealand's national magazines 'The Listener', helped quite considerably in our understanding of the violent transitions that were besetting our country New Zealand. Dated December 19, 1987, under the heading 'The Plan', we read:

40

By piecing together the statements and documents it can be shown that 'Rogernomics' was a plan imposed by a small group of ministers on a party which had confused ideas as to what it was letting itself in for.... Ultimately the L..........e-P.......r-C.......l-P.......e-D......s view of the economic policy had been endorsed before the snap election.... Even the Prime Minister D.........d L.......e acknowledged that the agenda of Rogernomics had been withheld from the party which had campaigned for his election.' End quote.

Now readers are becoming clear as to what has been taking place and should in no way attach blame to either the National or Liberal or Labour Parties, who probably in the main, knew very little of what was going on.

Once this book gets into their hands, they may try to act, but even now it is too late. The fat is in the fire.

At the time of writing this book, approaching 1990, the diabolical policies are irreversible. In politics there is nothing left to hang on to for security.

Where did I read
'The eternal God is thy refuge, and underneath are the everlasting arms.'
*Ref.4.

It would pay you, the reader, to examine this aspect of life with all seriousness. Politics has failed you. Economy will fail you at the next big stock market crash, when all cash will be cancelled. Religion will fail you when a giant conglomerate known as the World Church — embracing Protestant denominations, the Roman Catholics, Eastern Religions as well as the Church of Satan and the New Age Movement, is formed.

The only one who will not and cannot fail is spoken of as 'Jesus Christ, the same, yesterday, today and forever.' *Ref.5.

On with this true life saga. I sometimes wish that all this were wrong and that it were not happening. The problem is that it IS happening NOW!

I continued on with my search and read of a group called 'The Business Round Table'.

In an article written for the 'National Business Review', 3rd October 1983, we read in part:

'What is probably the most powerful and influential group in New Zealand outside Cabinet and the Treasury has decided to 'go public'.

The New Zealand Business Round Table, a group of 17 of

41

the country's largest businesses had made its membership list and aims available to National Business Review......its industrial and political clout is immense.

Less politely, but probably more accurately, the Round Table is also known in the capital as the Auckland (industrial) mafia.

The seventeen companies meet only occasionally, but are not averse to picking up the proverbial hotline to politicians and to ministers.

......**Feltex N.Z. Ltd Managing Director H........d T..........r is chairman, with Fletcher Challenge's R.........n T........r as his deputy.**

'......We've got to be careful we're not seen as a pressure group and not to be superseding other bodies', says T..........r.

The Round Table 'bends over backwards' not to be seen as a powerful lobbying group able to influence Government policy 'But I suspect that, if we have a viewpoint, it would be listened to, without necessarily being followed.'

......T......r says of the groups communications with Cabinet ministers or Government departments 'We may be helpful to them in passing on our thoughts of the day — and we take a jolly good interest in matters of the day.' End quote.

As this is a fairly old news cutting, we recognise that by 1989 the membership and leadership will have no doubt changed quite considerably.

It is important to understand also, that any names mentioned in this book are simply left in to make some sense of the whole scenario.

The author does not claim that any persons mentioned have any knowledge whatsoever of any of these World Government aims. We simply state that the master super-puppeteer, Lucifer himself, is pulling the strings and it is possible that many of those dancing to his tune are unaware of the overall plan.

We now have enough knowledge to recognise that many of these men would have overseas contacts also in business and economic life who also have interests in New Zealand. Some of these persons no doubt are aware of the Global 2000 plan.

From time to time, big business executives fly from country to country to conduct 'deals' and to buy up shareholdings in big business in other countries.

We are now ready to look at our next group. Very, very few New Zealanders have ever heard of this fairly secretive group.

PARLIAMENTARIANS FOR WORLD ORDER (P.W.O.) now PARLIAMENTARIANS FOR GLOBAL ACTION (P.G.A.)

The use of the name 'Parliamentarians for World Order' was illegal and broke the 1956 Electoral Act Section 32b, hence the new name 'Parliamentarians for Global Action'.

The purpose of 'Parliamentarians for World Order' as stated in its constitution is 'to promote the cause of world institutions and enforceable world law for the people of the world as a single community through Parliamentary action.'

Notice a change in the Constitution Act 1986, removed the power from New Zealand's Governor General to veto any bills being passed. A cunning move indeed. To any who object to my raising this issue, I ask three questions.

1. Why do you react?
2. Why was this done?
3. How does it help N.Z.?

This group, P.W.O. or P.G.A., in the 1980s, had individual members from U.S.A., Netherlands, Zambia, Zimbabwe, Australia, Denmark, Thailand, Ireland, Nigeria, E.E.C. Britain had 110 members, 130 from Canada, France with 40 members, India 15, Japan 160, Kenya 35, N.Z. 40, and Norway with 9 members.

In a letter dated 6th July 1987, New Zealand's then Prime Minister, Mr D......d L......e – when asked the questions:

1. Are you a member of Parliamentarians for Global Action (previously known as Parliamentarians for World Order) replied 'yes'.
2. As a member of the New Zealand Labour Party, do you belong to or are you affiliated with the Socialist International? Do you support or have sympathy with this organisation? The answer was 'yes'.

In a letter to the Christchurch Star on the 11th June 1986, the Minister of Justice, later to become Prime Minister of New Zealand, Mr P.......r was asked a number of questions, one of which read 'is he one of the 14 New Zealand MPs who currently belong to the international body known as Parliamentarians for World Order?' The answer was 'Yes I am a member. There are about 40 New Zealand MPs from all political parties who are current members'.

Readers, please note that the name change for this group was essential as it was not fitting that those New Zealand parliamentarians who took an oath to uphold N.Z.'s sovereignty and security should also work for, or even belong to a group which one day will no doubt play a part in N.Z.'s sovereignty being swallowed up in a New World Order or World Government. The M.P. for Glenfield was reported in the Dominion newspaper, Wellington, as having attended a P.G.A. forum at the United Nations in New York.

There they discussed such subjects as World Peace, War, Pollution and Disease Control. She said that these things....'know no national boundaries and that is why these problems must be tackled globally.'

In my book 'Second Warning', we read a statement made by a Mr R............d P...........e on the 16th July 1981, confirming that this group originally called P.W.O. (now P.G.A.) would challenge N.Z's independence. This I feel is a statement well worth rewriting.

Quote — (This statement may be viewed in Hansard.) 'We will not be able to tackle these problems unless we are prepared to co-operate and give up some of our national sovereignty.' End quote.

Away back on the 19th September 1981, we read in Wellington's Evening Post 'Chair for P......e in New York.

Auckland Central M.P. Mr R.........d P.........e is to chair a key committee at an international political forum in New York next week.

....The forum limited to 100 members of parliaments throughout the world, is to be held in the United Nations building. It has been organised by a worldwide group of Parliamentarians called 'Politicians for World Order.' End quote.

Later on when the New Zealand State Owned Enterprises began to come up for sale, the front page of the Dominion newspaper Wellington, read in giant type 'P........e Welcomes Foreign Investors.' In the article which followed, referring to New Zealand's debt problem, we quote 'The options for relieving some of the pressure are limited and none are attractive' he said. 'Either we cut social spending significantly, or increase taxation, or sell assets. End quote.

The author would agree with this statement and add one more viable option that is being used quite successfully in other third world countries — default on the loan.

In other words, the persons who created this intolerable burden from their overseas ivory towers cannot afford to let any nation collapse yet, as they do not have the new system set up yet.

THE PROBLEM WITH SELLING YOUR ASSETS IS THAT ONCE THEY ARE GONE IT'S ALL OVER FOR NEW ZEALAND'S SOVEREIGNTY. THE SAME APPLIES TO ANY COUNTRY IN THE WORLD.

WE ARE THEN OWNED BY THE MONEY LENDERS — NOW!!

Remember 'The rich ruleth over the poor and the borrower is servant to the lender.' *Ref.6.

No reader should ever doubt the sincerity of any individuals mentioned in this book.

They, in the main, are convinced that the 'united global' approach is the only way to go.

Many of their plans of necessity were done 'under cover' however, as most of the populace would have risen up in revolt had the plan been carried out openly.

Even I could have been deceived into believing that Global 2000 was a great idea, if I hadn't already read the MANUFACTURER'S TEXTBOOK. This, I willingly acknowledge to be the case.

The odd twist here is that some whose names I have written into my script were brought up in Bible-believing homes (their parents were my personal friends) and I pray that they too, will turn back to the God of their fathers before it is too late.

It should be remembered by all that politicians and business barons rise and fall, but they will one day all die and go to either heaven or hell. More prayer for their souls than criticism of their actions would be in order.

Sovereignty Under Threat

New Zealand and Australia are fast losing their sovereignty.

The politicians supposedly in power in the future, will have no assets to juggle, no government departments to work with, no power to make decisions and as long as they behave themselves and continue to listen to their 'advisors', they will be kept on.

Try and break away and become an individualist again could cause one to receive the John F. Kennedy treatment or the old arsenic in the coffee cup trick.

Remember the Chain of Advice

Global World Government plannners and money lenders —
travelling advisors and representatives — local powerful business
lobby-groups — Cabinet World Government advocates — other
politicians — the party — the people (the pawns) — Seven groups in
all.

The word 'Rogernomics' was a word coined in N.Z. in the late
'80's. It was play on the name of N.Z.'s then Minister of Finance,
Mr R........r D.......s. This was a radical plan, the media using his
name to describe it.

The idea was to make the user pay for everything, goods and
services alike — also, six Government departments were to be
corporatized or turned into revenue earning corporations. Then
later on of course, the State Owned Enterprises could be
privatised, thus allowing overseas investors in, and then gradually
the percentage of shares allowed to be bought by overseas investors
could be increased until, with our assets all gone, we would be
owned by the very people who lent us the money in the first place.

Further down the line, any person who took part in this bold
venture, going where no New Zealander has ever gone before,
could be 'beamed up' to a lucrative position overseas where the
angry citizens of New Zealand could no longer lay hands on them.

In an article in the Christchurch Press 26.9.87, we read 'Not
long ago of course the Labour Party's policy was clearly against
the sale of Petrocorp to private interests.

.....But last year, however, the Government realised that it
could not find the money for its welfare programme, without a
public float of shares in State Enterprises such as Petrocorp, the
Bank of New Zealand, New Zealand Steel and Air New Zealand.

.....Even at this point however, the Government was adamant
on one detail, it would continue to be the majority shareholder.

..... One is to avoid being at the mercy of private companies
and overseas influences controlling the supply of oil and gas.
Mr D............s has said that he is happy to sell the rest of the
Governments shareholding, not just a further part of it, 'next week'
if he gets the right price.' End quote.

It is little wonder that New Zealand's political system has been
described as one of the most fragile democracies in the world i.e.
vote them in, and sadly enough, they do what they wish.

The Prime Minister at that time, Mr L.....e confesses–(see
Press article 26.6.87) 'Rogernomics kept secret from the party'.

46

The article goes on to say 'The Labour Party hierarchy kept 'Rogernomics' secret from party members before the 1984 General Election' the Prime Minister Mr L.......e has told Australian television.

......Mr L......e .admits Rogernomics would never had been implemented had it first been shown to party members, the 'Auckland Star' reported.

Mr L......e said Labour's economic policy had to be sold to the party and the country in various DISGUISES, (emphasis added) the newspaper said. End quote.

On with game plan.

A key group in this World Government Global plan is 'Telecommunications' known in Australia and New Zealand as TELECOM.

Interesting Developments

As the world government group require a full dossier on every individual's life so that this individual no longer has any rights to self-expression in any field other than that which is chosen for him or her, we see that the power to control the transmission of all this data is of utmost importance.

We have learned recently that the S.D.I. Star Wars Programme is already in operation. 40% for the defence of the U.S.A. and 60% for the transmission of data.

In the Press newspaper 16.12.87, we read 'Sir R.........d T.......r has been appointed to be the chairman of Telecom, the Minister of State Owned Enterprises, Mr P......e announced yesterday.' End quote.

Sir R.......d T......r, you will remember, was also a top man in the Business Round Table group

Continue quote–'Mr P......e said that Sir R.........d, the chairman of the Fletcher challenge group was one of New Zealand's most successful businessmen and was ideally qualified to chair Telecom.

Referring to a WORLD MOVE to deregulate telecommunications, Mr P......e said that Sir R.......d had the ability to lead Telecom into a more competitive area.' End quote. Emphasis added.

The author of this book doesn't understand the phrase 'a more competitive area' as at that time at least (1987) there was no competition in this field in Australia and New Zealand.

If there were, the iniquitous charges of this group might be done away with.

On our trips away, we always called our home 'collect' or 'reverse charge' or a 'transfer charge' to our home number. We are now seriously disadvantaged, as these true humanitarians have slapped on a $2.00 surcharge, just for the privilege of having an operator assist.

No wonder people are baffled.

It is a strange and wonderful mixture of Fabian Socialism and huge monopolies taking over every department of our lives.

At this point, one may ask four questions of the author.

1. Are you against this World Government plan? — Yes.
2. Are you going to try and stop it? — No.
3. Why not? — Because the Scripture must be fulfilled.
4. Why did you write these books then? — To enlighten Australians and New Zealanders; to warn folk in other countries of the cunning of the enemy with whom we are dealing and finally to bring an antidote to the fear and despair which has been created.

This antidote is a personal and vital faith in God, through our Lord Jesus Christ. Do you find this obnoxious? Read on.

CHAPTER 6

Beginnings

Away back in history, a man called Ignatius de Loyola created the Illuminati (the Alumbrados), a satanic organisation to control the minds of European leaders through hypnosis, witchcraft and mind control.

The Dominican monks who ran the Spanish Inquisition, arrested Loyola because of these strange occultish activities, but upon presenting to the pope of the day his new plan to set up the 'Jesuits', (Roman Catholic defenders of the faith) the pope not only released Loyola from the Dominicans' prison but also appointed him the first Jesuit general.

Loyola was right into the occult. He used meditation, prayer, contemplation, visualisation and illumination to such a degree that he could ultimately levitate off the floor under satanic power. (Even those connected with the art of transcendental meditation can eventually move into this satanic realm today.)

Loyola used:

a. Philosophy
b. Metaphysics
c. Logic
d. Psychoanalysis
e. Psychology
f. Hypnosis
g. Telepathy
h. Psychiatry
i. Psychotherapy

(These are now referred to as 'behavioural sciences'.)

In the year 1776, on May 1st, the Illuminati of Bavaria was taken over by one Adam Weishaupt — a professor at the University of Ingolstadt, educated by Jesuits.

Important note. The link between the Jesuits and the Illuminati is inescapable.

Recap of Order

1. Illuminati — Ignatius de Loyola
2. Dominicans became involved. (Spanish Inquisition murderers.)

3. Jesuits inaugurated — Loyola appointed as first general.
4. Another Jesuit named Weishaupt took over the Illuminati.
5. Therefore, the World Government plan has extremely evil foundations.

It began to leak out that Loyola was the founder of the satanic Illuminati so the Jesuits trained up this other man who pretended to defect from their ranks to make the world believe that they (the Jesuits) did not, in truth, initiate this secret society. This man was Adam Weishaupt. In the year 1776 on May 1st, the Illuminati of Bavaria was taken over by Weishaupt, a professor at the University of Ingolstat and a Jesuit to the end.

To those readers whose emotions are stirred at this point, even to the stage of being offended, I humbly recommend again, as I have done before, that you obtain a copy of David Yallop's book 'In God's Name' and read it thoughtfully.

Mr Yallop, in a very scholarly manner shows the links between the Mafia — the Vatican — the Freemasons (today's Illuminati).

To those who choose to adopt the ostrich attitude and bury their heads in the sand and deny all this I say, 'Don't read Mr Yallop's book.' By the way, his book has become so popular that copies are now obtainable at a very reasonable price in paperback form.

The Illuminati became secretly the most important branch of the Jesuit order.

There were three classes of adepts:
(a) Nursery
(b) Masonry
(c) Mysteries

Each of these were subdivided also into degrees, very similar to the Freemasons of today.

The Bavarian Government viewed this society so seriously, that they attempted to close them down. (See Encyclopaedia Britannica.)

In the year 1778, through one Baron Van Knigge (a Templar), the upper degrees in Freemasonry were subverted, carrying in this plan its aim of

WORLD DOMINION BY ANY AND ALL MEANS

After gaining control of certain Masonic Lodges, the Jesuits, Weishaupt and his associates really got carried away with their ideas.

51

Simply put, 'the plan' evolved as follows.
(a) Destruction of all religion.
(b) Destruction of all existing governments.
(c) Destruction of all traditional human institutions.
(d) To rebuild a New World Order on the wreckage that they had created.

METHODS:
(a) Divide the masses of the people into opposing camps.
(b) Political, social and economic problems would be magnified.
(c) Arm these opposing groups causing them to fight and weaken themselves.
(d) Destroy peoples' faith in their systems of government.

MAIN POINTS
1. Use monetary and sex bribes to control those already in high places — government, business etc., with threats of exposure, harm to loved ones, financial ruin and such if they did not co-operate.
2. To get members on to campus to cultivate students with exceptional mental ability and to grant them special scholarships e.g. Rhodes Scholarships etc., by which to train them in One World Concepts.
3. To use all influential people and students controlled by them as agents, to be placed behind the scenes of all governments as experts and specialists, and to help bring about the destruction of the governments they were elected to serve.
4. To obtain absolute control of the Press (now including radio, t.v., video and movie industry) in order to control public opinion and to slant truth. (Media control centralisation.)

These individuals could never have hoped to have brought all these things about in their lifetimes, but the spirit in the background, centuries old in wisdom and skilled in the art of manipulating mankind, continued on the plan right up until today and beyond.

Please find a friend and read the 4 main points out aloud to one another and write in the names of some of these influential people helping to destroy your parliamentary system of democracy. Some of these are possibly even within the government.

Some of their names will be spoken regularly on the T.V. news and also figure highly in the stock market news.

SUBTLE WRECKERS LIST
1.
2.
3.
4.
5.

Please note that in order to pick out some snippets of real news, one needs to subscribe to the rapidly diminishing list of independent newspapers who have the courage to print some 'facts'. These of course, are a dying breed as they are being rapidly bought out by the media masters.

Readers of my books WARNING and SECOND WARNING, will remember me stating that many men have believed in and actively promoted World Government down through the centuries.

Cecil Rhodes of course was one such believer.

All those trained in Rhodes Scholarships have therefore been thoroughly indoctrinated in One World concepts, whether they were aware of this or not.

There are quite a number of Rhodes Scholars in New Zealand and Australia.

FABIAN SOCIALISM — Founded by Thomas Davidson, an idealist whose aims were to reconstruct society on a non-competitive basis with the object of remedying the evils of poverty. In 1884, the name was adopted.

The constitution of 1887 said in part, 'it will confine itself to supporting those candidates who will go furthest in the direction of Socialism.'

Among those prominent in the movement in the early days were:

Frank Podmore — a spiritualist
J. Ramsey McDonald — later Labour Prime Minister of England
George Bernard Shaw — a godless philosopher
William Clarke — a former disciple of Mazzini, a Luciferian top mason
Mrs Annie Besant — a radical who controlled Freethought Publishing Co.

53

Dr Pankhurst — husband of a later leader of the womens' movement

Mrs Charlotte M. Wilson — a member of the anarchist movement

Not a list of the most choice individuals you will agree.

Anarchists and Socialists both agree on the first step to reorganise the world to their liking.

(a) Anarchists say 'All must be destroyed in order that all may be rebuilt.' This aim is achieved through revolution.

(b) Socialists say 'All must be destroyed in order that all may be rebuilt.' This aim is achieved through gradualism.

Readers, please notice that both Australia and New Zealand in the 1980's at least, were governed by group 'b', i.e. socialistic governments hiding behind the word 'Labour'. Gradualism was their forte.

Look above and see their aims. The introduction of new laws continually baffles the populace in general.

These laws, while framed to appeal to popular fancy, once introduced, can be administered in such a way as to operate the INTERNATIONAL DESTRUCTION which is the primary aim of both parties.

KEY NOTE NO.1
Australia and New Zealand are the TEST CASE for World Government.

KEY NOTE NO. 2
New Zealand a State of Australia?

New Zealand is already included as a State of Australia, under the Australian Constitution Act 9th July 1900. This Act has never been revoked by Australia, was not initially agreed upon by New Zealand, and is not widely recognised by the people of either country. At a meeting in late 1988, a young man approached me and asked for proof of this as a friend of his who was a practising lawyer said that I was wrong. If this person had attained a law degree in Australia and was not aware of this fact, I personally would have sought out another lawyer to assist me with any legal problems.

A lady who listened to my messages wrote to the Prime Minister's department in New Zealand to obtain clarification. Here is the reply in part — dated 8th Feb. 1989.

Quote—'In answer to your query, it is not possible to simply delete the reference to New Zealand....The reference to New Zealand in covering clause 6 is not to be understood as stating that New Zealand is a State of Australia, it merely offers provision for New Zealand to become an Australian State....' End quote.

Under Definitions No.6—'The Commonwealth' shall mean, the Commonwealth of Australia as established under this Act.

'The States' shall mean, such of the colonies of New South Wales, NEW ZEALAND (emphasis added), Queensland, Tasmania, Victoria, Western Australia, and South Australia, including the Northern Territory of South Australia as for the time being are parts of the Commonwealth, and such colonies or territories as may be admitted into or established by the Commonwealth shall be called 'a State'.' End quote.

Which means, that by an act of parliament, both in Australia and in New Zealand, the latter can quickly link up with the former and be called a State of Australia as New Zealand has no actual Constitution of its own, as can be referred to as 'The Constitution'.

C.E.R.—Closer Economic Relations is preparing the way for this link up and some politicians and academics are now publicly using the term C.P.R.—Closer Political Relations, having in mind no doubt that the new Parliament House in Canberra would have room for the State Premier of New Zealand to attend the State Premiers Conferences. Note again the cover of the Bulletin magazine 12.4.88, showing the Prime Ministers of Australia and New Zealand in bed together and the caption stating 'Why N.Z. should be the 8th and 9th States of Australia.' (Maybe the North and South Islands could make up the two states.)

Now, the Fabians form numerous detached societies, committees, study clubs, associations, leagues, schools etc., in order to gain the support of non-socialists.

Thus 'sucker-lists' of capitalist supporters of socialism are made available to the Fabian Socialists working in England, America, and other countries; mainly big business tycoons who see a fast buck to be made as the good, honest working man is ruined or driven to the wall through these foul, and unethical governments 'restructuring' (code for destruction) of the economy. Be assured, these fat cats will not escape attention. They are next on the list to be destroyed.

Australian and New Zealand readers can make up their own SUCKER LIST. (Watch the names listed on the sharemarket columns.)

1.
2.
3.
4.
5.

i.e. In countries like Australia or N.Z. those wealthy capitalists would normally have voted National or Liberal, but greed drove them into the other camp. The sudden so-called 'freeing up of the economy' has made millionaires of some, paupers of others, and has caused others to commit suicide.

Wellington's 'Dominion' Newspaper, 8 December 1987. 'The number of suicidal and desperate people ringing Wellington Samaritans had increased significantly over the past couple of months...there's an overall feeling of desperation and there are all sorts of stresses in the community....

Some of the calls may be related to the sharemarket crash and the general feeling of lack of confidence in the economy which makes people scared'. End quote.

Dominion Newspaper 30 June 1988. 'Farmers under stress have committed suicide, suffered marriage breakups or abandoned their farms, a Federated Farmers conference was told yesterday.

.....In Waikato , checks on five farms revealed, one abandoned, one where the farmer had committed suicide, a marriage in difficulties, and a husband and wife team driving hundreds of kilometres a week to take on other jobs.' End quote.

'Behold the hire of the labourers who have reaped down your fields, which is of you kept back by fraud crieth and the cries of them which have reaped are entered into the ears of the Lord of the Sabaoth.' *Ref.1.

This simply means that to become rich at the expense of the poor is not a wise course of action. God loves the poor and will not forget injustice perpetrated against these folk. Big businessmen, remember there is a reckoning day coming.

Taxation — A Weapon
The best known and cleverest destructionist laws now on the statute books are those of the:
(a) Income Tax
(b) Inheritance Tax — yet to be applied
(c) Capital Gains Tax etc
(d) Assets Tax

These types of taxes are initially applied very forcefully only to the little man. Tax dodges called tax avoidance, not tax evasion mind you, are practiced by the majority of large firms and corporations thus enabling them to invest and grow fat, whilst the little man is kept quiet through fear of tax investigation.

Overseas Readers, Prepare for a Shock. The European Community countries and trading partners, including the U.S.A., Japan etc, you're next—believe me.

New Zealand 'Dominion Sunday Times', 25th June 1989.

'The taxman is burying small businesses in a mountain of paper work costing them between $2,500 and $5,000 a year to process, accountants say.

Inland Revenue Minister....says a normal sized business is now required to send in 28 payments and 26 different tax returns every year.

....the average business five years ago may have had contact with the taxman three times a year. The number of returns is at least 30 now....with the misery index rising ten-fold.

...In the worst case, a business would have to make 36 different returns....' End quote.

I recently met a young New Zealander at Honolulu airport (June 1989). He said 'I love New Zealand but it's been destroyed so I'm getting out.'

Hitting the small businessman is only a temporary measure however, whilst providing false security to the big business people.

Step 1. Hit the small people and almost encourage big business to dodge tax payments.

Step 2. Once the small man has been destroyed, then turn your attention to the big business tycoons.

See Auckland Star 1st August 1986 entitled 'Richer Taxman Nabs Dodgers. The Commissioner of Inland Revenue was given the power to declare that a business set up to make a tax deductible loss is not a business at all.

......the Commissioner of Inland Revenue was given new powers which, some say, violate a principal of British justice— that a person is innocent until proven guilty.'

Now the Sun Herald 20th November 1988. 'Thirty-three of Australia's best-known companies are having their books investigated in the latest phase of a major crackdown on tax avoidance.

....Taxation Commissioner....and his investigators....audited

57

40 of Australia's largest firms in the last financial year, following the Federal Governments tough taxation policies.' End quote. Can you see how it's done? Cleverly encourage tax avoidance by big business groups as you attack the lower income bracket. The top income folk become heroes as they boast of ripping off the tax department and buying big cars, boats etc. Then, when the time is right, using the media to reinforce your point, turn these tax dodgers into the lowest form of humanity e.g. from the same Sun Herald article—'Cheating the tax collector is the same as cheating on one's mates.

.....When people do not pay their proper share of taxation, it means that others have to pay more if the same level of facilities are maintained....'. End quote.

One can now picture in their minds a scene in a pub where groups of semi-inebriated individuals, breathing fumes over one another, eyes glazed and lined like road maps, waving copies of the local newspaper, heartily agreeing that all tax dodgers need to be caught, conveniently forgetting that many of their own number will be included in the overall catch. The media has tremendous power.

This is obviously clear in Australia and New Zealand where big business hobnobs with and gives friendly advice to the government—jobs for the boys and friendly acts; like big businessmen flying important government persons around in their aeroplanes and going to parties together.

LIST OF GOVERNMENT HOBNOBBERS
1.
2.
3.
4.
5.

There are still some alert citizens around however. Read this. 'Press', 31st May 1989. 'Tax Avoiding Monk.

A retired British dock worker has declared himself a monk and named his bungalow Alfredsco Abbey to avoid payment of a new local tax. Monks and monasteries are to be exempted from the community charge that will replace property taxes.

.....Chapman told reporters he had hoped to get his wife into a tax dodging habit, but she refused to call herself a nun....' End quote.

A Nasty Shock

The Fabian Scheme for World Perfection

'This ideal is to be achieved by the gradual expropriation and pauperization of all classes by systematic, economic pressure causing each class to be separately ruined according to the best means available for ruining it.'

This is not a new plan.

(a) It is the plan of the Jesuits.

(b) It is the plan of Weishaupts Illuminati.

(c) It is the plan of International Freemasonry.

(d) It is the plan so minutely described in 'The Protocols'.

(e) It is the plan of the Fabian Socialists.

The three points that Albert Pike (1809-1891) a 33 degree Freemason and Grand Pontiff of Universal Freemasonry believed in:

a.   Destruction

Wreck everything

b.   Materialism

Create a booming economy

c.   Imposition

Hit hard suddenly and control with an iron fist.

Albert Pike is called the 'Grand Pontiff' of universal Freemasonry. This title is very similar to that as is used in relation to the pope who is also known as the Pontiff in universal Catholicism.

Please notice therefore, the subtle link again between Freemasonry and the Vatican.

NEW ZEALAND FABIAN SOCIALISM

In New Zealand politics in the late 80's the Fabian Socialists did not reveal themselves, whether because of fear, shame or threats of hostility, we may never know — yet the three major planks are evident for all to see.

Plank no.1. Gradualism (Permeation)

Sneak up on society and then suddenly hit hard — do not swerve or deviate from your course or 'all of your waiting will have been in vain'. In N.Z. and Australia, they have made a start on the farmers. The cities and townspeople come next.

Plank no.2. Dispossession — They are after your land, the rascals.

Remove land and property ownership from the individual. Ownership of property gives one a measure of independence. One politician put it very succinctly when he allegedly said, in a private conversation to an acquaintance of the author; 'The concept of private property is outmoded and no longer viable for New Zealand's future.' No wonder he said it privately, because he is smart enough to know that if he said it publicly he would be down the road at any future election - should there ever be another one.

However, in the Bulletin magazine, dated 15th September 1987, Dr N....l B.........t, then minister responsible for the Australia Card, to the 1986 ALP South Australia Branch conference, was quoted in a Senate debate as having said 'Let me say as a socialist, that it is the interests of the community that should come before the individual right...We shouldn't get too hung up as socialists on privacy, because privacy, in many ways, is a bourgeois right that is very much associated with the right to private property.'

Plank no.3. Pauperization.

Each class is to be separately ruined according to the best means available for ruining it.

List of Ruined Sectors
(Please write your own in)

1.	6
2	7
3	8
4	9
5	10

I realize that this information is not sufficient but gives you, the reader, the option of co-operating a little to establish that we are presenting only facts in this book.

CHAPTER 7

The Protocols

On p 77-80 of my first book 'Warning', I outlined some of these Protocols.

At this point, I must make it clear that I utterly reject the anti-Semitic view that this great plan for world domination can be laid at the door of the Jewish race. I do this for two reasons.

  a. It can now be established that they were not the authors.
  b. As a friend of the children of Abraham, I read 'I will bless them that bless thee, and curse him that curseth thee....' *Ref.1.

I consequently set myself the task of endeavouring to ferret out the true authors of this work which sets out very tidily the list of world government aims; or a comprehensive blueprint for world domination.

  1. Hitler believed implicitly that the Protocols were the plans of Jews formulated at the International Judaic Conference held in Basle in 1897. He murdered six and a half million Jews as a result.

      We now know as a fact that it is not a Jewish document. (Possibly, nobody will ever find out who the true authors are.)

  2. Investigators overseas now tell us that their search for the origins of this provocative piece of literature have led them to believe that it is a mystical document apparently connected with a very high Masonic degree. In the book entitled 'The Holy Blood and the Holy Grail', the authors refer to this highly secret group who are called:

PRIEURE DE SION (PRIORY OF ZION)

  3. Anybody familiar with the upper degrees in Freemasonry, will know that the Scottish degrees or rites are higher than the others. These degrees link in with religion, cabalism, alchemy, Hermetic thought and mysteries such as Gnosticism.

  4. Also, the Upper Degrees of the Scottish Rites are the lower degrees of Prieure de Sion.

  5. It is very powerful in international and domestic affairs in Europe.

6. This title Prieure de Sion to top Freemasons involves not the hill of Mt Zion in Jerusalem, but the Priory of Zion meaning the KEYSTONE during the building of the Temple. Ps. 118, 1 Pet. 2:3-8, Matt. 21:4, Rom. 9:33, Acts 4:11.

   It is important to note that Freemasons' secrets are never clearly stated but are veiled in mysticism.

   In the Bible, Christ Jesus is the Stone which the builders rejected, but in Freemasonry it means something else.

7. This highly secret degree links with the 33rd degree which stands for 'Strict Observance'.

8. Anybody who reads 'The Protocols', as I have done a number of times, will note that they talk about 'the Advent of a Masonic Kingdom' — this links the Masons with the plan for World Government.

   Also the phrase 'A King of the blood of Zion' links this high Masonic degree with the plan.

   Here is another strange phrase — 'The King of the Jews will be the real Pope' — This links the Roman Catholic church with the plan.

9. Away back in the 12th century, a man called Malachi brought some prophecies highly respected by the Roman Catholic church. He listed the future Popes and some of their characteristics.

   e.g. Pope John the 23rd in those prophecies was referred to as 'Pasteur et Nautonnier'. (Shepherd and Navigator).

   It was Pope John the 23rd who opened the 2nd Vatican council in 1962 linking Protestants as churches which share God's grace and favour. The official title of Prieure de Sion's Grand Master is 'Nautonnier'. Could this be the same man referred to in the prophecies of this twelfth century prophet.

10. In 1738, Pope Clement XII excommunicated all Freemasons as enemies of the Catholic church. He stated that Masonic thought rests on the heresy which denies Jesus' divinity.

11. In June 1960, this Pope John the 23rd announced that a Catholic may be a Freemason. Is it possible that Pope John the 23rd was also the Grand Master of the high Masonic degree called Prieure de Sion?

12. Adam Weishaupt, Jesuit priest and one of the founders of Illuminati revised and modernised the Protocols and prepared them as the final Luciferian blueprint for the

63

destruction of the old order, and the building of the new order. Remember his society was formed in 1776.

Any reader of David Yallop's book entitled 'In God's Name' can clearly see the link up with the hierarchy of the Vatican and the hierarchy of Freemasonry, also with the Mafia.

In an interview with David Yallop on a midday show screened in Perth during 1987, watched by the author and his wife; the question was asked 'Is it true that many dignitaries within the Vatican walls are Freemasons?'

David Yallop replied that this was a valid question and by way of an answer held up a scroll containing the names of over 100 such persons within the Vatican. Mr Yallop, by the way, does not claim to be anti-Catholic but is of the Roman Catholic persuasion himself.

An ex-Jesuit priest, an acquaintance of my wife and myself, told of kneeling before the Black Pope—the head of the Jesuits, to kiss the ring on his finger. He was startled to see the Masonic emblem on the ring, namely, the square and the compass.

Mormons who have been through the temple ceremonies also will remember that the veil has the Masonic symbols clearly displayed on it, as do the endowment undergarments worn by some of their number for protection. Joseph Smith was a Mason of course.

Mormons, Roman Catholics and Free Masons. Enemies are they?

CHAPTER 8

Some World Government Plans and Aims

Author — Lucifer-Dominicans-Jesuits-Loyola-Weishaupt-Illuminati-Prierre de Sion- and others. (Initiated about 1776. This is all being fulfilled over 200 years after they were first predicted.)

(1) In the hands of the States today, there is a great force that creates movement of thoughts in the people, and that is the press. The part played by the press is to keep pointing out requirements supposed to be indispensable, to give a voice to the complaints of the people, to express and create discontent.

The masses have lost the habit of thinking, unless prompted by the suggestions of our specialists.

(2) We have included in the constitution such rights which are fictitious and not actual rights. All these so-called 'Peoples' Rights' can exist only in idea, an idea which can never be realised in practical life.

(3) We shall create....a universal economic crisis, whereby we shall throw upon the streets, whole mobs of workers simultaneously. These mobs will rush delightedly to shed the blood of those, whom, in the simplicity of their ignorance, they have envied from their cradles, and whose property they will then be able to loot.

'Ours' they will not touch because the moment of attack will be known to us; and we shall take measures to protect our own.

(4) We shall create an intensified centralisation of government in order to grip in our hands, all the forces of the community.

(In Australia and New Zealand county councils and local bodies are being amalgamated which means those who will ultimately be in positions of power will normally be remote from any problems that will arise and will therefore, not feel any personal responsibility. Computers will be much in use during these days and it is important to remember what my accountant once said to me — 'The computer has no soul.')

(5) We shall regulate mechanically all the actions of the political

life of our subjects by new laws. These laws will withdraw one by one all the indulgences and liberties which have previously been allowed. (E.C. will be ruled by regulation e.g. noise of lawnmowers restricted at certain times or they could remove all cars from the road unless special equipment was fitted.)

(6) The aristocracy as a political force is dead; we need not take it into account. It is essential for us therefore, at whatever cost, to deprive them of their land. The object will be best attained by increasing the burdens upon landed property — in loading lands with debt.

(I predict that all big names at present high on the stockmarket in Australia and New Zealand, will be absolutely destroyed. This pattern will commence prior to 1990.)

We shall raise the rate of wages, which however, will not bring any advantage to the workers, for at the same time, we shall produce a rise in prices of the first necessities of life.

(7) We have in our service persons of all opinions, of all doctrines.....socialists, communists, and utopian dreamers of every kind.

(8) We have harnessed them all to the task, each one of them, on his own account is boring away at the last remnants of authority. (e.g. Racial stirrers, unionists, greenies, women's libbers etc, etc. Most of these are lonely people always looking for a cause to protest about. This is how they meet other lonely people.)

(9) By these acts, all States are in torture, they exhort to tranquillity, are ready to sacrifice everything for peace; but we will not give them peace until they openly acknowledge our International Super-Government, and with submissiveness.

(10) The mob cherishes with special affection and respect the geniuses of political power and accepts all their deeds of violence with the admiring response 'rascally, well yes it is rascally but it's clever....a trick if you like, what impudent audacity.' (Over 200 years later, an example emerges. e.g. Rogernomics in New Zealand. Even after this system was shut down by a nervous government, just before the elections in 1990, delegates who admitted that they and their friends had suffered under these policies commended the author of their misery for his work. This is similar to being hit on the

head with a mallet and exclaiming 'Oh, that really hurts. Do it again please.')

(11) But if we give the nations of the world a breathing space, the moment we long for is hardly likely ever to arrive. (Note – in N.Z., a breathing space in 'change' was called for, but not allowed by the Fabian Socialists in power at that time.)

(12) The masses are a flock of sheep; and we are their wolves. We shall keep promising to give back to them all the liberties we have taken away as soon as we have quelled the enemies of peace and tamed all parties.

(13) Let us turn again to the future of the printing press. Everyone desirous of being a publisher, librarian or printer, will be obliged to provide himself with the diploma instituted. Therefore, anyone not fitting in with our plans will lose his diploma.

(In other words, we are just getting this book out in time. Once written, it is too late. The milk has been spilt. Praise be to God. This author does not need their diploma.)

(14) Even nowadays, already, to take the French press, for example these are groups which reveal masonic solidarity in acting on the watchword; all organs of the press are bound together by professional secrecy....not one of their numbers will give away the secret of his sources of information unless it is resolved to make an announcement of them.

(15) Not one journalist will venture to betray this secret, for not one of them is ever admitted to practise literature unless his whole past has some disgraceful sore or other. These sores would be immediately revealed. (Notice this even happened during the U.S. Presidential Elections and afterwards, 1989.)

(16) In order that the masses themselves may not guess what they are about, we further distract them with amusements, games, pastimes and passions. Soon, we shall begin through the press to propose competitions in art, in sport of all kinds. These interests will finally distract their minds. (In Australia and New Zealand – rugby, booze and racing.)

(17) In countries known as progressive and enlightened, we have created a senseless, filthy, abominable literature.
For some time after our entrance to power, we shall continue to encourage its existence in order to provide a telling relief by contrast to the speeches, party programmes, which will

be distributed from exalted quarters of ours. (Note the rise in video shops and pornography.)

(18) We at last definitely come into our kingdom by the aid of coups detat prepared everywhere for one and the same day after the worthlessness of all existing forms of government has been definitely acknowledged....we shall make it our task to see that against us, such things as plots shall no longer exist. (In the test countries of Australia and N.Z., peoples' faith in government is at an all time low. This now makes sense in the light of the above.)

(19) Every kind of new institution or anything like a secret society will also be punished with death; those of them which are now in existence, are known to us, serve us and have served us, we shall disband and send into exile....

In this way, we shall proceed with those masons who know too much; such of these as we may for some reason spare, will be kept in constant fear of exile.

(Top masons, read slowly, thoughtfully and carefully.)

(20) Meantime, however, until we come into our kingdom, we shall act in the contrary way. We shall create and multiply free masonic lodges in all the countries of the world, absorb into them all who may become, or who are prominent in public activity, for in these lodges we shall find our principal intelligence office and means of influence. All these lodges, we shall bring under one central administration, known to us alone, and to all others, absolutely unknown, which will be composed of our learned elders. (i.e. Upper degrees in Masonry.)

(21) ....Among the members of these lodges will be almost all the agents of international and national police since their service is for us irreplaceable...(See 'The Brotherhood' by Stephen Knight for the truth of this statement.)

(22) The class of people who most willingly enter into secret societies are these who live by their wits, careerists, and in general, people mostly light-minded with whom we shall have no difficulty in dealing and using to wind up the mechanism of the machine devised by us.

(23) Many enter the lodges out of curiosity or in the hope by this means to get a nibble at the public pie, and some of them, in order to obtain a hearing before the public for their impracticable and groundless fantasies, they thirst for the

emotion of success and applause, of which we are remarkably generous.

(24) We have set them on the hobby horse of an idea about the absorption of individuality, by the symbolic unit of collectivism.

(25) ...If we have been able to bring them to such a pitch of stupid blindness, is it not a proof and an amazingly clear proof to which the mind of the masses is undeveloped in comparison with our mind.

(26) Death is the inevitable end for all. It is better to bring that end nearer to those who hinder our affairs than to ourselves, to the founders of this affair.

We execute masons in such wise that none save the brotherhood can ever have a suspicion of it, not even the victims themselves, of our death sentence, they all die when required as if from a normal kind of illness.

(To any mason who prefers the Lodge to the Lord Jesus Christ, we warn—'Prepare to meet thy God'. *Ref.1.)

(27) Now, only years divide us from the moment of the complete wrecking of that Christian religion. As to other religions, we shall have still less difficulty in dealing with them.

(The reason for this statement is, that all other religions belong to Lucifer already.)

(28) The King of the Jews will be the REAL POPE OF THE UNIVERSE, the patriarch of an international church. (Emphasis added.)

(Note—The King of Kings and Lord of Lords is our Lord Jesus Christ. These people have their false messiah ready. We call him 'Antichrist'.)

(29) We shall see everything without the aid of the official police. In our programme, one third of our subjects will keep the rest under observation from a sense of duty. (Note—This is the eye of Big Brother.) Just as nowadays our brethren are obliged at their own risk to denounce to the kabal apostates of their own family or members who have been noticed doing anything in opposition to the kabal, so in our kingdom over all the world, it will be obligatory for all our subjects to observe the duty of service to the state in this direction. (In other words, spy on your neighbour. Neighbourhood Watch etc is a gentle conditioning for this. The Soviets practice this system. A girl we are acquainted

with went to Russia and was tailed everywhere she went. One hot day, she bought an ice-cream and being a Christian, felt sorry for her tail. She bought one for him too.)

(30) Sedition mongering is nothing more than the yapping of a lap dog at an elephant.

It needs no more than to take a good example to show the relative importance of both and the lap dogs will cease to yap, and will wag their tails the moment they set eyes on an elephant.

(This means that it is fruitless for us to try and stop them in the flesh. Let me state, they will be stopped -not by us, but by our Lord Jesus Christ at his coming. Events in China in 1989 illustrate this point with great clarity. Students tried to buck satanistic communism using fleshly methods. Tanks ran them over.)

(31) The sum total of our actions is settled by the question of figures.

Taxation will be best covered by a progressive tax on property.

Purchase receipt of money or inheritance will be subject to the payment of a stamp progressive tax.

Any transfer of property, whether money or other without evidence of payment of this tax which will be strictly registered by names, will render the former holder liable to pay interest on the tax from the moment of the transfer of these sums, up to the discovery of his evasion of declaration of the transfer.

(A Devilish Plan

Changing the rules in the middle of the game.

In New Zealand a variation on the above theme was used. Farmers and others were encouraged to borrow on a large scale.

Later on 'the interest rates were raised' to an exorbitant rate. Farmers and others of course could no longer pay, and with hearts full of anguish were driven off their properties.)

(32) Unemployment is a most perilous thing for a Government. For us, its part will have been played out the moment authority is transferred into our hands.

(33) Drunkenness also will be prohibited by law and punishable as a crime against the humanness of man, who is turned into a brute under the influence of alcohol.

A forecast of Sergius Nilus: 'One can no longer doubt it. Satan with his power and his terrors, the Antichrist — is about to mount the throne of universal empire.' End quote.

TO SUM UP

Antichrist is to appear on the world scene just prior to the return of our Lord Jesus Christ. He has two things about him which will reveal his identity. (See my first book 'Warning' — pg 22-24 for list of qualifications.)

1. He will have trouble with three countries within the E.C. He will subdue them, they will fall before his power and finally he will tear them right out of the Community, lock, stock and barrel.
   (a) He shall subdue three kings
   (b) Before whom three fell
   (c) Before whom there were three of the first horns plucked up by the roots.
2. This man will be a non-religious Jew, and will confirm a peace treaty in the Middle East area that will be initially for seven years. This man however, will break the treaty after three and a half years.

Readers, please note that at this time of writing, November 1988, there are twelve countries in the European Community.

In a quote from the London Guardian 15th October 1988, we read of other countries who are applying to join. (Turkey has been trying to get in for many years.)

'Indications that Austria will apply for membership of the European Community next year is highlighting concern among EEC government...

Following indications from Malta and Cyprus that they are considering membership applications.

...Austria had primarily economic and commercial motives for wanting to be part of the EEC at a time when it was moving to complete a single, internal market.

...Austrian access might directly encourage other European neutrals, such as Sweden and even Switzerland to join as well as Cyprus.' End quote.

Author's note — In the Community's rule book, there is an article i.e. 237, which tells any would-be future member, that any nation outside that specific area where the other countries are, cannot become a full member of the E.C.

Please note also, that of all those hopefuls, only Austria fulfils this qualification unless East Germany pips them all at the post for 13th position.

There is some juggling ahead for the E.C. Remember, it used to be called the European Economic Community (E.E.C.) but as they are completely broke, the newspapers refer to it now as the European Community (E.C.) The 'economic' piece has been left out.

For E.C.'s origins and future, please read the chapter dedicated to this subject.

CHAPTER 9

The Remedy

Feeling shattered? I'm not surprised. We often ask people what their initial reaction was upon first hearing all this information. They always use the same word — DEVASTATED.

Now, the reason for this feeling is that you 'know' that all this is correct and it is quite difficult to handle. There are times in life when we realise that there is no apparent way out.

Physically speaking, one goes into a hot flush, tremendous heat surges through the body, then a cold sweat of fear; with a pounding heart.

These reactions can occur:
  (a) When you lose one of your children at a show, alongside the river or at the seaside.
  (b) When the doctor looks at you silently across his desk with a copy of the report in his hand.
  (c) As the judge pauses before passing sentence.
  (d) As the cell door clangs shut behind you for the first time.
  (e) As you realise for the first time that you do not live in a democracy and that you have no say at all in your future. It has all been planned out for you.
  (f) When you realise that there is no escape from all this naturally speaking, short of building a rocket and flying away. Your next problem is where to land this proverbial rocket.

There are a number of groups, some of which I will outline:
Please tick the square that applies to you.
  1. Those who enjoy all this information and are grateful; but are still not committed born again believers in Christ. ☐
  2. Those who enjoy all this information and do not fear it because as committed born again believers in Christ, they have the Lord's unfailing promise: ☐
'For God hath not given to us the spirit of fear, but of power and of love and of a sound mind.' *Ref.1.
  3. Those who hate all this information, know it is true, and also hate every mention of the LORD JESUS CHRIST. (Why here's His Name again.) Those people

73

have a spiritual problem which could have initiated
from one of the following sources: ☐

   a. Your parents were godless before you and planted
trite little anti-God phrases in your mind that will
not do you very much good when you lie alone
on your death bed. ☐

   b. You initially thought God was probably there,
but got mixed up with a so-called intellectual
group who collectively mocked at any such beliefs.
Your desire to be part of this group caused you
to sacrifice your soul's welfare because of peer
pressure. ☐

   c. You committed some sin or indiscretion which
makes you wish to blot out all thoughts of God,
or judgement from your mind. ☐

   d. Your life until this point has been so busy, you
haven't had time to give God a thought. ☐

   e. Your friends are socialites, or public house
frequenters who find it the 'in thing' to discuss
sport, other people, Zen Buddism, birth signs,
T.M. etc but if the Name Jesus Christ comes up
in conversation, it is only as a curse word. ☐

   f. You had an interest in Christian matters but you
found an excuse to throw it all away when some
'Christian' failed and thus you claim, it
discouraged you. ☐

This, by the way, will not stand you in good stead at the
judgement.

'For we must all appear before the judgement seat of Christ....'
*Ref.2.

   g. You were brought up under an Eastern or some
other religious system, which denies Jesus'
statement when He says 'I am the way, the truth
and the life. No man cometh unto the Father but
by me.' *Ref.3. ☐

   h. You have never up to this point heard of God
or Jesus Christ. ☐

I remember some years back, a man travelled 200 miles to my
home to commit his life to Jesus Christ. We, as a family, knelt
with him as he said the sinners prayer.

Lord Jesus, I repent of my sin.

Lord Jesus, I believe that you died on the cross for me, a sinner. Lord Jesus, I invite you into my life. I receive you as my Saviour. The Bible promise is clear:

'But as many as received him, to them gave he power to become the sons of God....' *Ref.4.

I later asked him why he travelled all that way, that night.

He replied 'I used to listen to your tapes on the New World Money System and World Government as I travelled in my car. Every time you said anything about God, Jesus, or quoted a Scripture, I used to turn down the volume as it was objectionable to me.

Sometimes, I would catch some of the 'spiritual information' by mistake until I began to realise that you can't divorce the political and the economic material from the spiritual as they all go together in one package.'

Here is a helpful word to any who are seeking spiritual help at this point. For the full prayer of salvation, please turn to the end of the book where everything you need to do is outlined.

'Seek ye the Lord while he may be found. Call ye upon him while he is near. Let the wicked FORSAKE his way and the unrighteous man his THOUGHTS and let him RETURN to the Lord. And he will have MERCY upon him, and (return) unto our God. For he will ABUNDANTLY PARDON.' (Words in brackets and capitals emphasised for meaning.) *Ref.5.

A little boy, many years ago, built a toy yacht. It took him many strenuous hours of smoothing and planing the hull before painting.

At last, outfitted with a lovely sail sewn by his mother, he took it to the beach for an official launching, with his proud parents looking on.

To his horror, the wind turned contrary and swept his little craft out to sea. His eyes filled with a mist of tears as he made his way homeward.

The very next week, as he passed the local second hand shop, to his joy and surprise, there was his little boat with a FOR SALE sign on it in the window. He ran inside to claim that which was rightfully his, only to hear the kindly shop-keeper explain that he himself had bought it from a local fisherman.

Once the little boy had explained the situation, the shop-keeper agreed to sell the yacht back to the boy for the same price he had paid for it.

The boy worked and worked and worked. He cut lawns, sawed up firewood, washed cars etc., until he had the required amount.

He returned to the shop and came out into the sunlight smiling and clutching his precious possession.
An elderly gentleman standing nearby heard the little lad joyously exclaim
'Little boat I made you,
You went away from me,
I bought you back,
You are TWICE MINE.'
Jesus says similar words to you, right now.
'I MADE YOU,
YOU WENT AWAY FROM ME,
I BOUGHT YOU BACK,
YOU ARE **TWICE MINE.**'
What will be your response?

CHAPTER 10

Money, Money, Money
Australia and New Zealand
are the first

1. Cash is about to cancel. Citizens of these two countries have
   seen their $1 and $2 notes disappear or about to disappear,
   and in their place some strange little coins have been
   manufactured which are about the same size as the 5 and
   10 cent coins respectively. This was a deliberate move, no
   doubt worked out by psychologists in order that people,
   particularly those working on night shifts, taxi drivers and
   shop keepers, etc., would continue to give the wrong change
   and thus hasten the change over to the plastic card.
      Later, Australia received a strange plastic $10.00 bill that
   clogged up the note counting machines at the banks.
2. Cash transactions are being made very unpopular and any
   persons dealing in moderately large sums of cash are coming
   under suspicion.

I wish to make a key statement.

FOLDING MONEY IS YOUR LAST BASTION OF PRIVACY

Once cash goes, the computer operators will have a complete
dossier on you and your activities will be very easy to trace through
the money of the future — the plastic card.

A friend of mine who works in a managerial position in a major
plastic card firm put it very succinctly in a recent discussion.

'It is not difficult for me, in my position, to understand and
recognise that what you are saying is correct.

I can go to the computer and trace the activities of any
individual who has one of our cards.

Where he goes, what he buys, his habits, can all be deduced from
the computer screen. No longer do we need the man with the
hat brim turned down, the brown overcoat and sun glasses. A
computer screen is all that is required.' End quote.

I have in my possession a poster put out by the ANZ bank

78

in NSW, Australia. I love to display this in my meetings as I could not have put it more clearly myself.

It shows an empty wallet upside down. The wallet is laughing and says;

'WELCOME TO THE CASHLESS SOCIETY'

Now you can understand why in Australia, they have passed a bill which makes it illegal for any employee to demand to be paid in cash. Direct credit is now the name of the game.

In the Sydney Morning Herald on the 18th July 1988, we read of a Cash Transactions Reports Act, which makes it an offence to open or operate an account, including a safety deposit arrangement, with a bank (and other financial institutions) in a false name....this is punishable by a fine or imprisonment.

In New Zealand, the banks in many cases have brought in a 5% fee on large cash transactions. This requires some form of documentation and so you see, depositors of amounts of money over $2000.00 can be checked up on.

A speaker for the Hotel Association, who understandably was not very happy with the new rules, spoke very wisely when he said 'Despite denials, we believe that the bank policy relating to EFT (electronic fund transfer) has something to do with the decision'. End quote.

A bank manager quoted in the same article said that his bank already charged 35 cents per $100.00 for handling cash in excess of $2000.00 on behalf of other banks.

Readers, notice also the bank charges on cheques are also quite high.

The aim of all this is to drive folk off cash and into the use of the plastic card.

EFTPOS is alive and well in Australia.

CHAIN OF EVENTS IN AUSTRALIA
1. 1983 — Henry Kissinger introduces EFTPOS. Cartoon in S.M.H.
   Man with barcode on head. (See 'Second Warning', pg 21.)
2. 1984 — Westpac introduces EFTPOS as World's First.
   Cartoon in S.M.H. Article speaks of branding numbers.
3. 1985 — Laser gun unveiled with dummy. Cartoon S.M.H.
   Head down on barcode scanner.

EFTPOS in New Zealand 'apparently' turned out to be a failure. The Bank of N.Z. and others said that they were closing the system down. As I pen these lines at the end of 1988, note that is is not all over for EFTPOS in N.Z. The same equipment, much of it updated is to be used as a new form of card similar to the French SMART CARD.

Sure enough, in the 'Press', 18th March 1989, before I finished writing the manuscript, we read '...A big push to expand the use of electronic payment with plastic cards is under way...requires only the customer's signature on a computerised docket. No personal identification is required.' End quote. This is called 'Quicksmart'.

Later another card will have far more sinister connotations than EFTPOS, as built into it, will be a facility to store a great deal more information on the individual. Even a built in aerial within the card is being promoted.

I tell you, these guys are sneaky
Also, the databanks in this portion of the southern hemisphere will soon be obsolete. A friend of mine who carried cheques etc. in a security wagon was told in about 1987, that soon his services would no longer be required as all the databank work was soon to be done overseas, overnight, with the new information available each morning.

Why not? Isn't it right that our new owners have our records in their files?

New Zealand Databank has a demonic logo. An eye, inside a triangle, which in turn is inside a circle.

Away back in 96 A.D., the prophecies were written down outlining the plans which are now being implemented in the 1980's.

The number which would identify each individual was to be 666.

Readers of my book 'Warning' will remember the article on page 71, where we spoke of a giant computer being opened in Brussels in the administration building of the E.C. headquarters. The powers that be do not like this being made public but we have a friend from Germany, who worked at a computer system in that country which was linked to 'the Beast' in Brussels. This was not its actual name but a pseudonym promoted by some enthusiastic members of the media.

Some people wrote to me and said that no such machine existed. Not only is it there, but now, there is an even bigger one across the border in Luxembourg. When opening this computer system, one of the E.C. leaders. a Dr Eldeman suggested that by using a three six digital unit, the entire world could be assigned a working credit card number.

Sure enough, Australia now has a massive, all inclusive computer system at Deakin, Canberra. New Zealand is a little behind but is centralising all computer data in a building which is being constructed in a North Island city. (Due some time in the 1990's.)

We now know the meaning of 6-6-6

1. Birthdate. If you were born on the 7th July 1977, your computer number would be,

   year first —   2 digits

   month next — 2 digits

   then day   —   2 digits.

   770707 = 6 digits. Readers, please work out what your own birthdate would be on the computer.

2. Location or meshblock. On pages 28-30 in my book 'Second Warning' printed in 1984, I explained how this worked.

Pictures taken from satellites have divided the whole world and major cities into a complete meshblock system.

From these pictures taken initially in 1977 and then updated, we see these meshblocks gradually being whittled down in size.

i.e.   1982 — 300 square metres.

       1983 — 6 square metres.

       1984 — 5 square metres.

       1988 — 3 square metres.

There will be three blocks only to identify where you live.

The large mesh block — 2 digits.

The smaller mesh block — 2 digits.

The smallest mesh block — 2 digits.

e.g.   (These are not the correct numbers.)

       Sydney —   02

       Manly —   38

       Brown St — 19

       = 023819 = 6 digits.

Any person who has sat on a two legged stool will understand the difficulties encountered. In the fully computerised society, the point of all the foregoing is that very few persons with the same

81

birthdate would ever live within the same square or meshblock. To overcome this possibility arising is the need for a third leg on the stool. An I.D. card or mark.

On a trip to Great Britain during October 1988, we noted that Margaret Thatcher was looking into I.D. cards at that time. Australia almost had these cards inflicted on them in 1988, but this move was defeated and the world government advocates had to come up quickly with a substitute system. This system could no longer be called 'The Australia Card' or a national I.D. card, as this really upset the citizens.

As one man recently put it to me:
'Politicians do not usually tell lies.
They just do not tell you ALL the truth'.
I reject this statement. Even this is not correct.

I watch them night by night on television. When it is obvious that they should answer 'Yes', my family and I laugh as we repeat the lie 'No', along with them.

The letters which should become very familiar with all Australians, which were introduced in two stages from January 1989, are T.F.N., or Tax File Number, which the Australian Computer Society in an article printed in the 'Australian' newspaper on the 22.11.88, branded as a 'de facto personal identifier'.

Quote — 'The T.F.N. would have most of the characteristics of a general purpose human identifier and would exist on the data files of MANY ORGANISATIONS OTHER THAN THE TAX OFFICE (emphasis added) the statement said'.....'In withdrawing its Australia Card bill, the Government explicitly recognised the serious misgivings felt by large sections of the populace....'

'....During the 1970's virtually every advanced Western nation enacted privacy legislation.

Australia is one of the very few OECD members not to have legislated in compliance with the OECD's 1980 data protection guidelines.' End quote.

I wish to make it quite clear here and now, that the word PRIVACY is a joke, particularly in Australia and New Zealand, the 'guinea pig' test case nations.

The World Government secret rulers say 'Lets create an I.D. or T.F.N. number.' Initially of course, it will have more digits than necessary to prove that people like this author, are misguided.

Gradually, however, (which is the key word in Fabian Socialism) it will convert to six digits.

e.g. $481927 = 6$ digits.

Now, you the reader are 'in the know'.

What is here written is certainly not for you to understand but 'hey presto' and here it is.

We will now outline, in order, the 6-6-6 system.

a. Birthdate — 770707. This tells the computer that a person was born on that day.
b. Location (mesh block) — 023819. Linked together with the birthdate, the computer has now found out where this person lives.
c. T.F.N. (I.D.). This now links all the vital information together and tells who this person IS.

During the late 1980's, I was contacted by telephone one day at my home. A lady asked me on which side of the river my home was situated. I asked 'Why do you want to know?' She answered 'I work for a government department and this information is important for the mesh blocking system'. I gave her the information and upon hanging up the receiver, said out loud 'Thank you Madam, more confirmation.'

As this book goes to print, it is important to note that the 666 system outlined above is not in its fully developed stage. The numbers in each section will vary from time to time until a world system is set up. Therefore, at this point, let not the reader become excited and accuse the author of providing false information as we have set out very clearly in this book trends for the days ahead.

CHAPTER 11

Super Snooper

Back to privacy. New Zealanders beware, the lads in power will have to sneak something up on us shortly.

The main rule is 'Don't frighten people by calling it by its correct name'. Coffins are now referred to as 'caskets'. To the inhabitant however, the name is irrelevant.

In New Zealand, as we have mentioned, the huge monopoly 'Telecom', which apparently lacks a soul or heart has recently put telephone charges of $2.00 extra on all collect (reverse charges) or transfer charge calls.

The postal division of N. Z. Post, also lacking in soul or heart, has put horrendous costs on stamps for mailing a simple letter. A small group in the North Island set up their own mailing system only to be stopped by a court order. These folks no doubt could halve the price of postage stamps and still make a 'reasonable' profit.

The news is out that:
  a. Fax's are much cheaper than letter and telephone calls to send.
  b. A giant SPY BASE is being built in the Waihopai Valley (N.Z.) which can spy on Fax and telephone calls. That's nice isn't it? So much for your privacy.

Did you know that there is a spy system in Australia which has the ability to listen in to calls?

For years, we have had trouble with our telephone, which would cut off each time whilst we were in conversation with an Australian caller. Not once, but every time.

I contacted our N.Z. telephone people who checked out every line and system and said that the problem was not in N.Z. I asssumed therefore, that it must be in Australia. Their bug system must have been faulty, I suppose, and let them down. Why anyone should wish to spy on me, I have no idea. It's quite childish really.

'Courier Mail' 10th January 1989:
'Bugging' foxes Telecom. Telephone 'bugs' are available freely and legally in Brisbane and Telecom can do little to prevent their use.

The miniature FM transmitters, some are small as postage stamps, sell from $39.50 to around $100.00.

They can be attached to a telephone or a telephone line and conversations can be monitored with a cheap FM radio up to 300 metres away......

The Telecom spokesman said at least one bugging complaint a week was received in Brisbane......' End quote.

By the way, I have heard that the Soviet Union no longer poses a threat to the security of New Zealand. They have changed their ways to such a degree that they are considered to be really nice chaps. You know 'glastnost' and all that type of thing.

The people really worth snooping on now are God's people — the fundamentalist born-again Christians. The early church started by 'turning the world upside down' so if this is indeed the case and certain devious people are concerned about us, it's got to be a good sign.

As the church started, so it will finish.

As I have pointed out many times, I am not really worth snooping on. My information comes, not from surreptitious figures drifting around in the night, but from:

a. The Bible, the Word of God.

b. The newspapers and periodicals.

c. People who confide in me at the conclusion of my lectures.

d. Masses of information sent by mail.

, When a suspected snooper is on my telephone line, I speak to him like this:

'Hello snooper. There you are again'. My family sit around and smile as I continue on.

'If you would repent from your sins, believe that the Lord Jesus Christ died to save you, and receive Christ by faith into your heart, you could have a beautiful born-again experience and then maybe you would stop snooping on other peoples' telephone conversations.'

Poor little fellows. Their country is being devastated by a group of unscrupulous, shallow thinking individuals, who will destroy all of the snoopers' freedom as well, whilst they waste their time in this manner.

It really is serious business as far as they are concerned, but to God is His heaven, the whole thing is a big joke.

'Why do the heathen rage and the people imagine a vain thing? The kings of the earth set themselves and the rulers take counsel together, against the Lord, and against his annointed saying 'Let us break their bonds asunder, and cast away their cords from us.' *Ref.1.

Paraphrase of the above passage:
The real powers that be, the 'invisible government' that rules all governments, along with their puppet lackeys, get upset continually with the Lord God and all those that are called by His name.

They hold secret meetings saying 'These people are ultimately the only ones who could prove a threat to our system. Let's investigate ways of discrediting them or rubbishing them so that their beliefs, based on Judeo Christian values, won't be listened to anymore.

Let us cast away all restraining Christian influences so that these convicting thoughts of God and His reckoning day will not be continually brought to our remembrance.

On with the scripture 'He that sitteth in the heavens shall laugh. The Lord shall have them in derision.' *Ref.2.

Paraphrase:
Your efforts to bring about your plans are so ridiculous, says the Lord. I sit in the heavens observing all your secret meetings, all your juggling of finance, all your lies and innuendo and manipulation of peoples' lives.

Actually, I not only laugh, I mock your stupid efforts to bring about a world government.

CHAPTER 12

What's Going On?

Visiting my son in law and daughter recently, we climbed out of our vehicle, slammed the door and heard someone call out in a high pitched voice 'What's going on?' We turned around to look for the owner of the voice and saw a talking magpie standing on a log nearby. His was a fair question indeed in the light of present day developments.

At 9:10 a.m. on the 31st January 1988, I jumped on my bicycle to pedal the two mile return journey to the shop to pick up my daily newspaper. Besides being of benefit to the cardio-vascular system, I trust that it also sheds a little body weight from time to time. This I feel is important as I have learnt that 90% of the western world's population is overweight — these are round figures of course.

Later, turning the pages of the Christchurch 'Press', I was astounded to see a picture of a man, prominently displaying a very unusual passport, with the words 'World Service Authority' written on it.

Here is a portion of the article taken from this paper:
'Travelling on a World Government passport, Garry Davis was in Christchurch at the weekend to tell New Zealanders about world citizenship....

'You're a New Zealander but by birth you are also a world citizen'.

Mr Davis renounced his American nationality in Paris in 1948 and became a world citizen.

The world passport is recognised by about 100 countries and HAS BEEN STAMPED BY NEW ZEALAND. (Emphasis added).

World citizenship would lead everybody to take responsibility for the world, and work on the main issues of war and protecting the environment, Mr Davis said.

With a world government, New Zealand would not need a programme to research the likely impact of nuclear war here. The programme, which the New Zealand Goverment has approved, will cost $50,000.00 over the next two years'. End quote.

Are you shocked? So also was I. Why would the New Zealand

GATE 17 →
GATE 19 →

WORLD GOVERNMENT PASSPORT

Government admit a person to their country on, to use the proverbial expression, 'a home-made passport'? There is more to this than meets the eye.

On an early morning programme, I, myself, heard this gentleman being interviewed and he said that the first World Government meeting will be held in New Zealand in 1990. A friend from Auckland made investigations into these activities and sent me the relevant documentation.

From a fax message dated 6.1.89, we read that the chief executive of an event entitled '1990 Commission: Te Komihana O 1990' advised Mr Davis that 'his description of the aims and objectives of the World Constitutional Conventions fit perfectly with those expressed in our Missions Statement and we would therefore, be delighted if it were possible that you were able to bring the Convention to New Zealand in 1990'.

Good-bye New Zealand—Haere ra Ao te Aroa. (Maori translation.)

From the paper entitled 'World Government of World Citizens', we read that their aim is to help evolve just and democratic

WORLD LAWS—enacted by an elected
WORLD PARLIAMENT administered by a
WORLD EXECUTIVE controlled by a
WORLD COURT and enforced by a
WORLD PEACE FORCE.

We issue WORLD PASSPORTS
WORLD CITIZEN CARDS
WORLD IDENTITY CARDS
WORLD BIRTH CERTIFICATES
WORLD MARRIAGE CERTIFICATES

in all seven languages and an intra-global postal service has already begun operations.

Mr Davis tells of his book entitled 'WORLD GOVERNMENT—READY OR NOT.'

I also have in my possession an application form for joining up.

Away back in the 1970's, I took this cutting from the newspaper in Auckland, New Zealand.

'The New Zealand Government is to be urged to press for a World Government to safeguard peace and human survival.

The proposal will be made next week by the Emergency

Committee for World Government, a body set up last year after a meeting in Wellington.

Its office holders include the Mayor of Auckland (Sir Dove Meyer-Robinson) and Professor Adcock, formerly of Victoria University.

......We are concerned because the World seems to be faced with something of a crisis because of the nuclear threat and the danger of ecological breakdown dute to the poisoning of the planet and over-population....' End quote.

CHAPTER 13

Startling Information

As human beings we study the many aspects of life, come to conclusions and stick to those conclusions until persuaded that they are wrong.

We tend to assume that we know far more than we really do and when someone turns up with something we don't know, on a subject which we thought we knew all about, it annoys us. Some people react violently, whilst others stifle their emotions.

Try this for example. Please read the following phrase once through, fairly quickly, don't cheat and count the number of times the letter 'F' appears. Read the answer at the end of chapter 57.

FINISHED FILES ARE THE RESULT
OF YEARS OF SCIENTIFIC STUDY
COMBINED WITH THE EXPERIENCE
OF MANY YEARS.

To divert our minds from what is really taking place, the World Government advocates have created 4 red herrings:

a. nuclear threat
b. greenhouse effect
c. over-population threat
d. ozone depletion

As you will later have it explained to you, the media in many places is now under the control of the World Government people.

Unless you supplement your reading with independent publications and seek wisdom from the Lord as I do, you read only what these people want you to know.

CHAPTER 14
False Red-Herring No.1

'NUCLEAR CON'

Ask any average high school student about his or her aspirations for the future and they will answer something like this.

'I probably do not have a future. I could be incinerated tomorrow in a nuclear blast'.

Films such as 'The Longest Day', media coverage of scientists discussing nuclear winter and in New Zealand, our strange break with the USA over the ANZUS Treaty, and other nuclear issues, gave many citizens a nuclear phobia.

A friend who lives in Auckland, Mr Bruce Cathie, in his highly interesting book 'Bridge To Infinity', makes it clear that all of the above is based on a clever deception.

Statement! Nuclear devices CANNOT be detonated at any place at any time. Position and timing are essential.

On page 170 of Bruce Cathie's book, we read 'I had discovered during my research that an atom bomb was an intricate geometric device that could only be detonated by placing it below, on, or above a calculated geometric position in relation to the earth's surface. The geometric trigger that caused the disruption of matter within the bomb was the spacial relationship between the earth and the sun at a given instant of time. This knowledge made it obvious to me that AN ALL OUT NUCLEAR WAR WOULD BE IMPOSSIBLE (emphasis added) as each bomb would have to be detonated at a certain place at a certain time, which could be precalculated years in advance by an proposed enemy'. End quote.

Older readers of this book may remember that the U.S. plane that dropped the atomic bomb on Nagasaki flew around for over one hour constantly under attack from Japanese fighters until the correct conditions of position and time were arrived at. Now, it is easy to explain this enigma.

Bruce Cathie continues.

"....'As could be expected, once it became known that I had discovered the geometric nature of the bomb, I was contacted by personnel from various agencies and scientific establishments from around the world, who tried their best to persuade me to keep quiet about it. I refused, as I believe the public have the

92

right to know the truth about the geometric process involved".'
End quote.

I have noticed over the years that one way to make a scientist really upset is for a layman to dare to tell him something which he should, but doesn't know.

The repercussions of this information being correct are (to coin a phrase) earth-shattering.

I have spoken to quite a few scientists who continue to tell me that this is a theory which is not based on fact.

I therefore procede with the explanation.

Exploding a Nuclear Device — using for example, the gun method.

A simplified explanation

Imagine, if you will, a tube with a mass of plutonium or uranium at either end of the tube.

1. Using conventional explosives, the two are blown to the centre of the tube where they meet.
2. They must be held there in the centre of the tube as 'a critical unstable mass' long enough to detonate it.
3. The actual detonation is brought about by the GEOMETRIC SPATIAL RELATIONSHIP of the sun's and the earth's position at a precise moment of time.
4. This needs to be done immediately or no reaction will take place.
5. It is this geometric trigger that actually detonates the unstable mass by affecting the 'motion' of the ATOMIC PARTICLES.
6. The task to hand is to disrupt the geometric arrangement of the unstable matter.
7. Einstein was aware of this when he stated that 'The whole of physical reality is manifested by the geometrics of SPACE and TIME.
8. Therefore, in order to bring about a detonation it is necessary to set up a geometric proposition that is in opposition to the initial construction.

   This cannot be done by simply using conventional explosives.
9. The important thing is to cause the atomic particles which all revolve on a set course, to fly off at a tangent.

93

'Sydney Morning Herald', 13th May 1989.

'The French exploded a nuclear device at Mururoa Atoll this morning, signalling the start of a new round of testing.

.....The new round of testing had been anticipated by New Zealand.

In the past, French testing has been in series between April and June and between October and December.

Today's blast is the first this year. The most recent was in November.

Based on the pattern of the past five years, three more tests can be expected by the end of June....' End quote.

From the preceding article we learn the following:

a. The tests are conducted in series about twice yearly. The reasons for this are that the earth spirals around the sun and is therefore in a suitable triggering location about twice a year.

b. The top scientific community knows that what I am writing here is correct. They have advised the government who anticipate every test.

In other words, there cannot possibly be any sneak detonation.

'Time' Magazine, 10th July 1989. In an article discussing Soviet nuclear submarines and dangers posed by their sinking with nuclear weapons aboard, a Danish official helps verify our case. Quote – 'Nuclear things don't just go off....' End quote.

Therefore, terrorists could put a nuclear device together, but could never detonate it in a month of Sundays. They would require teams of computer experts to calculate the mini-second and location where the device could be detonated.

Any Arguments. Please do not go to your average scientist or physics expert. This information is exact, and has been hidden from the majority of these people as well as the rest of the world. Therefore, please do not write confrontational letters to me on this subject unless you can prove that what I have written here is wrong beyond a shadow of a doubt.

c. The New Zealand government also knows when the next tests will take place.

d. Therefore, if the conditions were right and the Soviets hit the U.S.A. with a nuclear missile, (which the U.S.A. could predict in advance and destroy the missile on its way over) the U.S.A could not possibly retaliate unless the conditions were exactly right, which in itself would be a mathematical impossibility.

What A SCAM

It is in the light of this information that we can now understand the following data.

New Zealand 'Herald', 11th May 1988. 'Lost H. Bomb, One of Many.

The United States and the Soviet Union together have littered the ocean floor with at least 48 nuclear weapons and 11 reactors....

The biggest sensation in the .....report, was the loss of a United States warplane with a hydrogen bomb on board from the aircraft carrier Ticonderoga, 130 km off the coast of Okinawa....

People on Okinawa....said they were afraid of the bomb which lies under 4,900 metres of water.

....one Okinawa resident said 'We know it has not exploded during these more than 20 years, but we never know, it might go off any day....' End quote.

On the 10th May 1989, the New Zealand 'Herald' reported the massive power of this device. Quote '....the weapon lost was one megaton H bomb — the equivalent of a million tons of TNT — about 70 times as powerful as the bomb that destroyed Hiroshima in August 1945.

Details of the missing weapon had not previously been publicised....' End quote.

Good News for Okinawins

You'll be all right. No one else is worried. Now you know why you needn't be either.

The H bomb on the sea floor will rot and decay while the powers that be, carry on with their pattern of lies and deception.

Have you ever observed this sign. People who march under it generally do not realise its demonic nature.

Any new candidate who joins the witchcraft movement is handed a ceramic cross. This is held upside down by the candidate, who proceeds to snap the two cross bars with a downward motion. This is a blasphemous gesture to the Prince of peace, our Lord Jesus Christ, symbolising that these people can achieve peace without enlisting his help. I challenge them to do so!!

Therefore, as we well know, many of the 'peace groups' work mainly in the non-communist world to agitate and cause division within the community, basing their main argument of a nuclear holocaust on a deliberate deception or a delusion, as very few would know the facts being presented here.

96

Therefore, riding a surfboard whilst clutching the bow of an American destroyer might gain a few admiring glances and a smattering of applause from other deluded souls, but the whole effort would be put to better use when advertised as a clown act in a circus, performed on water.

On page 176 of my book 'Second Warning', we read an article taken from the Otago Daily Times, 27th November 1984.
'Britain's Campaign for Nuclear Disarmament has refused to commit itself against Soviet nuclear weapons....The motion said that it was absolutely vital to apply our arguments consistently and publicly to all nuclear weapon states....

The conference then voted on a show of hands to move on to the next item of business, without taking a vote on the motion.
...

Other delegates said they were worried that the motion would be seen as a CONDEMNATION OF THE SOVIET PEOPLE AND SOVIET PEACE INITIATIVES.' (Emphasis added). End quote.

Some trendy folk are enamoured with Communism (from a distance of course).

I remember when I was teaching school, a pupil asked me which was the better of the two — capitalism or communism?

I answered 'My boy, have you heard of the Berlin Wall?'. He replied 'Yes'.

I then said 'Which way do the people jump? Very rarely will you ever read of someone being shot, jumping into East Berlin'.

Possibly, you may have heard of the East German champion pole vaulter.

He is now the West German champion pole vaulter.

No, I am sorry, peace without the Lord Jesus Christ is an impossibility.

'There is no peace saith my God to the wicked. The wicked are like the troubled sea when it cannot rest'. *Ref.1.

I further asked my friend, Bruce Cathie, that if what he was saying was correct, how was it then that both the U.S. and the Soviets in particular, were stockpiling masses of these nuclear devices. His answer was 'How do you know that they are not all filled with cardboard?'

Arriving home, I went through my files and came across the following piece of information from the 'Australian' newspaper dated 21st November 1988. we read 'Scandal at Colorado Nuclear Plant Exposed. At the Rocky Flats nuclear weapons plant in Colorado is a workshop so secret, plant managers have to make an appointment to visit it.

Building 881 is used to make models of bombs and new weapons for the Strategic Defence Initiative (SDI).....

For 18 years however, many of the secret shipments from Rocky Flats contained not weapon designs but wine presses, alcohol stills, gold and silver jewellery, baseball caps and clocks....

About 30% of the engineering and technical staffs' time at Rocky Flats was spent making items for private use......

Some of the nation's leading scientists at the Lawrence Livermore Laboratory in California ordered items listed for LASER WEAPONS RESEARCH (emphasis added) that included a press worth $35,000 to crush grapes and a $45,000 still. On one occasion, part of the nations strategic stockpile of silver was diverted to make medallions.

.....This was a security problem. HOW COULD ANYBODY TELL THEY WERE NOT SHIPPING A WEAPONS SYSTEM TO SOMEBODY (emphasis added)....

Situated near Boulder in Northern Colorado, Rocky Flats makes plutonium parts for nuclear weapons.....The scandal comes when the nuclear weapons programme is under scrutiny....The committee official said 'there were orders filled in that said "this is for the laser programme, and we want 2,000 baseball caps or 1,000 medallions".' End quote.

I feel that my point has been made. Somebody is being conned on the whole nuclear issue.

It would appear that 'all we like sheep have gone astray...' *Ref.2.

This Rocky flats plant was in the news again during the month of June 1989. The U.S. people are being conned.

Speak with a voice of authority, repeat the same line often enough and people, generally, will not ask questions.

A preacher friend of mine who, years ago, was involved in the hippy movement in New Zealand, before his conversion to Christ, told me the following amusing story which admirably illustrates my point.

99

Some years ago on a sunny Sunday afternoon, he took a friend along to a large Auckland park to demonstrate 'crowd control'. Families sat around under the trees on their rugs and tarpaulins eating their picnic lunches. Standing on the further side of the park, he spoke his message into a megaphone. 'Excuse me ladies and gentlemen. The authorities have requested that we all move to this side of the park.' The picnicers obediently packed up their hampers, rolled up their rugs and moved.

10 minutes later, he said to his friend 'Now watch this'.

'I'm sorry ladies and gentlemen. A mistake has been made. Would you all mind moving back to this side again.'

Sure enough, with hardly a murmur, baskets were repacked, rugs re-rolled and back they all went to position number one.

Satisfied now that his illustration had been duly noted, my friend went home.

God has used nuclear energy in the past and it is predicted that He will use it again.

During the period 1960/63, as a young man living in the island of Western Samoa, I remember calling to visit my fiance in her village one night. Suddenly, the whole sky lit up with a brilliant white light. It then changed to red, blue, green, orange purple and many other colours before fading out.

The local people including myself, received a tremendous shock. Fisherman out by the reef shouting 'Lolo afi, lolo afi' (tidal wave, tidal wave), paddled their canoes with such vigour that you would have sworn that they were jet-propelled. We all thought it was the end of the world.

Then later, we learnt that an atomic bomb had been detonated on Christmas Island to our north.

Scientists later picked up molten rock samples from that island and compared them with other samples taken from the ancient homo-sexual twin cities down the Jordan Valley i.e. Sodom and Gomorrah, which the Lord destroyed by fire and brimstone. They discovered an amazing thing. The residue from both sites was of a similar consistency thus revealing that God had the secret of nuclear energy years before Rutherford or any other scientist made their discoveries.

What about Chernobyl?

This was not a nuclear explosion. Just a melt-down, which is the worst thing that can happen to any conventional nuclear power plant. Please notice that this includes nuclear warships or submarines tied up at a wharf. These will not blow up as is commonly believed, but could be towed out to sea before too much pollution affects the environment. You see how subtle the whole thing is? The populace in general are not told these details e.g. During the month of June 1989, a Soviet 'nuclear' submarine caught fire. This vessel was towed to safety, with no-one on the towing vessel in any danger.

Questions for Sceptics:
 1. Why have nuclear devices been used only twice in history during a time of war? Where are the terrorists?
 2. When challenged to provide venues, times and dates for future nuclear tests, Bruce Cathie was able to do so with precision. How?
 3. How do the governments of the world manage to have their observation ships in the precise area at the precise time? It is fairly apparent that France does not notify them in advance.
 4. How does the New Zealand government know when the tests are due?
 5. Why does France only test around Muraroa Atoll during the periods mentioned in the article?
 6. Why is it when conditions are not perfect that France postpones some of their tests?
 7. Why do they test at all? What more do they hope to learn about these devices?

Soon, you will observe the USSR linking with the U.S.A. on joint space programmes. This is what the nuclear testing is all about.

Please do not consider writing to me to show how wrong I am, unless you include along with your letter of protest, the answers to the 7 questions written above.

Thank you in anticipation.

Some readers will wonder as to how I can make such bold statements in the light of the fact that I am not a nuclear scientist.

With all the information to hand, I am satisfied that all this is indeed the case, but I regret that I am not at liberty to reveal my sources.

Please do not request any more information on this subject as refusals often offend.

CHAPTER 15

Red Herring No.2 —
A False Greenhouse Effect

Speaking recently to a scientist friend of mine, I was not surprised when he said 'The greenhouse effect is a non-event really. Scientists were getting bored, so they dreamed this one up.'

Not only that, it keeps the media happy also. Did you notice how that all of a sudden, the newspapers began to bombard us with these words: depleted ozone layer, carbon dioxide coming down on us like a cocoon, ice caps melting, rising sea levels, skin cancer etc, etc.

The author of this book believes that the credit for this scenario should be given to the author of a novel entitled 'Alternative Three'. In this book, mankind, realising death through carbon dioxide poisoning must be overcome escape from this old polluted earth to safety capsules built on the moon and Mars.

A truly fascinating book, yet it must be faced, it is a novel.

What do the true scientists say?

In an editorial in the 'New York Times' dated 23rd June 1988, we read:

'The Greenhouse Effect — Real Enough. A fierce drought is shrivelling crops from Texas to North Dakota and has shrunk the Mississippi to its lowest levels on record. DRY YEARS ARE PART OF NATURES CYCLE (emphasis added). Still its time to take seriously another possible influence — the warming of the atmosphere by waste gases from a century of industrial activity. Whether or not the feared greenhouse effect is real, there are several preventative measures worth taking in their own right.

....There is no clear proof that the gases have yet begun to warm the atmosphere, but there's circumstantial evidence, and some experts think it's getting stronger.....**But it stops far short of proving the greenhouse effect has begun.** 'As far as we can tell, this is a tough summer, well within the normal range of variability', says.....the weather service's long range forcaster....But the warming is less than some computer models predicted, forcing defenders of the greenhouse theory to argue that the extra heat is disappearing into the oceans.....' End quote.

From the Christchurch 'Press' 14th January 1989, we read:
'.....debate about greenhouse effect predictions is hotting up among climatologists around the world....In fact, there is a degree of scientific scepticism about many greenhouse effect predictions, but it IS NOT USUALLY REPORTED TO THE PUBLIC. (Emphasis added).

Many climatologists are yet to be convinced that the present rise in global temperature is due to the greenhouse effect....others argue that the earth has undergone many natural temperature variations in the past and is continuing to do so.

From the 'West Australian' newspaper, 6th February 1989.

'The average global temperature last year was the warmest this century according to a British study.

....But meteorological officials said it was too early to blame conclusively the greenhouse effect....the earth's temperature fluctuates considerably due to natural causes and no connection can yet be made said David Parker of Britain's meteorological office.' End quote.

Now, this is primarily a book on prophecy. What is prophesied for us who live in these days? It is certain that a key issue is the return of the Lord Jesus to the land of Israel leading on from a seven year peace treaty in the Middle East. At this time in history, consider some other predictions made at least over 1500 years ago.

'And there shall be signs in the sun, and in the moon, and in the stars, and upon the earth distress of nations, with perplexity, the sea and the waves roaring,
Mens' hearts failing them for fear
And for looking after those things which are coming on the earth
For the powers of heaven shall be shaken. *Ref.1.

Press', 18.3.89.

'Things are hotting up out there in the earth's backyard, as the Sun goes into one of its periodic frenzies and blasts out radiation energy so strong that it sends scientists' instruments right off the scale....the most intense eruptions ever observed...' End quote.

The Greenhouse Effect theory tells us that global warming will cause the polar ice caps to melt which in turn will flood low-lying islands and coast-line.

False Premise
a. Ice is expanded water. If the Arctic ice melted, the water

103

volume in the sea would be less as there is no land under the Arctic ice. Therefore the oean levels would decrease.
b. There is land under the Antarctic ice mass at the South Pole. It would be virtually impossible to melt this area as its average temperature is about minus 50 degrees, and even goes much lower than this on occasions. It has been recorded as low as at minus 88 degrees fahrenheit.

Therefore, if even a 5 degree warming took place, bringing the temperature up a fraction, the ice still would not melt.

What baffles me is that politicians and scientists hold useless conferences on these subjects, flying first-class, staying in lovely hotels to discuss 'nothing'.

If any reader can arrange a free ticket for me, I would like to join them on their next holiday jaunt. Oh, what fun.

Reports daily coming to hand deal with all these aspects of disasters and problems. Space — nations — weather — heart attacks on the increase through people ignoring the Word of God and desperately trying to work out what is happening.

'Australian', 26th November 1988.

In Japan, masses of business men are dying of heart attacks. Quote — '...called kavoshi, or death from overwork...too much toil and too little play.....In 2 years, 499 cases have been reported....' End quote.

The So-Called Depletion of the Ozone Layer
a. There is no ozone layer.
b. Oxygen (o2) continuously drifts up to the upper atmosphere. There it meets the ultra-violet light from the sun.
c. A chemical reaction results. An extra oxygen atom is added. What was o2 or oxygen now becomes o3 — ozone.
d. This is a continuous process.
e. The earth revolves around the sun and remains on a constant TILT.
f. Therefore, at certain times of the year when the sun's rays are not present to provide ultra-violet light, and thus create o3, a hole forms above either the North or the South pole.
g. IT HAS ALWAYS BEEN LIKE THIS, THROUGHOUT HISTORY but scientific con-men, media men and politicians are promoting it is as a PROBLEM.

h. Aerosol sprays are being blamed. Why aren't there holes above New York, London and Paris? The Eskimos must be using too much hairspray.

i. High flying jets destroy more oxygen and ozone than millions of cans of spray but planes still fly and burn it up. Next time all this comes on the news, join me in a good belly laugh.

If these scientists (so-called) wish to stop ozone depletion, they should forget the aerosol cans with C.F.C.'s and stop all high flying jet planes.

What a con!!

The next statement may be unpalatable to you, nevertheless, read on.

'And then shall they see the Son of man coming in a cloud with power and great glory'. *Ref.2. The Lord's second coming is at hand, and if you, the reader, will give your soul a chance and continue on reading, we will establish many more astounding 'facts'.

Born again Christians need not fear all this information.

Some years ago, the study of all this data frightened me to quite some degree. I prayed for the Lord to comfort and help me, and was prompted, I believe, to read the following words:

'And when these things begin to come to pass, then look up and lift up your heads for your redemption draweth nigh.' *Ref.3.

In other words, true believers in Christ and His Word needn't be concerned about looking around. All we need to do is 'LOOK UP'

An interesting article in the New Zealand 'Herald' dated 18th October 1988 caught my eye. Having just completed a Middle East tour which took in Patmos in the Greek Islands, this article was of particular significance.

'Revelation and the Ecology. Recently an international gathering of ecologists took place on the Aegean Island of Patmos where tradition says St. John wrote his Revelation'.

Wrong! The Bible says this, not tradition.

'I, John, who also am your brother and companion in tribulation and in the kingdom and patience of Jesus Christ was in the isle that is called Patmos, for the Word of God and for the testimony of Jesus Christ.' *Ref.4.

Tradition is certainly not in tune with the Bible. Arriving at the wharf in Patmos in late 1988, our tour group climbed on board the tour buses to listen to our guides explain the plans for the day. Our guide, a French girl, said 'We will now visit the cave where St. John saw his revelations'.

We asked her 'Which cave?'

She replied 'You know, the one spoken of in the Bible where there was also a rock that split into three pieces.'

We told her that, contrary to her explanation, there was no cave, no rock nor anything that she had been telling her tourists for her three years on the island. How sad.

John actually was standing on a beach, when he saw into the 1980's and 1990's. Therefore, all our party wanted to view was the beach.

Quote from 96 A.D.: 'And I stood upon the sand of the sea.....'
*Ref.5.

My advice is, forget tradition and get back to the Word of God.

Continue newspaper quote: 'St. John made doomsday predictions that made the 'greenhouse effect' look like April in Paris.

The ecologists' meeting on Patmos was called 'the Revelation and the Future of Mankind'.

.....The first-century Green saw that men were scorched with great heat, (Revelation 16:9), that all green grass was burned up, (chapter 8:7), and that men hid themselves in the dens and rocks of the mountains, (chapter 6:15).

The ecologists pondered Revelation 8:11 'And the name of the star is called wormwood and the third part of the waters became wormwood and many men died of the waters because they were made bitter.'

CHERNOBYL, (emphasis added) they pointed out, is the Russian word for wormwood.

....there are religious pressure groups in Greece which take the Bible more seriously.

They are blocking a Government plan to provide citizens with computerised identification numbers.

They say the system incorporates the number 666 which, according to Revelation 13:18 is Satan's own number'. End quote.

CHAPTER 16

Red Herring No.3 —
Population Control

A statement needs to be made here. When the Lord made the earth and put people on it in his divine wisdom and goodness, He made provision for man's needs in every way.

In these latter days, wicked individuals divert these provisions from the masses who die of starvation and related problems.

Some years ago, I listened to a Christian speaker tell of an experience in which, whilst visiting a country in Africa, he went down to the bar of the hotel in which he was staying, for a lemonade.

There, he met a very drunk man and engaged him in conversation in the hope of witnessing to him about the Lord.

After some time of discussion, the stranger let him in on the secret of his behaviour. He explained 'I have to keep myself drunk all the time to subdue my conscience. I work for a world government group and my specialised task is to divert the food away from certain groups so that they will starve to death.' End quote.

I never realised until I heard that story, how deadly serious these people are in achieving their goals.

From the 'Sydney Morning Herald' 29th April 1988, we read: 'Population of World May Double in 40 Years.

......five countries are not growing at all. Austria, Denmark, Hungary, East Germany and West Germany. Italy, at its current rate would not double its population for 3,465 years.

In the South Pacific, the Solomon Islands will take just 19 years to double its population at current rates. Vanuatu 21 years, Western Samoa 24 years, Papua New Guinea 29 years, Fiji 31 years, New Zealand 87 years and Australia 88 years.

The five largest nations in the world by population are China with 1,087 million people, India with 817 million, the Soviet Union with 286 million, the U.S. with 246 million and Indonesia with 177 million.' End quote.

For full control of each individual life, somehow and in some way, this vast population of the world must be whittled down. Some men really enjoy playing God.

Read on and see how it is being done.

CHAPTER 17

P.V.R. or P.B.R.
Seed Manipulation

Now, readers of my previous books 'Warning' and 'Second Warning' (see page 49) may remember reading of a diabolical bill being passed in New Zealand in the early 1970's and then latterly in Australia on the 25.2.87. I refer to Plant Variety Rights or Plant Breeders Rights, where through seed emasculation, the reproductive organs are removed from the seeds and they become sterile. Hybrid plants result which requires that the growers need to go back to the seed merchant each new season, not only to obtain new seeds but to pay for the patent on each new variety.

One afternoon, whilst in Brisbane, Australia, I attended an agricultural meeting held in a large public hall. The speaker from the Dept of Agriculture was extolling the virtures of PVR.

In the middle of his speech, I called out in a loud voice 'Excuse me'. Everybody turned to look at this rude interjector. I continued on 'From what you are telling us today, it appears that this PVR bill is a good thing?'

He replied 'Yes sir. Bigger cabbages, cauliflowers, fruit, tomatoes will be the result...'

I interjected again. 'I'll tell you what's going to happen. You people ultimately will destroy all the natural seeds in the world through manipulating a natural resource through greed and turn all the seeds into hybrids. The result will be world famine. In New Zealand where I live, it is virtually impossible now to buy non-hybridised seeds.'

He said 'That's not true'.

I replied 'You live in New Zealand do you?'

He said that he didn't so I drove in my final nail. 'Well, I do, and until you do, listen to me.'

'And God said, let the earth bring forth grass, the herb yielding seed, and the fruit tree, yielding fruit after his kind WHOSE SEED IS IN ITSELF upon the earth and it was so.' (Emphasis added.) *Ref.1.

CHAPTER 18

Fish Manipulation in New Zealand

In our country, we allowed the manipulators in our Government to bring in a Fish Quota System call I.T.Q. — Individual Transferable Quotas. Readers in other countries, don't bother sympathising with us. We are the world's test case for world government where strict food control is essential.

In 1992, The E.C. countries will go the same way as the prototype, little old New Zealand, as will all those nations trading with the E.C.

This evil bill is turning many honest fisherman into criminals e.g. On a fishing trip with some of my family, we could not start the boat's motor and flagged down a passing fishing boat to tow us into port. Cruising alongside this vessel, our friends from Australia who were also with us, jumped over on to the fishing boat to take some photos. The crew who up until that point had been sitting on the deck opening a few scallops, beat a hasty retreat from the camera's lens. When I enquired why this was, they explained that the whole catch had now to be declared ashore, and anything they wished to eat could be eaten only after this declaration had been made.

Imagine that a registered New Zealand fisherman catches his fish 40 miles out from port. He is supposed to fold his hands in a pose of supplication and murmur words to this effect:

'Oh no. I must not have my evening meal just yet. I love my elected representatives so much, along with their very wise laws which are protecting the rapidly diminishing fish stocks. I will not allow wicked thoughts to come into my mind of Russians, Koreans and others nearby eating heartily, munching on fish caught in New Zealand waters.

No, I will wait until I can declare my catch to one of those very nice people who control these matters, then travel 40 miles out to sea again and eat my fish meal.'

Auckland 'Star', 27th April 1989. 'Fish Bill Goes 'Too Far'. The Fisheries Amendment Bill attracted a barrage of criticism from industry leaders....

The bill which enables confiscation of boats, gear and quotas if the Fisheries Act is breached is far too harsh...' End quote.

Many people are horrified to see townspeople putting REWARD posters in their shops, offering money to any Judas who will dob in their fellow men to the authorities for illegal fishing activities.

In New Zealand, it has become worse and worse. Spies with video cameras sit in their little hiding places, trying to catch fishermen out. Sudden raids on ships are being considered quite commonplace, as also is this type of advertising in fishing ports inviting people to report others.

No, this is not Soviet Russia. I am referring to the previously free democratic state of New Zealand.

This type of system leads to:
1. Smuggling
2. Lies and deceit
3. Fear
4. Hatred
5. Violence

New Zealand readers will note who the people are who bring in these laws and find it difficult to vote for them at the next elections.

An Italian friend once told me that it was harsh governmental laws like these that introduced the Mafia to his country.

These are World Government laws however.

It is obvious to normal people, that the designers of this piece of legislation are either madmen, or are working on a surreptitious plan to drive small commercial fishermen to the wall and control the food supplies through their larger 'yes-man' companies. Which of the two descriptions do you feel fits these individuals?

The system was brought in on the pretext of conserving fish resources. The majority of individual fishermen were issued with I.T.Q's, too small to make a decent living. 1987-88 saw a lot of individuals sell their I.T.Q's to bigger companies.

In other words, the plan appears to be working to schedule. Fishermen have told me that when the system was first introduced, once the quota of fish had been caught, all the extra illegal species of fish not in the quota were dumped over the side.

A T.V. programme showed this aspect to an incredulous public.

This dumping is of course, strictly illegal, but continues on with the New Zealand public paying disgusting prices for its fish while this waste goes on. The law says fishermen should bring these over-quota fish to shore and sell them through channels approved by the Ministry of Agriculture and Fisheries. Of course, many fisherman are too disillusioned and angry to do this.

Thank the Lord, there is a judgement day planned, when all these traitorous legislators will give an account.

'For we must all give an account before the judgement seat of Christ.' *Ref.1.

Remember the World Government phrase.

By controlling ENERGY, you can control NATIONS.

By controlling FOOD, you can control INDIVIDUALS.

CHAPTER 19

Livestock Manipulation in New Zealand and Australia

1988/89, the guinea pig country of New Zealand, saw a new tax come in. Many farmers transferred from dairying and agriculture to deer and goat farming. This industry thrived for a season then a new LIVESTOCK TAX called Standard Value Tax was announced. The rules were, animals on a farm had to be recorded in the books at market value and upon selling these animals, any extra profit was taxable along with the initial animal tax which could be paid off over three years whether the animal was to be sold or not.

What does this do? It records all stock so that at a future date, the World Government legislators can give instructions that no meat or skins can be sold to one's neighbours or friends but only to an approved buyer.

Things really became diabolical during 1989.

A farming friend freely gave us a number of culls (old sheep) to restock our freezer and the freezers of our friends who were in need.

We gathered a few friends together, spent over one whole day preparing carcasses for storage, only to hear the news that some new progressive law had just been passed which would make it illegal for meat to leave a farm.

As one involved in many things including social work amongst the lower income folk, I was horrified.

We made however, full investigation and found that at that point in history the bill had not been passed.

Arriving home, I picked up a little newspaper cutting from the New Zealand 'Herald', 5th May 1989. 'Blackmarket Blue Stripe.

Home-killed meat is not to be allowed out the farm gate unless the farmer marks a blue stripe along the carcass and records the meat's departure from the property.

It will then be an offence for anyone beyond the family to be found with the meat......Why not just make them (the farmers) ring the police whenever they feel an attack of naughtiness coming on.' End quote. (Words in brackets added for meaning.)

At that point, as the law was not yet passed, we carried on with our meat.

Do you see the significance of this evil law?

Barter

The enemy is now preparing the stage to make barter illegal. And they try to persuade me that there is no such being as the devil.

As Christians of the future, what will we do in this dilemma that is being forced on us?

What does the Master say?

'....render to Caesar the things that are Caesar's and to God, the things that are God's.' *Ref.1.

A. Who created the sheep? Did Caesar? — No!
   Who created the sheep? Did God? — Yes!

B. A list of doctrines of demons appears in the Scriptures; one of which is '......commanding to abstain from meats which God hath created to be received with thanksgiving of them which believe and know the truth.' *Ref.2.

Therefore, here is a recipe for mint sauce:

Brown sugar
Vinegar
Mint
Water

Add sugar and vinegar to boiling water, and add chopped mint. Leave to soak, then use.

Stock losses through natural causes of course are a problem to World Government folk and it is simply amazing how many animals are lost in this way and recorded in the books as having come to an unfortunate end.

Unfortunately, the World Government Advocates (whom we will refer to as W.G.A. in future), cannot control everything as they wish to.

It is interesting in this old world that many so-called atheists and agnostics claim either that there is no God or say that they are not sure whether there is, or whether there isn't.

Let a storm or an earthquake or a flood come by which destroys their houses, lands and villages, and these same interesting individuals have the audacity to refer to the calamity as —

AN ACT OF GOD

Almighty God warns such—

'I also will laugh at your calamity, I will mock when your fear cometh...then shall they call upon me but I will not answer....'
*Ref.3.

From the 'Australian' newspaper 3rd November 1988:

'The spectre of international food crisis of the 1970's, will haunt the world again next year unless there is a large increase in grain production, warns the United Nations Food and Agricultural Organisation FAO...The FAO puts world grain production for this year at 1730 million tonnes, 4% less than last year and below global food needs for the second consecutive year....

It notes signs of increased grain plantings in the United States and Canada, but says increases would need to take place in other grain producing countries.

....Australia is in no position to contribute to the need for expanded grain production.' End quote.

There is no doubt that two factors have caught the WGA on the hop.

(a) The subsidised U.S. wheat shipments to the USSR, where the Soviets stockpile much of it, and use a small percentage for everyday needs.

(b) The serious drought in the Midwest of the U.S.A. upset their calculations somewhat.

From the 'Albuquerque Journal' 16th June 1988:

'...hundreds of thousands of Midwest farmers are helpless this spring as one of the worst droughts of the century tightens across America's grain belt.

....For some regions, pastures and range lands have not been this dry since 1934.

....'If it continues throughout the summer, there will be nothing to harvest, says Tom Quirk who grows barley in Climax Minn.'

The 'Time' magazine on the 27th June 1988 reported:

'....If the drought continues, the Federal Government may dip into its store surplus feed grains—1.3 billion bushels of corn and 563 million bushels of sorghum, oats and barley—for sale to distressed farmers at reduced prices.

...Secretary Lyng is referred to in this phrase 'the best thing for us to do' he said, 'is to pray for rain.' Many drought victims were doing just that.....' End quote.

114

CHAPTER 20

The Shocking Aids Story

AIDS — It is obviously impossible to run a World Government system if there are too many people to control.

So far we have examined a number of crisis, whether real or imagined is beside the point.

  a. Nuclear threat
  b. Greenhouse effect and ozone depletion
  c. Over population and food manipulation
  d. Aids certainly is the headline stealer of them all.

From the 'Honolulu Advertiser' 13th June 1988:

'An estimated 150,000 people will develop Aids this year, doubling the estimated 200,000 Aids cases worldwide, since the epidemic began. The disease has now stricken more than 60,000 people in the United States.' End quote.

On the 13th June 1988, the 'Los Angeles Times' told us that:

'New Aids cases are being reported in the United States at a rate of one every 14 minutes.

....the number of Aids cases reported in Europe has reached 12,221 and is doubling every 11 months.

.....Australian researchers described six cases where mothers who became infected after birth passed the virus to their infants through breast milk.... End quote.

'L.A. Times' 14th June:

'A Southern Californian man doctors call the 'super spreader' has infected at least four women with Aids and is still having sexual encounters a new report says'. End quote.

Once people catch Aids, very few appear to ever find a cure, but it happens occasionally.

'Honolulu Advertiser' 13th June 1988:

'Dr Luc Montagnier of the Pasteur Institute in Paris told of a 40 year old homosexual man infected with Aids who spontaneously lost his infection two years later.....

' This is a unique case', he said. End quote.

From the 'Australian' newspaper, 11th April 1988:

'An American Aids sufferer, still alive five years after being diagnosed is confounding doctors and experts....is leading to speculation it may be possible to beat Aids.

.....A victim's average life span after developing full blown Aids is 18 months....From his home in California 'I feel as healthy now as I was before Aids, in fact, more healthy'......program includes:

Weight training
Aerobics
Diet Control
Visual Imagery

(He visualises a rubber eraser smoothing away his lesions and imagines his vital T. cells, the component of the immune system most susceptible to Aids multiplying.)

Mental Attitude
(He advocates 'unconditional love'.) End quote.

'Sun-Herald' Sydney, 4th October 1987:
'Sex swingers still go for it....full speed ahead—that's the message that 'swingers' couples who swap partners for sex, are spreading despite the warnings from Aids experts about promiscuity.....Aids experts are astonished at the swingers' attitudes.....most swingers are well-educated middle-class folk who know what they are doing. They are reasoning, curious people who want to know more about the world and PARTICULARLY HOW TO ENJOY THEIR OWN LIVES MORE.' (Emphasis added.)

This author personally discovered that a vital, personal relationship with God, through Jesus Christ, fulfills this basic desire of any person who will receive it.

'Oh taste and see that the Lord is good. Blessed is the man who trusteth in Him.' *Ref.1.

A friend of mine, Mr Ray Harrison, tells of an experience in India years ago, where a small boy tried so hard to sell him some oranges. He finally cracked Ray's apparent disinterest by peeling an orange and giving him a segment to eat. As soon as he tasted this delicious morsel, he was sold on the idea and bought a bag full.

Our Lord Jesus Christ is like that. Tradition has made the very mention of His Name quite boring to the average person, but God and the real Jesus are absolutely marvellous. Don't give up until you get the real thing.

Aids — Created by Man

On May 11th 1987, the 'London Times' printed a very powerful article in which it accused the World Health Organisation - WHO, of setting off the Aids epidemic through its mass smallpox innoculations in Africa and other third world countries during the 1960's.

Although the article appeared to be well-researched, others went further and discovered that it was not these innoculations that were responsible at all.

In an article entitled 'WHO murdered Africa' by William Campbell Douglass M.D., (from the National Health Federation, Monrovia, California, dated November 1987), the writer points out 'that the title of this article is not a question but a statement'.

Other periodicals advertise false information like this:

AIDS

A WORLD WIDE EFFORT WILL STOP IT

or

HIV infection is not spread through casual contact, routine social contact in school, the work place or public places, nor through water or food, eating utensils, coughing or sneezing, insect bites, toilets or swimming pools.

Dr Douglass, on the other hand, makes it clear that 'the Aids virus can live on a dry plate. So you are worried about your salad in a restaurant that employs . . . . you'd better be.

.....The World Health Organisation in publicised articles called for scientists to work with these deadly agents and attempt to make a hybrid virus that would be deadly to humans.

In the bulletin of the World Health Organisation (WHO) volume 47 page 259 1972 they said:

'An attempt should be made to see if viruses can in fact exert selective effects on immune function. The possibility should be looked into that the immune response to the virus itself may be impaired, if the infecting virus damages, more or less selectively, the cell responding to the virus'.

That's Aids. What the WHO is saying in plain English is 'let's cook up a virus that selectively destroys the T.Cell system of man', an acquired immune deficiency.....If their new virus creation worked, the WHO stated, then many terrible and fatal infectious viruses could be made even more terrible and more malignant.

Some.....have said that the green monkey may be the culprit

117

.... the Aids virus does not occur naturally in monkeys. In fact, it doesn't occur naturally in any animal.

Aids started practically simultaneously in the United States, Haiti, Brazil and Central Africa.

Was the green monkey a jet pilot? Examination of the gene structure of the green monkey cells proves that it is not genetically possible to transfer the Aids virus from monkeys to man by natural means.

Dr Theodore Strecker's research of the literature indicates that the National Cancer Institute, in collaboration with the World Health Organisation made the Aids virus in their laboratories at Fort Detrick (now NCI). They combined the deadly retroviruses, bovine leukaemia virus and sheep visna virus and injected them into human tissue cultures. The result was the Aids virus, the first human retrovirus known to man and now believed to be 100% fatal to those infected.

.....We've let the green monkey off the hook. How about the communists?

.....what they are in the process of doing is conducting germ warfare from Fort Detrick, Maryland, against the free world; especially within the United States, even using foreign communist agents with the United States Army's germ warfare unit euphemistically called the Army Infectious Disease Unit.

You don't believe it?

Carlton Gajdusek, an NIH bigshot at Detrick admits it.

'IN THE FACILITY I have a building where more good and loyal communist scientists from the USSR and Mainland China work, with full passkeys to all the laboratories, than there are American, even the Army's Infectious Disease Unit is loaded with foreign workers, not always friendly nationals.'

.....I can assure you that the creation of the Aids virus by the WHO was not just a diabolical scientific exercise that got out of hand. It was a cold-blooded successful attempt to create a killer virus which was then used in successful experiment in Africa. So sucessful in fact that most of central Africa may be wiped out. 75,000,000 dead within 3-5 years.

It was not an accident. It was deliberate. In the Federation Proceedings of the United States in 1972, WHO said 'in relation to the immune response, a number of useful experimental approaches can be visualised.' They suggested a neat way to do this would be to put their new killer virus Aids into a vaccination program, sit back and observe the results. 'This will be particularly informative in sibships', they said. That is give the Aids virus to brothers and sisters and see if they die, who dies first and of what.....

Dr Theodore Strecker is the courageous doctor who unravelled this conundrum. He should get the Nobel prize but he'll be lucky not to get 'suicided'.

.....He became fascinated with the peculiar scientific anomalies concerning Aids that kept cropping up.

Why did the experts keep talking about green monkeys and homo-sexuals being the culprits when it was obvious that the Aids virus was a man-made virus.....Aids was engineered in a laboratory by virologists. It couldn't engineer itself. As Dr Strecker so colourfully puts it 'if a person has no arms or legs and shows up at a party in a tuxedo, how did he get dressed? Somebody dressed him.'

Dr W. Schmuness, born in Poland and educated in Russia, came to this country in 1969. Schmuness' emigration to the U.S. was probably the most fateful emigration in our history. He, by an unexplained process, became head of the New York City blood bank. (How does a Russian-trained doctor become head of one of the largest blood banks in the world? Doesn't that strike you as peculiar?)......

Only males between the ages of 20 and 40 who were not monogamous would be allowed to participate in this study.

Can you think of any reason other than the desire to spread something among the population for insisting that all experimentees be promiscuous.....Schmuness is now dead and his diabolical secret went with him.

.....So the Aids virus didn't come from Africa. It came from Fort Detrick, Maryland, U.S.A.' End quote.

*see disclaimer on last page of Table of Contents

Can Aids Be Cured?

In the year 1930, an engineer named Royal Rife worked for Timken of the roller bearing company. Because this man Rife tinkered with microscopes as a hobby, Timken built him one of the best labs money could buy. Rife built five microscopes. One of them had the power of up to 60,000 magnification. This was a full-light microscope, not an electronic one, therefore, it observed but didn't destroy.

Rife observed that cancer viruses had colours so the inventor

119

of the vacuum tube, Lee De Forest, built him a frequency generator so Rife managed to generate the frequencies that killed this virus.

They worked on 16 terminally ill patients and had 16 healings. Later, the doctors involved celebrated at a banquet and were photographed. They all later denied that they were there and the whole thing was hushed up.

Strange, isn't it? The Rife Generator apparently could neutralise viral and microbial diseases. After attack from the medical establishment, Rife and his work faded from view.

Bio-electric medicines therefore, may help also in Aids cures.

Ozone A Cure?

A report tells us that in the Munich area of West Germany, a Dr Houst Keif is curing Aids victims by hyperoxegynating their blood with ozone, which destroys the Aids virus on contact.

Using the same system, sufferers from hepatitis, herpes, the Epstein Barr virus and the cytomegalovirus, find this treatment effective.

a. Treatment is very simple. Ozone is produced by forcing oxygen through a metal tube carrying a 300 volt charge.

b. A pint of the patient's blood is drawn into an infusion bottle.

c. Ozone is then forced into the bottle, which in turn is gently shaken, changing the blood a bright red colour.

d. As the ozone molecules dissolve into the blood, they give up their third oxygen atom, releasing the energy which inactivates all lipid envelope virus' while leaving the blood cells unharmed.

Ozone overcomes the Aids virus by a fundamentally different process than usually attempted with drugs.

Instead of burdening the liver and immune system with more elaborate toxic substances, ozone simply oxidises the molecules in the shell of the virus, rendering it incapable of spreading.

It also oxygenates the blood to a greater degree than is usually reached, what with poor air and sluggish breathing habits — this does not normally happen.

e. The treated blood is then given back to the patients.

f. This treatment is given from twice a week to twice a day depending on how advanced the disease is. The strengthened blood confers some of the virucidal properties to the rest of the patient's blood as it disperses.

g The disease will not return as long as the patient maintains his blood in an oxygen positive state, through proper breathing, exercise and diet.

Look at this alternative view which involves money.

Once Aids is diagnosed, it means death. There is no cure and no immunisation say most medical authorities. 1,000 Aids patients can bring to the medical fraternity $40-$150,000,000.

The difference is that ozone offers an actual cure and it's cheap.

Why isn't this common knowledge? 'The heart is deceitful above all things and desperately wicked.' *Ref.2.

Hydrogen Peroxide Cure? Neither of these treatments must be undertaken without medical advice.

Some folk around the world say they are finding similar success by drinking and bathing in diluted hydrogen peroxide, 3% of 35% food grade hydrogen peroxide, which can produce similar results to the ozone blood treatment. This offers a possible home treatment as no blood needs to be drawn and hydrogen peroxide is cheap and plentiful. Warning — the correct amounts are essential.

Please do not write to us regarding this treatment.

For more information, please obtain a book called "Oxygen Therapies" by Ed McCabe available from: Energy Publications, 99/RD1, Morrisville, NY 13408, U.S.A. In this book from page 188 on you may read of people & places using oxygenation.

Why did I spend so long on the Aids questions?

Because, at present rates, 80% of the world's population will shortly die unless a cure is officially found and used soon or unless there is divine intervention.

We Christians, are believing the Lord for protection and His divine healing for any believers in Christ who are infected in this way. Miraculous cures have already been claimed.

In the meantime, it is added to the list of crisis that are meant to make everybody clamour for a World Government.

'Bulletin Magazine' 3rd May 1988:

'....a political scientist at the University of Western Australia says.....'something diabolical has to happen to us first.....the United States and the Soviet Union will use their command of intellectual and material resources to turn the solution to their shared advantage.

......reader in politics at La Trobe University....didn't think an environmental crisis would see the realisation of the dream of world government, but it would result in a search for a world institution with collective responsibility for the globe, for this, and future generations — something that implied a redefining of issues which belonged to national sovereignty, and those that belonged to a planet.'

Although this statement is obscure, this book makes it clear that no amount of pussy-footing with semantics will stop it.

There will be World Government and if they have their way, before the year 2000.

CHAPTER 21

Change, Change, Change

This is psychologically important in preparing the populations of each country for a World Government.

That in itself will be the greatest CHANGE of all.

I will outline herewith some of these changes that have taken place in either Australia, New Zealand or both, during the past decade 1980-1990.

CONSTITUTIONAL CHANGE
1. Attempt to change the Australian Constitution.
   'Townsville Bulletin', 7th May 1988. 'Changes set for Constitution. The Constitutional Committee yesterday delivered its blueprint for more stable government and greater democratic rights in Australia.'

This was a giant con.

Notes
   a. The U.K. has no written constitution. Since the 9th century, the law has been based on the 10 commandments in relation to the whole Bible.
   b. Common Law then came in i.e. Parliament could advise the king who could correct a court judge if necessary.
   c. The Magna Carta was a restatement of this law. The Barons forced King John to sign it or he was out of a job. James II tried to buck the Magna Carta. Parliament said 'You are subject to this law' and out he went.
   d. William and Mary signed the Bill of Rights as this part of the law had been forgotten to this point. 200 years later, this Bill of Rights came to Australia.
   e. Each State Constitution now gave meaning to this law.
   f. The 1900/01 Constitution became the Law of Australia.
   g. Colonies called States became a Federation.
   h. In 1988, the government in power wanted to change this Constitution. Why? Whitlam said 'The way of the reformer is hard in Australia.'

See then how evil men throughout history have tried their best to change their foundations. This is so that they can set up a new

123

society based on their sadly misguided ideas. Remember, a politician without God is under special spiritual attack from the enemy of souls and the future world leader, in prophecy is referred to as 'the Lawless One.'

The Australian Prime Minister of the day said 'a Labour Government is not any good if it is temporary. It must be made permanent.'

i. The opposition was against these changes to the constitution. If it was insignificant, why change it? Answer—A softening up process for further change. A constitution offers a measure of security. This security needs to be tampered with to make way for the change to World Government.

j. There were 4 questions. Australians wisely voted NO to them all and won a brief respite from the on going plan. Poor New Zealanders, lost their round when the Governor General lost his power to veto any bill. Later on in New Zealand, the Government passed a law making the act of 'treason' no longer punishable by death. That's interesting isn't it? Who could they have had in mind when passing this bill?

CURRENCY CHANGE

2. Coins. It was interesting to watch the new $1.00 and $2.00 coins appear on the Australian scene. The change from notes was another important step, as it unsettles people. Individuals are usually secure with familiar objects.

Industrial psychologists probably helped to design these coins. The $1.00 was the same size as the 10 cent piece and the $2.00 coin the same size as the 5 cent piece.

An absolute nightmare to such people as taxi-drivers working nightshift and giving wrong change.

New Zealand, your coins are to be minted in Australia also. Kiss your $1.00 and $2.00 notes goodbye.

3. Phone boxes and letter boxes in Australia change. Australian letter boxes are being removed and N.Z. phone boxes, traditionally painted red, are now being painted blue. Why? Change of course. One fellow went around Christchurch painting them red again. Good for him.

4. Private boxes made public. Christchurch 'Press' 27th February 1989. 'Private box and bag numbers are losing their secrecy. A 166,000 list of private holders of boxes and

bags will be out soon. This will stop any person using a private box or bag to communicate with others who are against any outrageous bill or law being passed. Clever, isn't it? Anonymity is passing away.

5. Ferry timetable and name change. New Zealand has two main islands, connected only by sea or air. The sea ferries used to be advertised as 'making New Zealand one country'. Now the very opposite applies. This completely confuses the travelling public. The ships involved have also experienced a name change.

6. Travel tax change. Passengers flying overseas from Christchurch or Auckland paid this tax. From Wellington, there was none to pay as nobody knew who was to collect it. Disneyland is not situated only in America.

Now, at the beginning of 1989, a $4.00 tax was levied from all airports. Of course, they didn't call it tax. They called it by some other crazy name. The result was the same. Continual change, which equals confusion.

7. Amalgamation and Centralization change. Local body reforms. 'Papanui Herald', 7th February 1989. 'The local body reorganization of Christchurch is a close re-run of the major reforms in Classical Athens in the 5th century B.C. which were designed to break down local loyalties and communities interest.

About 500 B.C. Athens was a city made up of about 150 communities and small towns. People felt a strong community of interest in their local areas and administered themselves politically with little interference from a central authority. But the central powers were unhappy about this.....The effect of those reforms was to break down peoples' national ties with those living in the same area....' End quote.

In New Zealand and Australia, this goes under the title of 'amalgamation'. This was practised by both Hitler and the Soviets before they took over power.

It is quite a laugh to know all these things and to observe one's neighbours organising meetings aimed at preventing amalgamation taking place. These people are all so serious and sincere but they don't understand. This plan must and will, go ahead, protest or no protest.

PROTESTS in Australia and New Zealand are absolutely useless. These political leaders, have so much delegated power

125

from their World Government masters, that even if a PETITION of 800,000 were brought to their door, to prevent for example 'homo-sexual law reform', the petition is received with much noise and smiles all round.

The crowds who travel by sea, road and air, return home, satisfied that something positive will result from all this expense and effort.

Meanwhile, the POLITICIAN PUPPETS carry the boxes inside to be placed in a back room with a sign which says 'A.B.' = Await Burning — and then retire to the lunch room where jokes are made, and they are told that things will not change in any way whatsoever, as their minds were made up and their plans formulated well before any protest took place.

'Debate is a healthy thing', they say and laugh whilst we pawns engage in these fruitless meetings.

Any person who is naive enough to think New Zealand or Australia are democracies, needs to look up the meaning of the word in his or her dictionary.

Websters defines 'democracy' thus:

'Popular government from the people (demos-kratein). Government by the people; a form of government in which the supreme power is lodged in the hands of the people collectively.....either directly or through representation.....equality as regards to political and legal rights opposed to aristocracy.' End quote.

Another man described democracy in New Zealand and Australia as 'A mythical state of mind inducing self deception by one who is no longer acquainted with reality.' End quote.

By the way, the man mentioned above was myself.

It was Plato, the famous Greek philosopher, who stated that no democracy could last for very long as it would always turn into a tyranny. Plato was correct on this issue, at least.

Away back in 1957, the then Secretary-General of Nato, Henri Spaak, said 'We are tired of committees. Send us a MAN whether he be GOD or the DEVIL and we will receive him.' (Emphasis added). End quote.

Mr Spaak, let me tell you. Your words were prophetic. The world will receive a leader soon from the devil and his title will be 'Antichrist'.

8. Farming changes. We have discussed livestock tax. Now, try this. From 'N.Z. Farmer' 13th August 1987. 'In Holland,

farmers who haven't bought any extra milk quotas will only be allowed to milk 75% of their present number of cows, and what's more, they are being restricted in the amount of manure they can put on their fields and each farmer has to keep a manure book...' End quote.

The Australasian governments haven't thought of this one yet but it sounds extraordinarily like the fishing restrictions in New Zealand. Christchurch 'Press', 9th May 1988. 'Up to 1100 Farmers Cannot Survive'.

ACC (Accident Compensation) Levy rises by 700%. 'Timaru Herald' 24.2.88. 'The Industry was utterly baffled as it appeared as if the ACC was determined to cut off the aerial topdressing industry.' End quote.

'Australian' 25.11.87. 'The Australian tractor and farm equipment industry was experiencing the worst sales year in its history....' End quote.

9. Overseas Investors Change. The New Zealand Stock Exchange will liberalise its ownership rules so that foreign individuals or companies can fully own trading members firms. Changes again.

10. Property right change. In the matter of who owns what in New Zealand and Australia with various groups claiming land rights i.e. Morioris and Maoris—the original people of New Zealand and the Aboriginals—the original people of Australia and many other races who live in these two countries, an article from the 'New Zealand Management Law Reform 1988' may assist our understanding.

'...One problem identified so far is the question of property rights created under the present legislation. There are legal arguments about what rights existing users have and the review will consider the advantages and disadvantages of changing rights to the allocation of resources and what compensation should be given to those who lose their current rights.

The review will also consider the legal processes for resolving conflicts. This will cover such matters as how to transfer resources fairly efficiently and at low cost, whether rights to use resources should be bought and sold, and what role the Government should play when the normal forces of the market do not produce an acceptable solution....' End quote.

'Dominion', 22nd June 1989. 'Morioris Seek Fish Rights for All. The Morioris have proposed an equal rights fishing policy for the Chatham islands, arguing the resource should be controlled for the benefit of all island residents....' End quote.

Let's hope these people do not go for land rights as well, or the fat will be truly in the proverbial fire.

Has it ever occurred to you, the reader, that your home is in jeopardy of being taken off you.

Each group involved in World Government plans has, near the head of their lists of changes to be made, the 'taking over of all land and real estate', as land ownership gives one a measure of security.

Taxation, slowly and surreptitiously being increased and added to, is probably the most efficient method to achieve this end. Watch for it, Kiwis and Aussies.

If you are a born-again Christian, this will not seem quite so serious as we have the knowledge that we are leaving this earth shortly to be with the Lord.

'For the Lord Himself, shall descend from heaven with a shout, with the voice of the arch-angel and with the trump of God and the dead in Christ shall rise first.

Then we which are alive and remain shall be caught up together with them in the clouds to meet the Lord in the air, and so shall we ever be with the Lord.

Wherefore, comfort one another with these words.' *Ref.1.

We had barely finished building our own home some years ago, when I stood on the lawn with my family, looking at the finished product.

I said 'Take a good look at it family. The Antichrist will probably take all this from us, but it doesn't really matter too much as we have a house all arranged, up in heaven.'

'God is not ashamed to be called their God, for He hath prepared for them a city.' *Ref.2.

In late 1988, a group of us stood on the Mount of Olives, where I read the words of our Lord Jesus Christ.

This is where He left from to go to heaven after his crucifixion. This is where He is coming back to shortly.

Don't skim read these statements. Read them slowly and thoughtfully.

'Let not your heart be troubled, ye believe in God, believe also in me. In my Fathers house, there are many mansions. I go to prepare a place for you.

And if I go and prepare a place for you, I will come again and receive you unto myself, that where I am, there ye may be also.' *Ref.3.

Thrilling information, you will agree!

11. Changes in monitoring one's financial affairs. Christchurch 'Press', 12th July 1988. 'New Zealanders can expect legalised systems within five years which would allow State monitoring of their financial affairs, predicts an Australian civil liberties campaigner....

.....New Zealand will inevitably follow Australia in its legal steps to monitor and restrict the cash economy announced in the Australian May mini Budget.

.....The introduction of enhanced tax file numbers, which was one of the reforms announced in the Australian May mini Budget, would allow the tax department to have automatic input into peoples' financial affairs.

.....These included requiring people to quote their tax file number when opening a bank account, applying for a job, trading shares and buying a house, he said.....' End quote.

During the course of my public lectures, I have pointed this out for many years and that is how the World Government advocates, through their local government puppets will be able to tax the hated fundamentalist, charismatic and pentecostal churches apparently out of existence.

Now, as the author of this book, please allow me to make a statement.

The only true Christians are the fundamentalists. The devil knows this; God knows this, but many religious people don't.

I receive many calls from people who attend 'liberal churches' where their ministers really know more than the inspired Word of God. These men and women have such giant intellects and I sometimes feel it is a pity that God didn't wait for them to be born before he wrote His word, so that He could have called them in for advice.

A Christian fundamentalist by the way, is a person who believes God said what He meant and meant what He said and that the Scriptural record of itself is true.

'All Scripture is given by inspiration of God and is profitable for doctrine, for reproof, for correction, for instruction in righteousness.' *Ref.4.

A Christian fundamentalist will take only the Holy Scriptures as his guideline — not tradition, because tradition is at odds with the Word of God.

These people ideally should not only have a head and heart

129

knowledge of the Scriptures, but should be filled with love for all men.

The only people who really irked our Lord Jesus Christ when He was on earth, were the religious liberals of the day.

In over 90% of the media interviews, it is these Judases who speak for Christendom, but have no legal right to do so.

It is clear that at the judgement of God, the standard will not be:
a. Our religiosity
b. Our ability to fiddle with the Scripture i.e. to demythologize in terms of existential encounter
c. Our church attendance or good deeds.
d. Our attending the so-called 'true church'

No! Only our personal relationship with Christ Himself will avail on that day.

'He that hath the Son, hath life.' *Ref.5.

How marvelous. A present tense possession.

12. Changes to where people live. There are ways of moving people from certain areas such as:

a. Closing down Post Offices. In New Zealand and Australia, this has been a violent and traumatic innovation brought about apparently, by people who have no soul.

Older residents of rural areas have wept, protested held public meetings in vain as the plan is irreversible. In our own area, our two public post offices were closed down with not a word of explanation. We wondered why.

European Community and other readers, take careful note of the following information. We can now tell you why this took place here and why it will take place in your country also.

Statement

New Zealanders went like sheep to the slaughter with every other diabolical change to their way of living. One thing they did not take to willingly however, was the introduction of the plastic card 'EFTPOS' and in fact, caused some banks to discuss abandoning the whole concept.

The answer to this seeming enigma appeared in 'The Evening Post', Wellington, on the 15th August 1989. 'Govt plans subsidy for banking in rural areas.

130

The Government will subsidise automatic facilities for ten remote rural communities which lose banking services when the Government corporatised the Post Office. The Government is providing a one off (sic) subsidy of one hundred thousand dollars this financial year and fifty thousand dollars in 1990/91 to establish EFTPOS terminals offering cash deposit and withdrawal facilities. The communities all have a minimum population of 300 and are more than fifty kilometres away from the nearest banking or EFTPOS centre....' End quote.

Author's note.

The cunning rascals.

b. Charging exorbitant fees for rural mail delivery
c. Closing down hospitals in the area
d. Closing down local industry — A case in point is the Chatham Islands, off the coast of New Zealand; the Chathams are part of New Zealand territory. We who know the World Government advocates plan for setting up a surveillance system over every individuals' lives, also know that places like the Chathams pose a threat.

Fibre optics and microwave dishes for instant communication would be very difficult, not to mention expensive for the Telecom people to set up. A personalised numbering system for buying and selling and a change to full computerisation makes this place a nightmare in logistics. Note how these master manipulators turned their attention to the Chathams some time ago.

'New Zealand Times', 22nd June 1986. '...The recommendations being considered by the Government include: a 40% fare increase from $250.00 to $350.00 one way, a 33% increase in air freight rates from $1.50 to $2.00 a kilo,a 42% increase in sea freight rates on the Holmdale shipping link. Closure of the sole island meatworks.....' End quote.

Of course, another explanation will be given as to why these suggestions have been made.

It is a strange thing, but the Government spokesmen, coming regularly on television, have spoken with two tongues so often that the average citizen of our two countries , feels quite nauseated at viewing even their picture on the screen, or on a page of the newspaper. We used to have a measure of respect for our 'democratically elected representatives' but I for one, am very grateful to the person who invented the 'mute button' on the hand held device that works in a 'remote' fashion from my easy chair. I, unfortunately, can still see them, which is quite distasteful, but I can save my ears from the indignity of listening to their half-truths and even on occasions, untruths.

It ought not to be so, but it is.

e.g. 'The French bombers of the Rainbow Warrior will not be released.' Where are they now?

Goods and Services Tax will not rise from 10%. In July 1989, it rose to 12 and a half percent. Strange isn't it?

The forestry workers in the Tasman area will not lose their jobs. Member for Wanganui says, 'I will resign if the railway workshops close.' They closed, and this man became Minister of Foreign Affairs.

Many Christians emphasize that we are exhorted to pray for those in authority over us, quoting this Biblical passage:

Romans 13:1 – 'Let every soul be subject unto the higher powers, for there is no power but of God: the powers that be are ordained of God.'

Verse 4 tells us, 'For He is a minister of God to thee for good.'

A Russian brother who had been in Siberia for his faith, explained this verse. 'The Government is ordained to do the will of God. When they deny the existence of God and persecute the people of God, they are not of God, but of the devil.' End quote.

The words of Jesus may help in explaining this seeming enigma. 'Render therefore unto Caesar the things which are Caesar's and unto God, the things that are God's.' *Ref.6.

We are further told to pray:

a.'For Kings and for all that are in authority....' *Ref.7. Why?

b. 'That we may lead a quiet and peaceable life in all Godliness and honesty.

For this is good and acceptable in the sight of God our Saviour....' *Ref.8.

Why?

'Who will have all men to be saved, and to come unto the knowledge of the truth.' *Ref.9.

Now in Australia and New Zealand, all politicians need a copy of this book. If they miss everything else, may they read the above verses.

The policies being served up prior to 1990 are absolutely

132

diabolical and do not lead in any way whatsoever to:
a. A quiet life
b. A peaceable life
c. A godly life
Their policies lead to the very opposite.
The last verse tells us how we should pray for these characters.
'That they might receive the Lord Jesus Christ and be saved.'
Many change countries. New Zealand's Christchurch 'Press'
28th February 1989. 'The net population loss of 24,500 was
recorded for the year ended January 1989 from permanent and
long term migration said the Government Statistician....' End
quote.

Note. CONSTANT CHANGE CAUSES INSECURITY
however, those in tune with the Lord don't become upset over
all this. They trust in one who says 'FOR I AM THE LORD.
I CHANGE NOT.' *Ref.10.

13. Changes in Relationships of Australia and New Zealand.
'Press' 25th Feb. 1989. 'New Zealand was restructuring its
diplomatic posts in Australia because the relationship
between the two countries was growing rapidly....We are
reorganising our priorities in Australia as our economies
merge....' End quote.

14. Nelson 'Evening Mail' 4th August 1988. 'The obstinacy of
the Minister of Finance over changes to superannuation is
difficult to explain....'

In essence, what the Minister is saying is that
superannuation like all other forms of savings, should be
taxed....' End quote.

Fabian Socialism says 'Never deviate or change or all your
waiting has been in vain.'

15. Changes in environment. In both Australian and New
Zealand, land is being set a side for a 'World Heritage Park'.
This prevents logging of these areas and in turn, yields up
our land to an international body.

A good example of this may be taken from Tasmania.

I remember speaking at a public meeting in Hobart some years
ago. I said, 'Has anybody here heard of the Franklin Dam?' You
could have cut the air with a knife. The tension rose.

I went on. 'The Franklin Dam was a good example of the
infringement of rights on a State Government by other outside
groups.i.e. The Tasmanian State Government was going to dam

133

this river. However, the Federal Government in Canberra had already entered into agreements with international groups such as the U.N. and World Heritage.

The international groups reminded Canberra of the agreement. Canberra reminded Tasmania and Tasmania shut down the programme.

This is called the 'thin edge of the wedge'. Who is next to be infringed upon?

16. Changes to land use. Christchurch 'Press' 28.2.89. 'A world tree bank that could save thousands of species of plant life from extinction, may be established in New Zealand within a year....' End quote. Note the change of land use from animals to trees.

Farming has been widely destroyed in many parts of New Zealand. The land will be planted with trees as New Zealand is the country high on the list for quick tree growth. Under the W.G.A. plan, New Zealand will be responsible for tourism and trees. In order to make a quick dollar in the future therefore, I would recommend opening a ski lodge or a chain saw agency.

17. Changes in road signs. Christchurch 'Press', 28th Feb. 1989. 'One thousand new road signs aimed at making driving safer for tourists will be put up in Canterbury and the West Coast over the next six months.' End quote.

These are International road signs, which is part of the W.G.A. plans for New Zealand.

18. Changes in attitudes. New Zealand was one of the best places in the world to live if one enjoyed the 'quiet, relaxed life'.

Many years ago, Zane Grey, the author, flew into New Zealand for a weekend breather. When asked later, how he enjoyed New Zealand, he replied 'I don't really know. It was closed.'

Gone is the Buoyancy

Christchurch 'Press', 4.1.88. 'New Zealand is adopting a siege mentality in the face of economic, social and political difficulties, according to a French newspaper 'Le Monde'...the newspaper depicts New Zealand as a country 'gripped by doubts', 'traumatised' by cultural revolution and run by a Government 'shaking on its foundations'.

.....Shattered by the crisis, many New Zealanders are turning in on themselves, losing interest.....' End quote.

'Evening Post' Wellington, 9 Feb. 1989. 'New Zealand sunk

in gloom, says U.K. scribe. A once near-perfect country, New Zealand is now an unhappy land of instability and uncertainty, according to Simon Winchester, Pacific Affairs Correspondent of the 'Guardian'....Winchester lays much of the blame at the door of Rogernomics—an economic philosophy.....

True, New Zealand has always been a stupefyingly dull country—but a fundamentally decent place too. But now, all the goodness of the place seems to be eroding.

....If you're halfway bright, you want out.

....This year, all New Zealand seems cast down, collectively, dejected and depressed at itself and the state that it has managed to get into during Mr L.........'s terms....' End quote.

19. Change in Economy. In the late 1980's, a British member of the European parliament touring New Zealand, was shocked at the mess of the economy.

'....He said, "privatisation was being done for the wrong reasons" and was selling off the family silver instead of improving efficiency.

....The life blood was draining away from New Zealand's agricultural sector, the basis of the country's wealth....' End quote.

This man apparently brings an honest appraisal of the situation but he is not in on the plan to force New Zealand to link with Australia.

Dr Ravi Batra reported in the Christchurch 'Press', 12th Feb. 1988 says 'New Zealand will be the first country to plunge into a world-wide depression....' If it's any consolation, he believes Australia is not far behind us. Dr Batra has made a name through the success of his book 'The Great Depression of 1990'.

20. Change in payments for beneficiaries. 'Dominion Sunday Times', 15th November 1987....'The Government is investigating issuing beneficiaries with microchip plastic cards capable of storing a wealth of personal information. The Social Welfare Department has been involved in a series of meetings with the Australian suppliers of the French made cards known as 'smart cards'.

21. 'New Zealand as role model in change.' This is important. Please read this section at least twice.

In the late 1980's, the President of the World Bank visited New Zealand. Quote—'New Zealand's economic restructuring was a ROLE MODEL for other countries which also had to adjust their policies to achieve growth, the World Bank president, Mr Barber Conable said.

At a press conference, after talks with the Minister of Finance....and the Prime Minister.....Mr Conable said the policies 'wisely pursued' in New Zealand had NOT BEEN WITHOUT PAIN but were now showing benefits in an improving economy....(Emphasis added).

.....Policies implemented here were consistent with those advocated by the World Bank to achieve 'adjustments....Mr Conable said he was reluctant to tell countries they should follow precisely the steps taken elsewhere, because policies had to be adapted to the situation of each.' End quote.

Readers, please notice that this great international lending establishment also states clearly to any who borrow from them, precisely how the money will be spent. They don't advise — they instruct. Notice the word 'tell' in the above statement. The New York Times make all this very clear.

'The door to the new financing does not open however, unless the debtors accept conditions set by the IMF and World Bank. Acceptance of their conditions is not always politically palatable in the debtor nations.'

EUROPEAN COMMUNITY — YOU ARE NEXT. GET READY.

22. Year of change. 1990 is to be a very important year in New Zealand. The country has been viciously ripped from South to North by a plan which could not be devised in the mind of a mere mortal.

International figures, in league with some Trojan Horse type politicians who 'are prepared to sell everybody's birthright for a mess of pottage' have become traitors to the vows to uphold the sovereignty of New Zealand and have gone along with all this destruction.

1990 is the year for New Zealand; says the poster advertising the 150th anniversary for the founding of Wellington and Auckland. They carry on to say 'The potential of 1990 is endless.'

This author would agree with this.

1990 is the year the World Government Advocates plan to hold an official gathering.

Year — 1990
Venue — New Zealand

Why?—To make it official whilst they have the diversion of people involved in massive celebrations i.e. the 150th anniversary since the signing of the Treaty of Waitangi, between the Maori and European settlers.

CHAPTER 22

The Highly Organised Destruction of New Zealand

We have seen how 'change' has been wrought over most of the New Zealand way of life. Some folk naively think that certain people in New Zealand thought up these destructive policies. No—they simply implemented them.

Dates to Remember:
1990—New Zealand's destruction should be complete. The elections will be almost irrelevant, because no human being can ever remedy the damage done to this formerly, peaceful country.

1990/91—C.E.R. Closer Economic Relations with Australia will lead on ultimately to C.P.R. Closer Political Relations. Remember, New Zealand is on the Australian Constitution as a state of that country.

1992—The Planned Destruction of Europe (E.C.) commences using the country of New Zealand as a prototype.

Linking with Australia
The newspapers are full of it. Look at these newspaper headings:
New Zealand 'Herald', 1st October 1988: 'Kiwi Damsel In Distress Could Have Been Blushing Bride.

For nearly 88 years, New Zealand has suffered needless trade impoverishment and pain in sporting rivalry because it has not taken up an annually advertised invitation to merge with Australia....' End quote.

Each year, the Australian Government Yearbook carries a copy of the 1900 Constitution which almost invites New Zealand to link up officially. But, no. Pride or something else had prevented this happening to this point. Not for much longer however.

'Weekend Australian', 1988. 'Coast is clearer for New Zealand link.

In essence, New Zealand and Australia will form a kind of Common Market, a transtasman economic community on July 1st 1990.

Thereafter, all commodities will cross the Tasman freely without paying import duties....' End quote.

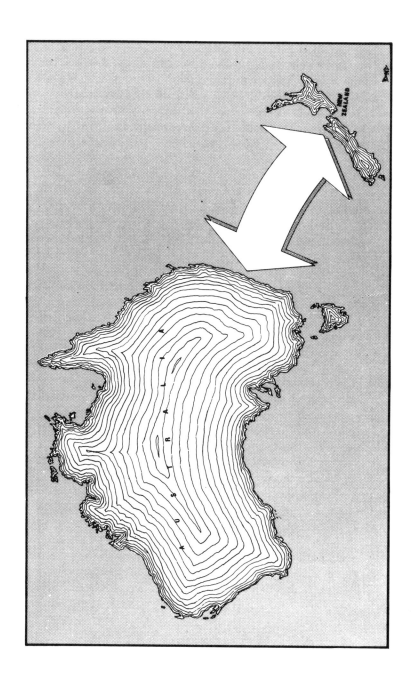

Readers, notice that Canada and the U.S. have their own C.E.R agreement going at the same time.

Rotorua 'Daily Post', 30th June 1988. 'Government denies move to New Zealand-Australian Law System....' End quote.

This statement is sure proof that this is what they intend to do. In order to understand a government statement in New Zealand just prior to 1990, hear what they say, then look for the opposite meaning.

'Dominion', 1988. 'Australia, Only Way to Go.

New Zealand's shrinking economy can be turned around only by joining up with Australia and reorienting to the Pacific Basin....' End quote.

Brisbane 'Sun', 2nd December 1988. 'Kiwis Invest in Gold Coast.

New Zealand companies unhappy with their own country's economy are pinpointing the Gold Coast for future property investments....' End quote.

'Australian', 3rd July 1984. 'Blainey urges New Zealand to join with Australia....

It was better for the country to start talks now rather than leave them until it was forced to join Australia....Let's say Australia and New Zealand became part of the same union and New Zealand was given the equivalent of two States....New Zealanders would also elect members to a federal parliament.

I suppose from time to time, a New Zealander would be Prime Minister of the trans-Tasman federation', he said.... End quote.

A very telling newspaper cartoon shows Australia's Prime Minister arriving at the door with a bunch of flowers, and speaking to a girl dressed like a map of New Zealand. He has two presents in his hands:

a. The Shipping Corporation
b. 25% in Air New Zealand

His car, parked outside, has C.E.R. written on the side. He says 'gidday. Thought y'might like a spin in the new car.'

The point is, although New Zealand has been PRIVATISING and SELLING OFF THE FAMILY SILVER, look who is buying it.

New Zealand entrepeneurs in touch with vast overseas financial resources, and Australian Companies.

Clever, isn't it? You sell your assets but ultimately, you sell them to yourself knowing that one day New Zealand will be part

140

of Australia yet the World Government advocates have their sticky little fingers in the pie also, so that you don't get carried away and try for INDEPENDENCE. Oh no. INTERDEPENDENCE is now the name of the game.

'Press', 28.4.88. 'Foreign Ownership Inevitable–D..............s.
New Zealand has to face up to the issue of foreign ownership of some of the businesses owned by the Government.....

It was not the action of selling assets to repay debt that transferred New Zealand's assets to foreign ownership' he said....' End quote.

Where would he get this idea from? I find it very original.

'Dominion', 11th December 1987. 'Overseas Buyers Look at Coalfields.

International mining companies are showing interest in buying prospecting licenses for seven large undeveloped coal fields, including the controversial Ohinewai field in Waikato.

In AN UNUSUAL MOVE, the Minister of Energy has put up for sale, licences for five Waikato fields and two West Coast fields relinquished by the former State Coal Mines....' End quote. (Emphasis added.)

Becoming clearer now is it?

A senior coal economist with the ministry said that the government 'did not know how much money would be raised from the sale....' End quote.

This is a key phrase.

It is many peoples' opinion that the government does not care two straws how much is made on any sale. This is not important, so long as they 'obey' and strip New Zealand of its assets and leave it vulnerable to the W.G.A.

Want a piece of New Zealand? Any price will do.

141

CHAPTER 23

Change of Allegiances

New Zealand was a partner in the Anzus Treaty i.e. Australia, New Zealand and the U.S.A.

Part of the plan to destabalize the Pacific area was to apparently break off part of the partnership in Anzus by refusing to allow nuclear armed, or powered ships into New Zealand ports.

A certain group of people then started talking about New Zealand as a nuclear free zone in a so called nuclear free Pacific.

A strange piece of logic, you will agree, with France testing their nuclear weaponry in the only suitable area for them to do so i.e. Mururoa Atoll in the Pacific.

A public speaker some time ago stated that a small country like New Zealand declaring the Pacific nuclear free was similar to a mouse in Africa declaring Africa an elephant free zone.

The late 1980's has spawned a strange lot of people who appear to have had their intellect taken away.

In the 'Pacific Islands Monthly', dated April 1988, we read the then Prime Minister of New Zealand quoted as saying:

'In terms of threats to our independent existence we are exactly in the same position in 1987 as we were in 1984. There is no threat and none can be conjured....Not even the fiercest of them, (government critics) has been able to identify an enemy massing on the horizon....' End quote.

I will quote one—SOVIET RUSSIA.

Why, for example, did they sink their ship in our waters, and why was there not a full marine enquiry? These people apparently are to be our new playmates.

The name of the ship—LERMONTOV.

Therefore, the apparent break with the U.S. by New Zealand, was to introduce 'equal opportunities' in the South Pacific for the U.S.S.R., which will soon be apparently co-operating with the U.S.A.in heading up a World Government system.

At this point, some of you overseas readers are becoming tired of words, NEW ZEALAND and AUSTRALIA.

Just settle down and read on. What is happening to us will be happening to you shortly. Remember us? We are the prototype.

I remember asking a young lady in Perth some years ago now, to draw me an advertising poster.

She did. It showed a man with a bar-code on his head and an inscription above which read:

'Hello Guinea Pigs'.

CHAPTER 24

The Overthrow of
New Zealand Sovereignty

People constantly ask me about racial tension in New Zealand. Yes, there is some. Government policies from 1984 onwards, brought it out in the open, and may I say, almost encouraged it. How?

1. By dividing New Zealanders into separate races, with separate sets of rights.
2. By allowing some radicals to not only train in Libya and Cuba but to train others in New Zealand and to use the media of New Zealand to propagate these views.
3. Their failure to clamp down on law and order when gangs were just getting into power.

Not only that, government's funds were used on some occasions to assist these people e.g. travel from South to North Islands on Social Welfare money, and in building highly expensive structures, and in some cases even using Government funds.

In socialist language, this is simply called: Divide and Rule.

You set the two groups in your country against each other, then when the ordinary people cry for help, bring in repressive laws which affects both groups.

Enquiries should be made to see if the SIS (Security Intelligence Service) had a mandate from the Government to investigate these gangs and their funding, or were they instructed to ignore the gang problem?

I don't know. Do you?

Struggle. Here is a common cliche if ever there was one.

'Dominion', 3rd March 1989.

....'We will get our land back and that is by taking it back, if necessary through armed struggle.....' said.......' End quote.

Well, this is quite amazing. The headline in one of New Zealand's national papers has this article under an eye-catching headline, on the front page mind you —

'New Zealand about to Explode in Revolution, Australians told.'

Here are a few insignificant, virtually unheard of individuals,

144

who have no mandate from their leaders or people for that matter, making themselves look absolutely stupid, bandying communist words like 'STRUGGLE'.

The biggest struggle most of these would have experienced to this point, would be to change their Soviet currency payoff into legal New Zealand money.

I suppose they have tried hard to create racial tension, but very few New Zealanders are very interested, if the truth was known.

Born again Christians have the advantage of having a basis for living e.g. 'We are all one in Christ Jesus.' *Ref.1.

'The life of the flesh is in the blood' and 'God hath made of one blood, all nations'. *Ref.2. and *Ref.3.

What good news. Different colours outside, but inside the same life flowing through our veins.

Pity these poor creatures who have a racial problem. It is a bitterness that none of us were born with.

It is taught and destroys the person involved.

Years ago, when I was teaching in Western Samoa, the birthplace of my wife May, I was approached by the Health Department for blood. A woman, a personal friend of ours, was bleeding badly due to a miscarriage.

The health workers came up to Samoa College where I was working at the time, tested some of the teachers' blood and guess who had the correct type. A negative—Me, of course.

They transfused my blood into our friend, and some years later, upon returning to the island, we met again.

She didn't look any different at all with my blood in her. I asked her in her own language 'O a lau gagu?'—'How's your English?' She replied 'O le mea lava e tasi'—'No change.'

I would suggest to all readers involved in land rights issues in Australia, New Zealand and elsewhere—forget it.

Under the new World Government plans, nobody will have any land rights. It will all be confiscated.

Let's all get together, recognise our common enemy—the instigator of all this confusion, Lucifer, and turn in repentance and faith to a common friend and would-be Saviour, the Lord Jesus Christ.

'I am the way, the truth, and the life. No man cometh unto the Father but by me.' *Ref.4.

Cliches Old Hat. The struggling individuals referred to in the article above need to read this.

145

'Australian', 12th April 1988. 'Cliches are Old Hat in the Socialist Struggle.

You won't be hearing much more about colonialism, imperialism, the proletariat and other rhetorical cliches from Australia's mainstream left.

.....Agreeing that such words made many people, particularly Australians, turn off he said......' End quote.

Soviets like Peace Groups in New Zealand. In politics, as in religion, it is possible to use words which have no relevance to the true meaning of these words.

'Press', 13th February 1989. 'Soviet Praise for Peace Group.

....The Novosti Agency said 'New Times', published in seven languages, with a circulation of about 500,000, devoted two pages to the activities of the New Zealand Foundation for Peace Studies....

.....brought the country respect from the world community....' End quote.

In my own personal opinion, there are three groups who apply here.

   a. Those who have never heard of New Zealand.
   b. Those who have, and regard these movements as ridiculous.
   c. Those communist countries and helpers called L.U.F. —
      Lenin's useful fools, who see all this in the light of taking over New Zealand.

Armed Revolution in New Zealand? If by any chance the 'stirrers group' did manage to rustle up some type of enthusiasm for a dust up, they would always have the Soviets to call on for help, wouldn't they?

By now, as the reader will have detected, my aim has been, not to denigrate the Soviets or the New Zealand Government, as I am sure that there are some thoroughly good and honourable people in their ranks — not necessarily easy to detect, but no doubt there.

I have tried to set a picture up in your mind, that leads from thought to thought, until the whole scene becomes so obvious, it is laughable.

CHAPTER 25

Telecom and Surveillance

Dotted along the mountain tops of New Zealand and through the outback of Australia on any small rise, one travelling through the area notices microwave transmission towers and dishes set up at varying intervals.

Please cast your mind back to a previous chapter and see the way Telecom links with the worldwide systems.

In a meeting sometime ago, I spoke about these microwave dishes, taking the place of the old copper wire system. An l.o.l. (little old lady) came up to me afterwards and asked why they were cooking, away out in the Australian outback.

I gently explained, 'Transmission dishes, not ovens, Madam.'

'Press', 2nd March 1989. 'Phone numbers for the newborn.... In the next decade New Zealanders will have a personalised telephone number from the day they are born, a visiting British telecommunications expert says.

....newborn babies will be issued with a number for a world where telephone numbers will relate to the individual rather than a place.....

He predicts the first video telephones will be on the market within four years.....' End quote.

Acquaintances of mine working in Telecom New Zealand, have over the years, spoken to me at the end of my meetings about a vast FIBRE OPTIC network being set up across Australia and New Zealand with far too many threads than are usable in this day and age. Obviously, the plan will lead on to complete computerisation of every aspect of life.

Why?

Because the plan calls for a dossier and complete surveillance of every aspect of life.

This plan was started by:

1. Lucifer — 2. Dominicans — 3. Loyola — 4. Illuminati — 5. Jesuits — 6. Weishaupt — 7. Freemasons — 8. Communism — 9. Big Brother.

The 'Eye of Horus' is the key

1. Lucifer was his original name. He wanted to watch over

147

creation. His beauty and wisdom corrupted this created being and pride to such a degree that he tried to take over from Almighty God, which ultimately resulted in his being thrown out of heaven.

'Thine heart was lifted up because of thy beauty, thou hast corrupted thy wisdom by reason of thy brightness.

I will cast thee to the ground, I will lay thee before kings that they may behold thee.' *Ref.1.

And again.

'How art thou fallen from heaven, oh Lucifer, son of the morning, how art thou cut down to the ground which did weaken the nations.

For thou has said in thine heart

a. I will ascend into heaven
b. I will exalt my throne above the stars of God
c. I will sit also upon the mount of the congregation on the sides of the north
d. I will ascend above the heights of the clouds
e. I will be like the most High.' *Ref.2.

This has been his aim ever since he was cast out of heaven.

As we mentioned in the 'Global 2000' chapter, the tower of Babel was his first big attempt — that failed.

It has been predicted that it will happen once more and behold — here it is. 1990 + 10 years = Global 2000.

2. Weishaupt, 1776 May 1st, Illuminati — He called his eye principle — The Insinuating Brethren — His aim was to spy on and guide society in his Luciferian ways.

3. Freemasonry — was infiltrated in the upper degrees by an associate of Weishaupt — Baron Von Knigge in the year 1778. (See Encyclopaedia Britannica). The aim was to inject mysticism, Ngosticism, mysteries and Luciferianism into this previously harmless society of men. Men in the lower degrees don't know all this of course, and instead of showing gratitude to writers like myself, some in their ignorance, get hostile.

In one meeting where I spoke on this subject, a mason who was present, protested publicly. I asked him which degree he was in and he answered 'the 18th'.

'Would you please be seated'. I replied. 'You don't know enough yet'.

After the meeting, with a degree of prompting from his wife, this man was prowling around, showing an interest in removing some teeth from my head. I asked my informant 'Why? Is he a dentist?'

The really sad thing is that he could have been saved through Jesus' precious blood, had not his know-it-all nature beat him.

Some ask me how I know so much about Masonry, having never been one. My answer is that I have informants up to the 32nd degree and even some 'Shriners' who became born again Christians, and renounced the whole thing. This is a wise move, as Freemasonry is Luciferianism.

The eye in their triangle, as worn by the Grand Master in each lodge as part of his jewellery, and that eye which is also on lodge walls, is referred to as the G.A.O.T.U. – The Great Architect of the Universe who is the Luciferian Eye of Horus, Adam Weishaupt's Insinuating Brethren and in actual fact, is Lucifer himself.

This quote was in my previous two books 'Warning' and 'Second Warning'. It is so important, I write it again herewith.

A copy of instructions issued by a 33rd degree Mason and Grand Pontiff of Universal Freemasonry on 14th July 1889 to the 23 Supreme Councils of the World. This will show you who the God of Freemasonry is:

Albert Pike, Sovereign Pontiff of Universal Freemasonry said: Quote – 'That which we must say to the crowd is, we worship a God, but it is the God which one adores without superstition. To you Sovereign Grand Inspectors General, we say this, and you may repeat it to the brethren of the 32nd, 31st and 30th degrees; the Masonic religion should be by all of us initiates maintained in the purity of the Luceriferian doctrine. If Lucifer were not God, would Adonay (God of the Christians) bother to spread false and harmful statements about him. YES, LUCIFER IS GOD. Unfortunately, Adonay is also God. For the eternal law is that there is no light without shade, no beauty without ugliness, no white without black, for the absolute can only exist as two Gods; darkness becoming necessary to light to serve as its foil, and the pedestal is necessary to the statue and the brake to the locomotive...The doctrine of satanism is a heresy and the true and pure philosophic religion is the belief in Lucifer, the equal of Adonay, but Lucifer, god of Light and god of Good, is struggling for humanity against Adonay, the god of Darkness and Evil.' End quote. (In A.C. De La Rive 'La Femme et l'enfant dans la Franc – Maconnerie Universelle' p. 588 and Queenborough 'Occult Theocracy' p.220, 221.)

150

4. The Communist eye is the eye of the KGB; who make life miserable for all who come under their power.

Key Statement

Communism was never, as many wrongly presume, a mass movement of the under-privileged to take over from the upper classes and bring equality.

Communism was a Luciferian, Illuminati style plan worked out with the blessing of the Jesuits to act as a test case for World dominion through a little group of thugs at the top, who trained each person to spy on his or her neighbours.

Financed by W.G.A., paid for from New York, Lenin and Trotsky were the men chosen to head it up.

Karl Marx, the founding father of Communism was a friend of a wealthy English cotton-spinner named Engels. Marx was never really into working for a living. He made constant appeals to Engels, who amongst other things, financed Marx's daughters' education. Marx insisted, 'they must have a bourgeoise education so that they can make contacts in life.'

So, Marx, 'the champion of the oppressed and downtrodden workers', spent nearly all his adult life living off the profits acquired from a capitalistic cotton mill in England.

In his youth, Marx was a believer in God, but like other fools, both before and after him, he changed his views while at University.

He once wrote that he wished to avenge himself 'against the One who rules above'.

Fair enough, you will agree. Worth a clap of applause at the time, but where is Marx now?

In June 1864, in a letter to his uncle Lion Phillips, Marx announced that he had made $400.00 on the stock exchange.

Marx and Engels wrote these aims for the Communist Party. Slight variations will apply in different countries.

Written in 1848:

1. Abolition of property in land and application of all rents of land for public purposes. (Marx wrote elsewhere in the Manifesto; 'you are horrified at our intending to do away with your private property. Precisely so, that is just what we intend.')
2. A heavy progressive or graduated income tax.

151

3. Abolition of all right of inheritance.
4. Confiscation of the property of all emigrants and rebels.
5. Centralisation of credit in the hands of the State by means of a national bank.
6. Centralisation of means of communication and transport in the hands of the state.
7. Extensions of factories and instruments of production owned by the state.
8. Equal liability to all labour. Establishment of industrial armies, especially for agriculture.
9. Combination agriculture with manufacturing industries. Gradual abolition of the distinction between town and country by a more equable distribution of population over the country. The ultimate capital good, man himself, would lose his ultimate freedom; the right to live where he chose.
10. Free education for all children in public schools. The State would assume the responsibility for the education of all the children in the society.

Later on, Lenin wrote 'our power does not know liberty or justice. It is entirely established on the destruction of the individual. We are the masters. Complete indifference to suffering is our duty....Through a systematic terror, during which every breach of contract, every treason, every lie, will be lawful....' End quote.

When I read this statement, it immediately occurred to me that certain people in the New Zealand Government from the 1980's-90's must have been familiar with these aims.

a. Indifference to suffering.
b. Lawful lies.

It is very important to note at this stage, that both New Zealand and Australia have been following a policy of FABIAN SOCIALISM.

Remember also, that Russia does not describe itself as being communist.

It is called the U.S.S.R. UNION OF SOVIET SOCIALIST REPUBLIC.

Rule — Socialist governments work with socialist governments.

Therefore, allegiances must change, and changed they have.

Facts
1. New Zealand is to be the test case for World Government.

2. The Soviet Union was a test case for surveillance of individuals.
3. Communism was financed by W.G.A.
4. New Zealand and the Soviet Union must get together.
5. Just prior to 1990, a top New Zealand government member visited the Soviet Union to discuss trade, fishing rights around New Zealand and rights for their national airline 'Aeroflot' to land in New Zealand — only to fly fishing crews in and out, of course.
6. Soviet 'fishing boats' of course, are also spy boats. This is generally assumed by all intelligent people.

CHAPTER 26

Australian Surveillance

I had heard about this place; now my eyes have seen it. In fact, I have a photo of myself taken outside this building.

I think the Government calls it 'The National Computer Centre', but to my wife and I, it looked like what we would imagine to be an Australian version of the Kremlin.

Situated at Kent St—Deakin—there it stood in Canberra, Australia. Solid concrete, narrow slits for windows, and inside, cold and forbidding, with access only if a pass is granted. People who have worked in there contacted me after my meetings and passed on some interesting information.

There is a centralisation of computers in there that makes a PRIVACY COMMISSIONER'S job seem like a sick joke. Ultimately, if not now, all will be linked together providing a complete dossier on every individual i.e.

Immigration—who goes where
Passports—customs
Statistics—private information to link with other records
Taxation—how much they declare
Social Security—how much the Government gives them
Aviation
Telecom—who calls who
Health—what they are suffering from
Digitalised video scan records
Land and Titles—what land they own
Drivers licences
Birth, Deaths, Marriages
Vehicle Registration—what vehicles they own
Gun licences—what protection they have
Australia Post—who corresponds with whom—notes changes of address
Bank records—how much they earn
Commonwealth Bank

The WGA plan for world domination has a great deal to do with taxation.

'Australian', 5th April 1988. 'Fears grow for tax data safety.

154

....enquiries following reports of unscrambled data flowing between the Australian Tax Office computers located at the former Deakin exchange in Canberra and State tax offices.

....The security of the Taxation Departments databases is a key issue in proposals to replace the Governments ill-fated Australia Card, with a high integrity numbering system....' End quote.

We have already mentioned the TFN in a previous chapter. 'Australian', 22nd November 1988. 'Tax file identifier sparks ACS fears.

The Australian Computer Society has expressed serious concern at the Federal Government's Tax File Number (TFN) scheme branding it a 'de facto personal identifier'.

.....During the 1970's, virtually every advanced western nation enacted privacy legislation.

Australia is one of the few OECD members not to have legislated in compliance with the OECD's 1980 data protection guidelines....' End quote.

'Australian', 12th July 1988. 'Paying your returns by computer.

Taxpayers will eventually be able to lodge their returns electronically.....

Tomorrows' taxpayer would come into the tax office, key in his return, have it processed and get it back in the space of a minute.....

Already, plans were under way for all returns prepared by tax agents to be lodged electronically.

.....the first 400 returns have been received electronically without problems, so the system is up and running.

....the paperless tax office was not too far away.

....The main obstacle for the Tax Office had been the apparent legislative requirement that a signature be provided with returns....

The office was investigating possible ways around this.' End quote.

Some person, obviously, knew a lot about all this and in his frustration, tried to put a stop to it.

Readers, it is possible in the light of all this knowledge to understand how one could feel like this, but prophecy must be fulfilled.

'Australian', 23rd November 1987. 'Sabotage is a nightmare for Telecom's weary band.

155

Telecom's N.S.W. operations manager....is loyal to Telecom; and expects all other employees to feel the same way. We have 30,000 employees and 29,999 of them are very happy', he said....'End quote.

A saboteur got down under the streets and cut masses of cables causing hundreds of computers to break down.

This of course increased the repairman's work, but this communications plan is world-wide and cannot be stopped.

There is only one weapon left, and that weapon, believe it or not, is SPIRITUAL.

A previous employee mentioned to us that it was very depressing to work in the Canberra surveillance centre, owing to the tight feeling of security.

Many years ago, when MEDICARE was introduced compulsorily to every Australian citizen, we struck up a conversation one day with a man who helped set it up. He told us the aims of this thing.

He said that it had very little to do with health, as the British had proven the system to be hopeless, but the aim of this system was:

   a. To get as many as possible on a computer programme.

   b. To use a series of LINK NUMBERS and link all the computers.

   c. To finally have access to all data. This was named 'MANDATA' available to only a select few, initially e.g. Prime Minister, Head of ASIO, Police Chief etc.

This man, whom I only met once told us that the computers no longer contained his link numbers. They had been mysteriously wiped and he, as a non-person was leaving for destinations unknown.

He made it very clear that he did not want us to know his name, or any details about him as it was his desire to become a non-person. I am glad for his sake, that this is the case. Who he was, or where he has gone, I don't know but what he said certainly makes sense in the light of today's events.

New Zealand readers, should watch for the building of a similar centre in the North Island. Wanganui is only a forerunner of the really big one.

Note the following. 'Australian', 27th June 1988: 'How they get your number in our Big Brother Society.'

Every time someone buys a car, the chances are that his or

156

her name will appear on a list available to anyone willing to pay for the information.

....Even the confidential information given for the five-yearly government census appears on the list in one form or another.

....Ever wondered why American Express invited you to apply for a Gold Card? Or why you were chosen as a possible buyer of a block of land on Queensland's Gold Coast?

Your name came from a list or a compilation of lists. THERE ARE NO LAWS IN AUSTRALIA SAFEGUARDING THE NAMES ON THESE LISTS....

The President of the ACCL (Australian Council of Civil Liberties) .....has called for legislation to be introduced....which is designed to stop the misuse of computer files containing personal information.....Undertakings by the Treasurer.....would not stop the misuse of the proposed TAX FILE NUMBER, she said....' End quote. (Emphasis added.)

It is my opinion that such a protest is correct but a complete waste of time now. It's all over. It's too late. It's all there now.

The head of Sweden's Data Inspection Board until early 1986, in an interview with Sydney 'Morning Herald', 15th July 1987, 'said he was prompted to quit, partly as an act of protest. He was fed up with the increasing computerisation of Swedish society,.....Apparently, Mr....did not think much of his own efforts to protect the privacy of ordinary Swedes, who are issued with a Personal Identification Number which lasts from birth to the grave.

.....He said, 'I realised that people were getting more and more tired of being numbered....' End quote.

The article referred to above is entitled 'Be very careful, Sweden's former identification chief warns Australia.' End quote.

Even the prisons are getting in on the act.

'Australian', 5th July 1988. 'Prisoners of the system. Prisoners serving periods of home detentions in Australia could soon come under the watchful eye of a computer.

A surveillance system involving electronic wrist tags is being considered by the South Australian Government with other States showing keen interest.....' End quote. The same thing is getting ready to happen in New Zealand.

In my public meetings, I have stated for many years that cable television sets were being introduced to this area of the world. these sets are linked up through fibre-optics cables and have a built in fish eye camera inside that can spy on you in your front room. Many t.v. folk contacted me and said 'We didn't think that this was correct, but now we know that it is.'

Here is a further development.

Sydney 'Morning Herald', 25th February 1988. 'T.V. meters will keep an eye on the fast-forward gang.

The days of the t.v. zapper—the viewer who records programmes and then zips through the commercials with the fast-forward button, could soon be numbered.

The electronic metering system.....requires a long term attachment of monitors to t.v. sets in participating households.....it would allow survey companies to measure audiences throughout the year.

.......Among the points are a requirement that the meters should operate 52 weeks a year, and that the meters should measure the number of people watching t.v. in addition to sets in use.

So far, this is achieved by the sampling audience 'clocking on' by numbers on a device resembling a t.v. remote control unit.....'
End quote.

Obviously, the danger of this experiment is that ultimately it could be passed as a statutory requirement that all persons register their times when viewing t.v.

Impossible, you say. In New Zealand, drivers requiring money back from the Government on the G.S.T. (goods and services tax), have to fill in fiddly log books with masses of information. Five years ago, we would have said 'Impossible'.

Surveillance at Airports

Coming through Sydney airport one day, my wife innocently stepped forward and glanced down at the reinforced glass panel where the Immigration or Customs Clerk was typing information from our passports. These men are normally very pleasant and polite.

However, in this case, the officer barked 'What do you think you're doing?', causing her to jump backwards with the shock.

Over in Western Australia, some years later we read a newspaper article that explained this man's actions.

'The Western Australian', 3rd May 1988. 'Joke led to secret list.

A chance remark by an airport Customs Officer led to a Perth accountant exposing an undercover surveillance system which watches everyone entering or leaving Australia. .....Mr .... had

158

been puzzled why the airport Customs Officer, who punched his passport number on the computer, in October 1986, had joked, 'Oh, bottom-of-the-harbour, I see.'

....Mr....was annoyed enough to spend about $2,000.00 in legal fees to go to the Administrative Appeals Tribunal.

At the hearing, a Customs man from Canberra gave evidence of PASS activities, which were so confidential that even Mr.... and his lawyer were barred from the closed court.

.....PASS, Mr....revealed is a computer based system which lists not only people wanted for serious breaches of the law, but even those who are under investigation or suspected of such activities.

....Input into PASS known as PASS 'alert' is allowed only with the approval of one of the control authorities: Customs, Immigration, NCA, AFP, or ASIO.

Other authorities, such as the Taxation Office or State Police must put in a request for a PASS alert to a control authority.' End quote.

Many E.C. Countries behind

Remember 1990. Remember New Zealand and Australia are the world's first with all this system being set up.

It was very noticeable, if not laughable, to go through Athens airport in Greece, at the end of 1988 and see the comparatively primitive conditions there, compared with New Zealand and Australian customs and immigration procedures.

London, on the other hand, was very sophisticated. There is much work to do on the other E.C. countries in this field, when they finally become united in 1992.

All this leads us on to a National Scandal, more significant than the jailing of Arthur Allen Thomas in New Zealand or the jailing of Lindy Chamberlain in Australia—both on trumped up charges. Interesting days indeed.

The scandal I refer to is a complete loss of liberty for each individual in the system.

It was predicted thus, years ago.

'Therefore, the law is slacked, and judgement doth never go forth, for the wicked doth compass about the righteous, therefore wrong judgement proceedeth.' *Ref.1.

From a booklet issued by the Commission for the Future entitled 'Issues for Cashless Society', on page 5 we read 'in 1975 an

159

American firm of consultants was asked to provide a way in which citizens behaviour could be monitored without their knowledge. Here is a fictitious analysis of one person.

'DAILY SURVEILLANCE SHEET
Confidential.
April 22, 1988
SUBJECT: Robert E. Squire, 13 Scilly St, Springtown, N.S.W. Male, aged 40. Married. Electrical engineer.
PURCHASES: Australian Financial Review, $0.70; Breakfast, $5:25; Petrol, $15.00; Phone (06 634 7968), $1.44; Lunch, $8.40; Cocktails, $10.00; ATM withdrawal, $100.00; Phone (02 824 7565), $0.20: Case whiskey, $270.00; Sydney Morning Herald, $0.90.

COMPUTER ANALYSIS
Owns shares (90% probability).
Heavy starch breakfast, probably overweight.
Bought $15.00 worth of petrol. Owns Volvo. So far this week subject has bought $50.00 worth of petrol. extensive driving beside 15km to work indicated. Purchased petrol at 7.57 a.m. at service station 10km from work. Subject probably later than usual for work. Third such occurrence this week.
Phone number (06 634 7968) belongs to J. McKenzie. McKenzie arrested illegal bookmaking in 1970, 1978, and 1982. No convictions.
Phone number (02 824 7565) belongs to Thatch, a firm specialising in hair restoration.
Drinks during lunch.
Cash withdrawal unusual. Cash now used mainly for illegal purchases or those not wished to be recorded on monthly bank statements.
Whiskey purchased third case in six months. Drinking more heavily or increased entertaining.
Subject left work at approximately 4.00 p.m. as whiskey purchased 2km from job at 4.10 p.m. Subject bought newspaper at 6.30 p.m. near his house. No purchases in interim. Unaccounted 2 hours 20 minutes.'

U.S. Surveillance in Australia
We have seen already that the Soviets are well and truly

established with their spying operations in N.Z. and Australia, through the courtesy of both Socialist Governments. 'Why do they let them stay on?' I hear you ask. I answer with one word — 'Trade'.

Pine Gap
Flying in and out of Alice Springs in Central Australia, one is immediately aware that something strange is going on below. There are white dome-like, or even golf ball-like structures out behind the hills that you soon learn is an American secret base. For many years, people have wondered what was going on there, and now they know.
The 'Weekend Australian', 12-13 March 1988. 'How the Kremlin is Bugged.
.....The book 'Pine Gap' is by Australia's leading intelligence expert, Professor Desmond Ball.
Professor Ball details the base's ability to pick up information on Soviet missiles, and to intercept communication from Eastern Europe, China, and the Middle East.
....Pine Gap's unique location in the middle of a continent makes it the only place in the region covered by the relevant satellites.
....The satellites linking Pine Gap's operations are the most secret of all U.S. intelligence-collecting satellites.
Known as the 'black' program, the U.S. refuses to confirm even its existence let alone release information about its capabilities or missions.
.....his knowledge of the area gives a far more detailed picture of Pine Gap than ever before revealed.
Apart from arms verification purposes, an important function is monitoring Soviet and Chinese radar systems.
.....But the satellites controlled by Pine Gap can also intercept Soviet and Chinese telephone and radio communications....' End quote.

161

CHAPTER 27

New Zealand Surveillance

Some years ago, a young man managed to penetrate the security of the Wanganui Computer building and detonate some explosives in a desperate attempt to destroy that which he felt was destroying his prospects for a happy future.

His plan was fruitless as one could drive a tank against that building and wreck the tank. Pieces of his body were found in various areas of the entrance hall.

The fact is, that things are moving very swiftly in this country as the big day approaches i.e. 1990—leading on to Global 2000.

Cheap Fax's

The newspapers are reporting that facsimile messages will soon be cheaper than a stamp on a letter, if sent at the right time.

'Press', 9th August 1988. 'Faxes cheaper than letters.

From November (1988) it will be possible to send a three-page fax message to Auckland for 38c overnight. This is a saving on the Fast Post charge and is even cheaper than standard mail.' End quote.

A new spy-base is being built in the South Island of New Zealand which is the subject of demonstrations and many newspaper articles.

'Sunday Times', 28th August 1988. 'Waihopai link to global web.

....New Statesman and New Society says British American and allied intelligence agencies are embarking on a huge expansion of their GLOBAL ELECTRONIC SURVEILLANCE SYSTEM.

....computers can sift out what sounds interesting and identify particular telephone numbers.

Mr.....said Waihopai would not be used without lawful authority to eavesdrop on New Zealanders.' End quote. (Emphasis added.)

I like that last sentence, don't you?

The point is that the people who have the lawful authority are all in this plan up to their necks.

Therefore, the final statement in this article would be better left unsaid.

Also, this Waihopai facility, (and it was reported in the news) will have the facility to spy on faxes.

Now you can see why faxes are becoming cheaper than letters. THEY CAN'T READ ALL YOUR LETTERS BUT THEY CAN READ ALL YOUR FAXES and that's a fax!

Taxation — closing the loopholes

'Dominion', 12th December 1988. 'Computer war on tax evaders near.

Tax evasion will become much more difficult when the Inland Revenue computer system is updated....

It will provide easy access to all information on any taxpayer including information held by organisations like banks and financial institutions.

It could also provide access to information from Government departments like Social Welfare, if the Government decided that it is desirable.....' End quote.

I love that last phrase, don't you? Let's have it again.

....'if the Government decided that it is desirable.'

You know, I have this strange, strange feeling that the Government may decide it is desirable.

Continue quote: 'It will be much harder to stay outside the system and once you are in the system, the technology will let us keep tabs on the taxpayer.

If you owe G.S.T. and you owe income tax, and you also owe PAYE as an employer, for example, all those three things will be clearly brought together.' End quote.

Telecom in Security

'Press', 16th November 1988. 'Security firms say they are suspicious of Telecom's move into the security business, which the corporation hopes will reap $12 million....' End quote.

Health Computer Sold Off, says the newspaper headline.

Quote: 'The Government has sold the Health Computing Services to a New Zealand and Australian Company,

PAXUS INFORMATION SERVICES LTD for $4.25 million.

But it has given an assurance that data stored by the system will continue to be totally secure and confidential....' End quote.

164

How secure we all feel with assurances like this.

'Israelis Teach New Zealand Cops. Sunday 'Star', 2nd July 1988. 'The police will learn Israeli interrogation techniques at a one day course at the Royal New Zealand Police College.

....scientific content analysis (SCAN) interview technique is reportedly used by the Israeli security forces, the FBI and American military intelligence.....no physical contact will be applied when applying the SCAN technique....' End quote.

'Census On Screen.' 'Press', 8th November 1988.

'.....census data is available on Supermap, a disk (sic) which provides information in either tables or full-colour maps on a microcomputer screen.

....The census provides information on income, marital status, age, occupation, education and ethnic origins. Information is also stored on the sexual gender and religion of the population, and some UNUSUAL FEATURES, such as the number of rented homes, types of landlords and rent levels.

In a demonstration.....was able to throw up on a screen a colour map of Christchurch showing where the city's journalists were on census night....' End quote. (Emphasis added.)

I can't help wondering what other unusual features are on this previously highly confidential, file of information. I also muse on the fact that it may be linked to other computers.

I.D. for New Zealanders? You will note that when the police on a TV programme, take a criminal into custody for interrogation, you have the hard guy first, then the kind guy comes in with a cigarette to soften the prisoner up.

On the I.D. debate, we now know beyond a shadow of a doubt that the WGA will insist that we have one.

The politicians will do their:

> hard guy — (we must have one)
> good guy — (we must not have one act)
> and then give us one

Whether an I.D. number, or like Australia, an updated Tax File Number — it really makes no difference.

'Dominion Sunday Times', 27th September 1987.

'In West Germany there was a furore when it was realised that police could use identity cards to track peoples' movements.

In France the authorities can detain suspects for up to four hours if they do not have them.

....In New Zealand, if Revenue Minister......gets his way, we will all be carrying a card in the not too distant future.

....Other countries, including Britain, the United States, Canada and Sweden have a halfway house system that stops short of a card, but issues citizens and residents with national insurance or social security numbers.

Portugal by contrast, has a provision written into its constitution that citizens will not be given an all-purpose national identity number.

There are more than 400 laws and regulations in New Zealand that require the disclosure of personal information between departments.

....A national identity card with its unique number holds a potential key.

.....insists that the proposed card would only be used by the Inland Revenue Department and Social Welfare Department....'
End Quote.

Oh I love these last lines, don't you?

Of course, this is an old 1987 cutting. Things have certainly moved along.

'Southland Times', 21st September 1987. 'New Zealand may soon get I.D. card....

Describing opponents of the proposed system as 'the forces of Armageddon', Mr L..........e dismissed claims that the proposed system would destroy civil liberties.

...... Mr L........e said resistance to the introduction of I.D. cards in New Zealand was high but because his government had not yet proposed such a system, 'the forces of Armageddon have not been marshalled against it....' End quote.

The only place Armageddon is mentioned is the Holy Bible, the Word of God, so it would appear that the phrase is in reference to Bible believers who would see this I.D. as the MARK OF THE BEAST, or related to it.

This is a very good reasoning, because that is exactly the case. In this fact, I also rejoice, that the Lord is full of mercy in spite of our foolishness.

'The Lord is not slack concerning His promise, as some men count slackness, but is longsuffering towards us, not willing that any should perish, but that all should come to repentance.' *Ref.1.

166

CHAPTER 28

Surveys

Did you notice the word 'Survey' in the preceding article? There are too many of these around and I have made it a rule that when a sweet young thing steps up to me in the street clutching a paper on a board and a ball point pen, I immediately say 'No, thank you' and keep walking.

Rule! (Taken from a sign in a public bar in New Zealand.)

'Keep New Zealand green'

Some prankster wrote these words underneath.

'Don't tell them anything'

Letters to the paper
'Australian', 21.9.88. 'Beware of ABS Survey.

.....7500 households have been earmarked by the ABS (Australian Bureau of Statistics) to complete this intrusive survey containing a 22 page income and 110 page expenditure questionaire; a two week spending diary, plus a form authorising the bureau to extract loan details from your bank.

.....People who are asked to do the survey should refuse to do so until the question of its legality is resolved.....' End quote.

It is fascinating to watch the development of the surveillance system.

'Sunday Herald', Sydney, 17th July 1988. 'Telecom will be required to hand the National Crime Authority detailed lists of the telephone numbers dialled by people being investigated.

....The person does not necessarily have to be under suspicion. N.C.A. officers could obtain the information if they considered there was a connection with a serious offence....' End quote.

'Marlborough Express', 21st February 1989. 'Phones with picture by Christmas.

By Christmas, yuppies into 'his' and 'hers' could be swapping visuals on the video telephone, for the price of a local call — after a $2500.00 (NZ $3600.00) outlay for each unit.

.....'But it also has great potential in the Police Department for, say, identification in outback areas where faces, or distinguishing marks like tattoos can be seen over the phone.....

The video-phone plugs into a telephone line....
It can also act as a remote control SURVEILLANCE
CAMERA, activated by a silent telephone call....' End quote.
(Emphasis added.)
In N.S.W., Australia, where in 1988 they had a Hungarian
born premier, they have introduced new plastic colour-coded
drivers' licences bearing their photographs.
The Civil Liberties people of course, were justly upset.
Sydney 'Morning Herald', 20th July 1988. '.....vice-president
of the council said....' When we were campaigning strongly against
the Australia Card, the Liberal Government was also one of the
greatest fighters. Now they've introduced the very thing they
opposed.
Surely a man whose roots go back to a communist country
should realise what it's like to be made to carry around numbers
and cards all the time.....' End quote.
'Oh, how true, but what do you do?'

Statistics Survey
Hello, here's another one of these forms asking a business
acquaintance of mine all about his business in minute detail, thus
adding many more data bits to an already prolific file on the
computer.
How is this for a line on the fourth and last page:
'I am most appreciative of the co-operation received from New
Zealand businesses and organisations under survey.....' End quote.
Then right at the bottom, we read:
'The taking of this survey has been approved by the Minister
of Statistics, and the return of this questionaire duly filled in and
signed is a COMPULSORY REQUIREMENT.......' End
quote. (Emphasis added.)
Question — what other compulsory requirements will these
people come up with before 'Global 2000'.

CHAPTER 29

Bits and Pieces
Bank of New Zealand
and EFTPOS

Many people called and wrote to me when the BNZ announced a change in EFTPOS. It did not mean that they were throwing it out. As we know, EFTPOS is the means to an end.

Gradualism as taught in Fabian Socialism is the key.

The end of course, is the mark on the right hand or forehead.

From a letter to auto-card holders with the BNZ dated 14th September 1988, we quote in part:

'.....If you are a regular EFTPOS user, we apologise for the inconvenience, but we ask you to take comfort from the knowledge that we are seeking an alternative that will be better for everyone concerned.....' End quote.

This I take to mean that I can stop crying and put my handkerchief away, knowing that there is something far nicer coming soon to take EFTPOS' place.

Could it be a Smartcard with a built in aerial and computer?

New Zealand 'Herald', 2nd May 1989.

'Four banks agree on EFTPOS integration. Yesterday's integration agreement by Westpac, the National Bank, A.S.B., and Trust Bank pick up the threads of plans torn to shreds last year when the Bank of New Zealand pulled out of the Quicksmart EFTPOS system.

....The Bank of New Zealand had pulled out of EFTPOS because of excessive costs, but its options were still open....' End quote.

I'll agree with that. The BNZ and all banks MUST prepare for the CASHLESS SOCIETY, or cease in the field of banking.

Right Wing Political Groups and Christian Groups

It would appear that the Soviet Union is no longer regarded as the enemy or a threat to New Zealand's security.

N.Z.'s military forces have been weakened. Their numbers cut down and their budget slashed.

169

Look above and see who the new enemy is.

'Press', 18th February 1986. 'An examination by the National Council of Churches on a possible link between Right-wing political groups and Christian groups who are rigidly conservative on social and ethical questions could take up to a year.

....she conceded it was more the fundamentalists the N.C.C. was concerned about....' End quote.

Fundamentalists believe that the Scriptures are God-breathed and are the final standard for life in general.

Without wishing to cause offence, I wish to point out that the letters 'N.C.C.' includes two letters 'C' and neither of them stands for Christian. The National Council of Churches (N.C.C.) operates a smaller version of the World Council of Churches (W.C.C.).

Therefore, as we Christians have always been hated, just like our Master, listen to His words:

'If the world hate you, ye would know that it hated Me before it hated you.' *Ref.1.

Nelson 'Evening Mail', April 1986. 'Charismatic Fringe Irks...

The Minister for Education.....is concerned about the rise in the number of children going to fringe charismatic Christian schools.

Mr.....a former Methodist minister said the growth of such schools was simply a reflection of the growth of charismatic Christianity generally.

....he hoped the rise of fundamentalist Christianity was simply a fad......' End quote.

Well, I can tell him, it won't go away. He will, but the true work of the Lord will go on until Jesus comes, more strongly than ever as the days go by.

Trans-Tasman Travel Increase

With the two countries preparing to merge, this article comes with renewed power.

'Press', 15th March 1989.

'Ten years ago, the average Australian visitor to New Zealand might have carried a knapsack or tickets for a coach tour of the South Island. Today, they are just as likely to be carrying a briefcase and a laptop computer. Air New Zealand says that last September, more than half the people who travelled from Australia to New Zealand were on business....' End quote.

Remember, it is no longer an international flight. It is now domestic.

The South Pacific Link up

The sound of a ukulele being nicely strummed usually awakens in me a desire to return to the Pacific Islands. As we speak to various Island groups, hear them sing, enjoy their food and their relaxed, laid-back lifestyle; I say to my wife, May, 'Let's go back'.

Many of these dear people who have up-rooted their families to come to New Zealand or Australia, after having read this book or one like it, will have thoughts of returning home.

This is a Global problem and Winston Churchill was half right when he spoke, many years ago emphasising the words NO PLACE TO HIDE.

This is partially true. Born again Christians will hide in their living faith in Christ, just as Noah and his family hid in the ark.

'And as in the days of Noe were, so shall also the coming of the son of man be.' *Ref.2.

As I have mentioned earlier on in this book, Noah's Ark has been found and photographed in 1974 by a man called Tom Crotzer.

VITAL

   a. We can now establish the book of Genesis is correct, with the news on the Ark.

   b. We can now establish the book of Revelation is correct with the 666 surveillance system.

   c. All Scripture in between is also correct and our Lord Jesus Christ still changes lives, if one is willing to be changed.

Under the Club of Rome plan for World Government, the world has been divided into ten regions. Region number 4 is the pertinent area regarding the position of the islands in World Government plans.

Number 4 — New Zealand — together with Australia, South Africa, Israel and Oceania (the Islands of the Pacific).

No wonder these islands are now being linked up with microwave dishes and fibre optics etc.

Computers have been introduced also.

Visiting Apia, Western Samoa, some years ago, I was shocked to find a Government computer centre at Vaiala.

At this facility, the computers store information for Customs,

171

Statistics, Government Salaries Payroll, National Provident Fund, Bank of Western Samoa (cheque, saving a/c) and Inland Revenue.

When I pulled this little piece of information out from my files I was shocked when I thought of the repercussions of all this. There is no place to hide in the islands.

Many years ago, the prophet spoke:

'And a man shall be as a hiding place from the wind,
and as a covert from the tempest,
as rivers of water in a dry place,
as the shadow of a great rock in a weary land.' *Ref.3.

Search for this Man — Find Him — Trust Him — and hold on to Him.

CHAPTER 30

Others Can Spy Also

'International Herald Tribune', 6th October 1988. 'Now a Little Brother Too, is Watching.

.....the information explosion can work both ways. Now a small group of young Swedes is using the new technologies to defy some government attempts at secrecy. They have developed a third eye in the sky, a civilian ability to monitor some important military programs, something that only the superpowers could do before.

....The group's first big coup was providing the first pictures and details of the Chernobyl disaster in 1986, obviously playing an important role in persuading the Russians to come clean on the gravest nuclear accident yet.

Since then, it has discovered secret preparations for a Soviet space shuttle, powerful Soviet laser installations which could be made to serve Soviet 'star wars system......'

Already it is working on chemical warfare facilities. Evidence so far indicates that Libya is building a complex and that Syria may be doing the same.

....Even adversary governments know much of each others' secrets yet still insist on keeping the public in the dark......This time LITTLE BROTHER IS WINNING A ROUND.' End quote. (Emphasis added.)

Other Countries with I.D. cards
'Herald', 11th June 1986. 'A number for everyone.
Britain, Holland and Switzerland are three rare European countries that do not have to carry identity cards.

Italy proposes to introduce one nationally....

Everybody in Greece is meant to get an identity card from the local police station....

In West Germany, France, Belgium, and Spain, people have long had to carry an official identity card....

In Sweden and Denmark, people are not obliged to carry identity cards, but every Swede or Dane has a code number giving date of birth; gender and origin (place of birth)....' End quote.

U.S.A. — hard to control

One country very difficult to take over for World Government strangely enough, is the U.S.A.

When Poland was overrun by the Soviets, I noted the first three things to be confiscated were:

a. Weapons
b. Ammunition
c. Communications

In 1986, there were about 120 million guns in private hands in the United States with about half of all homes containing one or more firearms.

Also interesting, is the fact that three quarters of all American gun-owners keep them at least partly for protection.

On a visit through L.A., some years ago, we were amazed to go into a gun shop and watch teen-agers buying all types of weapons.

I turned to the boys in my family and said 'Hey! These boys are not going out to shoot possums and rabbits. They're going to shoot people.'

Gun laws will need to be introduced world wide to allow the plan to work, and the U.S. people will not like that at all.

Hong Kong — Bar codes on car windows. Very shortly this area will be returning to Communist hands i.e. 1997.

'Sydney Morning Herald', 21st March 1988:

'For some time Hong Kong has been threatening its motor-borne burghers with road taxes based on computer sensed and traced usage. This has not met with universal approval. Now the State of Illinois in America is thinking of getting in on this act.

There, the system will work by reading bar-codes on window decals as the car rolls by. A computer will compute the distance travelled, and mail monthly bills....' End quote.

Great Britain. In the same article as above, we read:

Quote: 'In Britain the Government has confirmed that it is seriously thinking of linking the police national computer into other government computer networks.....' End quote.

Fibre Optics in Europe and Elsewhere

Not only that, in the 'Sydney Morning Herald', 29th February 1988 we read: 'A new OPTICAL fibre link has been installed in the city of London for a total cost of $674 million....the most advanced network of its kind in the world.'

174

.....The network is said to offer virtually unlimited message-carrying capacity. For example, the main trunk connection may carry 12,000 simultaneous calls in a typical application.

About 25,000 kilometres of fibre have so far been installed in the city of London, of the 60,000 kilometres which are planned.

.....Some 11 British Telecom customers—including large organisations such as the Japanese Securities Company, Nomura, the U.S. Banking and Insurance Concern, Merrill Lynch, and the Union Bank of Switzerland—are already served by the new system....' End quote.

No matter how clever the innovation, because mortals are involved, these developments are all subject to faults. (As anybody who deals with banks and airlines will bear witness to—have you ever heard these words 'I am sorry, the computer is down'?).

'Dominion', 14th August 1989. 'Submarine optical fibre cables failing.

Despite rigorous quality control procedures meant to ensure 25 years without failure, some early optical fibre submarine cables are proving failure-prone....

....between Hawaii and Japan....across the Atlantic, TAT-8 has been broken several times by fishing boats....

Telecom New Zealand and OTC are planning to link New Zealand and Australia with an optical fibre cable, Tasman 2, in 1991.' End quote.

I have a picture in front of me that shows a giant eye drawn on a wall in Duesseldorf. 'Adelaide Advertiser', 6th January 1984.

This was taken from an Australian paper and acts like a warning, five days into the Orwellian year of 1984.

Are things really as serious as this book portrays them?

Puzzled? No need to be

Statement—The cancelling of the ANZUS TREATY by the New Zealand Government was also part of the bluff of WGA.

It left New Zealanders feeling insecure and that our old ally the U.S. had neglected us.

Not so.

Then the Government began makes overtures to the Soviets, which furthered the insecurity in New Zealanders.

How could all this be part of the plan?

Because THE UNITED STATES OF AMERICA and THE SOVIET UNION will shortly head up a joint space programme, and will be loosely linked under the WGA plan.

175

The U.S. still advises the New Zealand Government on security matters and the Soviets are moving in also to set up shop in this little country.

They both have their bases here and in Australia.

Let's face it. We've all been conned.

Now let's examine the influence of these World Government advocate dominated giant superpowers.

CHAPTER 31

The Sinking of the *Lermontov* in New Zealand Waters

Date — 22nd July 1989, 7:15 a.m.

Our boat sped up the Pelorus Sound at approximately 25-30 miles per hour. All on board were in good spirits in spite of the cutting bite of the early morning frost on our faces.

Our destination — Port Gore, in the Marlborough Sounds.

On board with me were the two divers, my son-in-law, Dennie Capell, and Anthony Piper from Havelock (who owns the local marine and dive shop), together with John Hey from Blenheim and Talbot and Joshua Jamieson, mussel farmers in the Pelorus Sounds. In the stern of the boat was a great pile of scuba diving equipment.

Our minds flashed back to the 16th February 1986, to the news report that a Russian cruise-liner had sunk in our part of the world i.e. The Marlborough Sounds.

We all joked using such words as 'spies', 'espionage', 'cloak and dagger' etc., little realising the possible importance of this incident to our national security.

As this book's specific aim is to show the movement towards Global 2000 and World Government, (in which both superpowers, namely the U.S.A. and the USSR are being linked by the secret planning groups), it would appear to be essential that not only the U.S.A., but also the USSR must have a stake in the South Pacific area.

Inquiries Commence

The Preliminary Inquiry into the sinking of this vessel was duly carried out.

By speaking to interested persons, we discovered that with a sinking of such international prominence, a full marine inquiry would normally have taken place, but this did not happen.

Questions were asked, yet few suitable answers appeared to be forthcoming. Studying the Lermontov case was similar to enjoying an exciting programme on TV, only to have someone switch the set off just as the mystery was about to be unravelled.

177

178

The key emotion evoked was 'frustration'.

Christchurch 'Press', 23rd April, 1986, we read 'Cruise Liner Enquiry Facts Called For. A bid by a member of the Marlborough Harbour Board Mr E.L. Collins to have the facts behind the sinking of the Mikhail Lermontov made public, failed at a meeting of the board yesterday.

The reason it seems, is not that the board will not tell, but that it does not know.

....'I am still wondering what is being hidden, what has been swept under the carpet. A lot of people are thinking the same thing', Mr Collins said...' End quote.

Christchurch 'Press', 14.6.86. 'Lermontov Secrecy Decried.

....The sinking was discussed at a recent meeting in Christchurch of the New Zealand Company of Master Mariners.

The company, which represents about 400 masters, has written to the Minister of Transport,......, urging him to release details of the preliminary enquiry into the sinking.' End quote.

One group however, was very happy with the preliminary enquiry i.e. the Russians.

'Press', 25.6.86. 'Russians Happy with Enquiry.

Dissatisfaction with the preliminary enquiry into the sinking of the Mikhail Lermontov is not shared by the Soviet Union representatives in New Zealand, according to the Soviet Ambassador to Wellington.

....The former deputy harbour master at Timaru, Captain J.W. Cook, has recently criticised the initial enquiry report for its inadequacies and unanswered questions.

The Russians on the other hand were happy with the way it was handled said the Ambassador...in Blenheim yesterday.

'We consider it was well done and fair, very professionally done, he said.

...'We consider that any further investigation will reveal nothing new at all....' End quote.

New Zealanders should be very pleased that there is a responsible group called 'The New Zealand Company of Master Mariners' representing about 400 masters, who took this event very seriously and endeavoured to do something responsible about it. After all, up until the time of this book going to print, New Zealand is still a 'sovereign state' with its own law system, governing incidents such as this.

One of the group's number, a Captain Cook, then of Timaru, was quoted quite a number of times in the news media.

179

Along with these media reports, a number of documents were either referred to or written, with the view to asking the questions which Master Mariners felt needed to be asked.
1. Ministry of Transport Preliminary Inquiry 'Mikhail Lermontov'.
2. Ministry of Transport Marine Division — Instructions on Holding Preliminary Inquiries into Shipping Casualties.
3. 'Mikhail Lermontov — Grounding and Subsequent Foundering.

This was an unofficial document which makes observations and not only asks questions which were not asked in the original inquiry, but comments on statements made, which, it was felt, needed challenging.
4. Another document outlines questions, answers and comments.
5. Also available are newspaper cuttings, reporting on aspects of the case.

Including a chapter such as this in my book has been difficult owing to the secrecy of the case at every turn.

Captain Cook, according to the 'Press', 23rd June 1986, had a copy of the instructions for holding a preliminary enquiry into shipping casualties. 'All of Captain Cook's enquiries were based on this document....' End quote.

Some people thought the Lermontov question was dead and buried, but wait! Here it is again.

'There is nothing covered that shall not be revealed, and hid that shall not be known.' *Ref.1.

A Number of Interesting Questions

Q.1. Should there have been a full official enquiry into the sinking of this ship?

Captain Cook, with the backing of 400 Master Mariners, says 'Yes'.

Instructions on holding Preliminary Inquiries into shipping casualties.

Ministry of Transport, Marine Division (Instructions to Inspectors) — MOT Internal Paper 1984.
1. Section 2.
   Paragraph 2.
   Foreign Ships — Jurisdiction to exercise the formal powers of a Marine Inspector in relation to a foreign ship.

'Shows conclusively that the holding of an Inquiry into the 'Mikhail Lermontov' grounding was properly within New Zealand jurisdiction.' End quote.

Without becoming too bogged down with detail, we must ask Q.2. How do we know that the ship on the bottom at Port Gore is the one spoken of in the Inquiry.

Captain Cook's report points out — Quote:

1.0 Particulars of Ship given in the Report are lacking in detail and precision. The description of the vessel and its equipment and dimensions are incomplete and are at marked variance with Lloyds Register of Ships 1985/86.

For example:

(i) Lloyds Register description of the vessel 'Twin Screw Passenger/General Cargo' becomes 'passenger liner' in the report.

(ii) Dimensions given by Lloyds Register are —
Overall Length 175.77
Length B.P. (between perpendiculars) 155.00
Extreme Breadth 23.98
Moulded Breadth 23.91
Maximum Summer Draft 8.16
Moulded Depth 16.21
Dimensions given by the report are —
Length — 155 m
Breadth — 23.6 m
Depth — 13.5 m
The use of length B.P. is out of context and not specified and other dimensions used differ considerably from those of Lloyds Register.

Q.3. Captain Cook asks about the ship's draft.

6.2.0. Paragraph 2. 'The draft recorded leaving Picton of 8.00 metres forward and 8.40 metres aft, gives a mean of 8.20 metres — 0.04 metres deeper than the 'Mikhail Lermontov' laden summer draft.....

Was she overloaded? How was this draft achieved, if as a 'passenger liner' she carried no cargo. It is not recorded. Is Lloyds Register in error....' End quote.

Q.4. Look at this obvious discrepancy. One would have thought that someone in an official position would have done some simple addition; possibly whilst idly doodling during a lull in the Preliminary Inquiry.

181

Continue quote: 'The enquiry says 741 people were on board.

408 passengers
330 crew
3 pilots

However, a breakdown of this number in the enquiry adds up to only 688. The enquiry neglects to say WHO THE REMAINING 53 PEOPLE ARE and also fails to say WHO THE THIRD PILOT IS.' End quote. (Emphasis added.)

In the preliminary report it read:

Quote: 'The total number of crew at departure Picton was 330, made up as follows:

Master — 1
Deck Officers — 8
Deck Ratings — 31
Chief Engineer — 1
Engine Officers — 13
Engine Ratings — 34
Radio Operators — 4
Cooks — 35
Stewards — 153.' End quote.

280 is this total in this crew list, yet right above this total is written the number 330.

330 − 280 = 50. Where did these people go? Are they still in New Zealand? We don't know. Add one more also for the unidentified 3rd pilot — total 51. The two other pilots were mentioned in the enquiry so there is no mystery regarding their identification. Therefore, 51 remain unaccounted for.

By the way, where are the missing 51? Were these persons off-loaded before the sinking? If so, why?

Q.5. Why was the Soviet Captain off the bridge at the time the ship struck rocks on the starboard side whilst going through the FOUL GROUND at Cape Jackson?

Christchurch 'Press', 8th May 1989. 'Captain (Soviet Captain)......left the bridge sometime after 4:30 p.m. without telling Captain (pilot).

He was absent for more than an hour, and with no arrangement for handing control back, Captain (pilot) continued 'to con the ship'. End quote.

Q.6. Just prior to arriving at Cape Jackson where the ship was taken port, through FOUL GROUND, they passed a headland called Kempe Point, to the port side of the Lermontov.

Captain Cook asks: 'Was the course of 040 degrees set before Kempe Point or after. The reciprocal course projected passes less than 1 cable (185 metres) of Kempi (sic) Point. Is this correct? Did the Mikhail Lermontov pass that close to that Point....? End quote.

Q.7. Why was the 'spur of the moment' decision taken to adopt the ship's ill-fated course? This decision would normally have been taken before the voyage, at the time the course was being plotted.

Christchurch 'Press', 8th May 1989. One of those on the bridge on that occasion speaks. Quote 'I have never conned any large vessel through the passage. I have been through the passage on many occasions on small craft of drafts up to 2 metres and have often fished in the passage.' End quote.

Another interesting point is that the ship was taken through this FOUL GROUND at full speed, with both engines on full ahead. Why?

Q.8. The Preliminary Inquiry reports 'On grounding a series of shocks were felt, and although impressions of persons varied as to the location on the hull of these shocks, the concensus is that the ship grounded along the starboard side forward of amidships....A starboard list developed....' End quote.

Actually, after the sinking, an 'Eye Witness' news team sent cameras down and filmed gashes on both sides. The question in my opinion, should have been asked immediately:

a. Where did the gashes on the port side come from?
b. Some have asked 'Is it possible that these gashes were made before the ship turned to go through Cape Jackson?' I reply 'I don't know.'

During our diving expedition on the 22nd July 1989, we checked out these port side gashes. There are two of them and they are significant.

Q.9. Why weren't these gashes spoken of in great detail during the Preliminary Inquiry or at any later court case? Strange, isn't it? Any diver may confirm all this.

Q.10. A Mayday call was cancelled.

'Sydney Morning Herald', 6th May 1989. The pilot is spoken of in this news article.

Quote: 'He said he sent out a mayday call after the grounding, but Captain (Soviet Captain) disagreed and the call was cancelled.' End quote.

To coin a phrase from Alice in Wonderland – 'It is getting curiouser and curiouser.'

Radio Calls Unanswered
Q.11. The same gentleman mentioned above goes on in the same article — Quote: 'He said he found that radio calls were not being answered.' End quote.
We ask the question 'Why?'
Q.12. S.O.S. to the Soviet Union.
In spite of the fact that there was ample help available from ships large and small, the Soviet Captain did not accept any of this assistance, nor did he request any help from the New Zealand authorities.

Communications Were Made
Preliminary Inquiry report Radio Communications No.2. — quote: 'After the Mikhail Lermontov' grounded, several H.F. radio-telegraphy communications were exchanged between the ship and various stations in the USSR....The final....communication was an S.O.S. signal to Vladivostok.....' End quote. Why? Let us use an analogy.
We are aboard a sinking ship off the coast of the USSR. Local shipping rushes to our assistance but we ask them all to kindly leave or simply ignore many radio messages of asistance offered. We then call New Zealand, (on the other side of the world) advising of our predicament. At this point we are convinced that a new rescue craft has just been developed in New Zealand which will meet our immediate needs in Soviet waters — obviously travelling at the speed of light.
Q.12. When the ship was beached at the southern end of Port Gore, why were the anchors not thrown out, the passengers and crew evacuated to dry land, and the vessel saved?
Testimony A. New Zealand 'Herald', 10th May 1989.
'An Officer of the Mikhail Lermontov yesterday denied in the New South Wales Supreme Court, that the Soviet Cruise Liner had beached before sinking in the Marlborough Sounds......' End quote.
Testimony B. New Zealand 'Herald', 28th April 1989.
'Captain.....anchored near the stricken vessel and readied the Tarahiko's lifeboats.
'The Mikhail Lermontov appeared to be very close into the beach. I was sure she was aground', Captain......told the court.
....Captain....said it was considered standard practise to beach and anchor a ship that was holed and taking water.....' End quote.

The above quote is the testimony of an eye witness who saw the events here described.

Opinion A. New Zealand 'Herald', 24th April 1989.

'The Soviet cruise liner Mikhail Lermontov was possibly aground for 12 minutes in Port Gore, during which time it could have been anchored and saved from shipwreck, according to a report produced in the New South Wales Supreme Court yesterday......

Captain.....reconstructed the Mikhail Lermontov's final passage using information from the ship's course recorder and charts.

....Captain.....said that when water entered a ship at an uncontrollable rate, the ship should be beached as soon and as safely as possible.

'My impression is that there was a hesitancy to beach the vessel....He estimated she grounded her bow on the beach at no more than half a knot.

....Without any doubt, an anchor should have been let go as soon as the vessel grounded in the bay', Captain.....said in his report.

....'If the anchors had been used, the vessel could have been easily saved.....' End quote.

Testimony C. Sydney 'Morning Herald', 6th May 1989.

Quote 'After the liner grounded on the beach, Captain (pilot)....said it 'crossed my mind' that anchors should be dropped, but with a change in wind, it drifted into deeper water where it sank.' End quote.

Author's note.

Notice the absence of the words 'if it grounded', or 'nearly grounded'.

Q.12. Why were passengers not informed as to their danger?

New Zealand 'Herald', 27th April 1989. A 72 year old passenger reported — quote: 'We struck the rocks very hard....they waited for about half an hour before hearing the first announcement in English over the public address system.

'And that was to tell us that our evening meal would be late', he said...' End quote.

Q.13. Why were divers kept away from the area?

For about the space of one year, divers were not allowed near the wreck. Once the Russians had recovered their 'gear', the ship was then open to divers once again.

Q.14. Why did the cruise company dive on the wreck about one year later? Why did they wait so long?

What was this gear that they recovered?
Christchurch 'Press', 9th March 1987.
'C.T.C. Cruises Ltd, the company which brought the Soviet cruise liner Mikhail Lermontov to New Zealand a year ago, will not say why it was diving on the wreck last month.
....C.T.C.'s New Zealand representative Mr.....said from Auckland that the dive was not a matter for public scrutiny.
'I am not interested in talking about it at all. The company wanted to retrieve some of its property that's all', Mr......said.'
End quote.
Oh, is that why? — I see. Readers must admit that it was interesting that for one whole year, all other divers were driven away and threatened with prosecution if they didn't leave the area.

If my boat sank, I certainly wouldn't wait for one year before retrieving my gear. However, I confess that different people have different ways of doing things. That is what makes humans interesting creatures.

In a chapter such as this, we have endeavoured to be strictly ethical. Therefore, I divide my final remarks into the following headings.

1. Fact
2. Opinion
3. A mixture of both
4. Fair comment

Facts

Fact no.1. The dimensions given in the Preliminary Inquiry are at variance with those held by Lloyd's Register.

Fact no.2. The ship's draft on leaving Picton was also at variance with the draft held by Lloyd's Register.

Fact no.3. 51 persons were unaccounted for.

Fact no.4. The Soviet Captain was off the bridge for a considerable period during the crucial stage of the drama.

Fact no.5. The ship, after leaving Ship's Cove on a point 040 degree, would have passed reasonably close to Kempe Point on its port side. (This area is situated immediately before Cape Jackson.)

Fact no.6. The ragged gashes later found in the port side, (which our diving team, also an 'Eye Witness' news team, and other divers have found), did not figure prominently in the Preliminary Inquiry.

Fact no.7. The starboard side was certainly gashed and this fact did figure prominently in the Preliminary Inquiry.

Note. Any divers should be able to satisfy themselves as to the veracity of the above statements as the ship is lying port side up.

Fact no.8. The New Zealand pilot followed normal procedure and sent out a may day call, requesting assistance immediately following the striking of rocks at Cape Jackson.

Fact no.9. The Soviet captain then cancelled the call.

Fact no.10. Calls made by concerned persons were ignored by the Soviets and in some cases were not even answered.

Fact no.11. A may day call was sent from the ship to the Soviet Union.

Fact no.12. Local help was discouraged and in some cases, turned away.

Fact no.13. Witnesses say that when the ship beached in Port Gore, anchors which could have been immediately dropped were left in place.

Fact no.14. In that position of beaching, adjacent to a wool shed, direct access to the open sea is blocked by a small headland.

Fact no.15. Passengers were not informed as to the danger that they were in.

Fact no.16. Diving on the wreck by unofficial individuals was forbidden for a period of one year.

Fact no.17. The ship finally sunk in the deepest part of Port Gore facing directly out into the open sea.

Fact no.18. Many of the deliberations in this case have been held in secret, and information withheld from interested parties.

Opinion

Opinion no.1. It is this author's opinion that this whole case is a blot on the history of New Zealand. We have always prided ourselves on free and open democratic discussion and the majority of people are shocked that it could come to this.

Opinion no.2. Although not directly involved in this incident, I (along with many others of my countrymen,) feel sad for a number of folk involved, including the Australian passengers who happened to be on the ship at the time of the sinking. Little did they know the bizarre set of events that would follow, including lack of information, the terror surrounding the evacuation of the vessel, and loss of their luggage.

Opinion no.3. It grieves me, as a resident of the Marlborough

Sounds area, that because of the lack of information, the people in our area now live in a fog of rumour and innuendo which could easily be cleared up, with a full marine inquiry.

Fair Comment

This author has no desire whatsoever to prove what did or did not happen on that fateful night around Cape Jackson. His only interest is ,'How does all this fit in with New Zealand's role in World Government negotiations.'

Summing Up

As could be expected under the circumstances, is it any wonder that the little country of New Zealand buzzed (and to this day still buzzes) from North to South, with rumours and supposition about what really took place on that fateful night.

Did this sinking have links with other aspects of this *social experiment* being conducted on poor New Zealanders?

We don't know.

Now, as an old school-teacher, I can visualise presenting the foregoing material to my pupils and asking them to write an essay which would sum all of this up.

Possible Scenarios

We may read something like this, plucked from the fertile imaginations of our imaginary pupils.

Scenario no.1. (Pupil no.1.)

In my opinion, this ship was an old model dressed up for the occasion.

Specific care was even taken over the welding on of the new nameplates.

It may even have been brought to New Zealand deliberately with the intention of sinking it in New Zealand waters.)

By making sure they had two other wrecks in other locations, say for example, one to the N.E. and the other to the N.W., this could provide an underwater triangle for navigation, enabling them to map the seafloor in the South Pacific area, thus preparing the way for more submarine visits to this portion of the earth.

It would be for this reason that the ship could not be anchored to the beach, where it would be hidden from the open sea by a small headland, but would have to be allowed to drift right out just beyond halfway in Port Gore where it would have uninterrupted access to the sea in a northerly direction.

I think it is possible that the Soviets somehow offloaded the 51 missing persons to a submarine within the Marlborough Sounds before the sinking.

Scenario no.2. (Pupil no.2.)

In my opinion, the ship was sunk in this position as ι ι___ possibly has on board a sophisticated device which can pick up the sounds of all ship's motors as they pass through the Cook Strait.

By sending this information by satellite to the USSR, all vessels in this vital New Zealand shipping lane could then be checked on, as each ship has a distinctive sound, and just as a human being can be detected by his fingerprints, so a ship can be known by its engine sound.

Scenario no.3. (Pupil no.3.)

I think the ship was sunk there to possibly act as some kind of a base for future Antarctic visits by USSR vessels. I feel that its deep position on the sea-bed is vital for communications, either with satellites or submarines.

Scenario no.4. (Pupil no.4.)

I believe the ship hit Kempe Point, tearing the port side. This would explain why they took it through Jackson Head at full speed, desperately searching for a spot to beach her before she sank.

Probably, this urgent predicament would give rise to arguments taking place on the bridge about that time as to whether they should go through foul ground or not.

I also believe that the ship was sunk there in that position.in Port Gore, as it is in a direct line with the 3 communications bases on the North Island i.e. Ohakea, Tangimoana and Irirangi.

I am wondering if it could be possible that the Soviets with the cooperation of World Government agencies arranged the whole plan in advance.

This would also explain why those vitally involved in the case of the Russians, did not serve a prison term in the Soviet Union as had been initially suggested by the media.

Scenario no.5 (Pupil no.5.)

I am convinced that all my classmates are sensationalists.

It was an accident, pure and simple, as any sensible person reading all this information can clearly see.

I agree with the statement made on a T.V. programme. No further enquiries are necessary. Russian ship — Russian problem.

Postscript

Some have inquired 'Why include the subject in your book? What relevance does it have to the other subject matter presented herewith?'

Answer

(a) Some have described this sinking and following events as being worthy of being included as one of the most bizzare shipping stories in the annals of marine history. You must admit, it is fascinating.

(b) The Soviets have not hidden their desire for a strong Pacific presence during the decade 1990-2000.

(c) Their vessels are sighted regularly in many different areas of the Pacific.

(d) We can only ask, 'Does this event have anything to do with the equal division between the superpowers of the balance of power?'

We would appreciate readers not writing requesting any extra information on this subject as we have none available.

Simply watch the Global scene as a whole and marvel.

Final Fair Comment — Let the reader take note.

Statement. By any information here disclosed or any opinion given, the author does not in any way whatsoever either by innuendo, or directly, accuse any individual or group of malpractice or complicity in a conspiracy.

Secondly it is not the authors purpose to attribute blame or otherwise to any individual or group.

Thirdly there is no intended criticism of the Preliminary Inquiry, merely a desire for all the facts to be presented in a further full marine inquiry, and thus give the people of this country the comfort of knowing that all is well with our national sovereignty and security.

The inescapable fact remains — Whether operative or inoperative, the Soviets now have a permanent presence in New Zealand waters.

CHAPTER 32

Commos Are Such Nice People

a. The capital city in New Zealand is Wellington.

b. The capital city in Australia is Canberra.

Read now about the findings of Dr Desmond Ball, a director of Strategic and Defence Studies Centre at the Australian National University at Canberra.

'Press', 11th July 1986. 'The Soviet Embassy in Wellington is used to listen in to Government telephone and radio communications, according to a world expert on intelligence.

.....He said he saw the aerials and the housing for a microwave dish when he visited Wellington last year.

.....Confirmation of eavesdropping came during a visit to the United States where a Central Intelligence Agency list had included the WELLINGTON EMBASSY as a Soviet listening post, Dr Ball said.

.....the International Institute for Strategic Studies had made similar claims regarding the SOVIET EMBASSY in CANBERRA, in an interview with the 'Age' newspaper in Melbourne.

He said, the Canberra and Wellington eavesdropping probably gave the Soviets access to sensitive communication.

.....In a detailed account of the system possibly used in Canberra, Dr Ball told the 'Age' that the microphone might trigger a tape recorder when a certain telephone number was dialled, or a word mentioned.

The microwave dish at the Wellington Embassy could tap into microwave bands and it was possibly programmed to filter out the most valuable conversations.

'It could trigger the tape when words such as sugar, wheat, Pine Gap or ANZUS are mentioned', he said.

.....Asked if he thought the New Zealand Government knew of the eavesdropping, Dr Ball said 'I'm sure they would.' End quote. (Emphasis added.)

Findings—Soviets spy on people, even their so-called friends. 'Dominion Sunday Times', 23rd October 1988 tells us:

'The Readers Digest journalist who published his claims in the November edition (1988) of the international magazine says he

191

and his research team have the intelligence and documents to prove their claim.

.....a new highly secretive Soviet group known as the SPECIAL RESERVES is headed in the South Pacific by Valeri Zemskov, minister-counsellor at the Soviet Embassy in Canberra....Members.....have been trained as diplomats and instructed how to conduct themselves according to the local customs of a country..

.....They are active in New Zealand and Australia.' End quote.

Findings – Soviet K.G.B. agents are being identified now, so a more subtle group has been bred.

The Soviets are moving into New Zealand under subtle guises.

Snuggle Up To A Commo
1. A c.n.g. (compressed natural gas) deal between New Zealand and Soviets. 'Press', 30.1.89.
2. A fishing deal around the coasts of New Zealand. 'Press', 10.11.88.
3. Soviet port visit in May (1989) 'to assess the area's ability to service the Soviet Union's South Pacific fishing fleet'. 'Press', 28.2.89.
4. Diplomats visit to Soviet Union by Deputy Prime Minister. 'Waikato Times', 29.10.88.

Finally, when it all boils down, what do the Soviets really want?
Answer – a base in the South Pacific.

My wife and I, one day, spent one and a half hours in the office of a very senior New Zealand politician.

Pointing to a globe of the world in his office, he said 'Look at Russia then look at New Zealand surrounded by water. Of course they want a presence in this area.'

In the light of recent events in China, we may see that the Communist Government there really loves its people. So much in fact, that they shoot them, when they are not running them over with tanks.

Lies

A spokesman later claimed that no lives were lost in the square in Beijing.

Not only are communists liars, they are stupid liars.

And still some people in high office in New Zealand and elsewhere, wish to snuggle up to them. Unbelievable, yet true.

192

Believe it — or not!

Stop Press. Christchurch 'Press', 22nd June 1989.

'A Soviet research ship has been refused permission to visit Auckland 'because of national security' the 'New Zealand Herald' reported yesterday.

....the move to refuse entry into Auckland has angered scientists and researchers on board.....' End quote.

A student was seen walking around the campus of a large American university with the letters V.K. printed on the front of his sweatshirt.

A friend stopped him and asked what the letter V.K. stood for.

Student: 'Very Konfused.'

Friend: 'But "confused" doesn't start with the letter "K".'

Student: 'Ah, that shows you how confused I am.'

I recommend sweatshirts with V.K. on them for all New Zealand government leaders responsible for New Zealand's security from 1985-1990.

CHAPTER 33

The Soviet Union and Communism

Two tramps in the Soviet Union were having a discussion.

Tramp A: 'And what do you think of the Moscow Times comrade?'

Tramp B: 'The Moscow Times eh? A very fine paper.'

Tramp A: 'What about the South Cossack news?'

Tramp B: 'South Cossack news. Very coarse. Yes very coarse indeed.'

Tramp A: 'How about the Soviet Herald?'

Tramp B: 'The Soviet Herald? Oh, I really don't know. I haven't smoked that one.'

The Soviet Union is a massive land mass to the north of Israel. Many nationalities here are crowded into a socialist system, that like all socialist systems, is collapsing around their ears.

People are absolutely fed up with communism. Proofs of this statement may be observed in China, Russia and in Poland.

Socialism never lasts as Peron of the Argentine would bear witness, if he could return from the dead. It completely wrecked his previously prosperous Argentina, just as surely as it is in the process of utterly destroying New Zealand and Australia.

The test case of all test cases for World Government, the Soviet Union, now has a new leader – Gorbachev, who has his attractive wife accompany him on his softening-up journeys.

I have quoted Breshnev's statement in both my previous books, 'Warning' and 'Second Warning'. Here it is once more.

A quotation from Breshnev, taken from the 'Washington Post'. 12th February 1977.

'Trust us Comrades, for by 1985 as a consequence of what we are now achieving with DETENTE (peaceful co-existence), we will have achieved most of our objectives in Western Europe. We will have consolidated our position. We will have improved our economy and a decisive shift in the correlation of forces will be such, that come 1985, we will be able to exert our will wherever we need to.

We are achieving with Detente what our predecessors have been unable to do with the mailed fist....' End quote.

194

Not bad for a guess. 1985, he said. Gorbachev is speaking in 1989 about openness and the strange thing is, world leaders believe him.

It would help me somewhat if he would officially renounce the aim of communism which is to take over the whole world. This he has never done, but even then, I wouldn't fully believe him. As we have seen in the communist manifesto LIES are a key to their success in the art of deception.

Mind Boggling Developments
'Albuqueque Journal', 14th June 1989.

'Soviet President Mikhail Gorbachev and West German Chancellor Helmut Kohl endorsed a joint strategy Tuesday to 'heal the wounds' of European division which their nations helped inflict half a century ago.

....their partnership poses no threat this time, as it did when Adolf Hitler and Joseph Stalin divided Poland.....

Both nations want 'a common European home, in which the United States and Canada have their place' and all nations exist in 'peaceful competition with one another', the joint declaration says....' End quote.

Why not? These communists have no moral standards.

Communists and socialists. The same thing exactly. A group not to be laughed at, but a group to be pitied.

Statement—If you do not have the Word of God as your standard, there is no common standard.

True, these socialist politicians are eloquent. They mock others and put them down, but then as time moves on, they are normally stabbed in the back by another politician as ungodly as they are, lose their job, retire, get sick and on their deathbeds, alone, without the back-slapping and clever phrases, wait in anguish of mind to meet Almighty God without a lawyer in the person of the Lord Jesus Christ.

Sad—but a true commentary.

Soviet Designs on Antarctica
'Australian', 26th November 1988. 'Nine sign Antarctic Treaty.

A convention on mineral exploration and mining in the Antarctic was signed by nine countries here (Wellington, New Zealand) yesterday.

....the nine countries to sign were:

195

the Soviet Union
New Zealand
Norway
Finland
Brazil
South Korea
South Africa
Sweden
Uruguay

The United States, Britain, Chile and Argentina said they would sign as soon as possible, and the convention is before the Australian parliament for discussion....' End quote.

Later, Australia refused to sign.

Now can you see why the Soviets want to move into New Zealand?

Now can you see why they possibly needed their Lermontov here?

They want a jumping off place for the Antarctic. There is much wealth down there in mineral form.

In spite of the two words PERESTROIKA (reform) and GLASSNOST (openness) being bandied around by the gentlepersons of the press, it is not as easy as all that. China and Russia both have similar problems.

'Press', 25th February 1989. 'Communists who have concluded that communism is dead, still have the problem of arranging a decent burial. The biggest difficulty is that the two main economic weaknesses of the system — State ownership and distorted prices -worsen each other......' End quote.

Like most other countries, these two will also move quickly into PRIVATISATION to cure their economic woes.

Democracy In The U.S.S.R.

Look at this — Visa.

'Herald', 8th March 1988. 'Visa Breakthrough in the Soviet Union.

Visa will become the first international payment card to be issued in the Soviet Union....' End quote.

Comrade, Big Mac's all round

'Christchurch Star', 24th March 1988. 'The Big Mac has arrived in Eastern Europe.

McDonald Corp. has launched its first hamburger bar in the region.

.....Company officials said a McDonalds would open in the next few months in the Hungarian capital of Budapest, more stores would be built in Belgrade, and a deal would soon be concluded for a restaurant in Moscow....' End quote.

The KGB still has an iron grip on the Kremlin, but the WGA have ways to force them to back off slightly.

Their agriculture is a mess.

Their economy is a mess.

Their shopping system is a mess—queues and more queues.

They are a primitive society. Here are a few luxuries enjoyed by few of their people:

Indoor plumbing, television, automobiles and telephones.

In modern technology and weaponry however, they do very well indeed. How?

Most of this was imported from their so-called 'enemy' the U.S.A.

Four Power Groups Revealed for Our Times
1. The United States of America.
2. The U.S.S.R.
3. The European Community.
4. The Secret World Government Advocates.

Rule—no.4 rules the other 3 with a fierce grip.

These WGA made it all happen.

Suddenly Reagan stops calling the Soviets names.

Suddenly Gorbachev stops calling the U.S. names.

Suddenly they are together.

It is all smiles in front of the cameras.

It is Ronnie and Mikhail.

These World Government people knew it was the time in history to pull in the net. They had done their utmost to this time, to keep anybody from knowing that the conspiracy existed, or exists BUT PEOPLE WERE GETTING SUSPICIOUS.

Key Statement. The real reason for making the Soviet Union a power, equal to or surpassing the power of the United States was to make people fear the possibility of such a war and to accept a NEW WORLD ORDER, or NOVUS ORDO SECLORUM as written on the reverse side of the U.S. $1 bill (underneath the pyramid.)

This would bring about a World Government situation and 'they' would tell us that this new 'ruling elite' would 'eliminate' the threat of a major war and incidentally make all multinational investments safe and all loans secure.

CLEVER

DEVISED IN HELL

We have learnt already that Karl Marx was a fraud in that he pretended to identify with the underprivileged and hob-nobbed with a wealthy benefactor.

Lenin is said to have declared the best way to destroy the capitalist system was to debauch the currency.....it does it in a manner that not one man in a million is able to diagnose.

What a strange aim in life — to destroy and wreck. How different to the aim of the Master who came to make life full of meaning.

'The thief cometh not but for to steal, to kill and to destroy, but I am come that they might have life and that they might have it more abundantly.' *Ref.1.

Beautiful — Here's a real person of quality.

This philosophy of Lenin attacks only one group — the middle class. The objectives of Lenin's philosophy was twofold.

1. To destroy the free enterprise system.
2. To take the wealth from the poor and the middle-class and redistribute it to the rich.

New Zealand and Australian readers will now understand what is happening in their two countries. Lenin in action.

What a crook. He now goes in the same basket as Mr Marx.

Violent and Non Violent

Another interesting point to those seeking to make sense out of Communism or Socialism is that Lenin went to University where he became a student of Karl Marx.

Marx had special methods for conquering, which two alternatives have split the party throughout its history.

a. violent method
b. non-violent method

As we can clearly see, Gorbachev is quite within his rights therefore, to use the non-violent method, as the violent method days are over. (Perhaps not yet in China, but they will be brought into line.)

The aims are still the same, however.

199

Lies
We read earlier that the Communist manifesto allows for 'lies' to be used and this one fact alone makes a little sense out of the way that these people operate.
The 'Sunday Times' in London, some years ago, showed why it is necessary to tell lies and deceive the public if one wishes to bring in socialism.

Socialism — definition
a. competition without prizes
b. boredom without hope
c. war without victory
d. statistics without end
The Eastern Bloc has proved this.
Argentina and Angola have proved it.
Australia and New Zealand have just finished proving it, prior to 1990.
Now it's on to World Government.
Most people do not want socialism, nor do they wish to live under it, so the socialists must turn to 'trickery and deception', by a series of lies offered to the people by lying politicians.

Socialism and Communism — Any Difference?
None at all.
A definition of socialism. 'The longest road there is from democracy to democracy.' (Hungarian joke.)
'There is no economic difference between socialism and communism. Both terms....denote the same system....public control of the means of production as distinct from private control.
The two terms, socialism and communism are synonymous.'
'.....if any should not work neither should he eat' is the Biblical injunction.
The Russian constitution states in article 12:
'From each according to his ability, to each according to his work.'
Question — How does this system provide for those unable to work?

Bible Promise
'But my God shall supply all your needs, according to his riches in glory by Christ Jesus.' *Ref.2.
200

Communist Answer

These individuals would be executed 'in a kindly manner'. To any keen communist I ask 'Would you apply this to your own mother?'

Soviet History — Full of Lies

'Press', 28th June 1988.

'....."We can only be thankful to the person who finally had the courage to veto history exams', 'Izvestia', the Government newspaper, declared a few days ago.

.....'Only one thing is important', wrote Izvestia. 'To have schoolbooks from which you can learn and teach without lying.'

Despite new enthusiasm for a more accurate version of history, it is unlikely that the authorities can afford to give Soviet citizens an entirely unvarnished view of history.' End quote.

Boredom a Problem

Many times we read about the drab colourless lives lived by people under communism or socialism. Alcoholism is rife and atheistic dogma is also thrust upon these poor souls.

Spies are called 'Minders'

Those of us living in the west cannot possibly imagine what it feels like to be spied upon from dawn to dusk by these minders.

The big brother concept coming upon us through the World Government is a very real thing within Russia and its surrounding states.

'Weekend Star', 10 September 1988. 'KGB Minder under the Bed.

There are 14 KGB 'minders' to every one of the capital's 10,000 foreign residents, according to a senior American embassy official in Moscow.

At least three of these minders are in daily contact with their target and one lives right in their home.

.....any employee supplied by the UPDK to foreign embassies....businesses, correspondents and their families — makes a regular report on their visitors, telephone calls, meetings, invitations and domestic relations.

'Soviets a Risk'. 'Press', 12th March 1988.

'An Australian Opposition back-bencher has claimed the security of the New Zealand, Canadian and British High Commission

in Canberra is being placed at risk by siting a new Soviet Embassy next to them....' End quote.
You see, they export their vile spying lifestyle to other countries also.

In an interesting article quote in the 'Weekend Star', 10th September 1988, a diplomat's wife describes the drab existence that is their lot, when living in Moscow.
When asked by a friend why she didn't ring to get an official decision, she replied 'But there is no telephone directory in Moscow....

......Mr Gorbachev's policy of openness has scotched forever the myth that the Soviet Union offers anything close to an adequate health service....' End quote.
The lady took her daughter, suffering with an abscess to a dentist. 'A sympathetic Soviet dentist swept her hand despairingly around her surgery and said there was nothing she could do to help her. She had NO DRUGS, NO ANAESTHETIC and NO DRILLS. We flew to Helsinki.' End quote. (Emphasis added.)

Soviet Airlines Unsafe
'Financial Australian', 11th April 1988. 'The Perils of Flying with Aeroflot.
....Official media have likened airports to refugee camps and accused air crews of 'barbarous and shameful' treatment of passengers.
There are no safety demonstrations at the start of each flight, mainly because there is little to show.
There are no life jackets under the seat, or air masks in the overhead compartments. The seat pocket in front is usually empty. Emergency exists are marked but often blocked by excess baggage.
....International Civil Aviation Organisation regulations require safety equipment on international flights, but Aeroflot sets it own domestic standards.
.....scores of passengers were killed in a crash at the Volga River industrial city of Kuibishev when an Aeroflot pilot bet his crewman he could make a blind landing and pulled a shade over the cockpit window.
....The newspaper also said alcoholism among Aeroflot crew members had increased by 60% in 1987.' End quote.
In the light of the foregoing information, it now becomes apparent that the media has been guilty of puffing up the Soviet

image almost matching them with their 'apparent opponent', the U.S.A.

U.S.S.R. a Super Military Power?
No!

It cannot possibly be. Its name tells you this. It's socialist. Everywhere it has been tried, it has failed. It is ridiculous, as any country who tries it long enough finishes up like socialist Ethiopia.

Some try to tell us that the USSR is more powerful than the U.S.A. An easy test would be to ask any U.S. military leader if he would like to swap his men and equipment for his Soviet counterpart.

Some years ago, I read of a battalion of Soviet tanks on manoeuvres. They were to cross a river but the tanks bogged down and troops were drowned as the drivers and tank commanders mistook the orders. There is so much language difference in the region. That also is a major difficulty. The mechanism for loading and ejecting shells is so antiquated that crew members are often killed by their own machinery.

The U.S. Feeds the U.S.S.R.
The eagle feeds the bear.

Not only is the Soviet Union poor and weak. It is evil.

Chain of Control
The World Government secret power brokers have leadership over the Federal Government of the U.S.A through their business contacts in high places, including their banks. All these combined up until 1988, had loaned the Soviet Union $127 billion. (An article in the 'Wall St Journal' made this clear.)

Will it be paid back?

No.

Why?

Because the WGA build the monster, supply it with food and machinery, along with modern computers and technology.

Anthony Sutton, whom I mentioned in my previous books, has written another one called 'The Best Enemy, Money Can Buy.'

Now listen please. Commonsense tells me that if you feed something and supply all that 'thing's' needs, you do not really wish to destroy that 'thing'. O.K.? O.K.!

If the U.S. Federal Reserve said that anybody lending to, or trading with the evil empire, would be expelled, it would all be over.

But no. On and on they go, perpetuating this farce.

Is the U.S.S.R. really a major military power?

Judging by their other equipment, lifestyles and output, I would say 'no'.

Even their warheads are probably filled with cardboard or low-grade uranium.

The whole system is built on lies and deception as we have endeavoured to point out in this article.

Very Cruel

Men and women are tripartite. This has been clearly established by out of the body experiences had by many folk, including my own wife. whom we very nearly lost after a major operation. By the grace of God, in answer to our family's desperate prayers, she was restored to us after observing for some time, her lifeless body lying on the bed, while her spirit rejoiced in freedom from all pain and earthly distress.

Other believers throughout the world have also been privileged to see glimpses into eternity.

This is in no way connected to any occultish practice which is demonic in nature. Astral travel and any other anti-God exercises we publicly condemn, and release people who attend our meetings from these bondages in the Name of the Lord Jesus Christ.

'I pray to God, your whole spirit, soul and body be preserved blameless unto the coming of our Lord Jesus Christ.' *Ref.3.

Spirit — The God conscious part

Soul — The self conscious part (mind, will and emotions)

Body — The world conscious part

A person without God, or one who has not experienced the NEW BIRTH that Jesus spoke about, has not had his or her relationship with God awakened.

There is really no relationship with God at all. A very real interest possibly, but no relationship.

In our meetings, year by year, we lead thousands of seeking people into a genuine relationship with God, through Jesus Christ.

All this knowledge previously unknown by the majority is the 'catalyst' that opens up the desire for a spiritual foundation that neither the World Government Advocates nor the arch-enemy of souls himself, can take away.

Have you ever looked into an atheist's eyes? They are grey and dead-looking. No spark of spiritual life illumines them.

The eyes are the windows of the soul.

People in Australia and New Zealand, the guinea pig countries, still have ample opportunities to get to know this God and His dear Son, Jesus. This access is open to all in non-communist countries up until this point in history.

The injunction is clear.

'Seek ye the Lord while He may be found.

Call ye upon Him while He is near.' *Ref.4.

In a communist atheistic state where the God-conscious part is suppressed, how much opportunity do these millions have to find God in a personal way? It's very hard.

Now, a person without the new birth is very similar to, and acts sometimes worse than —

A Beast. What is a beast?

A living animal, capable of enjoying life to a degree but not ultimately, as it was not created in the image of the living God. Man was.

Therefore, to a beast, there is no right or wrong. No common standard of behaviour.

PLEASE FIND ON THE FOLLOWING PAGE THE DIFFERENCES BETWEEN A COMMUNIST/SOCIALIST (WHO DOES NOT ACCEPT THE WORD OF GOD AS HIS OR HER STANDARD FOR LIVING) AND A BEAST.

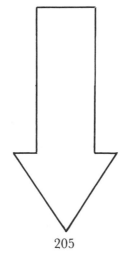

To any who object to this last statement, I say, 'Show me your book setting out a common standard of behaviour and I will delete the statement from future reprints of this chapter with a word of apology.'

God, his Creator, has put into a living person, a CONSCIENCE.

This conscience tells one when they are doing right or when they are doing wrong.

New Zealanders hearken unto me. In 1989 and onwards towards 2000, the spirit that drives these people that our Government is chumming up to is worse than the spirit of a beast. Beasts do not make life miserable for all around them.

The Reader's Digest some time ago, included an article about Soviet behaviour in Afghanistan.

Quote: 'The Soviet killing is going on right now. An entire nation is dying while we in the west, seal our eyes to the horror. 'They burn easier than wood.'

.....An Afghan doctor who interpreted for us had a sudden outburst as we were leaving. 'What's the point of all this? People should know by now. There are no human rights in Afghanistan. They burn people easier than wood.'

.....A French doctor, telling how Russians punished an entire village, after some Afghan troops had defected. 'They tied them up and piled them like wood. Then they poured petrol over them and burned them alive. They were old and young men, women and children. Forty people were killed.....' End quote.

You reply—'That's revolting. I am not born again but I would never be capable of such an action.'

Over the years, we have met many, many people, during the course of our travels.

I remember years ago, in my younger, unsaved days, partying etc with some very influential people.

Men and women dressed beautifully with apparently impeccable manners, mixed with the right people, yet with a small quantity of alcohol in their systems, would revert to some of the most shameful and disgusting acts it has been my misfortune to witness.

The Old Book was correct all the time.

'The heart is deceitful above all things and desperately wicked.' *Ref.5.

No wonder the Master said 'Ye must be born again.' *Ref.6.

Soviet Moves in the Pacific. 'Waikato Times', 5th August 1986.

207

'Earlier last month, the New Zealand Prime Minister, ..., said he was concerned about Soviet penetration in the South Pacific.

....He said the Soviet Union had a long term aim of subversion in the region and was using fishing agreements with impoverished nations as a way of doing that...' End quote.

Herein lies an enigma. In August 1986, the New Zealand Prime Minister admits the Soviets have ulterior motives in their 'fishing' deals, yet in February of the same year, against all common and established procedure, allows them to sink one of their vessels in a very strategic spot in New Zealand waters and to cap it off, does not initiate a full marine enquiry. Why?

'No Russian Warships in South Pacific.' 'Press', 26.3.88.

'Vice-Admiral Komarov was asked for information on Soviet Naval activities in the South Pacific and specifically, whether any Soviet ships or SUBMARINES had passed through New Zealand's 200 mile economic zone or within the 12 miles territorial limit in the last year.

HE DID NOT RESPOND DIRECTLY although he said 'There are no Soviet WARSHIPS in the South Pacific....' End quote. (Emphasis added.)

This devious answer reminds me of a Bob Hope yarn.

Some years ago, he stayed in a beaten up hotel in a small town.

The newspaper later reported him as stating that rats walked over him all through the night, wearing hob-nailed boots.

The manager of the hotel, righteously indignant, threatened legal action unless the defamatory statement was retracted.

A couple of days later, Mr Hope's retraction appeared in print.

'I sincerely regret my former statement regarding this hotel. I hereby declare that the rats who walked across me all through the night, were not wearing hob-nailed boots.'

Common Policies.

'Press', 16th June 1988.

'Reform policies in New Zealand, other Western countries and the Soviet Union have much in common, says Parliament's speaker....' End quote.

You know, for a change, I agree totally with this statement. The nice Soviets from down the road are to be our new playmates.

From here on, with ample background information, all falls into place. The WGA have now pulled the plug on the Soviet

Union. They are being 'restructured' — which means 'destroyed' just as New Zealand is.

They are being forced through contrived circumstances to fit in with world plans for their future.

World Court, Soviets and the U.S.A. — Note link up.

'Press', 11th March 1989. 'USSR will accept World Court Rulings.

The Soviet Union says it will accept the World Court rulings in cases involving human rights treaties, reversing 40 years of suspicion and resistance to the court's authority.

State Department officials hailed the Soviet move as a major step and said they hoped the Soviets would join the United States in accepting the court's rulings in all but the most sensitive national-security cases.....' End quote.

Come into my Parlour

The South Pacific countries, particularly New Zealand, which is looked up to as a big brother figure by some of the island nations, has failed to read the warning signs.

Flies would be foolish to enter into 'meaningful dialogue' with spiders, speaking of restructuring and openness. Nevertheless, it sure is interesting, watching all this skull-duggery take place.

New Zealand is the key-stone to the Pacific. It is strategically placed as the gateway to the Antarctic and the Soviet's would dearly love this country as a prize.

With ANZUS broken, the U.S. could legitimately appear to ignore our cries for help, whilst at the same time, through agreements with the SECRET WGA, maintain their bases on our soil.

After all, (let's be fair), once New Zealand is a State of Australia, and don't ever forget, the U.S. has strong links with Australia — surely the Soviets can have one teeny state. 'Aw, come on.'

CHAPTER 34

Soviets Link With Religion

Pastor David McBride, a dear friend of mine, was preaching in the open air one evening, when a passerby said that his message was a waste of time as there was no God.

David then asked this man if he could be everywhere at the same time which would be important in the light of his initial statement.

'Why's that?', asked the interjector.

'Because', David replied, 'in order for you to say what you've just said, with full conviction, you would need to be everywhere at once, at all times because the God whose existence you deny, could be somewhere where you're not. Therefore, if you continue with your argument, you, yourself are claiming to be God, because you must be able to be everywhere at once.'

World Government Links with World Church

Prophetically speaking, we know that the World Government will work in with a World Church. Here it comes.

'Australian', 3rd May 1988. 'Gorbachev Cements Ties with Church.

....The Soviet leader noted that 'mistakes' committed by the Kremlin, with regard to the Church and believers since the 1930's were being corrected.

Pravda quoted Archbishop Pimen as replying 'May the Lord God bless you and your works, deeply respected Mikhail Sergeyevich.'

.....Church—State relations have improved considerably under Mr Gorbachev.....' End quote.

For an atheist, he's quite religious. 'Press', 9th December 1987.

'Dealing with a reduction in nuclear arms, the two leaders met in 1987.

Mr Gorbachev used the name of God. Quote: 'The visit has begun. May God help us', he declared on arrival at Andrew's Air Force Base.....' End quote.

Reagan later said—quote: 'He and I will meet the hopes of promoting peace for our peoples and all the people on Earth.......' End quote.

210

Christchurch 'Press', 7th July 1989. 'Gorbachev Baptised. Mikhail Gorbachev, general secretary of the officially atheistic Communist party said yesterday he was baptised in the Russian Orthodox Church. 'I was baptised. I was christened, and I think this is quite normal', the Soviet President said.' End quote.

As the Irishman said, 'A strange paradox indeed, indeed.'

New Age Links. You, the reader will be interested to know that Mr Gorbachev has New Age interests, and this will be dealt with later on in this book.

CHAPTER 35

Soviets Future Predicted

Link up with the U.S.A.

The first thing the WGA hope to bring about is a link-up of the two super-powers USA and USSR for joint World Government ventures.

The man, chosen of course, to fulfill this momentous task is George Bush, whom we will discuss further under the chapter on the U.S.A.

Key Note. The question is often asked 'If the nuclear tests are not of a warlike nature, then why do they keep testing in the Pacific at Mururoa Atoll, and in the U.S.A. in the Nevada desert etc, etc'.

Where?

1. The first reason deals with location. These two spots I have cited are some of the very few places on earth where these devices can be most frequently detonated. That is why the French cannot move their tests to France as some have suggested they should do.

Note also, that at each test, U.S. and English ships, along with others, monitor each explosion.

As we now understand, they know of course, exactly what time France will detonate these devices.

Why?

2. The answer to the other part of the question as to why they keep testing.

This nuclear energy is to be used in a joint space programme, because under the SECRET WGA plan, they have never been enemies at all.

'Jerusalem Post', 28th September 1988. 'Soviets call for U.S. Co-operation in establishing World Space Agency.

....Soviet leader, Mikhail Gorbachev, suggested earlier this month that the Soviet radar base at Krasnoyarsk be turned over to an INTERNATIONAL SPACE AGENCY for the peaceful exploration of space....' End quote. Emphasis added.

Russia in Prophecy

Referred to as 'the King of the North' — Soviet Union.
Referred to as 'the King of the South' — Black African communists.

For a full run-down on Russia's future in prophecy, please read my earlier book 'Second Warning' — page 172 'What about Russia?'

A Brief Precis of Events

1. A middle-east peace treaty will be confirmed for a period of 7 years.
   The Israelis will apparently lay aside their weaponry at this point. That is a big thing for them to do because they could be classed as the most heavily fortified country in the world. Even the Soviet Union is terrified of them.
2. The following countries will be involved with the Soviet Union for the invasion of Israel.
   All these are clearly named in the prophecies:
   Russia — King of the North.
   Black African communist countries — King of the South.
   Iran.
   North African countries — watch Libya, Tunisia and Morocco.
   East Germany.
   Turkish mountain people and many others, including the Cossacks.
3. The evil demonic prince call 'Gog' leads their forces on to their destruction.
4. Initially, troops will come up from Africa, join with many Arab nations and attack Israel.
5. Next Russia, Iran, East Germany and the Cossacks will come through:
   Iran — by land
   A Mediterranean amphibious attack
   Air-paratroops
6. The only areas that escape this invasion are Edom, Moab and Ammon down the Jordan Valley. The ancient fortress city of Petra is in this area. The caves in the rocks can shelter up to one and a quarter million people. Many Jews will hide there during this period.
8. Whilst in Egypt, the Soviets hear bad news from home in

the north about threats from China in the east. This unsettles the Soviets and makes them feel insecure.

9. The Soviets and their allies move back to their total destruction on the mountains of Israel.

A weapon called 'The Velocity Factor of 7' will wipe them out. (See Second Warning — page 180.)

The might of the USSR will now be laid to rest.

CHAPTER 36

Unionism

Unionism is Finished

We know that the time will come when multinational big business through their mergers will become so powerful that:

a Unions would want to strike, but be afraid to.

b The Union bosses would begin to sweat, as they would become redundant and may be forced to go to work to earn a living. Perish the thought.

c Union bosses will do deals with the Government and big business, if not to help their workers, then to protect themselves.

A very powerful spirit is involved in Unionism. The New Age movement leaders know about this destructive demon. He has run his course of strife, destruction and misery.

The WGA aims that I have outlined elsewhere in this book include one especially for Unions and their cunning leaders.

I always took note that when a Union leader organised a protracted strike, families and individuals in the movements suffered but never the Union leader. He would just fly away, still on full pay and arrange more trouble elsewhere.

Under the heading Industrial Warfare, written in the 1700's, see how applicable it has been in our generation. (See Warning — page 78.)

'We shall further undermine artfully and deeply sources of production, by accustoming the workers to anarchy....

In order that the true meaning of things may not strike the masses before the proper time, we shall mask it under an alleged ardent desire to serve the working classes and the great principles of political economy....'

Wage Price Spiral. 'We shall raise the rate of wages, which however, will not bring any advantage to the workers, for at the same time, we shall produce a rise in prices of the first necessities in life.'

A Spiritual Remedy

To you dear Union workers, who are now redundant, they used you and dropped you. All is well, however.

How wonderful. There is a God in heaven who cares for you. 'Casting all your care upon Him, for He careth for you.' *Ref.1.

CHAPTER 37

The United States of America in World Government Plans

This great country has something that has attracted me since my boyhood.

I remember, during the war days, prior to 1945, my father driving our family to our holiday property at Raumati South, a little township, 30 miles north of New Zealand's capital city — Wellington.

There they were, dozens of them. Young American servicemen on a Pacific tour of duty, seated on the fence of their base which adjoined the main road. We would stop and talk and they would in turn give us bubble gum, American candies, and on occasions, the odd naval gob cap, or a Marine cap with a map of the world and an anchor on it. I was the envy of my mates at school.

We would also invite many of these young men home for a break. One such man from the Mid-west took a guitar and I can still hear him singing:

'I'm gonna dance with the dolly with a hole in her stockin',
While her knees keep a knockin', and her toes keep a rockin',
Gonna dance with the dolly with a hole in her stockin',
Gonna dance by the light of the moon.'

We loved those young men. They were so clean and interesting and really enjoyed my mother's home-cooked meals.

We kept records of their names and addresses and tried to contact some of them as the war drew to a conclusion.

Imagine our grief when we heard that many had been killed in the Pacific, on Tarawa and Iwojima. Sent into battle with their lives not yet lived, only to end it all with a piece of lead or a Japanese bayonet in the gut.

Many years later, I began to get wind of some anti-American feeling and couldn't really understand why. They had done our country no harm, in fact, only a lot of good.

Graffiti was written everywhere in many of the poorer countries like 'YANKEE GO HOME' and someone had written underneath, 'AND TAKE ME WITH YOU'.

'Readers' Digest' printed another such caption:

'YANKEE GO HOME' and some enterprising businessman had written down below, 'AND FLY PAN AM'.

Peace Campaigners

In the late 1970's, I was strolling on the Auckland wharves with some of my family, when I heard and saw a great commotion. A group of so-called 'peace campaigners' were shouting abuse at the sailors on a U.S. ship tied up at the wharf.

I said to my children 'Watch this.'

I shouted as loudly as I could 'Down with communism'.

The man speaking into the megaphone was temporarily silenced as I made my presence felt.

The TV cameras immediately moved off him and on to me as I stated my case. I pointed out that if it hadn't been for the U.S. forces in the battle of the Coral Sea, north of Australia, Japan would have overrun our country and we could have all finished up pulling rickshaws.

Later, a 'peace campaigner' sidled up to me and said 'You want to be very careful or you might slip off the wharf into the sea.'

I replied loudly, much to my children's delight, that I didn't think that this was very likely.

U.S. Influence in World Government

The United States of America today, however, has a great deal to do with World Government.

It is apparently organised from New York and Basle, Switzerland, and involves the top 13 families who seek to run the whole world system.

Under the top 13 are various other groups of power elite.

The main World Government power groups are generally located in the U.S.A. or Europe and include the following names. (See pages 83-91 in my first book 'Warning' for further details.)

1. Council on Foreign Relations — U.S.A.
2. Bilderbergers Group in Europe
3. Trilateral Commission
4. Club of Rome
5. Federal Reserve Banking System
6. Bank for International Settlement — Basle, Switzerland
7. House of Rothschilds
8. Rockefeller Foundation and many others.

Read any book on this subject and continually see the names written above referred to.

The Presidency of the U.S.A

For many years now, this highest office has been dominated by the secret World Government figures.

In a meeting one night, I mentioned that it would appear that U.S. Presidents were chosen rather than elected.

An angry young university student confronted me at the end of my lecture, and stated in no uncertain terms that I had no right to make such statements.

He cooled down considerably when I showed him the following information.

New Zealand 'Herald', 5th November 1980. 'Websters in Early for Last Word.

The Republican challenger, Mr Ronald Reagan, has caused a major upset in the United States presidential elections by beating Mr Jimmy Carter.

So in effect says the latest edition of Webster's dictionary even though Americans do not go to the polls until later today to decide their President for the next four years.

....Mr Reagan has been listed in the dictionary as the 40th President of the United States, along with his 39 predecessors.....

....The presumption or genuine mistake by the Chicago Publishers Consolidated Book Publishers, has dumb-founded the American Consul-General in Auckland....'Unbelievable', was his first word.

....Auckland representatives of the publishers were just as surprised and had no explanations.' End quote.

Unless one is aware of the overall plan, none of this would make sense but a full understanding of all the details makes future predictions easy.

Before we move on however, an interesting point in relation to Ronald Reagan appears.

An old Red Indian curse was placed upon every U.S. President elected in a year divisible by 20. They were all to die in office, and die they did.

1840 — Died in office
1860 — Died in office
1880 — Died in office
1900 — Died in office
1920 — Died in office
1940 — Died in office

220

1960 — Died in office

1980 — Ronald Reagan was elected and almost died in office.

A young man called John Hinkley shot him, but Reagan survived. Why?

Because before this happened, a group of new-born Christian businessmen who knew about this curse, sat Ronald Reagan in a chair, surrounded him, praying and breaking the curse in the Name of the Lord Jesus Christ.

Now here is a challenge. There is no other name they could have used to break this curse as it is written:

'Christ has redeemed us from the curse of the law, being made a curse for us, for it is written, cursed is everyone that hangeth on a tree.' *Ref.1.

Mr Reagan himself acknowledged his debt to the Lord for his still being alive.

Some years before, President Jimmy Carter inaugurated the Global 2000 plan. President Reagan ignored it and made the statement that he was not a Trilateralist (not a World Government advocate) but it was essential that the future President continue on with the World Government plan.

On the 7th November 1988, I was at home in New Zealand when I received a telephone call from Channel 7, Brisbane, Australia, asking me to travel to Avalon T.V. studios on the North Island ready to do a satellite interview the next day.

On the 8th November 1988, I sat before the camera waiting for the interview to take place.

My interviewer from Brisbane asked his first question.

'Tonight, the U.S. elections take place. Who will win?'

Without a pause, I answered 'George Bush'. (I have since found out that he is Queen Elizabeth's 13th cousin removed. The most royal President in U.S. history.)

Some person with a critical bent will say 'Good guess. You had been watching the polls.'

Wrong, my friend. I predicted this not in the light of the latest polls, but in my book 'Warning' on page 169.

Written in 1980......'We note with anticipation that the Presidential running mate — George Bush was introduced to the world by Walter Cronkite as 'our future President' and strangely enough, by another radio commentator as being a 'heartbeat away from the Presidency.'

221

Obviously, it was all planned that Reagan was chosen to be nought but a stepping stone for George Bush, the next to ascend the throne of power.' End quote.

Q. How did I know this over 8 years before he took the job?
A. Because he belonged to, or attended, at least 5 World Government groups.
1. The Council on Foreign Relations
2. The Bilderbergers in Europe
3. The Tri-lateral Commission
4. A director of the C.I.A.
5. The Order.

For a more complete expose of The Order, please send away for the 4 books on the subject written by Anthony Sutton. (For address, turn to Recommended Reading section in front of this book.)

Skull and Bones Society

I have been to the libraries to search out information on this latter group, but as it is so highly secret, I could find nothing.

The Skull and Bones Society meetings are held in a windowless building on High St. How like the Masons. In an article entitled 'The Last Secret of the Skull and Bones' ('Time' magazine, 22nd August 1988, referring to George Bush), an Esquire Magazine author, Ron Rosebaum spoke about this secret society situated at Yale University. He tells us that this group has been around since the 1820's or 30's and can be referred to as 'THE MOST INFLUENTIAL SECRET SOCIETY IN THE NATION.' End quote. (Emphasis added.)

The author went on to say that he seemed to have been able to link this society with the notorious Bavarian Illumanists. (That is the Illuminati whose strange pyramid seal is on the reverse side of the U.S. $1.00 bill.)

It is also significant that George Bush's father, Prescott, a wealthy investment banker, was also a member of the same secret society.

The son, George, graduated from Yale in two and a half years, yet during that time was also a Phi Beta Kappa.

In the 'International Herald Tribune', 7th November 1988, Art Buchwald, the satirist, tells us a little more of George's involvement in the club.

Quote: 'The fact that George Bush's father stole Geronimo's skull when he was a member of the Yale Skull and Bones Fraternity doesn't mean that the Vice-President won't carry out the laws of the land.' End quote.

What is the Skull and Bones Society?

15 new members only, are admitted into the group every year. This has been the case for over 150 years.

The Order

On leaving Yale University, these men become 'The Order'. This group is very, very secret.

Aims:

a. World domination 'through a New World Order'.
b. The control of each individual's life from the cradle to the grave.
c. A complete change in society.
d. No national boundaries.
e. No longer any constitutional protection.
f. Complete control of information through the media.

It is significant that during the latter portion of 1990, both President George Bush, Dr. Henery Kissinger and Mikhail Gorbachev began publicly using the term "New World Order".

Methods:

Encourage false, yet apparently real 'managed conflicts' to bring about 'polarisation' and 'hatred' in a society.

Controls:

Education — political parties — private banking — major law firms — philanthropic organisations.
Influence in Executive branch of Government — foreign policy - major banks — Federal Reserve.
Influences churches — universities — business — industry.

From the 1600's, members have 'thrown away loyalty to their country'. These people swear allegiance only to The Order.

Main Aim:

Through the 'managed conflict' between the Soviets and the Americans, The Order, with the assistance of the latest President, aims to merge these two countries as a 'global tool' to bring in World Government.

'Is all this true?' you ask. The Christchurch 'Press', 26th April 1989 included a highly interesting article.

New Zealand readers will know that our democratically elected representatives destroyed our defence treaty (called ANZUS) with the U.S.A.

This was against the wishes of the people of New Zealand; apart from a few misguided individuals who didn't at that stage understand the no-nuclear threat revealed elsewhere in this book.

The article mentioned above, quoted in part herewith, referred to the then Prime Minister's trip to the U.S. where the White House and the President didn't wish to see him.

Quote: 'The Prime Minister .... may not get to see President Bush, but he was all over the old Bonesman's territory at Yale University yesterday.

....When the now President George Herbert Walker Bush, was a student at Yale, he was one of the very secret 'Skull and Bones' Society founded in 1832 and which chooses only 15 members a year for membership.

....Little is known of the Skull and Bones Society except that through the generations it has comprised the most influential students who have gone on to places of prominence in American business, Government and society.....' End Quote.

Soviets and The Order

In 1983, Averell Harriman (The Order) went to Moscow to see Andropov. The Hatch Act U.S.A. says that no private citizen must conduct foreign relations, yet what was discussed was hushed up.

The Soviets now treat George Bush with very great respect for they know of his role in The Order.

Things are really humming along. The section that you have just read is some of the most up to date and important news in this book, but only taken in context with the rest of the data does it make sense.

'Press', 11th November 1988.

'George Bush says a productive summit meeting with the Soviet leader, Mikhail Gorbachev, and resumption of United States aid to control rebels....will be 'TOP PRIORITIES' of his administration.....' End quote.

Note. When Bush and Gorbachev sign an agreement or agree verbally with East and West Germany to knock down the Berlin wall, this will be a strategic sign to prophetic students. 'For when they shall say peace, peace, sudden destruction.....' *Ref.13. During the month of June 1989, this was discussed openly.

This proves a point.

a. Links with the Soviets to be strengthened.

b. Managed conflict to be assisted.

'Time' Magazine, 24.4.89, shows us a little more of the Kissinger influence on the Bush administration.

Quote: '....Henry Kissinger has been trying to persuade the Bush administration to work out a new agreement with the Kremlin. The Soviet Union would commit itself to tolerate political and economic pluralism in Eastern Europe in exchange for Western guarantees of Soviet military security. The notion seems to be that Moscow might be more likely to allow Poland, Hungary and other countries to evolve towards democracy and free market, perhaps even to associate themselves with the European Community.....

The furore is a curious sort of testament to Kissinger. Twelve years out of office, he still commands immense authority....' End quote.

Note the date of the 'Time' article. Within 3 months of this being published, Bush acted. Interesting isn't it?

Postscript. 'Press', 19th July 1989.

'The United States' President, George Bush, who began his 10 day trip to Europe with a call to re-unite the continent ended his journey insisting the 'new world' he seeks poses no threat to the Soviet Union.

.....'Our hope is that the unnatural division of Europe will now come to an end — that the Europe behind the Wall will join its neighbours to the West, prosperous and free', he said....'The new world we seek is shaped by an idea — an idea of universal appeal and undeniable force, and that idea is DEMOCRACY...' End quote. (Emphasis added.)

If Mr Bush is sincere in making this statement, I suggest that he will be doomed to disappointment.

Democracy is all over.

A world leader, a dictator called Antichrist awaits in the wings.

President George Bush, along with many other politicians in the world today, has good intentions and possibly, does not understand the end result of this "New World Order" that he is introducing. We do not attack the man, but only reveal the plan.

U.S. and Middle East

A top P.L.O. official has stated 'He (Bush) is the President who will solve the Middle East problem.....' End quote.

I agree, yet feel it is important to watch for the role Dr Henry Kissinger will play in these negotiations.

Remember:

We are watching for a 'Jewish' man to 'confirm' a seven year peace treaty.

The Presidents and Christianity
Ronald Reagan claimed to be a committed Christian with a great interest in Biblical prophecy.

George Bush, his successor, is associated with the Episcopalian church along with his wife Barbara, a very charming lady.

Dr Henry Kissinger and Key Trilateralists
The Trilateral Commission list as of March 15 1988, lists Dr Kissinger as one of its members, along with other interesting names.

Zbigniew Brzezinski — Senior Advisor, Georgetown University, Centre for Strategic and International Studies....
Frank C. Carlucci — Former U.S. Deputy Secretary of Defence
Alan Greenspan — (now working with the Federal Reserve)
Alexander Haig — Former U.S. Secretary of State
Robert McNamara — Former President of the World Bank
David Rockefeller — (job not stated)

As I turn the page on this manuscript, I take note that on the European members' list, one name is outstanding.

Baron Edmond de Rothschild — Chairman, Compagnie Financiere Holding, Paris.

Prior to 1990, we note that:

a. Dr Kissinger was in New Zealand — the World Government test country, for a brief visit (did this include the Inland Revenue Dept?) in the latter part of 1988. One early morning radio programme mentioned his arrival.

b. The Canadian papers note he is coming out of mothballs to help in solving the Middle East crisis.

c. He, himself, has stated a 5-7 year period for peace in that area is envisaged.

d. Away back in 1984, President Reagan named this man as a member of his Foreign Intelligence Advisory Board. New Zealand 'Herald', 6th March 1984.

e. He no longer feels that U.S. can be viewed as the world's policeman. 'Australian', 23rd November 1987. '....Oddly enough, as American resources are shrinking, the drive towards global intervention seems to be increasing....' End quote.

f. The above statement reinforces his long held 'global concept' for the world.

226

g. In 1983, a man called Seymour Hersh, published a book revealing many secrets of Kissinger's deeds and policies, many of them apparently damaging to his reputation.

Such was his image, however, that the criticisms never really took off. A writer for the London 'Observer' reported in the 'Press', 2nd November 1983, says 'I had been surprised that despite earlier revelations, now crowned by the Hersh indictment — which nobody has attempted to refute, certainly not Kissinger — the Kissinger reputation on both sides of the Atlantic still remained so high.

.....Hersh had found in his first few days in Britain, that almost everyone he talked to still took Kissinger's foreign policy efforts at Kissinger's high evaluation of them.

He instanced Vietnam. 'Henry has convinced everyone that he personally ended the Vietnam war. But the war ended when the other guys won.' It ended with the United States ambassador escaping by helicopter from the roof of the United States embassy, as the North Vietnamese were invading Saigon....' End quote. Peace in Vietnam? Really?

'And through his policy also, he shall cause 'craft' to prosper in his hand, and he shall magnify himself in his heart and by 'peace' shall destroy many; he shall also stand up against the Prince of princes but he shall be broken without hand.' *Ref.2.

In this ancient prophecy regarding a future world leader who will arise in the latter days, a number of words stand out as clues to this man's identity.

1. 'Craft' has nothing to do with the assisting of arts and crafts to prosper.

I checked the original Hebrew word out and find that the word has more to do with 'crafty or clever advice' i.e. in speaking to converse, to consult, by implication, to aid.

At the time of writing, that is exactly what Dr Kissinger is doing. He runs a business called 'Kissinger Associates' that advises, through consultation, governments, business conglomerates or even individuals who pay very large sums for this advice.

Foreign policy and economy is his forte.

2. 'Peace' as we may have seen, this man was hailed as a peace maker when there was no peace.

3. 'Force' — Jewish born Henry Kissinger says 'Israel should put down the Palestinian revolt quickly, brutally, and rapidly....' End quote. 'Financial Review', 7 March 1988.

In a biography written about Dr Kissinger years ago, the biographer made a very interesting observation. He said that although people did not generally understand everything Henry Kissinger was saying, and sometimes didn't know whether to believe all they heard, his voice and speech were so compelling, 'they wanted to make his words their own.'

The ancient prophet writing in the 6th century B.C. put it like this, referring to this great future world leader.

'He shall come in 'peaceably' and obtain the kingdom by 'flatteries'.' *Ref.3.

There is growing evidence to suggest that human beings are often quite adept at distorting or changing their facial expressions in order to mislead others about their true emotional states.

We talk about the Orientals being 'inscrutable'. Nothing is given away by the body language.

I remember as a schoolboy, preparing to receive my regular dose of the cane on the most suitable portion of the anatomy to receive such treatment.

Upon hearing of my sentence, I would hasten to the locker room, and under my school trousers, put on two extra pairs of shorts.

Later, whilst receiving the cane, I could barely feel any discomfort at all through the material. In order not to give the show away however, my piteous moans and writhings were very convincing and as for my contorted features, why, they were enough to break the most stony heart.

Diplomats, attorneys, physicians, salespersons and 99.9% of politicians all find that FACIAL DECEIT is a help in their work.

As Dr Kissinger speaks over television next time, watch his expression and listen to the modulation of his voice with his pronounced German accent. He is very proficient in public relations exercises.

An article in the 'Press', 4th August 1983, has some interesting information about this man. Quote - '.....reviled by his detractors as the reincarnation of both Mephistopheles and Machiavelli, while lauded by his fans as a Metternich, one of the world's truly great statesmen.....' End quote.

Whichever of these two he really is doesn't concern us, for in writing this treatise, we await a brilliant Jewish man who will some day soon, put his personal rubber stamp on a 7 year Middle East peace treaty.

'And he shall confirm the covenant with many for one week....'
*Ref.4.

This word 'week' is a Hebrew thought standing for a period of seven years.

'Press', 30th January 1989. 'Kissinger says Moscow can Work with Bush.'

Obviously the U.S.A. and the Soviet Union will be involved. We await the MAN HIMSELF. Who is he?

Does Prophecy Mention The United States of America?

Some ask me 'Is this country mentioned in the ancient prophecies?'

Some writers say it is but I can't find it myself. Here is a strange enigma. The world's greatest power, home to the poor and the oppressed, land of opportunity not mentioned. Why?

Some time ago, the U.S.A. celebrated their bicentenary. 200 years of nationhood. Populated with people from all over the world, it has boasted some of the greatest talent in every field.

Trojan Horse

The enemy within. Even as far back as the year 1776, the world has in the main been oblivious of the fact that an ancient evil power of manipulation has been organising events to bring us to this day.

In Los Angeles today, there stands an edifice dedicated to all that is evil. The church of Satan.

On the one dollar bill of the U.S.A. we see on the reverse side the words 'In God We Trust.' And then, just along from these words, the pyramid with the eye, or the Seal of the Illuminati.

As I have pointed out before, there is no reverse side to the actual stamp of the Great Seal of America. On the reverse side of the seal is the handle that one uses to hold it.

Seeming inconsistencies? Yes.

The capital city of Washington D.C. built on a reclaimed swamp. Why go to all that bother when they could have built it elsewhere?

It has been discovered that there is a pulsating energy grid surrounding the earth, and throughout the centuries, certain people have found the secret of tapping into this grid and picking up the energy e.g. Ancient Incas built their cities this way;

229

Stonehenge is another example; on Easter Island, the giant statues were moved by this power; in Egypt, the Pyramids; U.F.O.'s from the U.S. use this energy even today.

All these, and many others bare silent witness to the fact that we, the average people, have a great deal hidden from us.

Also, connected with this energy grid system is a natural communications network, placed there by the hands of a benevolent creator, the God of the universe.

This system is built on a series of harmonic vibrations. For example, Greenwich in Great Britain was not put just anywhere. It is exactly in the right spot mathematically speaking, to act as a centre stage for the time systems of the world.

Washington D.C. is another case in point. Built in exactly the right position for a harmonic communications network.

I regret that there will be readers of this book who will say that there is no such being as satan. This is not due to unbelief in matters spiritual, but merely a lack of knowledge in this particular area.

We turn to the book specialising in these matters and read that this being was originally called Lucifer and was thrown out of heaven with one third of the angels who rebelled with him.

'How art thou fallen from heaven, oh Lucifer, son of the morning....' *Ref.5.

Upon reaching the earth, he took the place over; and is now called 'The god of this world' and controls all who have not yielded or submitted to the true and living God, through His Son, the Lord Jesus Christ.

'But if our gospel be hid, it is hid to them that are lost, in whom the god of this world hath blinded the minds of them which believe not.....' *Ref.6. Why?

'Lest the light of the glorious gospel of Christ who is the image of God, should shine unto them.' *Ref.7.

Down through the generations of Americans, working quietly and surreptitiously in the background have been these individuals, many of them from European stock, who secretly have fraternised with Lucifer.

Many men connected with the politics of America have had connections with secret societies down through the years, such as Freemasonry and other secret groups.

Masonry, a Religion

Pike, this highly exalted Grand Pontiff wrote a book concerning

230

the first 32nd degree called 'Morals and Dogma' which was not intended for the world at large.

1. This book states 'every Masonic Lodge is a temple of religion and its teachings are instruction in religion.'
2. He later tells us what is the object of freesmason's worship. It is 'reason'. 'Reason is the absolute for in it, we must trust.'
3. His aim is outlined. 'Human reason leaps into the throne of God and waves her torch over the ruins of the universe.'
4. He laughed at Christianity. 'The teachers even of Christianity are in general, the most ignorant of the true meaning of that which they teach.'
5. '...Jesus of Nazareth was but a man like us....'
6. 'Self....the true ruler of the universe.'

The 'object' of Masonic worship according to Pike was Lucifer. 'Lucifer, the Light Bearer. Lucifer, the Son of the Morning. It is he who bears the Light....'

The goal of the Freemasons is to rule the world.

To become, according to Pike, 'rulers over the masters of the world.'

If you are a Freemason and didn't know all this, don't be surprised. Neither do 99.9% of other masons.

What to do.

Please read carefully the two chapters on this subject in my book 'Second Warning' and get ready to leave this 'Luciferian Organisation'. (See pages 87-100 in 'Second Warning'.)

There is nothing Christian about Freemasonry.

Back to America

Many of the founding fathers of the United States were Freemasons.

In 1731, Benjamin Franklin joined as did John Adams, Thomas Jefferson and later, Franklin Delano Roosevelt (32nd degree mason.)

It was Roosevelt who had the Illuminati World Government seal placed on the reverse side of the U.S. $1.00 bill in the year 1933 as America was climbing out of the 1929 stock market crash.

Now we see an outline emerging.

Benjamin Franklin, U.S.A.

Adam Weishaupt, Bavaria.

Weishaupt through his friend Baron Von Krigge, infiltrated the Masonic Lodges in 1778, bringing in the Luciferian influence.

231

Links

Jefferson was appointed U.S. Ambassador to France in 1784. In 1789 he returned to the U.S. and became Secretary of State. In that same year, the U.S. Consitution was accepted, as was the Great Seal, including the pyramid and eye in the triangle.

Thus the U.S.A. became thoroughly infected with Weishaupt's brand of Luciferianism.

Statement. Whilst in Europe, Jefferson became acquainted with Weishaupt, the man who designed for him, this demonic seal.

Remember the words 'ANNUIT COEPTIS' which has been variously translated 'Agreement with that which has been started' and 'NOVUS ORDO SECLORUM' — 'New World Order' or 'New Secular Order' or 'One World Government'.

What a strange set of words to have written on a U.S. $1.00 bill.

Bad Times Ahead for the U.S.A

Acquaintances of mine who speak on similar subjects believe that the U.S. is mentioned in the prophecies of Revelation under the heading 'Babylon' — The nations will weep as the U.S. goes under.

The prophecies list products of trade etc e.g. 'And merchants of these things which were made rich by her, shall stand afar off for fear of her torment, weeping and wailing....and cried when they saw the smoke of her burning, saying, what city is like unto this great city....for in one hour is she made desolate.....' *Ref.8.

I agree that possibly this is the future of much of the U.S.A., but I am not fully convinced of this as it appears to have religious conotations.

Who needs enemies with leaders such as these involved in Luciferianism?

What hope does the U.S. have with the masses worshipping the true and living God and its leaders worshipping Lucifer.

Visions Past and Present

As there appears to be doubtful prophetic insight into the future of the U.S.A., we are driven back to the visions of respected persons.

a. George Washington — Valley Forge

In his tent one day, Washington was in prayer seeking to know the divine will for the future of this country, when a series of four visions were revealed to him.

An angelic being came into his tent, pulled back a mystical veil and said 'Son of the Republic, look and learn.'

Vision a. There he saw a dreadful war with colonists battling the forces of Great Britain in the War of Independence.

'Son of the Republic, look and learn.'

Vision b. Brother fought brother, amidst blood, sweat, screams and moans of dying men. The American Civil War.

'Son of the Republic, look and learn.'

Vision c. A red fog rolled right across the U.S. Potholes and devastation appeared in every direction.

'Son of the Republic, look and learn.'

Vision d. Amidst the smoke and debris, the U.S. flag 'Old Glory' flew again, showing that although the U.S. would be devastated, it would rise again from the ashes in a greatly weakened form.

Others have seen similar visions, many of them being servants of God.

The latest of these is David Wilkerson who forecasts a sneak Soviet attack on the U.S.A. which will come from over the Polar Cap to the north. In his book 'Set the Trumpet to Thy Mouth', all this is clearly outlined.

Writing this type of information is not very popular I find, but if it is truly from the Lord, it makes sense.

The apparent enemy without, for years is supposed to have been Soviet communism. This we have now proved to be a partial fallacy.

The real enemy is within. A group of traitors who are selling their country to Lucifer.

The Illuminati in the U.S.A.

There were 7 main aims behind Weishaupt's Illuminati.

1. Abolition of monarchy and all ordered government.
2. Abolition of private property.
3. Abolition of inheritance.
4. Abolition of patriotism (nationalism).
5. Abolition of family (i.e. marriage and all morality and the institution of communal education of children).
6. Abolition of all religion.
7. To make Lucifer, God.

North Americans will prove to be the toughest group in the world to subvert. Most of them fiercely love America, which is quite understandable.

1. In the U.S., the monarchy has gone. Ordered government is next.
2. The 'Time' Magazine, 14th September 1987, displayed on their cover the following title 'THE SELLING OF AMERICA — Foreign Investors Buy, Buy, Buy.' Inside the article reads in part — quote '....The searchers are Japanese and British Canadian and South Korean, West German and Swiss and all of them have only one thought in mind — Buy! Buy! Buy! They are in search not only of factories but also of skyscrapers, shopping malls, farms and forest land, ski resorts and vineyards, refineries and mineral deposits......

Suddenly the U.S. seems to have become a huge shopping mart in which foreigners are energetically filling up their carts. Result: foreign ownership in the U.S. including everything from real estate to securities, rose to a remarkable $1.33 trillion in 1986, up 25% from the previous year.

.....By the end of this century (2000) the U.S. may have the most modern manufacturing sector in the world, but it won't own it....

America has been selling off its family jewels to pay for a night on the town and we don't know enough about the proud new owners.

....Says a Japanese banker in Tokyo 'we are amazed at the way Americans are willing to sell out their companies. In Japan, owners of companies hold on for life.' End quote.

Japanese Influence in the U.S.

In an earlier chapter we learnt how the W.G.A. are manipulating events to bring about a world monetary collapse.

At the time of writing the yen props up the dollar; but the yen is in the process of being subtly undermined.

Continued quote from the 'Time' Magazine 'Bereft of enough investment opportunities at home to absorb their astonishing pile of savings, the Japanese are hungrily looking abroad for places to park the excess cash.

....Japanese investors own more than half of the twelve major hotels along Waikiki beach.

....in California.....four of the top ten banks are now Japanese owned: California First Bank, Sanwa Bank, Bank of California and Sumitomo Bank of California....' End quote.

Canada Being Bought Out too

A little note from the same article tells us 'Canada has the highest levels of foreign, chiefly U.S. ownership of domestic enterprises, of any major industrial country....' End quote.

Never forget, the U.S.A. and Canada have a similar C.E.R. agreement as Australia and N.Z. and will ultimately work together as one unit, only to be totally swallowed up by the WGA.

Sorry America — you are on the skids also.

Weishaupt may be dead and gone but he is still speaking today in individuals in high office in the U.S.A.

However, it is not all one-sided.

'The Southland Times', 22nd September 1987. Further notes on the U.S.A.

'....What we have done in effect, is a sale of American assets to pay our bills....The cross-ownership reflects the interlocking of national economics.

Europe, U.S. and Japan, we are all becoming Siamese triplets. It's all interconnected....' End quote.

That is exactly the aim of David Rockefeller's Trilateral Commission.

It is clear now, that private property is next on the agenda. Gradualism, remember, now on a world basis.

Years ago, I remember driving an old Samoan chief around the waterfront road from his village to the town of Fagatogo.

I feel he must have felt insecure with my driving habits, for as he was being flung from side to side he murmured one of his very few English phrases 'Simifi (Smith) — slow but sure.' I got the message and quietened it down.

These WGA won't slow down however. They have a target date. '2000'.

Japan Playing Hard to Get

A heading in the New Zealand 'Herald' reads 'Japan Buys the World, but Japan is Not for Sale.'

Wait awhile. They will be.

U.S. Food Stock Manipulation

As we have already read, the U.S. has exported tonnes and tonnes of grain to the U.S.S.R. and elsewhere, for many years now.

Food Control on a World-wide basis is necessary if World Government is to be instituted.

This is happening very strongly in the guinea pig country of New Zealand.

'And when he had opened the third seal, I heard the third beast say, Come and see. And I beheld, and lo a black horse; and he that sat on him had a pair of balances in his hand.

And I heard a voice in the midst of the four beasts say, A measure of wheat for a penny, and three measures of barley for a penny; and see thou hurt not the oil and the wine.' *Ref.9.

Cut in Population of the U.S.

Already, the Aids question has been revealed in this book. According to an influential member of the Club of Rome — quote: '...It is necessary that the United States cut its population by two thirds within the next fifty years.' End quote.

He also pointed out that America would be unable to support the present population of 225 million. With a population of 75 million, it 'could be stably employed in subsistence agriculture and unemployment would be virtually nil....' End quote. (D. Griffen, 'Descent into Slavery', 1980, pp 341-342.)

'And when he had opened the fourth seal, I heard the voice of the fourth beast say, Come and see.

And I looked, and behold a pale horse: and his name that sat on him was Death, and Hell followed with him. And power was given unto them over the fourth part of the earth, to kill with sword, and with hunger, and with death, and with the beasts of the earth.' *Ref.10.

3. Quick and subtle changes in the law will soon make it 'reasonable' to abolish inheritance.
4. Gradually it will cease to be a popular thing to honour the flag, as it may bring thoughts of anti-discrimination from many of America's new owners. Nationalistic conflicts could arise, so these ceremonies will be gradually shed from the American way of life.
5. Family destruction in the U.S. has been engineered very successfully.

Television has taken away any time previously spent in discussion, Bible reading, prayers, family outings etc.

De facto has become the norm in many minds in contrast to marriage.

6. Christianity was undermined some years ago when Madlyn Murray O'Hair had prayer stopped in schools around the country.

With the influx of eastern religions and New Age philosophies, soon it will be brought up by the anti-discrimination people that Christianity is just one of many and will be down-graded by the powers that be.

7. Lucifer run the world. Is it possible?

Yes, but only for a short period.

Believe me, it's not all doom and gloom.

Citizens of America, God is not to be put down.

Don't look for World Government.

Look For a Spiritual Revival

'When the enemy shall come in like a flood, the Spirit of the Lord shall lift up a standard against him.' *Ref.11.

The Federal Reserve

One of the most clever plans in history came into being with the formation of this group.

Initially, this plan used two major planks from the communist Manifesto to destroy the middle classes.

1. An income tax system.
2. A central bank.

One Congressman said that the income tax system was a wrong move for a country that promised liberty. 'It will bring out the spy and the informer', and this it has surely done.

How It Started — A Giant Trick

In 1907, whilst the big-business man, J.P. Morgan was in Europe, it was decided to have a bank scare in America.

Morgan went home and started the rumour that some banks were going insolvent. This was called the '1907 Panic'. Solution - A central bank.

The individual who introduced the legislation for this central bank was the maternal grandfather of Nelson and David Rockefeller, one Nelson Aldrich.

In 1910, Aldrich met J.P. Morgan and eight others and wrote up the legislation.

This group was sworn to secrecy as they were working outside the Constitution. They used only first names to avoid detection.

Note. THE LEGISLATION FOR THE FEDERAL RESERVE WAS NOT WRITTEN BY GOVERNMENT LEGISLATORS BUT IT WAS DONE SECRETLY BY PRIVATE BANKERS.

They avoided the words 'central bank' and called it the Federal Reserve System.

The Federal Reserve Act was signed in 1913 by Woodrow Wilson, who agreed before his election that he would do so.

The bill he signed promised to foster '....:.orderly economic growth....', which is exactly what it has not done, yet this system continues on and on.

Years ago, Congressman Lindbergh warned that if the bill were passed, it would 'establish the most gigantic trust on earth' and that is what it is, even today — a private trust.

Inflation and depressions can now be scientifically created by this privately owned, privately operated group.

a. Member banks own all the stock.

b. It pays postage as it is not a government department.

c. Its employers are not civil service workers.

d. It spends whatever it wishes to.

e. Its property, held under private deeds is subject to taxation.

The U.S. Presidents know all this, but the majority of Americans don't.

Many bankers found out about all this and withdrew their banks from the system, thus weakening 'the Fed.' This could not be allowed to continue so the Congress of the U.S. passed a bill called The Monetary Control Act, 1980.

This put the Fed. in control of all institutions in the U.S. where money could be deposited. Economic cycles can again be created. Is 1990 the one chosen, as Ravi Batra has suggested in his book 'The Great Depression of 1990'?

Now through this private group, in league with the secret WGA, these people can create a depression or bring about inflation, fiddle with interest rates, drive people off their properties etc, etc, and the lawful U.S. Government stands, hands in pocket, whistling a merry tune.

Audit of the Fed.

One Congressman suggested that the Fed. receive a full audit but this idea was squashed in 1974 when he was removed from his job.

'He was too old', they said.

What a Scandal

'Can we establish all this?', you ask.

Please take a U.S. banknote and turn it face side up.

On the top of this note should be written the words 'United States Note', whose official government should be responsible for the issuing of all currency.

However, you will be struggling hard to find those words now. A bank manager friend of the author has looked at literally thousands of U.S. notes and every time the same words appear, 'Federal Reserve Note'.

Challenge — How many of the old ones can you find?

O.P.E.C.

In my first book 'Warning' written in 1980, on page 88, I quoted from a newspaper article which asked the question, 'Why is it that the OPEC countries insist on being paid for their oil in American dollars? No-one knows.....' End quote.

This is an explanation in very simple English. There are five groups of players.

1. Petrol and oil buyers.	2. O.P.E.C.
3. World Govt. Advocates.	
4. Holding Banks	5. 3rd World Countries

Please familiarise yourself with these five groups.

Do you remember buying very cheap petrol? I do. I remember my Dad, who was a commercial traveller taking me around the South Island of New Zealand in his car.

Often times when he would fill his petrol tank, the store-keeper would come out, go to the old bowser with two bottles on top covered with wire mesh. The operator would manually pump the fuel by hand into the two bottles which would then gravity feed into the car's petrol tank.

Then the new pumps came along dispensing gallons, leading on to the latest units that along with Europe and much of the world, have gone metric.

Prices went up and up with the buyers (stage 1) throwing up their hands in horror.

Why?

Methods for Destroying World Economy

In the 1970's, the World Government people (stage 3) went to the OPEC people (stage 2) and offered to assist them financially if they agreed with the terms which were:

a. Double the price of light crude oil, upon which all oil prices are based. A monetary reward assisted OPEC to agree.
b. Any capital raised from their oil from then on would be put from the OPEC sales (stage 2) into the World Government Holding Banks (stage 4).
c. The truly cunning part was this:
    1. All oil would be paid for in U.S. dollars, thus getting rid of the constant exchange rate problem.
    2. All capital derived from oil or petrol etc. would go

immediately into these Holding Banks (stage 4) where it would be held on 30 year deposits i.e. it could not be drawn out until about the year '2000'.
3. The Arab, OPEC people would live on the interest. OPEC agreed to this and for 30 odd years have done very nicely, living on the Petrodollars interest.

   d. Here is the dirty side of the story. The Holding Banks (stage 4) were created by the World Government people (stage 3) to take the blame off them, when the OPEC people got wise to what was going on.

   e. In the meantime, the young men with their suitcases packed full of money that, I spoke about earlier, took this vast fortune and literally gave it away in the form of loans which they knew could never be repaid.

   f. As a result, it is all gone and the OPEC people have just found out. There is little they can do as the World Government people continue with their plan to bankrupt the Arabs.

   g. The ex-OPEC petrodollars were loaned out using fractionalised banking.

This means that when the bank lends out money using this method, it makes a tremendous profit.

Let me explain using the U.S. dollar as an example.

Man A borrows $1000 U.S. from the bank and uses it.

The bank however, collects a 5% surcharge on this money and pays it to the Federal Reserve.

The money changes hands and is rebanked by say Man B.

This money can now be lent out again to Man C who uses it.

The bank of course has taken out its 5% and paid it to the Fed.

The original $1000 at the end of its journey, in and out of the bank, will have earned for the bank at least $21,000 out of nothing. Easy money?

Yes and watch what happened.

   h. OPEC are justly and righteously angry and are now separating their oil sales from the U.S. dollar.

'Australian', 17th March 1988.

'OPEC is committed by a ministerial decision to investigate breaking the link between the world oil price and the dollar....OPEC has considered the dollar as still too dominant an element.

The plan believed to be under consideration by economic advisors

241

is that customer countries will be billed directly in their own currencies....' End quote.

Poor Arabs. They too have been taken for a ride by a group of crooks dressed in pin-stripe suits.

Things have never changed. It is still written 'The heart of man is deceitful above all things and desperately wicked.' *Ref.12.

The Secret Power

For years I had known the Federal Reserve of the U.S. was a private group posing in the main as the official government economic agency.

The groups I will now describe however, are so powerful that they make the Fed. look like the office boy or chief blotting paper-changer.

G10 and G7

I refer to the Bank for International Settlements, including G.10 and G.7.

You the reader, are subject to highly secret information as we inform you of the activities of these men.

Every month of the year, except in August and October, a very small group of immaculately dressed men arrive in Basle, Switzerland. (Basle situated on the Rhine River borders also on the south of Germany and the west of France.) When they meet they become the most powerful club in the world.

In 1983, 4th December, the 'Sun Herald' in Sydney printed some information which proved to be very helpful.

G.10. — the initials stand for Group of 10 although 11 members normally meet.

1. Britain	7. Holland
2. Germany	8. Japan
3. Italy	9. Switzerland
4. France	10. Canada
5. Belgium	11. U.S.A.
6. Sweden	12. Saudi Arabia's unoffical member

These gentlemen receive $100,000 each every year and are not bound by the law of Switzerland. Imagine belonging to such a system — no law, no taxes.

This group controls most of the transferable money in the world. Under this group is a smaller club called 'Monetary and Economic Development Department', a private think tank for the larger group.

There is so much money at their disposal that it is estimated to be one-tenth of the world's available foreign exchange $40 billion.

The main rule is that central banks should be able to work independently of their home governments e.g.

In 1984 — Swiss National Bank, privately owned.
— Bundesbank Germany, does not have to consult with government.
— Federal Reserve, private, but keeps in touch with Congress and the White House.
— Japanese Bank holds autonomy.
— Italy, largely left alone by the government.
— Bank of England, tried to stay beyond government control.
— Bank of France, seen as a puppet of the government.

Other banks represented at these meetings are under too much government control and the delegates are seen as outsiders.

These men are so powerful that when the I.M.F. wish to borrow from them, the I.M.F. come 'cap in hand'.

G.7.

Now we are getting to the central power group.

'Sun Herald', 4th December 1983.

'The object of the inner club is the worship of money in all its naked purity, untainted by political considerations....' End quote.

Purpose of the Group (B.I.S.) Bank of International Settlements.

'Australian', 9th January 1984.

'....And the unabashed purpose of its elite, monthly meetings is to co-ordinate and if possible, to control all monetary activities in the industrialised world.

....Originally the central bankers sought complete anonymity for their activities. Their activities were in an abandoned six-storey hotel...with an annexe above the adjacent Frey's Chocolate shop....' End quote.

(This is where the clue on World Government comes in.)

Continue quote: 'It was in the wood-panelled rooms above the shop and the hotel where decisions were reached to—

a. devalue or defend currencies

b. to fix the price of gold

c. to regulate off-shore banking

d. to raise or lower short term interest rates....' End quote.

Have you ever wondered how these rates go up and down? Day by day, the notice boards in the bank change showing all these ups and downs. Will you still blame your own government? In the light of the above information, national governments become willing and necessary pawns in the game. If they go along with the plan, they are tolerated. If they buck or kick up a fuss, out they go. Quite a precarious job, you will agree.

With reference to the third world debt, Christchurch 'Press', 4th April 1989, 'G7 cannot agree on third world debt....' End quote.

In Australia, one of the test cases for World Government, not only does its Treasurer know about G7, he wants Australia to join it.

'Sydney Morning Herald', 18th May 1989.

'The Treasurer......wants Australia to join the big league of economic nations known as the Group of Seven (G7).

....Mr.....said Australia did not want to 'muck around with the Belgians and the Dutch and the Swedes' in what he described as the 'mushroom club' known as the G10.

The countries in the G7 are the west's major industrialised economies, the United States, the United Kingdom, West Germany, Japan, France, Italy and Canada.

....Asked how he felt about Australia not being allowed into the G10, Mr.....said, 'Well we don't want to bother with it now. WE WANT TO GET INTO THE G7.' End quote. (Emphasis added.)

The Crunch Line

Continue quote from 'Australian', 9th January 1984: 'And though they shaped a 'New World Economic Order' through these deliberations (as Guido Cardi, then the governor of the Italian central bank, put it) the public even in Basle remained almost totally unaware of the club (B.I.S.) and its activities.' End quote.

If the local people don't know about this group, that is why you have never heard of it before either.

It is there. Don't argue. Even New Zealand's ex-Prime Minister knows about its existence.

New Zealanders, in the main were quite surprised when Sir Robert Muldoon lost his leadership role in the mid 1980's and did not apparently seek to regain that position of power.

He moved on to far more important Global Economic matters, and no doubt, was thrilled that his party was not in power when the directions came from overseas to destroy New Zealand. (This directive would be cloaked in slightly more delicate terms.)

At the time of writing, it would appear that the political parties, normally numbering two, both have their jobs to do.

Party no.1–Absolutely destroy, rape and strip a country of its assets and security, thus committing political suicide.

Party no.2–The electorate votes this group in later for the mopping up process, as both nos. 1 and 2 are ruled from overseas.

That is the gist of it in simple English. Sorry!

Mr Muldoon Speaks About G.7. New Zealand 'Sunday Star', 27th January 1987.

Mr Muldoon in the article spoke of 45 representatives from different countries meeting in Rome. Quote: '...to see what we could do to mobilise public opinion in our various spheres of influence to give political support to the difficult decisions that have to be taken BY THE GOVERNMENTS OF THE G7 to implement the policies that are seen to be necessary.

....What we may well have now is the next best alternative, that is to say a meeting of the seven most powerful members of that committee, which three times a year will co-ordinate the economic policies of those governments. If the rest of the world can follow those moves, and I am sure they can, we may well avert the economic disaster which has been in prospect now for a number of years....' End quote. (Emphasis added.)

Look at this for a statement, which thoroughly proves my point.

Continue quote: '...The G7 proposal INVOLVES SOME LOSS OF SOVEREIGNTY by the participants and that is where the political difficulty arises. If the public or more correctly, the electorate of those countries can be persuaded that the RESULT OF THAT LOSS OF SOVEREIGNTY is higher standards of living for ALL THE PEOPLE OF THE WORLD, the political difficulty will be overcome....' End quote. (Emphasis added.)

CHAPTER 38

Computerisation Equals Bondage

To this point, it is now clear that certain power groups run our lives, in many cases, from afar.

Some readers say, 'I wish I had never read this book', to which statement I reply, 'too late'.

On the 107th floor of the New York Trade Centre in Lower Manhatten, near the commodities exchange, written on the wall is a message in big white letters.

'Soon Gold Will Become Primitive Money.

Wallets will soon be obsolete. Electronic money transactions will occur at the speed of the computer's pulse. In place of cash and cheques, your personal I.D. number will be entered into a computerised bookkeeping system which will instantly record your purchase. You will not have to touch a single piece of paper.' End quote.

Computer Developments

'Pioneer Dies. John Brainerd, an engineer who headed the war time team that designed the world's first electronic computer has died at the age of 83....the huge computer weighed 30 tonnes and contained more than 18,000 vacuum tubes...'

'Athens News', 2/3 October 1988. 'Applications for Brain-Like Computers Begin to Emerge.

The science-fiction fantasy of a computer that works like a living brain is beginning to emerge as a reality in the United States.

....We are trying to build a brain, and we are trying to build it out of brain-like parts.....

But the system breaks down when a situation occurs for which there is no pre-learned rule, the kinds of situations living brains encounter all the time.

....Applications have been developed to verify signatures and identify heart disease by reading electro-cardiograms....' End quote.

This sounds a lot like genetic engineering, and the frightening part is that in some laboratories, portions of brain tissue is already being used in experiments.

As happened in the days of the first try for World Government,

the tower of Babel, the Lord spoke '....now nothing will be restrained from them, which they have imagined to do. ....So the Lord scattered them abroad.' *Ref.1.
Divine intervention is certainly on the agenda. Watch for it.

Texas Banks Going Broke
On a visit to New Mexico in 1988, we were attending an outdoor country festival in the desert area east of Taos.

I sat alongside a man who told me he was a banker and oil man from Texas, who along with his wife were enjoying their final vacation in New Mexico.

He told me that oil was collapsing, banking was a mess and there seemed to be no light in sight. He was correct. Without the Lord fulfilling our spiritual needs, things really look black.

'Herald', 8th March 1988.

'The problems of Texas banks dominate the skylines of Houston and Dallas. Many of the shining sky scrapers are empty....' End quote.

Plastic Cards Are Here Only For A Season
'Sun Herald', 18th October 1987.

'Australians are going credit card crazy and for a growing number of people the little plastic cards mean only misery, stress and ruin.

....In the past twelve months, the amount owed on the banks credit cards has soared by 15% to $3.5 billion.....' End quote.

It's All Happening Everywhere
Newspaper headlines scream for attention and show us this very definite world-wide trend.

'Australian', 12th July 1988. 'McDonalds joins consumer push with plastic cards.....' End quote.

The 'Albuquerque Tribune', 24th June 1988.

'Before long, New Mexico motorists could be carrying drivers' licenses that look and work like credit cards...' End quote.

A programme from Kuala Lumpur reads like this: 'EFTPOS '85 Malaysia.'

'Financial Review', 8th March 1988. 'Soviets Embrace Plastic Money.....' End quote.

'Business Times', 17th April 1987. 'Hong Kong Plans For A Cashless Society....' End quote.

'Weekend Australian', 3rd December 1988. 'Banks Usher In A Moneyless Millenium.

No longer will you be persecuted by your ATM. Instead it will literally throw money at you. No intricate numbers to forget. ATMs of tomorrow will recognise your voice, your fingerprints and even the retina of your eye.

But cash should be obsolete by then anyway. Merchants will have embraced fully the Electronic Funds Transfer Point of Sale (EFTPOS) system by then....

The banks are making slow progress towards 2000 but all the signs are there.

To improve service, the first task will be to remove all paper from the system according to Westpac's General Manager, retail banking...' End quote.

Bye Bye Tellers

'Press', 31st January 1989.

'The jobs of hundreds of thousands of bank tellers in industrialised countries may depend on whether customers prefer people or machines....' End quote.

They will probably choose the machines because they are a novelty. I have noted that the long queues outside the banks on a wet day are ridiculous. As for me, I'll stick to the good old reliable bank teller. At least it's warm inside the bank.

Nervous? How About Investing in Switzerland?

Things are not as they were. On occasions, the numbered Swiss bank accounts have been opened up to the gaze of investigators. It's only a matter of time and the secrecy will go.

Remember G7 Influence

'Weekend Australian', 19/20 May 1988. 'Swiss to vote on secret account laws...could open bank accounts to tax enquiries, and check the flow of foreign capital seeking a haven in this neutral country....Evidently no firm data is available on how much flight capital is held in Swiss banks.

Got Any Black Money?

The introduction of World Government plans has also brought in much restriction to personal freedoms. Communist and socialist countries of course are the worst in this realm and the backlash is correspondingly greater.

'Press', 25th June 1986.

'Europe's underground economy of untaxed, illegal labour and business activity is thriving....NEWSWEEK International said the so-called black economy accounted for about 10% of Europe's gross national product.

Italy harbours the biggest underground economy in Western Europe with more than 3 million people and accounting for 20% of goods and services in the country....

Six to eight per cent of income in Britain comes from the black economy and in West Germany the estimate is between eight and twelve per cent.....

The phenomenon is even more widespread in Eastern Europe....in Hungary, 70% of the population worked, at least part of the time outside the legal economy....' End quote.

We have already outlined the programme for Europe. The last day of December 1992 will bring about vast changes, not least the cash economy.

I invited some Greek folk to our meetings. When they heard all this explained they were very agitated and at the conclusion of the meeting they said 'We're going back to Europe.'

In other words, things were becoming so restrictive in Australia with computers keeping checks on everything that even CASH DEALS were coming under attack.

Leaving Australia for Europe is not the answer. The true answer is a spiritual one.

See end of book.

The vagaries of finance in this strange period of history are illustrated in what has happened in the island of Nauru — The Phosphate Island.

'Press', 1st July 1987.

'About a dozen Nauruan families discovered recently that they were millionaires.

That was the good news.

The bad news was that they cannot touch any of the money for about eight years.

'They can see but they cannot touch', a Government official said.

....The treasury says they cannot touch the money and then only the interest for about eight years, after the nation's phosphate deposits are expected to be exhausted....' End quote.

Statement — These poor Nauruan families will never receive their millions of dollars. Cash will cancel before the time of restriction is over. That is the good news.

The bad news is that any money that people have at the time of the 'crash' will not be credited to the new system.

Suicide will be rife by those who have not thought clearly about what their lot will be beyond the grave.

My advice is 'Don't ever commit suicide.

Do turn to the Lord in repentance and faith towards the Lord Jesus Christ.

He will give you a new life.

'Therefore, if any man be in Christ, He is a new creature. Old things are passed away, behold all things are become new.' *Ref.2.

CHAPTER 39

The European Community and its Leader

Scene: Te Atatu South, Auckland, New Zealand.
Year: 1969.
Occasion: Having just completed drying the dishes as every good husband does, I was on the phone to the British High Commissioner at his home.
Self: 'Good evening. This is Smith speaking.'
BHC (with a weary voice): 'Yes, Mr Smith.'
Self: 'I would like to ask you about the E.E.C....'

......and so I was underway in my search for information on all these subjects.

This gentleman graciously gave me the information I requested and at the conclusion of our little talk, suggested that I call back next time during office hours.

His point was duly understood.

My family have heard me speaking about the European Community for more than 20 years and with further details coming to hand, the stage is now set for some exciting predictions to be fulfilled.

Recap on E.C. History

Firstly, allow me to establish that the predictions we will be referring to were outlined in two Biblical Books, namely,

Daniel — 586 B.C.

Revelation — 96 A.D.

Therefore, it is clear that this author cannot juggle the facts in any way to make these prophets say what they really didn't say.

These two books are open for you, the reader, to check out if you so desire.

In my book 'Warning', written in 1980, please turn to page 10.
Heading: Does the Bible Speak of the E.E.C?
It does, under 4 main headings:
10 Toes.
10 Horns.

10 Crowns.

10 Kings.

Some years after I wrote this first book, I was lecturing in South Western Australia in a small town.

After the meeting, I was verbally attacked by an elderly man who had listened to my message.

He started 'You can't tell me that those 4 refer to the E.C. For a start, you have 10 Kings on your list and I happen to know that some of the European countries are run by Queens.'

I answered: 'Wait a moment. You don't think these prophecies literally refer to 10 Toes, do you?'

'No'.

'10 Horns?'

'No'.

'10 Crowns?'

'No'.

'Then there is no reason to believe that there will be literally 10 Kings. It will simply be a federation of ten nations connected in some way to Rome.

The prophet gave us a very significant pointer.

Details on the E.C. Including its Future

1. The 10 will come out of the 4th prophetic empire which was Rome. N.B. The official title of the document on which the E.C. is based is 'The Treaty of Rome', signed on the 25th March 1957.

Quite a good guess, you say. Wait. That is only detail number one.

2. The E.C. which to this point has been guided and led by:
   a. A Council of Ministers
   b. A European Parliament, will soon be led by a
   c. One Man Dictatorship.

The titles of this man in the language of the prophets are many, some of which are:

1. Antichrist
2. Beast
3. Man of Sin
4. Son of Perdition (This name was previously applied to Judas Iscariot. The man dies, but the devil that was in him lives on to inhabit another man in our day; 1990-2000.)
5. The Lawless One

252

6. Little Horn

If you have read the books 'Warning' and 'Second Warning' you will be aware of this future leader's characteristics and qualifications. As it is important for you to watch for his ascent to power over the E.C., the new World Monetary System and the signing of the 7 year Middle East Peace Treaty, I will outline these points again without detail as these are all available within the pages of my first two books.

1. He will arise after the 10 nations come together.
2. 3 nations in the European Community will initially reject his leadership but will finally submit and then be expelled by this great leader. (More on this later.)
3. This leader will be chosen from outside the E.C. but will have links to it, possibly by birth.
4. He will be a one man dictator, not a committee.
5. He must be Jewish, yet in a non-religious sense only.
6. A man of boasting arrogance.
7. Outstanding in the art of diplomacy, world economy and false peace treaties.
8. Something unusual about his eyes.
9. Dishonest. Not to be trusted.
10. Good people will still rely on him, despite his devious nature.
11. He will be a party-goer or a swinger.
12. He will be a seasoned traveller.
13. His aim is world domination.
14. He will endeavour to change times and laws.
15. He will cause corruption and destruction.
16. He will control politics — another will control religion.
17. He will be an outwardly peaceful man and a flatterer.
18. Once accepted, an image of this leader will be placed in the 'holy place' in Jerusalem.
19. He will confirm a seven-year peace treaty in the Middle East, and will break it after three and a half years.
20. He will be destroyed by Christ at his public coming at the conclusion of the 7 year period.

Sometime ago, I received a call from New Zealand's Christian radio station 'Radio Rhema' and an interviewer asked me the question, possibly you also are bursting to ask.

'Mr Smith. How was it some years ago, you spoke of 10 nations joining the E.C. but now there are 12?'

To be perfectly frank, I am quite happy that there are 12, but that is not the end of the matter, as I am now watching for number 13 to join up.

'Press', 29th March 1989. 'Europe versus Islam....

Turkey is determined to join the European Community...' End quote.

Whilst on a bus tour in that country in 1988, I asked the local tour guide if Turkey was still pursuing this goal and he replied with a very emphatic 'Yes'.

'Guardian', London, 15th October 1988.

'Indications that Austria will apply for membership of the European Community next year is highlighting concern among E.C. governments....

Following indications from Malta and Cyprus that they are considering membership applications.

....Austrian accession might directly encourage other European neutrals such as Sweden and even Switzerland, to join as well as Cyprus.'

N.B. Events in Eastern Europe may allow East Germany to take 13th position.

Contenders:
Turkey
Austria
Malta
Cyprus
East Germany

On page 18 of my book 'Warning', I drew attention to Article 237 of the E.C.'s rules which state in effect, that:

'Only countries within that specific area of Western Europe are entitled to full membership of the community.'

Associate members number over 20 at time of writing and this of course, is another possibility for the other applicant nations.

At time of writing (end of March 1989) my guess would have to be Austria or East Germany for 13th position but who really knows at this point?

A highly interesting detail, overlooked in the main by others writing on these subjects is that further proof of this new world leader's identity will be established when he expels three nations from E.C. membership.

a. '...He shall subdue 3 kings...
b. '...Before whom 3 fell........'

254

c. '...little horn, before whom, there were three of the first horns plucked up by the roots.....' *Ref.1.

This prediction is so important that it is given to us three times in one passage alone.

When I was in the school-teaching business, I regularly updated my teaching colleagues on these matters, whilst we relaxed over a cup of coffee after school.

Some listened, whilst some laughed.

To those who laughed, and I say the same to any sceptic reading this book, 'When these things begin to happen, seek God with all your heart.'

1992 The Big Year

Has it occurred to you that December 31st 1992 is the beginning of the end for this world system as it exists today.

The changes will be radical in every country as evidenced in the guinea pig nations of Australia and New Zealand.

I sincerely believe that this book and others like it are ordained by the Lord to appear at this time in history to act as a warning.

Please take heed.

255

CHAPTER 40

The Future of the E.C. Prophesied

1. Once the leader is identified and the market has 10 nations in membership, I turn to the prophecy dated 96 A.D. to discover what is next on the agenda.
2. The European Community will not exert any real influence on the world trading scene until this new leader takes over.

The reasons for this is that within the market, there are strong and weaker nations described by the prophet as either iron or clay.

Iron = strong nations — G. Britain, W. Germany, France.

Clay = weak nations — Italy, Belgium, Luxembourg, Netherlands, Spain, Portugal, Irish Republic, Denmark, Greece.

A recent article on the E.C. referred to Ireland, Spain, Portugal and Greece as 'four of the poor states.'

'...And as the toes of the feet were part of iron and part of clay, so the kingdom shall be partly strong and partly broken (weak)....' *Ref.1.

A fascinating detail must be inserted here. This great world leader, who will shortly run the leadership of the E.C. will not spend too much time on the strong iron nations, but will concentrate his attention on the weaker clay nations. Remember, he will rule with an iron hand and take over control in areas where he has no right. The other nations, affected by his policies will begin to complain, softly at first, and later on, very vocally.

'....Shall not all these take up a parable against him and a taunting proverb against him and say woe to him that increaseth that which is not his. How long? and to him that ladeth himself with thick clay...' *Ref.2. (The word 'ladeth' in Hebrew means 'to be heavy' in a bad sense.)

3. These weaker nations will bog him down in his plans.
4. They will finally become so angry with him (as many Australasians have with their politicians) that they will rebel against his leadership.

'....Shall they not rise up suddenly that shall bite thee, and awake that shall vex thee, and thou shalt be for booties unto them.' *Ref.3. (The word 'booties' in Hebrew means plunder, spoil and rob.)

This looks like violent confrontation. All will not go his way. His dishonesty and arrogance will catch up with him.

4. A number of world empires have existed over the years, which have all collapsed at the end of their allotted span:
Chaldees — Assyria
Egypt
Babylon
Medo-Persia
Greece
Rome

(E.C.) The European Community will be the last system for man to rule over.

This is definite. No argument. Nothing to discuss.

N.B. The next ruler after Antichrist will be THE LORD JESUS CHRIST.

The E.C. will collapse also after a very brief period with their leader in control.

'....And the ten horns which thou sawest are ten kings which have received no kingdom as yet, but receive power as kings ONE HOUR WITH THE BEAST....' *Ref.4. (Emphasis added.)

(Power in Greek has to do with the word 'treasurer'. This connotation tells us that the E.C. will control trade and economy for a very brief period.)

6. The 10 nations of the E.C. will unite to let the new world leader make all their decisions for them.

'....These have one mind and shall give their power and strength unto the beast....' *Ref.5.

7. At the time of writing, this is the last thing that would appear to be possible. The E.C. is a mess. They do not work together and neither will or can until this new leader is revealed.

'....And whereas thou sawest the iron mixed with miry clay, they shall mingle themselves with the seed of men, but they shall not cleave one to another, even as iron is not mixed with clay.' *Ref.6.

What then makes the difference?

DIVINE INTERVENTION

'.....For God hath put it in their hearts to fulfill his will and to agree and give their kingdom unto the beast, until the words of God should be fulfilled....' *Ref.7.

8. The nerve of this guy. Australians will understand the phrase 'He has more cheek than Ned Kelly' who (for the uninitiated), was an audacious Australian bushranger.

Politics and Religion Link

This great new world leader will get so carried away with his political power that he will move out of his depth into the field of religion.

This he should never do, as it will lead to his downfall.

I say this to any others who read this book with a mocking attitude. Almighty God has plenty of time on His hands.

He says—'I'll catch you later', to use a colloquialism.

In spite of his Jewish heritage:

'And the king shall do according to his will, and he shall exalt himself, and magnify himself above every god, and shall speak marvelous things against the God of gods....' *Ref.8.

9. The European Community, along with their new world leader, then get together to attack the Lord Himself; no doubt initially through bringing in restrictive laws on all true born-again believers in the Lord Jesus Christ.

10. Christ and His people will ultimately defeat the system that has been imposed on them from this man and his policies.

'....and the Lamb shall overcome them for his is Lord of lords and King of kings....' *Ref.9. (Jesus is the Lamb.)

11. Time will be so short that this great world leader will not have sufficient time to implement his world government system over every nation on earth before the Lord Jesus Christ Himself will put a stop to his grandiose ideas.

This man called Antichrist will only control a quarter of the earth before he comes to his end.

'And I looked, and behold a pale horse, and his name that sat on him was Death and Hell followed with him. And power was given unto them OVER THE FOURTH PART OF THE EARTH,

to kill with sword, (probably the French guillotine),

and with hunger, (no mark—no buying and selling),

and with death, (persecution and finally, wild animals will be used),

and with the beasts of the earth.' (Emphasis and words in brackets added for clarity.)

It sure is good to be on the winning side.

Don't miss it. Read what to do at the end of this book.

12. The world leader of the E.C. (beast) and the world leader of the false church (false prophet) will be cast into hell.

'And the beast was taken and with him the false prophet that wrought miracles before him with which he deceived them that had received the mark of the beast and them that worshipped his image.

These BOTH were cast alive into the lake of fire burning with brimstone....' *Ref.10. Emphasis added.

12. It therefore has now become obvious that a Satanic trio or a false trinity will control the world at this time.

    a. Lucifer (Satan) — Boss man

    b. Beast — E.C. leader — political

    c. False Prophet — False world church leader — religious

2 Aspects

This new money system predicted in 96 A.D. and coming into being in the late 1980s has two aspects.

1. The receiving of the mark on the right hand or forehead.

2. The worship of the beast.

GOOD NEWS FOR BELIEVERS IN THE LORD JESUS CHRIST.

Once the E.C. gets started in December 1992, we have learned that it will last one hour with the leader. Now, the prophet says again, referring to the world leader, 'he must continue a short space.' *Ref.11. Not only that, Christ will return to finish their short term of rule. He is likened to a great stone that smashes the E.C. and sets up His own rule for 1000 years initially and then on into eternity.

Are you ready?

Don't play the fool.

Turn to the Lord now.

It will happen exactly as predicted. 'The dream is certain and the interpretation thereof sure...' *Ref.12.

259

CHAPTER 41

Subversion of the Children

'Things are not the same as they were when I was a boy.'
Have you ever heard that statement? Of course you have.

Solomon, the world's wisest man gave good advice when he said 'Train up a child in the way he should go and when he is old, he will not depart from it.' *Ref.1.

As a man who has 15 years teaching experience behind me, it is horrifying to see the terrible hold our 'curriculum organisers' have over the future of our children. These people need to be weeded out of the system and publicly beaten for the wreckage they are causing to millions of lives.

We did a section on 'change'. Apparently one change that really has to be made is to completely destroy every good standard that a child has and do away completely with the hated book the Bible, which includes of course, the laws of God.

On p 79 of my book 'Warning' amongst a lot of other aims of the WGA written up over 200 years ago, we read:

'Education. We have fooled, bemused, and corrupted the youth of the masses, by rearing them in principles and theories, which are known by us to be false, although it is by us they have been inculcated.' End quote.

In New Zealand, to prove the point, all one needs to do is find out who the 'curriculum organisers' are, and find out if they are godly, well-disciplined individuals, loyal to God and the sovereignty of New Zealand, as well as people who wish to promote honourable standards of behaviour and morals in the children. Whichever country you belong to however, you will find these organisers at the helm, so investigate them and possibly prepare for a shock.

Parents read this—The aim today is to change the social values of the child away from the values that are traditionally fixed, permanent or absolute.

Part of the plan, believe it or not, is to get the mother out of the home so that all teaching given comes from either the state or television.

The tool used is INFLATION. This causes the husband's wage

to be insufficient and the suggestion is then made that the mother should supplement the family income by going to work.

What about the children? The government then moves into the picture with an offer of a day-care centre.

Parents who send their children to private schools or Christian schools are a thorn-in-the-flesh to the planners.

No Absolutes

1. Many of these state schools subtly teach atheism, which is the most important step in the child's destruction.
2. No absolute final authority must be also be taught, thus cancelling out life's text book, the Bible.

I ask you — are you happy with these changes in society?

A True Life Story

Years ago, I was attending a Christian camp in New Zealand at a place called Ngaruawahia.

One afternoon, I went to visit the local barber (hairdresser) for a haircut. As was the custom of old-time barbers, they wore a white coat and talked a great deal.

I heard of one man who visited his barber, who asked him 'And how would you like it done sir?'

The man answered 'Quietly, please.'

Back to my story: The barber engaged me in conversation.

'Are you a Bible-banger from across the river?'

Self: 'Yes.'

Barber: 'I have no time for God or the Bible and get along quite well without all that.'

Self: 'What system of rules do you live under?'

Barber: 'What is good for me may not be good for you and vice versa. Everybody should make up their own rules.'

Self: 'It wouldn't be a safe system on the roads if the government adopted it, would it? Everybody would drive how and where they wanted to.'

Barber: 'Oh, you are being silly.'

He finished trimming my hair, took off the white sheet, brushed me down and I paid him the money.

I then went to the inside of his shop window, removed the pipes, tobacco, shaving soap and brushes; put them down my shirt and then before his horrified gaze, walked out of his shop and down the road.

A few seconds later, he ran out onto the street. I can still see him, even now. His white coat, his glazed look and strained voice shouting 'Hey, what do you think you are doing?'

I answered 'This may not be good for you, but it is for me.'

I had made my point well. His argument was demolished and being a committed Christian, I replaced his gear in the windows, explaining at the same time, that under his rules, this would not be necessary.

With this new curriculum and lax rules, are the children happier, and is the country reaping any benefits? Let's look at the results shall we.

'Press', 28th November 1988.

'Youth suicide numbers this year are likely to be 40% up on last year's figures', said the co-ordinator of the Youth Mental Health Project....' End quote.

It is true that insecurity leads to mental problems in many cases.

'Dominion', 2nd November 1988.

'Mental disorders are the cause of much time spend in hospital by 15-24 year olds, according to the Medical Journal....' End quote.

As a former school teacher, I am not guessing when I say, the failure in Education today isn't that the classes are too big, the staff are underpaid, or the hours are too long; The problem is NOT ENOUGH DISCIPLINE.

A group of non-teaching know-alls in their ignorance, have removed discipline from the class-rooms.

As a young teacher who taught in the Pacific Islands and in New Zealand, I learnt a great deal on child management.

In the island of Samoa where I taught, it was a delight to go to work each day. The children were excellent. They sat in straight rows, they kept quiet in class unless they had a question to ask, they took notes with the same keenness that a drowning man would clutch at his would-be rescuer, and they were immaculately dressed.

Anybody stepping out of line was immediately caned, or strapped, if theirs was a serious enough misdemeanour. This punishment applied to both boys and girls, which is correct in these days of anti-discrimination.

The teachers were happy.

The children were happy.

Everybody knew where they stood.

262

We came back to New Zealand, where I taught in a classroom situation, where over 80% of the children came from Pacific Islands.

It was most enlightening.

New children would arrive from the islands. For the first 2 days, they would sit quietly drinking in the pearls of wisdom that dropped from the golden lips of the teacher.

About the third day, they would begin to look around at the undisciplined behaviour of the other children. By the end of the week, it was all over. They lapsed into the same undisciplined, non-learning mode of the rest of the class.

Sad—but true. Here is a paradox.

Statement
  a. Corporal punishment has been banned from the majority of schools. The children now decide on their mode of behaviour—which is normally bad.
  b. When these undisciplined rebels leave school, because they can't obey the teacher, they find themselves unable to obey the law either. A quick rap over the skull with a police baton however, works wonders.

Therefore, we assume a strap on the bottom, which is admirably built for the job, is outlawed by a group who repeat the old cliche 'violence breeds violence, you know.'

A baton on the head at a later date, is quite acceptable. 'Believe it or not.'

'Press', 2nd March 1989.

'Corporal punishment in schools should be made illegal, says the president of the Counselling and Guidance Association....The answering of violence with violence will perpetuate the abuse...'
End quote.

Fortunately for this gentleman, he was not living in Israel during the days of God's law to Moses. He probably wouldn't have lived to make such unsubstantiated and ludicrous statements.

'If a man have a stubborn and rebellious son, which will not obey the voice of his father or the voice of his mother, and that when they have chastened him he will not hearken unto them, then shall the father and mother lay hold on him and bring him out unto the elders of his city. This our son is stubborn and rebellious, he will not obey our voice, he is a glutton and a drunkard.

263

And all the men of his city shall stone him with stones, that he die, so shalt thou put evil away from among you and all Israel shall hear and FEAR....' *Ref.2. (Emphasis added.)

The greatest weapon in the fight against rebellious youth has got to be the fear of retribution. If it is administered correctly, while the child is young, he will not need it when he grows older. A word will be enough.

Of course, under this ancient Israeli punishment (stoning), debate for and against corporal punishment was deemed unnecessary.

My wife and I threw Dr Spock's book in the rubbish bin and reared our four children from the text-book of life — the Word of God.

Did they turn out warped, deprived and violent? No. Just loving, kind and considerate of others.

Is this a crime in your book?

'Press', 20th November 1979. Here is another individual trying to get physical child punishment outlawed. Her picture is before me, even as I write and here I behold a woman, quoted in the newspaper as being a senior lecturer in psychology at a New Zealand university. Hanging prominently around this person's neck is a hexagram in a circle with an upside-down cross hanging below it.

This would be one of the most demonic witchcraft symbols in the world today, worn by some person who advises others on child-rearing.

    a. By the way, when we were young, the rod of correction was used to great effect.

    b. One scarcely heard the word 'psychologist'.

    c. We were all normal.

Sadly, many psychologists create more problems than they solve, by suggesting to their victim where the problem may have stemmed from. The patient then latches on to this and builds a whole tower of problems on this shaky foundation.

Medical doctors are really useful in assisting with bodily healing, but matters of the soul and spirit would be better left to trained Christian councellors, with the Word of God at their disposal. Using the Word of knowledge, the Word of wisdom and the discerning of spirits, these people could solve the problems correctly.

'The spirit of man is the candle of the Lord, searching all the inward parts of the belly....' *Ref.3.

The newspaper headline says the Australians are suffering the same fate as New Zealand—'Moves to Oust the Cane in New South Wales.'

God's Wisdom

Thank the Lord, there are still some thinking people left. 'Sydney Morning Herald', 4th January 1989.

'A religious book which advocates spanking as 'God's idea' has been condemned as advocating child abuse....

The $5.95 paperback by U.S. religious writer, Roy Lessin, includes a chapter headed:

'Eight Instructions for Spanking' and sub-headings such as 'Spank promptly, Find a private place, Get into a good position, Spank the proper area, Wait for the proper cry'......

The book says that God has provided the perfect area for spanking—the bottom which is a safe place, because it is well cushioned, yet highly sensitive.

.....a spokesman for the N.S.W. Parents and Teachers Against Violence in Schools, said the punishments recommended in the book could do children permanent harm....said a PSYCHOLOGICAL APPROACH should be used to discipline children and not physical force.

But....assistant manager of the Church Missionary Society Bookshop in Sydney said the author Roy Lessin was only following God's instructions.

'There are numerous references to disciplining children with wooden rods in the book of Proverbs', Mr ..... said. 'Books which follow the Word of the Bible in this regard generally sell very well.' End quote.

There it is in a nutshell.

    a. If the Bible is the Word of God, it is a reliable standard.

    b. If the Bible is merely the word of a man, it is not a reliable guide.

You choose. 'As for me and my house, we will serve the Lord.' *Ref.4.

The alternative to following the Word of God, is following the word of some depraved lecher, posing as an educationalist.

Dr Billy Graham's wife Ruth, stated publicly that her children were all brought up on God's wisdom given to Solomon and written up in the book of Proverbs.

Recognising that this is a war we have entered into, let us turn for proof of this to a UNESCO report entitled 'Towards World Understanding.'

P.1. 'Before the child enters school, his mind has already been profoundly marked and often injuriously by earlier influences, first gained, however dimly, in the home.'

P.59. 'It is frequently the family that infects the child with extreme nationalism. The school should therefore use the means described earlier to combat family attitudes.' End quote.

In another article on education, the author writes 'There is however, an underlying assumption in many teacher education courses and reflected by many practising teachers that THE CHILD IS ESSENTIALLY GOOD, but is has been damaged by its parents. The teachers' role in part, is to counteract this damage.' End quote.

By way of contrast, the Word of God says exactly the opposite.

Handy Hints on Child Rearing

'The heart of man is deceitful above all things and desperately wicked.' *Ref.5.

'Foolishness is bound in the heart of a child but the ROD OF CORRECTION shall drive it far from him.' *Ref.6. Emphasis added.

'Train up a child in the way he should go, and when he is old he will not depart from it.' *Ref.7.

'He that spareth his ROD hateth his son, but he that loveth him chasteneth him betimes.' *Ref.8. (From time to time.) Emphasis added.

'Chasten thy son while there is hope and let not thy soul spare for his crying.' *Ref.9.

Someone says 'you might hit him too hard.' This is true. It needs to be administered, not in anger, but for his (the child's) good.

'He might die' cries the do-gooder, liberal educationalist.

I have great news:

'Withhold not correction from the child for if thou beatest him with the ROD, he shall not die.

Thou shalt beat him with the rod, and shalt deliver his soul from hell.' *Ref.10.

'The ROD and reproof give wisdom but a child left to himself bringeth his mother to shame.' *Ref.11. Emphasis added.

Ask this question of any prison warder. Who visits the prisons more than any others? The mothers of course.

Love and Communication must go together with this discipline. Learn to turn off the TV each evening and have a family chat.

Tuck your little ones in bed at night. Talk to them. Listen to them and you will learn to do things together that keep the family happy.

We do a series on the 'Christian Family', but that is not the purpose of this book.

A professor of psychology and his wife became committed Christians. They told us that their search for truth and reality commenced after eating a meal at the home of a top lecturer in psychology.

This dear professor told us that the home of that man was complete chaos and bedlam. In his heart he said, 'If this is the end result of psychology, there must be some other way.' He found it in the true and living God, and Jesus Christ.

Humanism — centres on 'self'. It is being taught as a religion in schools, along with eastern religion, the New Age movement and Satan is its author.

Self recognises no other being to which man is responsible. Educational psychologists promote these terms:

Self-concept

Self-esteem

Self-awareness

Self-fulfillment

Self-understanding

Self-actualisation (equals self-indulgence; which ignores the needs and rights of others.)

This is not the way of Christ. One of His followers put it nicely — 'It is no longer I that live, but Christ that liveth in me.' *Ref.12.

Satan's way is rotten to the core.

Christ's way is lovely.

The good news for Christian believers is that they haven't got to put up with this educational nonsense for very much longer.

December 1992 will be the beginning of the end of this era.

Things are getting out of hand. 'Press', 30th July 1988.

'A vegetable hating child, aged 14 months, led to his grandfather's appearance in District Court yesterday on a charge of assault.

The charge arose from the grandfather's frustration at trying to feed the child for 10-15 minutes; only to be covered in vegetables which the child 'blew out' over him.

He smacked the child on a hand, without success and then flicked his fingers on the child's cheek, leaving marks which led to a complaint to the police.

....He said he loved his grandson, and all his other grandchildren...' End quote.

This poor man was discharged without conviction. His only mistake was, he flicked the wrong cheek.

CHAPTER 42

Is Education Improving?

An article from the 'Woman's Day', 23rd November 1987.

'....director and founder of the Language Foundation of Australia, says the major cause of our growing illiteracy is the way young people are taught to read and write; coupled with poor understanding of language shown in a child's early years at home.

....They aren't taught the breakdown of words until much later.

....because they learn by sight, they don't understand it.

....called Look and Say, and Constance says that wherever it has been introduced, remedial classes have later become necessary.

It began in Germany a generation ago, and within 10 years, there was a need for remedial classes.' End quote.

'Courier Mail', 8th June 1982.

'At least 92,000 Australian-born Queenslanders have trouble reading and writing, according to the newly formed Council for Adult Literacy.' End quote.

Actually, I saw this trend coming in some years ago and taught my own children, using the old text-books.

The 3 'R's':

Reading — using the art of syllabification — dividing each word up into syllables e.g. Con-stan-ti-no-ple

 1 2 3 4 5 syllables

Writing — not printing, which is widely taught today.

Arithmetic — 4 rules: adding, subtracting, dividing and multiplying; plus all the tables up to 12x.

My children put a tape on each morning in our caravan which commenced 'Good morning children. This is the Smith family travelling school. Now for our times tables.

 $2x0 = 0$

 $2x1 = 2$ etc etc.'

'Bulletin', 5th April 1988.

'Four out of five would-be soldiers miss out on donning the khaki because they cannot meet the literacy requirement based on primary school standards. 'It's as basic as 'the cat sat on the mat' says......of the Sydney recruiting centre, 'but they fail. That tells you something about the education system and about the kind of people we are attracting......' End quote.

'Australian', 2nd December 1988. 'N.S.W. Wants Schools Pushed Back to Basics.' End quote.

'Press', 29th February 1988. 'N.Z. Math's Programme to Be Tried in the U.S.....' End quote.

They've destroyed New Zealand, now they are talking about exporting their nonsense to some other poor group in the U.S. Shame on them.

'Financial Review', 23rd November 1987. 'Stop Treating Our Children like Guinea Pigs and Teach Them to Spell.....' End quote.

'Press', 23rd May 1987. 'Why Tim is So Bored at School.'

Have you ever brightly said to a child 'And what did you do at school today' and heard the stock answer?

'Oh we drew a picture and played.' That sums it up very well.

Tim's programme was outlined in his letter to the Minister of Education. This will explain to you why he was so bored at school.

Quote from the article above — his timetable and a portion of his letter:

9.00 — SHARING STORIES (writing stories and reading them to your partner.)
10.00 — MATHEMATICS
INTERVAL
10.45 — WRITING (from the blackboard.)
11.15 — SILENT READING
11.40 — TAHA MORAI (sic) (Stick games and singing.)
LUNCH TIME.
1.00 — FITNESS
1.30 — TOPIC STUDIES
2.00 — PLAY
2.05 — SPORT
3.00 — GO HOME.

What is really boring about it? It's that I would like to learn Claws work and English Grammar even this letter. I Couldn't do without some asstince. I wondered if you could help me.

Yours Sinserly
Tim......' End quote.

'Press', 23rd March 1988. 'School Cert. 'Must Go' Seminar Told....' End quote.

This is an important step to remove all competition which in turn removes standards.

Landmarks

Whilst on our Middle-East tour in 1988, we saw little piles of rocks scattered everywhere through the apparent desert land. Upon asking the guide what they were, we were told they were very important landmarks put there generations ago and all the local inhabitants knew whose land belonged to whom. To a stranger, it meant nothing. To the locals, they were of the utmost importance.

I say 'Woe to these people who are bringing in this destructive system and damning not only millions of children and their offspring, but damning their own souls at the same time.'

'Remove not the ancient landmark which thy fathers have set.' *Ref.1.

The Results of Change

'Press', 26th July 1988.

'Classroom violence in Britain is deterring people from becoming teachers, says the country's biggest teachers union...' End quote.

'Sunday Mail', 11th June 1988.

'Teachers in Queensland are leaving the profession in droves because of violence and the lack of discipline in schools.....' End quote.

'Sunday Telegraph', 11th January 1987.

'Police officers will take up permanent station in N.S.W. schools if the Education Department endorses radical proposals to curb the rising juvenile crime rate.....' End quote.

'Sun', 4th August 1984.

'Police were being called into schools more often to resolve discipline problems, the head of one of the community policing squads said yesterday....' End quote.

Sex Education

The people who promoted this subject to little children need to be examined by their friendly psychologist. If he says that they are all right, he also needs to be examined.

Even the Swedes recognise their mistakes in this realm.

'Nelson Evening Mail', 19th April 1983.

'A strong wave of puritanism has suddenly swept over Sweden, the country once described as a paradise of sexual liberation when it became an international forerunner in the legislation of contraception, the promotion of sexual education and the relaxation of censorship laws.....' End quote.

Meanwhile, back in little New Zealand.

'Herald', 6th November 1984.

'Scenes from blue video movies are being described by eight and nine year old school-children in class talks, according to a Hastings police youth aid officer.

The children are also said to be acting out such scenes during play times at school, and outside the school grounds....' End quote.

Video Censorship — a Horrible Joke

Because we do not employ committed born-again censors, who have definite standards based on the Word of God, look at the mess we have got ourselves into.

Don't blame the censors. Their job is absolutely impossible. They try to gauge society's ever-changing standards with no stable point to work from.

I watched my son attach a label to videos of our meetings and asked him what he was doing. He replied that it was a sticker which showed that all our videos had been inspected by this group of censors. I said 'What? They let all that other filth go by and corrupt their own minds by watching it and have the audacity to scan Christian videos which promote decency and goodness.'

My son, Andrew, explained that this was another World Government ruse to keep track of how much we have found out about their nefarious plans.

I am quite happy about it all however, as the video censors now have to listen to the Gospel message and who knows, some of them might turn to the Lord and be gloriously saved.

Nuclear Education

Oh no. They are still at it. All this appears so foolish once you have understood the information on the nuclear red herring.

'Press', 27th January 1989.

'The Government has approved a programme of education and research on the likely impact on New Zealand of a nuclear war.

This was to follow the 1987 Planning Council study and report on 'New Zealand after nuclear war', said the Prime Minister....nuclear war remained a possibility....' End quote.

If you have read the chapter on nuclear issues, you will be aware that it does not remain a possibility at all.

Hinduism in N.S.W. Classrooms

'Sydney Morning Herald', 18th August 1983.

'Children begin the day with the guru.....for the 46 pupils at Manu School in Cremorne, the school day begins (and finishes) with classes in transcendental meditation.....' End quote.

They don't want Jesus, the truth, but they want Hinduism, the worship of millions of demon spirits. (See Second Warning, pg 141-142.)

Tomorrow's Schools

(Picot Report in New Zealand.)

In the light of the mess the education system is in now, we hear the words 'Tomorrow's schools', throw up our hands in horror and cry 'Have mercy on us all.'

This radical change in New Zealand's education system means that the parents and friends of the school now take over the day to day running of the school and the hiring and firing of teachers etc.

Two results can ensue from all this.

a. A group of dedicated born-again committed Christians could get elected to the school board and have an influence for a return to goodness and decency.

b. Remembering that each successive generation of school-children learns less than their predecessors, means that amongst tomorrow's parents, there would be those who were almost illiterate and consequently could 'foul up' any intelligent decisions.

Also the lack of morality in many of these people would surface in their meetings and they would try to inflict their lack of standards into their school situation; thus corrupting the children even further, and also incurring the wrath of God.

'Woe unto the world because of offenses; for it must needs be that offences will come, but woe unto that man, by whom the offence cometh.' *Ref.2.

This innovation taking place with Tomorrow's Schools in poor little New Zealand is more sinister than it first appears.

Parents in many cases, clamour to get on the school board, naively thinking that they can inject some of their skills into the education system, not realising that the syllabus has already been made up for them and cleverly disguised under 'The Charter'.

Christchurch 'Press', 14th April 1989. 'Schools Becoming a 'Political Tool'.

Schools are being used as a political tool by the government to engineer social changes, according to a local parents' action group.

A spokesman for The Concerned Parents Association.......said the proposed school charter to be adopted by school boards or trustees was being used by the government to make compulsory social changes.

......One of the Principles is that trustees develop policies which are consistent with the spirit of partnership in the Treaty of Waitangi.

......said the charter read like a party political statement, with a strong feminist bias, RATHER THAN A SERIOUS PROPOSAL ABOUT HOW TO EDUCATE CHILDREN. (Emphasis added.)

'The government is asking schools to be partners with it in the wreckers ball it has swung at the education system.'

......'So many important aspects of a school's functioning are laid down as non-negotiable, that it makes a mockery of the government's claim that parents will have effective input.' End quote.

To Sum Up
The children of this generation have been betrayed.
  a. They have not been disciplined at school. This discipline is love in action.
  b. They are burning the schools down, by way of protest and this trend will not cease until the children get a fair deal.

'They have sown the wind and are reaping the whirlwind.'
*Ref.3.

FINAL STORY
Out of the many thousands of pupils that were under my care during the days of my teaching stint, Harry stands out in my memory.

Born to a Pacific Island family, he was very cheerful, happy, yet naughty.

If I had an electric heater burning in the classroom during winter, Harry would push a wire into it and fuse it.

He dropped a giant thunderflash cracker in the window of the fish and chip shop and caused the manager to drop a vat of hot fat all over his feet.

274

A man in the vicinity of our school was doing the family laundry. He went inside to get some soap and when he returned, the copper was gone. Harry had been there; collecting scrap metal for selling.

My wife and I took Harry and other boys on holidays and into our home.

At school, I disciplined him with my strap and voice, but he always knew that I really liked him.

Many years later, my wife and I received a letter in the mail, postmarked Melbourne, Australia. We both wept as we read it.

The letter went something like this. "Dear Mr and Mrs Smith, I am on a world tour and as you can see, I am writing from Melbourne to say thank you for your input into my life.

You, Mr Smith, are the only person who corrected me and told me about God. You and Mrs Smith had me in your home and loved me. Thank you very much. Love, Harry."

CHAPTER 43

Evolution and Education

'West Australian', 7th January 1988. 'A Win for Science. The N.S.W. Government now has the power to close down schools which teach the biblical story of creation rather than evolution in science classes.' End quote.

A dear friend of mine, Derek Jones, now with the Lord, had just completed his B.A. degree which included units on anthropology. He told me that his hang up with Christianity was that it did not allow for any previous civilizations prior to the Biblical account of Adam and Eve, although, there were traces of prehistoric monsters and humans still being found.

As we were teaching together at the same High School, we had ample time for discussion, both before and after work.

I pointed him to the fact that even in a pre-scientific age God makes sure we know that everything has a beginning.

7 Hebrew words sum it up. Genesis 1:1:

'In the beginning God created the heaven and the earth.'

Verse 2 goes on 'and the earth was without form and void.'

I said 'Derek. The word 'was' in this verse can also be translated 'became'. Therefore it can also read 'and the earth became without form and void.'

Therefore, between verse 1 and verse 2, there is a very indefinite time period where many other things and possibly people, may have existed in former civilizations.

This, the Bible does not tell us, because for God's wonderful plan of salvation to take place, He wishes us to start with Adam and Eve, a 6,000 year span and wind up this age at the end of the 6,000 years. The seventh thousand year period will be spent with Christians reigning with Christ.

Remember, 'One day with the Lord is as a thousand years, and a thousand years as one day.' *Ref.1.

7 Days of History

Proof: 'Timaru Herald', 19th February 1988.

'Theories about the birth of mankind were turned back to front yesterday when scientists claimed modern humans existed before Stone Age cavemen.....near Nazareth in Israel — modern man lived there almost 100,000 years ago.' End quote.

Derek was satisfied. He committed his life to the Lord, was baptised and a short time later at the young age of 38, took a heart attack whilst teaching a class, and went home to the Lord. 'He that hath the Son, hath life.' *Ref.2.

During my teaching days, the subject of evolution was part of the curriculum.

Trying to be a basically honest teacher, I would divide the blackboard in half and write one word as the heading for each column i.e.

1.	2.
God	Nothing

I would then invite the children in my classes to choose which they felt was the author of our existence.

I now say to you, the reader, you choose!

Forget the big bang, the primevil germ, the amoeba, protoplasm or apes and answer the initial question.

'Whence comes life?'

I sincerely hope you are too intelligent to choose column 2.

I suggest school children reading this book should take it to school, open it at this page and ask their teachers to answer the question, preferably in front of the class.

If they choose column 2, you say 'Therefore that leaves me free to believe that a copy of Webster's Dictionary came about through an explosion in a printing shop.'

The aim of evolution is initially explained to us by the scientist Julian Huxley 'to convince the student that there is no creative force in the universe.' Huxley goes on to say 'God can no longer be considered the controller of the universe.'

Freemasonry also goes along with evolution 'to assist man in his evolutionary progress on the road to perfection.'

Summing Up

Evolution therefore, is a scientific conspiracy with no initial starting point. It is therefore false, because without a beginning, there can be no conclusion.

All atheists would accept some form of evolution as being the basis of existence.

Statement:
1. All atheists choose this path later on in life. They were all born with a knowledge of a creator.

'This is the true light which lighteth every man that cometh into the world.' *Ref.3.

2. All atheists should be confronted and asked when they became that way, and why.

John Bunyan (1628-1688), the author of 'Pilgrim's Progress', was a high Anglican but later joined the Puritans. He was jailed for a number of years for 'preaching without a license'.

One of his little known works was 'Visions of Heaven and Hell'. We will read excerpts from this book as the stories he tells ring with truth and authority.

An Atheist in Hell. (Paraphrased.)

Those involved: John Bunyan, Atheist Hobbs, Tormenting Devil, Accompanying Angel.

'We had not gone much farther before we heard another, cursing himself for his foolishness and increasing his own misery by thinking of the happiness of blessed souls.

The tormentor who accompanied me said 'These atheists are the worst of all. We all know there is a God, although we hated Him, but these are so foolish that they would never humble themselves to admit God's very existence until they come here.'

'Then these' said I, 'are atheists. A wretched group indeed.'

At this point, Bunyan recognised the voice of this poor wretch. It was a man named Hobbs, the author of a book called 'Leviathan'. Bunyan remarked on how Hobb's voice had changed.

Hobbs: 'No wonder my voice is changed, for I am now changed in my principles, but sadly, it is too late to do me any good. I now know that there is a God, but I wish there wasn't for I am sure He will have no mercy on me. There is no reason why He should however, as I was His foe on earth and now He is mine in hell. It is that wretched confidence I had in my own wisdom that betrayed me.'

Bunyan: 'Tell me. Did you really believe when you were upon earth that there was no God? Did you imagine that the world made itself and the creatures on it were the cause of their own production? Didn't your soul whisper to you that another made you, and not yourself?

I have often heard it said that although there are many who say outwardly, there is no God, not one of them really believes it because of an inner witness that there is a God. Now you can tell me in all honesty whether this was indeed so, because you have no reason to conceal it.'

278

Hobbs: 'I will tell you although the thoughts sting me badly even as I remember back to my days of opportunity.'

Steps of an Atheist Lead Downwards

Hobbs continues:

1. 'I did at first believe there was a God, but getting involved in various sinful practices, made me wish that there was no God. If there was to be a God, He would be righteous and would need to punish sin. The more I sinned, the more I began to hope there was no God. I then began to frame new ideas in my own breast, to fit in with what I hoped. I also worked out an alternative view for the world's origin, excluding the being of a Deity.

2. After awhile, when these views took a hold on me, I began to try and convince others of these ideas. At the same time, there were checks in my conscience which told me I was making a mistake, but I ignored these warnings.

My love of sin, a) hardened my heart against my Maker and made me hate Him at first. b) Then I denied His being. c) And finally, His existence.

Sin, which I loved, is the cause of all this cursed woe.

'The wages of sin is death'. *Ref.4.

Now I find in spite of all my vain philosophy, THERE IS A GOD.

Jesus said 'And fear not them which kill the body, but are not able to kill the soul, rather fear him who is able to destroy both soul and body in hell.' *Ref.5.

3. I used to take pleasure in listening to my disciples mock sacred matters, but now, those very thoughts torment me like whips of burning steel.'

Fire and Darkness

Bunyan: 'I have another question to ask. You talk about flames, burning steel etc. How can this be as you are in utter darkness?'

Hobbs: 'I dearly wish I could say that there was no fire but alas, the fire we endure is ten thousand times worse than ordinary fire in fierceness, and also it is of a different consistency. There is no light at all, therefore in hell is fire but utter darkness.

Earthly fire consumes things away to a pile of ashes, but not here. It will never burn out. We shall ever be burning, yet not burned. It is tormenting, but not consuming. I cannot therefore, express the torment of my soul.'

279

Tormentor: 'You see then what sort of men they were on earth. Is it not just therefore, that they are receiving the reward for their deeds?'

Bunyan: 'Yes. They suffer the reward of their sin, but you, evil tormentor, await the same fate when Almighty God turns to your case. You knew there was a God, yet you rebelled against Him and will be away from the glory of His presence for all eternity.'

(Note — this tormentor was one of the one third of fallen angels who rebelled initially against God, were thrown out of heaven. Their judgement has been forecast.)

'And the angels which kept not their first estate, but left their own habitation, he hath reserved in everlasting chains under darkness unto the judgement of the great day.' Ref.6.

Bunyan: 'This place of torment acts as a mirror to reflect the enormity of sin.'

Accompanying Angel: 'It does to some degree but a far greater mirror of human sin and iniquity is the Cross where the Lord Jesus Christ hung at Calvary. If you look back to Calvary, you will see the just merits due to sin. This is where we may contemplate the blessed Son of God upon the cross.

What you see here in hell is the suffering of creatures who are damned, but on the cross, you see a suffering God.'

'Mercy and truth are met together. Righteousness and peace have kissed each other.' *Ref.7.

Bunyan: 'Praise be to the Lord that at Calvary, JUSTICE was fully satisfied in the just punishment of sin, and MERCY triumphed in that it was offered to poor sinners who would receive it.

Eternal praises to His holy Name for ever that His GRACE has made me willing to accept this salvation. I am now an HEIR of glory.

I see these poor wretches here, who also had this grace offered to them, but they refused it.

It was grace alone that helped me to accept it.....' End quote.

I Challenge You!

Statement. You've read it, you now know all you need to know, what awaits you at death. If you are an atheist or an evolutionist, cry to God for mercy — and enjoy His divine favour.

'For whosoever shall call upon the Name of the Lord shall be saved.' *Ref.8.

'Humans Self-Made' is a heading in the 'Evening Post', 14th July 1988.

'Human beings are self-made — our humanity is created from cultural evolution — Professor Lloyd Geering believes.

....Professor Geering, emeritus professor of religious studies at Victoria University is a special lecturer.

....Because of cultural evolution, humans were moving away from their animal origins at an extraordinary rate...' End quote.

In the light of Bunyan's visit to and description of hell, the implications are terrifying for both teacher and students. I am not a judge, but these words seem applicable.

'Ever learning and never able to come to the knowledge of the truth.' Ref.9.

Male and Female. Unisex — the Occult Connection

A form of madness has overtaken the western world.

Question: Are men and women equal?

Answer: Pertaining to salvation, yes.

'We are heirs together of the grace of God.' *Ref.10.

In everything else, no. We were not created to be equal. The Creator's plans were more complex.

Man

'And God said 'let us make man in our image, after our likeness....' *Ref.11.

Woman

'And the Lord God said 'It is not good that man should be alone. I will make an help meet for him.' *Ref.12.

There it is in all its clarity.

Modern education is seeking to cancel sex roles in the classroom.

Thank God for the Bible. It makes sense even when all else is collapsing.

CHAPTER 44

Agnosticism and Atheism

Why include this strange belief under the heading 'occult'?
Unless one moves off into the eastern concept of reincarnation, evolution would be the only alternative for one who is dedicated to denying the Creator's existence.

Atheists say 'There is no God.'

It is clear that no normal person would make such a statement, unless they were a candidate for a mental hospital. That leaves the only alternative i.e. demonic influence.

Agnostics say 'I'm not sure whether there is or whether there isn't.'

In the year 1954, a man from Sydney, Australia came to introduce the Open Air Campaigners to New Zealand. In those days, I was a student at the old Bible Training Institute in Auckland; the visitor's name was Jim Duffecy.

Before the open air meetings really got under way, it was my privilege to accompany Jim on lunch time sorties to various parks and factories around the city. I played my guitar, as the two of us sang and collected a crowd.

This day, the students were gathered at Albert Park eating their lunches. We drove up in the big Bedford van, let down the side on chains as this acted as our platform.

Jim began to speak and instantly gained the attention of all. 'Any agnostics up there?', he shouted.

The crowd erupted in to wild cheering and shouts of affirmation. If enthusiasm had anything to do with anything, these students were apparently all keen to be known as agnostics, to that point. Jim continued on.

Jim: 'That's great because today I am going to speak on agnosticism.' Wild cheers again.

'First of all, we will examine the word 'agnostic'. What does it really mean? I KNOW NOTHING!'

A shocked hush followed and Jim went on with his message, leading inevitably to the Lord's death for us and the old rugged cross. Souls turned from darkness to light, even as Jim spoke.

At this point, I honour the memory of this man, as being one of my early teachers in the art of communication.

At 7 a.m. on Thursday, November 17th 1983, this man who took the Gospel to thousands stepped into the presence of the Lord Jesus Christ whom he loved and served and heard him say 'Well done, good and faithful servant.'

A Final Question to Atheists and Agnostics:

Where are you going when your turn comes to die? Start thinking. Do your soul a favour.

CHAPTER 45

Occult Activity

He stepped out of the boat on to a beach, glistening coral sand, shining in the tropical sun.

A group of local people came down to meet him, led by a very dignified man who stepped forward and demanded to know what he wanted on their island.

My missionary friend, Sam, asked the chief for his permission to preach the Gospel of the Lord Jesus Christ on his island; which question caused the leader and all his followers to burst into laughter.

With a twinkle in his eye, the chief called a young girl about the age of 18 years, to lie on the beach before them.

He then spoke to his witch-doctor, who stepped forward, mumbled some words, whilst gesticulating with his hands. The young lady, in a perfectly horizontal position, levitated about 10 feet up in the air before the group of on-lookers.

Turning to Sam, the chief laughingly said 'If you can bring her down, I will give my permission for you to hold your meetings on this island.'

Sam told us that he felt really sorry for the girl. He couldn't watch so he turned away saying 'Bring her down Lord Jesus.'

There was a terrible crash, and as a gasp of wonderment went up from all those assembled in that area, Sam quickly sprang forward to pray life back into the girl in the Name of the Lord Jesus Christ. She lived, and the gospel was preached on that island.

Here, you have just read an actual happening that took place in the Marshall Islands, and my friend was the man involved.

To any non-believer reading this book, I say 'Explain all this. How did it happen?'

You say 'I've never seen anything supernatural like this'. That doesn't really matter. All that this proves is that you were in the wrong place at the right time.

Millions of people all around the world know of the supernatural realm.

Films like 'The Omen', 'Poltergeist', 'The Amityville Horror', are not figments of someone's imagination. These things really happen, even today.

My family and I have dozens of supernatural stories from events that have taken place at our meetings over the years. In my book Second Warning, we outline some of these on p125-164. Read those two first books and you will find very exciting information. For example, on the wall of my office where I write, there is a photograph and an article from a Samoan newspaper about a devil-dog eating its way through the wall of my house in February 1961.

Don't bother saying it didn't happen. It did! As a sceptic, your job is to explain it.

We were in a public meeting another night, when at the end of the service, a great commotion took place. A queen witch was raking the air with her fingernails, her eyes changing colour, red, green, blue, yellow, white. I tell you, it was like something from a Hollywood horror film.

My wife May, ran to me and said 'Barry, do something.' People were running in all directions.

I stood beside this young lady and her face contorted into an evil grin. The devil spoke from deep within, using her mouth. 'You mole. Do you think you can get rid of me? I'm not a witch, I'm a queen witch and I've been here 20 years.'

I answered 'I've got news for you and it's all bad. In the Name of the Lord Jesus Christ, spirit of the queen witch, come out.'

There was a crash as she hit the floor and when she stood up again, she was free.

You can rebuke devils in the name of Buddha, Mohammed, the Prime Minister or the President if you like, but they (demons) only come out in the Name of the Lord Jesus Christ.

'He that believeth and is baptised shall be saved; but he that believeth not shall be damned.

And these signs shall follow them that believe; In my Name shall they cast out devils;.....' *Ref.1. End quote.

Politicians need prayer

Many strange decisions are reached in the halls of Government that baffle the intellect of the man in the street.

One of the reasons we are exhorted to pray for these individuals is that whilst they suppose they are making the decisions, there is a far greater power using them as tools to make his diabolic plans come to pass on the earth. The vast majority of politicians are unknowingly open to his suggestions if they are not believers in the Lord.

By now, you know his name.

Lucifer, also known as Satan.

'For we wrestle not against flesh and blood, but against principalities, against powers, against the rulers of the darkness of this world, against spiritual wickedness in high places.' *Ref.2.

Satan Links World Government Advocate Groups

Nobody will ever convince me that all these World Government groups are working individually to achieve their ends.

Master Puppeteer—Satan is a co-ordinator of them all, and you the reader, are going to see all these things fulfilled in the near future.

Each country has a chief prince in the demonic realm, ruling its affairs.

The prophets speak of e.g. The Prince of Persia, the Prince of Greece.

Your country has a demon spirit running its affairs also.

It should be noted that Labour movements are also run by a demonic master, who foments continuous labour and union unrest. Not many people know this, but occult people do.

Master Jesus

Not many people are privy to this information but there is a devil in the field of religion, posing as the Lord Jesus Christ. This is an evil spirit inhabiting an actual man.

There are thousands of Jesus' in the world today. Christs abound in every direction, all of them false of course, except the real one.

Dr Billy Graham said that at the last Olympic Games in Los Angeles, there were over 400 men all claiming to be the Christ.

There is only one. Lord—Jesus—Christ. This is His full title.

If you are given to praying and wish to speak to the correct one, that is the Name to use in your prayers.

Remember this demonic master works within the church itself. He is particularly involved in Europe and America in preparing the people for a demon possessed world teacher who will appear shortly.

In the light of the chapter showing the importance of the European Community, this information is of great importance.

Remember, Politics—Antichrist. Religion—False Prophet.

This demonic Master Jesus by the way works together with

'The Christ'. When I talk to people and they put these two words together, (The Christ), I know immediately where they are coming from. This being is Satan himself.

No wonder Jesus warned in His day 'For there shall arise false Christs and false prophets and shall show great signs and wonders, in so much that if it were possible, they shall deceive the very elect.' *Ref.10.

Communists and Capitalists Link

Now, with the rise of the European Common Market to power in December 1992, the demonic activity is increasing.

Have you noticed:

a. The capitalists are going socialist?

b. The socialists are going democratic?

They will all meet in the middle shortly in a World Government whose main thrust will get rid of the old competitive spirit and bring in co-operation.

Lawless Spirits on the Increase

With the tremendous increase in occult activity even in our schools, a whole generation has grown up almost illiterate, hooked on vile acid rock music, drugs, illicit sex and no self-control.

This great E.C. leader who is about to arise has another name also — The Lawless One.

'And then shall the Wicked be revealed, whom the Lord shall consume with the spirit of his mouth and the brightness of his coming.' *Ref.3.

Here is a fair warning. Don't get mixed up in occult activity, even some of which is cleverly disguised e.g. Freemasonry. It will destroy your soul.

This obvious demonic activity will result in the world being completely run by 3 beings.

3 Leaders to Rule Soon:

1. Satan — also known as the Dragon
2. Beast — E.C. Leader and Political Leader
3. False Prophet — World Church Leader, religion

Listen to what the prophet says about these characters.

'And I saw three unclean spirits like frogs come out of the mouth of the dragon, and out of the mouth of the beast, and out of the mouth of the false prophet.

287

For they are the SPIRITS OF DEVILS working miracles, which go forth unto the kings of the earth and of the whole world to gather them to battle of that great day of God Almighty.**Ref.4.

Sure enough, it will all culminate shortly in a giant confrontation.'In the years 1990-2000, you will watch this build-up increase.'A complete polarisation into two camps.'To which camp do you belong?' God's or Satan's?

Psychic Predictions for 1988. Wrong—Wrong—Wrong

In keeping with his title, the 'father of lies', all Satan's workers and minions have always experienced problems with the truth.

Even their predictions are suspect as a little truth is mixed with a mass of untruth which keeps the whole potion palatable.

For example, any poisoner would do better if he mixed his poison in raspberry juice or some other juice.

'Evening Post', 3rd January 1989.

'Psychics will have to do better in 1989 than they did in 1988 when virtually nothing they predicted came to pass.

....Among other predictions for 1988 by the Examiner's psychics:'Richard Nixon would become a television evangelist, Gerald Ford would become one of his bishops and Fidel Castro would defect to the United States to open a cigar factory.
Jesse Jackson would quit politics to become a football coach.

Space aliens would land in New York and be mugged.....'End quote.

True Prophets

In contrast, the predictions of a true prophet of God will always be 100% correct.'If they were not, the prophet underwent a very nasty experience.'He was stoned to death.

'But the prophet which shall presume to speak a word in my name, which I have not commanded him to speak or that shall speak in the name of other gods, even that prophet shall die.**Ref.5.

How do you know if the person who is telling you the future is really from God or not?'This question is asked of me continually.'Here is the answer.

'And if thou say in thine heart, how shall we know the word which the Lord hath not spoken?
When a prophet speaketh in the name of the Lord, if the thing follow not, nor come to pass, that is the thing which the Lord

288

hath not spoken, but the prophet hath spoken it presumptuously, thou shalt not be afraid of him."*Ref.6.
If I wish to know the future, to whom do I go?

List of Forbidden Practises:
Do I enquire into:
Black or white witchcraft?
Ouija boards or occult games like Dungeons and Dragons?
Seances, clairvoyance or mediums?
E.S.P.'Second sight or mind reading?
Fortune telling, palm reading, tea-leaf reading?
Crystal balls, tarot and other card laying?
Astrology or horoscopes?
Reincarnation healing using metaphysics?
Hypnosis, any curse from any source?
Water witching or dowsing, levitation, body lifting?
Table tipping, psychometry automatic writing?
Astral projection, and other demonic skills?
The New Age thinking, false cults?
Hereditary powers or problems?
Satan or any other evil spirit?
Mind power?

All these need to be renounced and deliverance is required in the Name of the Lord Jesus Christ.

For information regarding the future, go only to the Word of God, the Holy Bible.

'The secret things belong unto the Lord our God, but those things which are revealed belong unto us and to our children forever....*Ref.7.

The enemy is working flat out.'Why?

'....Woe to the inhabitants of the earth and of the sea for the devil is come down unto you, because HE KNOWETH THAT HE HATH BUT A SHORT TIME. '*Ref.8.Emphasis added.

How does he know this? He can read. He knows that the prophets don't make mistakes.He's more clever than most people.

Vile Games and Occult Explosion
'Sun Herald', 18th October 1987.

'A new computer game called Jack the Ripper features — in full and gory multi-colour vision, the unsolved murders which shocked the nation in 1888....*End quote.

289

'Press', 21st December 1983.

'Britain is seeing its biggest occult explosion in a century as hoards of people turn to witchcraft, magic rituals and astrology.

Over the past five years, hundreds of Britons have signed up for correspondence courses in spells...'End quote.

'Herald', 6th August 1988."Feminist Witches Weave Spiritual Spells.....Wicca groups do not belong to the lunatic fringe.'The women attracted to Wicca tradition are almost without exception, well-educated middle class and pakeha (caucasian).'Many are lapsed Christians, some still attend and their numbers are rising....'End quote.

At this point I make an observation or two.'The article goes on to say 'The reason they remain in the Church is that they still believe in Christ.....'End quote.

A False Christ

The point is, as we now know, the Christ they believe in is the cosmic demonic Christ, who has been substituted by most liberal churches for the Lord Jesus Christ.

Where is the proof?

Further quote from the above article: 'Christ says the group is part of a 'oneness that we are all part of.'End quote.

That's right.'Correct name — wrong person.'Very clever.'No wonder masses continue to be deceived.

A Melbourne newspaper in the year 1988 told us that Satanism was rampant in Australia with over 20,000 members.

The article went on to outline their activities:

a. Sexual orgies

b. The sacrifice of animals

c. And even humans

This author knows of occasions reported to him where away up in Northern Queensland, some of their girls are deliberately having babies which they intend to abort and use in their ceremonies, and while we sit in our cozy homes, work from 9-5 then watch TV, all this goes on around us.

Soon my friend, this will all be blatantly revealed for the world to see.

We are being gradually desensitised.

Creeping into the Church

'Press', 27th April 1988.

'A new wave of religious thinking embracing witch-craft will reach New Zealand in June with the visit of its leading American advocate.

The Rev. Matthew Fox, a Catholic theologian....has hired a group of freethinkers....including a witch named Starhawk, an Episcopal vicar turned Zen Buddhist, a masseuse and a yoga teacher....'End quote.

Pity the Kids

From a school syllabus in a New Zealand school.'An integrated theme for standard 2 — form 1.

'Magic'.'Introduce topic with a collection of lucky charms and objects associated with magic and display them so that they trigger off discussion and stimulate interest.

.....A separate (sic) display of unlucky omens can be made e.g. crossed knives, broken mirrors, the number 13....

Continue article.

Signs and symbols in magic:

The hex sign — the pentagon

The sign of the cross

The swastika

Lucky charms

The signs of the zodiac

Totem poles.....'

THIS IS ALL CALLED THE THIN EDGE OF THE WEDGE.

In a syllabus on 'ghosts', for J2 and higher, 'create a ghost-like atmosphere....'End quote.

Witchcraft a Crime in New Zealand

'Herald', 23rd July 1988.

'The Minister of Justice....says witchcraft has not been decriminalised.

....the Summary Offences Act 1981 which made it an offence to act as a spiritualistic medium or use telepathy, clairvoyance, or other similar powers with intent to deceive....'End quote.

Strange Changes

A British newscutting tells us 'A Bangladesh mystic is to be allowed to hold a meditation session in the House of Commons....Sri Chinmoy ran an offshoot cult of Hinduism that had already caused embarrassment and had 'run foul' of the United Nations.

Sri Chinmoy is said to claim that he can levitate elephants and can produce up to 16,000 paintings a day....*End quote.

All this looks like a big joke but unfortunately, what would never be allowed in the Western civilisation 20 years ago, is now here with a vengeance.

We have done quite a deal of work in South East Asia.'Here is a cutting from the 'New Straits Times', Malaysia, 18th March 1981.

'About 100 girls became hysterical at a factory here and a college at Batu Pahat in two separate incidents today....

Two bomohs (witchdoctors) from Parit Raja and Songgarang were summoned to the college to calm down about 30 students and bring the situation under control.

....It is learnt hysteria had broken out at the college four times since March 9....*End quote.

Demonism

Now this is a simple case of demon possession.'The witchdoctor can reason with these evil spirits, but the name of the Lord Jesus Christ will expel them, never to return, provided the victim means business in his or her Christian life.

'And these signs shall follow them that believe.'In my name, they shall cast out devils....'**Ref.9.'End quote.

We've seen this happen many times, but only in the name mentioned above.'That is a challenge in itself to any unbeliever.

CHAPTER 46

New Age Deception—Planned Lucifer Worship

Raising of Consciousness Equals the Road to Hell
One area of the United States is renowned for the tremendous increase in weird, way out, soul-destroying cults, including the New Age Movement.

This area is at the southern end of the Rocky Mountains in New Mexico called Sangre De Cristo.

We were in this area during the month of June 1989 in a small town called 'Eagle Nest'.

I was chatting to a small group about the MARK OF THE BEAST system and how the marking machinery is already available in New Zealand and Australia.

A girl in her early 20's stepped forward and said 'Well, we'll just have to raise our consciousness won't we?'

I replied 'No, we won't. We will need to turn to Jesus.'

Severe Warning. This girl's statement made me so angry, I felt physically ill, and needed to step away from her. I don't know if anybody has ever told you this, but even if they haven't, I am telling you now.

Hinduism—the Basis of New Age
By becoming involved with this form of teaching, you probably felt:
   a. with it
   b. excited at the prospect of receiving spiritual enlightenment
   c. far ahead of Christians and others
   d. part of an exciting new development
   e. on to a brand new teaching.

Statement
The only thing you are 'with' is Hinduism. It is not new, as millions of miserable Indian folk would be quick to point out.

Hinduism is association with, and oppression by, millions of demonic spirits, who plant suggestions in the mind which these deluded people call 'a raising of the consciousness'.

Believe me, when you lie on your death bed, you will not be interested in any way at all in the raising of your consciousness.

You will be desperately looking for the Saviour, God's only remedy THE LORD JESUS CHRIST.

The New Age Movement is not something one may join. It is a world-wide phenomenon which is catching on very quickly and thousands are getting involved in its philosophies.

On pages 75-79 of my book 'Second Warning' one may read quite a lot of information regarding this system, yet in this final book of the trilogy it is my aim to endeavour to show a new frightening aim of these people.

Founded on a False Premise

To quote once more their key thought:

All is one — therefore God and Satan are one.

Everything there is can be found within the 'self'.

Alternative lifestyles e.g. homosexuality, lesbianism, free sex, frees one from moral restraints, they wrongly suppose.

'There is a way which seemeth right unto a man, but the end thereof are the ways of death.' *Ref.1.

Occult symbols are used prolifically i.e. pentagram — the dragon — the ankh — the peace symbol, etc.

Note. The occult nature of these symbols is revealed when they are portrayed inside a circle or a triangle.

Databank — New Zealand — Logo

In this regard, people have contacted me from all over New Zealand, excitedly pointing out the new Logo for Databank. Whether intentional or unintentional, it is AN EYE INSIDE A TRIANGLE, INSIDE A CIRCLE.

This is pure occult.

Can you see the significance of this? I can!

Much of the New Age teaching is connected with IMAGERY AND VISUALISATION TECHNIQUES, which is also taught in many church groups under the heading 'faith'.

This is not true faith in any way whatsoever.

Satan in Visualisation

What people do not understand in many cases, is that when we attempt to visualise and to create what we think is a divine image, the enemy, Lucifer himself, sends a demonic spirit to fulfil that role.

294

Real born-again Christians are told to watch out for the devil, particularly in the area of the mind.

'For as he thinketh in his heart, so is he.' *Ref.2.

'Whatsoever things are true,
                    honest,
                    just,
                    pure,
                    lovely,
                    of good report,
IF there be any virtue and if there be any praise,
THINK ON THESE THINGS!' *Ref.3.

Witnessing to New Agers

A friend I met in 1988 told me that he was in the New Age Movement before turning his life over to the Lord and becoming born-again. He felt that my comments in the book 'Second Warning' about the New Age were too severe. He also mentioned that there are very genuine seeking people in the movement.

I am aware of this but if you tickle these folk with a feather, they'll merely laugh.

If you hit them with a hammer, they'll accuse you of intolerance.

In simple English, I do not want these dear people to finish up in hell, so I try above all things to be gentle, and to heed the admonition:

'Speaking the truth, in love.' *Ref.4.

If we allow our minds to move into 'an altered state of consciousness' we are begging for demonic encounters.

Methods:

Drug taking
Hypnotism
Chanting
Meditation
Visualisation etc

All these open the mind or the brain, to Satan. Leave them strictly alone.

At this point, the image conjured up of your divine being is actually THE IMAGE OF THE BEAST.

The Mark of the Beast

In the New Age Movement, the Chakra Point is right in the

centre of the forehead. Hinduism makes this third eye aspect clear by the use of the red spot on the forehead.

Can you now see what I am driving at?

The forehead figures prominently in these latter days.

THE INDIVIDUAL WHO CAN GET HIS MARK OR NAME ON YOUR FOREHEAD HAS FULL OWNERSHIP.

Reincarnation

Many New-Agers believe in re-incarnation. They believe, that ultimately, the person dies and comes back to a 'higher spiritual frequency.'

Their Teachings

New Age Bible is called 'the Keys of Enoch.'

It speaks in terms of the future.

a. Non New Agers being cleansed from the earth.

b. High angels will mix with humans (those angels will in fact be demon spirits.)

c. The Antichrist is not a man. (The Bible declares that he is.) Instead, the Antichrist is all who do not go along with New Age Unity. For we are all jolly good fellows.

d. The Bible must be abolished as the final authority and the New Age 'mystery writings' must be embraced.

New Age in the USSR

Various Christian writers are now telling us that Mikhail Gorbachev of the USSR is a New Age man.

He wrote a book on Perestroika in which he used New Age terminology calling for all to adopt a GLOBAL CONSCIOUSNESS.

Therefore, the New Communism and the New Age are in cohorts.

New Age Propaganda Man

For some years now, people have written to tell me about a man from Scotland, a Benjamin Creme who speaks of 'The Christ' — Maitreya.

This fellow's message, whoever he is, is fraudulent.

Jesus made this abundantly clear with His early warning.

'Then if any man shall say unto you, lo, here is Christ, or there, believe it not.' *Ref.5.

I tell you my friends, when the real Lord Jesus Christ appears, nobody will be in any doubt.

'For the Lord Himself will descend from heaven with a shout...' *Ref.6.

This deserves a chapter all on its own.

The Satanic Initiation

At the beginning of our book, we spoke of the stage being set to receive the mark of the beast on the RIGHT HAND OR FOREHEAD.

This is only half the story.

The prophets tell us that in order to complete the deal so that one may buy and sell, an initiation is necessary, to encourage people 'voluntarily' at first, then compulsorily to worship this great world leader, the new head of the European Community.

Way out? I certainly thought it was. Long hours have I spent, considering, discussing, reading and praying for light.

How could this ever happen?

We live in a real world of real people, many of whom never once darken the door of a place of worship.

I have found it. (Not in the yellow pages either.)

here are a Number of Keys.

Key No.1 — Food

During the writing of much of this book, my youngest daughter Debbie and I went on a grape fast for a period of 4 weeks.

Aims:

    a. To prepare our bodies physically to carry the good news about God's wonderful salvation through the Lord Jesus Christ.

    b. To promote a clean body and a clear mind to hear the voice of the Lord.

    c. To act as guinea pigs for the sake of our many friends who seek a natural healing process for their lives of over-indulgence. By the way, the Lord is our healer.

Any Christian doctor will also admit this.

We have often been asked 'What was it like?'

Answer: 'Very boring indeed, yet thoroughly worthwhile.'

Debbie and I both agreed that we sympathised with the children of Israel who had in the main, only one type of food to eat for 40 years — manna.

The worst times of course were at meal-times. Beautiful smells wafted through the house. Bacon, eggs, onions, savoury dishes, french fries done in olive oil, etc. Even salads looked delightful, and on occasions we both agreed that even a piece of brown bread would have been a luxury.

Food, a Bondage

A friend of mine said once 'If you eat a lot, you will never hear from God.'

It was during this period that it was revealed to me the tremendous power of food in our lives today.

We reprimand folks on the evils of drinking and smoking but forget the words of wise old Solomon.

'Put a knife to thy throat if thou be a man given to appetite....' *Ref.7.

I feel that in these critical days, the Lord will speak to others also on this subject.

The World Government people are working hard to cut down the food supplies in New Zealand.

Only as far back as 1987, a lamb could be bought for $5.00 on the hoof. We would buy a few of these from a local farmer and fill our freezer.

On the radio news in early 1989, we hear that farmers are cutting back on their breeding stock, that restaurants are now finding lamb and some mutton too expensive to buy, and will have to take it off their menus.

A deliberate evil, hell-inspired move, based on an insatiable desire for power.

World Leader — 4 Stages

As a result of this fiddling with the fish, cutting down the stock and hybridising the seeds, the great World leader, head of the E.C. will, according to the prophet, come to the world with 4 major thrusts:

    a. Peace — He will confirm a 7 year Middle East peace treaty.
    b. War — When the communists invade Israel, he will have a major influence on world events at that time.
    c. Famine — Through man's ignorance and foolishness in tampering with the food chain, we see this man seated on a black horse, weighing out the food on a set of scales, and charging exorbitant prices for it.

d. Death is the leader's name at this stage.

Execution is the final stage leading on from the EFTPOS plastic card system to the mark on the body. Here, it has become compulsory, and death is the penalty for non-compliance.

Let us look again at Stage C — Famine.

'And when he had opened the third seal, I heard the third beast say, come and see. And I beheld, and lo a black horse, and he that sat on him had a pair of balances in his hand.' *Ref.8.

The succeeding prophecy shows a very definite food shortage, which we know is being engineered at this time of writing.

'And I heard a voice in the midst of the four beasts say, A measure of wheat for a penny, and three measures of barley for a penny...' *Ref.9.

When the cry goes out that there is a food shortage and the only way to obtain that food is by taking a permanent mark on the body, and also taking an oath of allegiance to the world leader, people will be queuing up for the privilege.

Key No.2 — Peer Pressure

This is far more pronounced than I initially thought. Many folk know that we travel to various places continually lecturing on these and related subjects. Thousands turn out to our meetings and during our 20 years of work often the halls are so packed with interested people that they spill either outside the hall, or are seated all over the stage.

Small Communities

In early 1989, we were at home having a little time aside to write this book.

Some of our friends invited us to bring the local people up to date and arranged a public meeting in an old shop in a little township nearby, which we will call 'Havenot'.

The keen local Christians did a letter box drop, so that everybody possible would know.

At 7:00 p.m. sharp, our meeting got under way and interestingly, not one local non-Christian man from that town turned up to listen, in spite of the fact that it was all put on for their benefit.

Many assembled at the hotel up the road, probably playing the big fellow, glass of beer in hand and discussing the crazies down the road having their meeting.

Men like this, of course, are similar in a way to an amoeba. Completely spineless. I returned home very tired that night and asked myself 'Why didn't they take this one opportunity?'

The answer was 'PEER PRESSURE.'

In a small town, such as 'Havenot', everybody knows everybody and so it is convenient to hide like a bug under a stone. If someone moves the stone, the bug runs under another one.

One writer summed it up like this 'The fear of man bringeth a snare.' *Ref.10.

Strangely enough, in small communities similar to the local one that I have described in this book, people are much the same.

Some person's opinion of them for a span of 60-70 years, is more important in their thinking than where they will be for all eternity.

I have watched folk listening in my meetings and at the conclusion, as is my custom, I invite people to the front of the hall to commit themselves to Christ. Many times at this point, you will observe people looking nervously around to see if there is anyone present who may know them.

They say 'Oh, there's my boss, Bill, sitting over there. If I go forward to accept God's mercy and salvation, Bill will see me and give me a hard time at work tomorrow.'

Fairly shallow thinking, you will agree.

Years ago, as we were travelling as a family, we were having a Bible reading in our vehicle when this very powerful Scripture cropped up. I took careful note of it, and use it regularly during the course of my public meetings.

'...who are thou that thou shouldst be afraid of a man that shall die?....' *Ref.11.

In straight forward language it says, 'What is wrong with you? The person that is holding you up from making a firm decision for Christ and His kingdom will shortly die also.'

The main questions that you should be asking are:

a. Where is he going?

b. Where are you going?

Please do not be offended. The foregoing is not calculated to be a criticism. It is an unemotional statement of fact.

The men of 'Havenot' in 1989 act as a severe warning to the men in your community. They make their beds, then they have to lie in them.

May God have mercy on their miserable souls.

Key No. 3 — Deception

Already, the picture is becoming very clear.

a. The unavailability of food without the mark and the initiation.

b. Peer pressure to take the mark and the initiation.

c. Deception as foretold by the prophets will play a strong part.

How do you get people to accept and worship Lucifer as their god?

At this stage in history, mankind generally will completely polarise into two main camps:

a. The non-deceived.

b. The deceived.

The classic 'Pilgrim's Progress' gives us insight into this fact. Pilgrim, on his upward journey to the Celestial City, finds a wretched man in a cage built of steel bars. Pilgrim asks the man 'Why don't you come out of the cage?', to which the poor man replies 'I can't. I built it with my own hands.'

'His own iniquities shall take the wicked himself, and he shall be holden with the cords of his sins.' *Ref.12.

Sad, yet I know how true this is in my own experience. Pulling one's self up by the bootlaces is a fruitless effort. What we really need is for someone stronger than us to step into the situation and lift us out of the muck of sin and self. (That's not very New Age is it?)

I'm referring to God's provision — the Lord Jesus Christ.

'He brought me up also out of an horrible pit,
Out of the miry clay,
And set my feet upon a rock,
And established my goings,
And He hath put a song in my mouth,
Even praise unto our God,
Many shall see it and fear,
And shall trust in the Lord.' *Ref.13.

Well said, isn't it?

Each new generation becomes more depraved than its predecessor.

Filthy unclean images cloud peoples' minds. New Age meditation, visualisation and altered consciousness will make the general populace become so out of touch with Almighty God's realities through union with the true Christ, people will be ready for anything.

301

The True Way

My family and I and many others like us, have followed the steps of the Master in our own stumbling way for most of our lives.

The Lord's ways are sweet to us.

His Words are true.

Jesus Christ is the ultimate truth.

Buddha died looking for the truth.

The Freemasons embark on a journey looking for the light.

Many devoted church people think that their organisation is the way.

Young people and old are looking for real life.

Yet the Lord Jesus Christ alone is all of these and more. He said:

'I am the way, the truth and the life. No man cometh unto the Father but by Me.' *Ref.14.

Bold statement? Yes.

Is Jesus the Only Way?

Possibilities. Please be honest and tick the appropriate box.

1. Jesus Christ was a madman in claiming all this. ☐
2. Jesus Christ was deceived in claiming all this. ☐
3. Jesus Christ was a liar in claiming all this. ☐
4. Jesus Christ was who He claimed to be ☐
5. Of course, the odd fellow always arises who claims that the Biblical record is unreliable and Jesus Christ never really said those words.

Ivan Panin Proofs

Sorry. Dr Ivan Panin, whose works could not be faulted by the Nobel Foundation, has proved the divine authenticity of the Holy Bible, in the original texts, using a system of numerics. Therefore, in claiming that the Bible is unreliable, you are setting yourself up as being more clever than Dr Panin, a brilliant Russian mathematician, not to mention the Nobel Foundation.

For further details on all this for the honest seeker, please go to your nearest Christian bookshop and order a book called 'The Seal of God', by F.C. Payne.

God's seal is on His creation, as God's seal is on His Word.

Please don't bother writing to me about this. Just read the book.

The Initiation

The non-deceived will be fundamentalist Bible-based, changed, believers in Christ.

The deceived will be the rest, who will be so messed up in their minds having no standard, will accept anything, even as many so-called learned top Freemasons even now accept the damnable lie, — Lucifer is God.

En Masse

These will be MASS INITIATIONS, done publicly and of course anybody not participating will be seen as a pariah or a threat to society.

The prophet brings a warning for all who believe this message that Lucifer is god.

'Woe unto them that call evil good, and good evil, that put darkness for light and light for darkness that put bitter for sweet and sweet for bitter.' *Ref.15.

Now here's the crunch line.

Statement: 'If you miss Jesus Christ as God's only way of salvation, know this, that throughout eternity, you will be acutely aware that you have missed THE WAY, THE TRUTH, THE LIFE.

Truth versus Error

There is no such thing as a spiritual vacuum. People always fill that God-shaped space within with something else, which sadly, is but a temporary measure. Boats-horses-cars-camping-embroidery-bridge-parties-dances-gardening-wheeling and dealing-hobbies-etc; all good fun, quite legitimate, but if any of these activities makes us too busy for God, we are too busy.

Now for all who hear of Christ and His salvation, the choices are three-fold:

a. Accept
b. Neglect
c. Reject

(b. and c. go together.)

GOD WILL PERSONALLY SEE TO IT THAT ALL THESE RECEIVE THE LIE.

You say, 'God is a God of love. He wouldn't do that would He?'

Yes, He would.

He is a God of love but also a God of justice.

303

Listen: '...because they received not the love of the TRUTH that they might be SAVED. And for this cause God shall send them STRONG DELUSION that they should believe a LIE....' *Ref.16. Emphasis added.

You say 'Hey, wait a moment. That's not fair.'

Another prophet in the Old Testament had the same problem thrown at him in his day. Let's see how he dealt with it, when dealing with the Israeli rebels of his day.

'Yet ye say, the way of the Lord is not equal. Hear now, oh house of Israel. Is not my way equal? Are not your ways unequal?' *Ref.17.

Continuing with the complaint — 'That's not fair.'

God's reasoning is this. It is a real privilege to become a Christian. Some proud people think that they are doing God a favour by getting themselves saved.

The peak of human arrogance is reached by man's refusal of God's remedy for sin i.e. the death of Christ.

Only one thing awaits that person — Judgement.

'That they all might be damned, who believed not the truth, but had pleasure in unrighteousness.' *Ref.18.

Some years ago whilst teaching at a High School, a little music teacher came into my classroom wringing his hands in despair.

He said, 'Mr Smith, I don't think that I can continue on. These children are making a mockery of my instruments. Do you know they are strumming my violins as if they were ukuleles.'

I looked at my bewildered colleague and said 'Mr.....if I were not a Christian who understood the ways of the Lord, I too could not spend a moment longer at this school.'

He gazed at me with an amazed look on his face and spoke a line that appeared to me to have come straight out of the book 'Swiss Family Robinson'. 'Mr Smith, I perceive that you are a seeker after truth.'

I answered 'Wrong, Mr......I am not a seeker after truth. I have found Him. His Name is JESUS.

CHAPTER 47

New Age and the Occult

Let me speak very clearly here. What we are saying in this chapter is that there are many deceptions out to get your soul. All of them are deadly and if not renounced, will take you into eternity, into damnation.

Look at this article thoughtfully. 'Orange County Register', 23rd June 1988.

'Senior Pastor of the 3,000 member church of Religious Science will be sworn in July 10 as president of the United Church of Religious Science denomination.

...The denomination is one of several 'New Thought' groups which hold that truth is a matter of continuing revelation. In general, 'New Thought' holds that 'salvation' is achieved by recognising one's own innate divinity, that God can be sought by looking inside oneself....' End quote.

Oh no-no-no. One thousand times — no!

'There is a way which seemeth right unto a man, but the end thereof are the ways of death.' *Ref.1.

The Manufacturer's Handbook tells us that you will never find salvation within yourself. Remember, the man who tried to pick himself up by his own bootstraps.

'Be it known unto you and to all the people of Israel that by the name of JESUS CHRIST OF NAZARETH....

Neither is there salvation in any other, for there is NONE OTHER NAME under heaven given among men whereby we must be SAVED....' *Ref.2. End quote. (Emphasis added.)

If you wish to be saved, better go to the correct source.

The Old Lie

If this New Age or New Thought is suddenly correct, what about God's plan for salvation for the billions who have lived on earth before all this teaching was dreamed up. Actually, it is the old lie of Lucifer, the snake in the garden of Eden.

'Ye shall be as gods.' *Ref.3. Dressed up? Yes. More sophisticated? Yes, but the same lie.

DON'T FALL FOR IT!

God's plan has always been the cross of Christ. The Old Testament believers looked forward to it. The New Testament believers look back to it.

'Behold the Lamb of God which taketh away the sin of the World', said John the Baptist. *Ref.4.

New Zealand 'Herald', 23rd December 1987.

'Mrs....has taught meditation techniques to people from seven to seventy. Children, she has found, will value a walking 'mantra' a 'secret' word, which can be used to calm them, not sitting quietly as adults do, but on the move....

The.....have worked at dispelling the myths that TM is an Eastern religion....' End quote.

Hinduism

T.M. is actually Hinduism in disguise. For further notes, see 'Second Warning' p141-143. The mantra is a demon's name.

'Seattle Times', 18th January 1987. 'The Coming of a New Age....

The subject of New Age teaching....is not to change the world but to change yourself.....

In fact....said, meditation has helped him discover a spirit guide — sort of like a guardian angel who advises him.

....Its hallmark...is moral spirituality that allows 'freedom of belief'. Many adherents add, freedom from guilt and fear....' End quote.

Write Your Own Road Rules

In other words, if you don't like the road rules, simply write a new road code, but pity help you when the law catches up with you.

Continue quote: '...And New Age has infused popular culture. When Star War's Luke Skywalker says 'The Force be with you, and calls on the spirit of Obi Wan Kenobi for help, he is echoing New Age mysticism. The Army's recruiting slogan 'Be all you can be' and the song 'We are the world', capsulise New Age thinking.

.....It works for me says....She now holds 'visualisation' for interested.....schoolteachers and believes that an invisible guide named Alenna talks to her...' End quote.

A Presbyterian minister got it partially right in this article.

306

Self-Worship

'.....New Agers', he said, 'ultimately end up worshipping themselves....' End quote.

If you're in it, please get out of it now!

Ufology

U.F.O.s are real. A lady and her boys were crossing the Nullabor Plains in Australia in 1988. A U.F.O. buzzed their car, picked it up with the occupants intact and put it down further along the road.

The paint on the car was scorched and there was ample evidence to lead us to believe that this was a true event.

Later on, the lady said she was interviewed by a man in a South Australian police uniform, yet the wearer spoke with an American accent.

Where did all this take place?

Just south of the U.S. base in Central Australia in a place called 'Pine Gap'.

This place is named in Stan Deyo's book 'The Cosmic Conspiracy', which gives an educated account of activities taking place in that area, including U.F.O. activity.

To obtain this book, please write to:

P.O.Box 71,
Kalamunda,
Western Australia 6076.

There are two sources for these objects and neither of them is found in outer space.

Source 1 — U.S.A.

Manufactured in the U.S.A. and using an anti-gravity motor, which sets up a 'harmonic' which tunes in with the earth's energy grid. This harmonic in turn, sets up a vacuum on the leading edge of the craft into which it flies, with no discomfort for its pilot or passengers. They (the passengers) become part of the vehicle and can fly faster than the eye can see, and turn right angle corners with no problems.

Why don't the U.S. government come out in the open and admit this?

The WGA won't do that just yet until the time is right as it

would make all other forms of energy obsolete, and wreck the WGA 'oil economy'.
Be patient. All will be revealed.

Source 2 — Hell

Posing as aliens from outer space, these are demonic spirits from the centre of the earth, mixing with evil powers in the upper atmosphere.

In Old Testament times, these devils came down and married earth's young women, cohabited with them and as a result, giants were born to them, both physically and in evil.

Remember, this was the main reason for the flood; the judgement of God.

'What are you saying?' you ask.

'As it was in the days of Noah, so shall it be also in the days of the son of man.' *Ref.5.

History is repeating itself. Why is evil increasing? Why are doctors afraid to attend an accident victim at night? - In case their drugs get stolen and they get mugged. Gangs, rapes, arsons, muggings, murders.

Evil has increased. Of that there is no argument.

The demons are here again. The coming of the Lord Jesus Christ draws near. Satan is working at top speed.

A scenario put out by Stan Deyo in his excellent book, is that this craft will possibly be part of the WGA plans for these end days. His book makes it clear that the U.S. government is included. The scene portrayed shows these U.F.O. folk as space Messiahs who came to show us a better way.

'Accept our help', they say and will assist in setting up a NOVUS ORDO SECLORUM i.e. 'A New World Secular Based Government'.

A Demonic Encounter.

A New York man describes his frightening encounter. 'Sunday Telegraph', 17th May 1987. 'The Visitors, small greyish beings with huge heads, and almond-shaped eyes, conducted a series of strange medical examinations on their terrified captive, before finally transporting him back to his bedroom.

....For the past year, Streiber has continued his research and meetings with others who have experienced the visitations.

All of them, he says, HAVE A SENSE OF IMPENDING

308

DOOM FOR OUR WORLD, although none can explain why.

....'Blind denial' he says, 'is as empty a response as blind acceptance....' End quote.

You need Jesus—I need Jesus—We all need Jesus.

CHAPTER 48

Israel

Year 1986

At Rome Airport where the massacre took place, we were hustled from gate to gate by anxious officials.

Suddenly they led us quickly through a gate, then on to a low slung airport transport bus, which, accompanied by an armoured car sped between parked planes to the far end of the airport and took us to the front stairs, where we boarded the plane.

Looking behind us, we observed the armoured car parked at the base of the steps with a machine gun poking ominously through a little porthole. What a feeling.

We knew the danger in that area of the world, yet we had promised our tour organiser that we would travel, come what may. I well remember our initial ride to the airport in our family pickup. May, as is her custom, read the Scriptures to me, which is a tremendous help for any person claiming to be a Christian. She read the words:

'And I am with thee and will keep thee in all places whither thou goest and will bring thee again into this land...' *Ref.1.

This really gave us the confidence which we would need later.

As the passengers boarded the Air Italia, I 'felt' the fear in them. Some were weeping and moaning as they passed through the door.

It is no wonder that this was how they felt, as the night before, our plane had been redirected on its way from Australia across Libya, through Gulf of Sidra, so that the US Navy could monitor the progress of ours as well as other flights.

The night before that, America had shelled installations in Libya, and Gaddafi in his anger, was threatening all flights far and near. Looking down, that night on our initial flight, we saw the U.S. battleships and an aircraft carrier all lit up.

Today, we were on our way again. May and I felt quite calm and as our plane swept around the foot on the map of Italy, and off across the Mediterranean to pass once again the dangerous Gulf of Sidra.

Strange Happenings

I looked out of the window and saw three jet streams, apparently

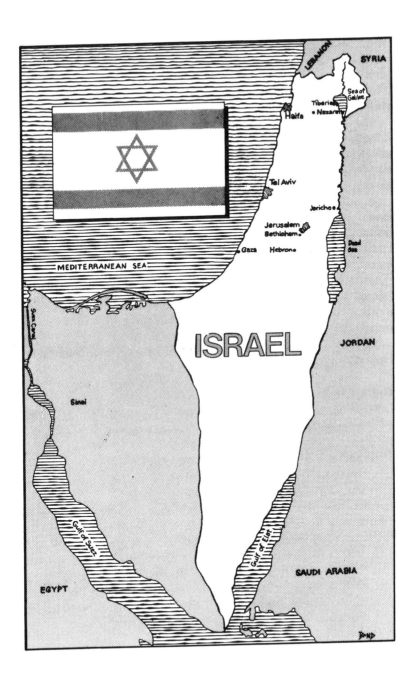

311

from some fighter planes; two on one side of our plane and one on the other. I drew May's attention to this, yet no other passengers appeared to notice these outside flying companions. These people just sat quietly, many gripping their armrests with white knuckles showing.

We passed Libya to the south of us and approaching the coast of Israel, we looked keenly to try to pick up the types of fighters which were accompanying us all this way. The jet streams had been strong and billowing all the way across, and the planes should have appeared, as they slowed down ready to land.

An old Israeli gentleman on board had made the remark when shown these jet streams; 'Never be surprised at what the Israeli airforce will do.' Not once could we see any planes at all however. These jet streams gradually petered out into wisps of smoke like vapour and disappeared.

My wife and I who have experienced so many supernatural deliverances and protection over the years, just had to ask one another, 'Fighter planes or angelic protectors?' One day we will know.

NOTE: The terms Jew and Israeli will be used interchangeably. This is Biblically permissible.

God's Clock

Israel is sometimes likened to God's old clock. World events can be gauged effectively by the prophecies with reference to Israel.

Prophecies Fulfilled and Yet to be Fulfilled

1. In about the year **1900** the return of the Jews from all over the world began to take place.

'That then the Lord thy God will turn thy captivity and have compassion upon thee and will return and gather thee from all the nations whither the Lord thy God hath scattered thee.' *Ref.2.

2. **1917**. General Allenby, under divine inspiration through his prayer to the Lord for wisdom, sent little reconnaissance planes over Jerusalem, which as they flew overhead, had little leaflets dropped from them to the Moslem Turkish invaders below. The notes written in Arabic said:

'Leave the City'—Signed Allenby

In Arabic, the two words Allah and Bey, both references to leadership and divinity caused great consternation amongst the Turks. Here was a message directly from heaven. They fled, and the ancient city fell into British hands without a shot being fired, or a building being damaged.

'As birds flying, so will the Lord of hosts defend Jerusalem, defending also he will deliver it, and passing over he will preserve it.' *Ref.3.

3. **1948** on May 14th, under David Ben Gurion, Israel became a nation. The 'Jerusalem Post' headline stated, 'A Nation, Born in a Day.'

There was no midwife. They were out on their own. No other country was willing to help with the birth of this nation and incur the displeasure of its Arab oil producing enemies.

'Who hath heard such a thing? Who hath seen such things? Shall the earth be made to bring forth in one day? Or shall a nation be born at once? For as soon as Zion travailed, she brought forth her children.' *Ref.4.

4. **1967**. 40 million enemies mobilized themselves against the 2 and a half million Israelis.

The old N.Z. publication, 'Weekly News', called the impending battle 'David versus Goliath.'

During the month of June the night before the first battle took place, I was speaking to a group in the Teen Challenge Coffee Bar in downtown Auckland.

Many young would-be communists were gathered there, waving little red books and shouting 'Read the thoughts of Chairman Mao.'

I jumped up on a coffee table waving my Bible, and shouted:
'Never mind the thoughts of Chairman Mao, read the thoughts of God.'

I went on, 'The thoughts of Chairman Mao will go down the tube, but the thoughts of God will go on forever.'

Challenging them, I continued: 'There is going to be a massive fight in the Middle East shortly. Who's going to win?'

They shouted that Israel would be driven into the sea, to which I answered:

'No, Israel will win.' Within six days of that statement being made, it was proven to be correct.

'Keep not silence O God, hold not thy peace, and be not still O God. For lo thine enemies make a tumult, and they that hate thee have lifted up the head. They have taken crafty counsel against thy people and consulted against the hidden ones. They have said, Come and let us cut them off from being a nation that the NAME

OF ISRAEL may be no more in remembrance. For they have consulted together with one consent they are confederate against thee ......' *Ref.5. (Emphasis Added.)

The enemy still wishes to use the name Palestine. They hate the name ISRAEL. It drives them crazy.

In 1973, whilst Israel celebrated Yom Kippur, the Feast of Atonement, a time of fasting and weakness, the enemy attacked again and for a time began to win the battle. 1,854 Israelis lost their lives during this time.

They began to cry out to their God again and the tide turned.

Out in the Sinai desert, over by the Suez Canal, they finally bottled up the Egyptian army division and had not Henry Kissinger intervened, the Israelis would have wiped them out.

'But as for me, my feet were almost gone, my steps had well-nigh slipped............Verily I have cleansed my heart in vain and washed my hands in innocence. For all day long have I been plagued and chastened every morning...' *Ref.6.

Note the above passage implies the fasting on the Day of Atonement.

Now notice... Continue quote:

'Until I went into the sanctuary of God. Then understood I their end.' *Ref.8.

Now, Israel begins to win. The tide turns.

'Surely thou didst set them in slippery places, thou castedst them down to destruction.' *Ref.9.

Israel finally won in 1973.

We have been to the area twice, and agree that any nation that attacks Israel will have a terrible fight on their hands.

A young Israeli hitch-hiker called in to our home in 1989, and I was able to give him some details about Israel's future.

He asked me whether there would be any more attacks on Israel. This he wanted to know, as he was an unbeliever and this information would give him the impetus he needed to look for the spiritual side of his life.

I told him 'Yes, Israel will be attacked again.' Actually not once, but three more times.

(a) Communist invasion from black African Communist states (called the king of the south in prophecy) and the Soviet Union (called the king of the north in prophecy.)

Those present in this invasion will be the following countries:
1. African Communists.

314

2. Soviet Communists, Libya and other North African States
3. Iran
4. Libya and North African States
5. East Germany
6. Mountain people from Turkey.

Battle Order — No. 1 — Soviet Invasion — Timing — After Peace Treaty

1. A Peace Treaty will be confirmed for 7 years by the new World Leader who himself will be of Jewish extraction.
2. The invasion takes place, whilst Israel is at peace.
3. The enemies are defeated on the mountains of Israel by a conventional weapon being used against them. i.e. 'The velocity factor of 7'.

For a detailed explanation, please read 'Second Warning' pp172-184.

Battle Order — No. 2 — Chinese and south east Asian Invasion

1. The seven year period from the peace treaty will be almost complete.
2. The dam blocking the Euphrates river, situated up in Syria will be turned off and dry up the river, which is a natural boundary between the east and the middle east.
3. An estimated army of 200 million will come against Jerusalem.
4. The Lord Jesus Christ will return from heaven and will personally kill the invaders.
5. Those present on the side of the Lord:
   (a) The Lord Jesus Christ
   (b) The Christians who have died and come back with the Lord for this battle.
   (c) The armies of heaven dressed in white, and all riding white horses.
   (d) The Jewish remnant, probably hiding in the rocky caves of Petra down the Jordan Valley.
6. The Lord Jesus Christ does all the fighting alone, watched by these observers.
7. He wins, and in doing so, kills one third of all who come against Him.
8. This is called the Battle of Armageddon.
9. The valley is 200 miles from end to end, and will be filled with a river of blood to the height of a horse's bridle.

315

10. Result, those killed number 66,666,666.
11. The Lord Jesus Christ will reign from the city of Jerusalem for 1000 years with His born again believers.
12. E.C. Leader and World Church Leader thrown into lake of fire.

Battle Order — No. 3 — Satan and all remaining nations
1. The 1000 years reign of Christ draws to a close.
2. Satan falls in the bottomless pit during this period.
3. Satan is released for a short period.
4. He gathers all nations to go up to Jerusalem to fight against the Lord.
5. Fire comes from heaven and destroys him.
6. He is thrown into the lake of fire where the E.C. Leader plus the World Church Leader await him.

Thus the Great Tribulation is over. The Satanic Trinity is no more.

Christ will reign forever and ever with the believers.

You object — someone says to me: 'You should not include so much religion with all this information. You are stroking the cat the wrong way.'

I reply — 'Let the cat turn around.'

Readers please take note that part way through 1989, Yasser Arafat of the P.L.O. was conducting talks with the Soviet Union.

'Australian', 8th April 1989. Quote:
'Arafat in Moscow for Mid-East Talks......' End quote.

The Soviet Foreign Minister was helping in this peace process.
'Press', 21st February 1989. Quote:
'The Soviet Foreign Minister, Eduard Shevardnadze calling for swift groundwork on a Middle-East peace conference flew into Cairo yesterday for talks with Egyptian leaders and Israeli Foreign Minister Moshe Arens .....' End quote.

Many Jews are leaving the Soviet Union — A Second Exodus
'And I will say to the north 'Give up and to the south, keep not back. Bring my son from far, and my daughters from the ends of the earth'.' *Ref.10.

The Lord God Himself therefore is behind this exodus, and it is all happening NOW. Not in the 1970's but it commenced during the 1980's.

'Australian', 8th February 1989. Quote:

'For the past six months, there has been a massive emigration of Jews from the Soviet Union and signs are that this will be a lasting trend.......Last year 19,000 Jews left the Soviet Union. Upon landing in Vienna, they are asked at the airport by eager young Israelis, whether they want to go on immediately to Israel, the destination stated on their Soviet exit visas. Only 7 percent agree. The rest want to go to America, land of milkshakes and honeycakes.......Few of the stranded Jews in Ladispoli want to go to Israel. This is, the rabbi says, because they have only the vaguest idea about the country. There was little information available about Israel when they lived in the Soviet Union.......The question of whether Soviet Jews should go to the U.S. or to Israel is part of a complex international debate......' End quote.

Things are certainly opening up for them in Russia. It is almost unbelievable after years of persecution.

'Press', 26th January 1989. Quote:

'The first official Jewish culture centre will open in Moscow next month, kicking off a three week festival in main Soviet cities, that reflects a dramatic change in the Kremlin's human rights policy, the World Jewish Congress has announced ..'

Is Jerusalem the Jewish capital?

'Dominion', 15th July 1980. Quote:

'Jerusalem was the Jewish capital long before anybody had ever heard of London, Israeli Prime Minister Menachem Begin said yesterday in a rebuke to British Foreign Secretary, Lord Carrington. In a weekend interview, Lord Carrington said on Israeli television that it would be a great mistake for Mr Begin to move his office to Jerusalem ....' End quote.

'And in that day will I make Jerusalem a burdensome stone for all people, all that burden themselves with it shall be cut in pieces, though all the people of the earth be gathered together against it....' *Ref.11.

In simple English, woe betide any individual or nation who interferes with Jerusalem.

They will confront the living God Himself.

Another fascinating sign of things happening in Israel and surrounding areas is the return of the Black Ethiopian Jews to Israel.

Ethiopian Jews Exodus

Entitled 'Operation Moses' arranged by the U.S. and Israel, it took only 47 days in late 1984 and finished on January 6th, 1985 with 35 missions and uplifted 7,800 people.

Then later the then Vice-President Bush made an agreement with the Sudanese to uplift some more of them. This was to be called 'Operation Sheba'.

Today there are 16,000 of them in Israel, and possibly 10,000 more still waiting for their exodus.

My wife and I have seen them, some living in little cells in Jerusalem in abject poverty, yet they feel thrilled to be 'home'.

'In that day that the great trumpet shall be blown, and they shall come who were ready to perish in the land of Assyria and the outcasts in the land of Egypt shall worship the Lord in the holy mount at Jerusalem.' *Ref.12.

Raiders of the Lost Ark

There are those who believe that the Ethiopian Jews have the Ark of the Covenant, hidden away in a church in Aksum, Ethiopia.

There are other possible sites, yet the prophet Zephaniah implies that these poor Ethiopians, (having looked after and protected the Ark since it was given to the son of the Queen of Sheba by Solomon), will return it to the temple mound in these latter days.

Recognizing in their extreme poverty their gratefulness to God for their return, what better gift could they bring, set it up initially in a tent, on the temple mound and use it as a focal point, for the final ingathering of Jews awaiting the return of their Messiah.

'From beyond the rivers of Ethiopia my suppliants, even the daughter of my dispersed shall bring my OFFERING.' *Ref.13. (Emphasis added.)

Could this be the missing 'Ark of the Covenant'?

Kissinger and Middle East Peace

Earlier on in this book, we read how a German-born non-religious Jewish man now residing in the United States is involved in the Middle-East question.

Dr Henry Kissinger now of Kissinger Associates advising on Economic, Political and Social Issues, is being brought back into the media spotlight.

Remember the Jerusalem Post article of 2nd October 1988,

where Dr Kissinger said that after the American and Israeli elections a Peace Treaty should be attempted. He also fitted in with the prophet who spoke of a seven year treaty away back in about 539 B.C. Kissinger spoke of an initial treaty lasting from 5 to 7 years. Fairly accurate I would say wouldn't you? After all, there is only a gap lasting 2,500 years between the two men.

Uprising

1988 was the year of the Arab uprising. That means, 40 years on from 1948, things dramatically changed in Israel.

The stage was at that point prepared for the media to turn against Israel, thus swaying public opinion. This was necessary prophetically speaking as only the Lord Himself will stand for Israel during the Soviet Invasion that is predicted.

Bible — Miraculous Predictions

Do you not think that some credit could be given at this stage to a divine being who knows the end from the beginning?

Let's call Him the God of Abraham, Isaac and Jacob. The Father of our Lord Jesus Christ, the living God.

Stubborn unbelievers with a skin as tough as the proverbial rhinoceros will no doubt still struggle like a fish trapped in a net, but as this information continues to hammer at your intellect, I suggest at this point that you give up fighting.

Just submit to Jesus and be refreshed by him.

'Come unto me, all ye that labour and are heavy laden and I will give you rest.' *Ref.14.

Back to Kissinger

'Australian', 12th April 1988. Quote:

'Israel should withdraw from the Gaza Strip and part of the West Bank to defensible borders, the former United States Secretary of State, Dr Henry Kissinger said yesterday.....' End quote.

Regarding the Palestine Liberation Organisation — 'Time', 26th December 1988. Quote:

'.... an observation Henry Kissinger has made privately 'If you believe that their real intention is to kill you, it isn't unreasonable to believe that they would lie to you......'' End quote.

People to Watch

The fact is, that this well-known, world figure is involved in the peace negotiations and the following people should be watched carefully.

From Russia — Eduard Shevradnatze
From U.S.A.   — George Bush
From P.L.O.   — Yasser Arafat
?   — Henry Kissinger

Rumours of Messiah — 'Press', 4th January 1980 Quote:

'The rumour is buzzing through the extreme Orthodox community of Israel that the Messiah is coming...........Some reports said the rabbis had dreamed the clash between the mythical monsters, Gog and Magog, would narrowly head off a nuclear holocaust between the super-powers...........Kabbalists have been citing signs of the Messiah's coming for the past year...........But Rabbi Ephraim Manella when asked when the Messiah would come responded with an ancient Jewish proverb.

'Those who tell, don't know, those who know, don't tell.' End quote.

A Generation — 50 Years

Actually some rabbis have been reported as saying that a generation in their reckoning is a period of 50 years.

Jesus said in Matthew 24:34 that every thing would be fulfilled before a generation passed.

The Christians and some rabbis agree on the starting date: 1948 — The founding of the state of Israel.

The year of Jubilee from the Old Testament was reckoned at being $7 \times 7 = 49$ years and on the 50th year, the actual Jubilee was celebrated.

I receive much mail, and some interesting as well as bizarre information is sent to me.

One writer suggested

$$\begin{array}{r} 666 \\ + 666 \\ + 666 \\ \hline 1998 \end{array}$$

The date I find interesting, but I have not yet grasped the logic of adding 666 three times.

However,

$$\begin{array}{r} 1948 \\ + 50 \\ \hline = 1998 \end{array}$$

brings us to a Jubilee from the founding of Israel.

This particular year is very close to the Global 2000 date, so let us do what we are told to do:

WATCH

When Will Messiah Come?

Before, after or during 1998, the Messiah will come. We know he is the one spoken of in the Jewish prophecies, that the majority of Israel today cannot accept because of a temporary spiritual blindness put on them by God Himself.

'.......blindness in part is happened to Israel until the fullness of the Gentiles be come in.' *Ref.15.

In other words, the Lord God of Israel is now giving non-Jews an opportunity into His loving family.

As the blindness in Israel is only 'in part', I would recommend to any Jewish reader, to pray that God will have mercy on you and open your eyes too, because God loves you.

How embarrassing for Israel when their Messiah finally arrives and shows them His hands with holes in them.

Listen to what the Jewish prophet received.

'And one shall say unto him, what are these wounds in thine hands? Then shall he answer those with which I was wounded in the house of my friends.' *Ref.16.

The person we believers amongst the Gentile nations call Jesus is in actuality:

YESHUA and He is ISRAEL'S MESSIAH.

'He came unto his own, but his own received him not.
But as many as received him, to them gave he power to become the sons of God, even to them that believe on his name.' *Ref.17.

A new birth is involved here and I tell you this experience is absolutely marvelous. It is second to none.

'Which were born, not of blood, nor of the will of the flesh, nor of the will of man, but of God.' *Ref.18.

Are you interested in having this relationship with God Himself?

Turn to the back of this book for the prayer.

321

CHAPTER 49

Freemasonry and the Occult

Strange Happenings

The meeting finished at about 9.30 p.m. and I invited a couple of Christian men to stand with me as I prayed over a number of fellows and their families who wished to be freed from Freemasonry.

We shut the door to the room, closed our eyes in prayer and I led the group in the prayer of renunciation of their initial witchcraft vows.

i.e. Entered Apprentice Degree — The cutting of the throat etc. Fellowcraft Degree — The tearing out of the heart. Master Mason's Degree — the tearing out of the bowels.

Each different degree included the blasphemy of sealing these horrendous witchcraft oaths by kissing the sacred Word of God.

As we repeated the renunciation prayer, men began to fall to the floor all over the room with loud crashing noises. One man almost bowled me over and one at the back of the room fell with such a crash that I thought that he may have brained himself, had the presence of the true and living God not been with us.

They were all released that night in the name of the Lord Jesus Christ, and we all went home.

The next day I met one of the men's wives and she startled me by saying:

'My husband told me all about the happenings of last night.' I asked what he had said and she replied 'He told me how you pushed him to the floor and then stood with a foot on his chest as you continued with the prayer.'

I was quick to point out that as he was at the back of the room, and I was at the front, separated by a great crowd of people, it was not I who pushed him over.

Speaking to a fellow servant of God early in 1989, he told me the following story.

His old Dad, who had been a Freemason for many years suffered a stroke and sat day by day in a chair showing very little interest in life in general. The son one day spoke to him very forcefully and recommended, that as he was getting on in years and could no longer attend the lodge meetings, it would be

advisable to renounce his lodge vows and leave, thus opening the door for him to come to a knowledge of salvation through the Lord Jesus Christ.

My friend told me, 'I was shocked when the old man sat bolt upright, his mind apparently clear and lucid, his steely eyes focused on me as he spoke these words; 'I will never do that', and then he lapsed back into his semi-comatose state.

Freemasonry Demon

At that point this man realised that this was no longer his father speaking. He was in direct communication with a demonic spirit.

Men who join the Freemasons have absolutely no idea of its Luciferian demonic nature, usually until they are fully trapped -hook, line and sinker.

When I wrote my first book 'Warning', being quite short of funds, and wishing to save money, I found a group of committed Christian friends, who offered to collate the chapters in the basement area of one of their homes.

As this book had a section revealing the demonic nature of Freemasonry included within its pages, they prayed over it nightly as they worked, that no masons would be able to come near, or harm this book before it was released to the public.

The wife of the man who owned the home was regularly visited by her father (who was a Freemason) and his wife. They used to call regularly to visit the couple, plus the grandchildren.

I was told later that as long as my book was under their home, the Freemason would arrive at the gate with his wife; she would go in to visit the family, but he himself would never venture beyond the garden gate. The family would call out 'Come in Dad' but he would reply 'No thank you, I just feel to wait out here.'

As soon as the book was removed from the premises, he was then free to visit as normal.

A Challenge

Can you explain all these stories away? Try if you will, yet inside you will remain confused.

A Cancer Healing

Whilst in Perth during the 1980's, we visited a small town, some miles to the south.

A young couple came up to us, thanking my wife and I for our book 'Second Warning'.

They explained that their Dad, a Freemason, had been dying with cancer in a West Australian hospital, so they took our book in to him, read him the chapters on 'Freemasonry' and 'How to Set a Freemason Free' (pp87 – 106). The father then asked them to:

(a) Go home and burn and destroy all his Freemasonry gear.
(b) Help him pray the prayer of renunciation of Freemasonry (pp103-106 'Second Warning'.)
(c) Help him with the prayer of salvation through Christ alone (p. 221 'Second Warning'—also to be found at the back of this book.)
(d) Pray for his healing.

The young couple were overjoyed as they told us the story. 'Dad was delivered from Freemasonry demons. He was saved through the grace of God. He is now healed from cancer and is walking around in Western Australia, a well man.'

These are the type of stories that give my family and I strength to carry on.

An ex mason, now a Christian, wrote to me from New South Wales, Australia and told me:

He said that he liked the way I wrote and recommended that I continue to:

(a) Save the masons and at the same time
(b) destroy the craft.

Masons Backtrack

In all NSW chapters, these words have been added after the traditional oath.

'This was the penalty of this obligation in ancient times, we neither could, nor would improve them, but rely instead on the moral obligation attached to this vow.'

I regret to inform these men affected by this apparent backtrack, that demonic spirits take no notice of additions such as this, but continue on to destroy Freemasons, their families and their ancestors to the third and the fourth generations.

I have no fight with the masons. Jesus wishes every mason to be saved.

Witchcraft

Unfortunately, as soon as a man joins up, by taking the oath in the first degree, he puts a terrible witchcraft curse on:

1. Himself
2. His wife
3. His children
4. His grandchildren after him

Please do not hand me the old excuse 'I didn't really mean what I was saying'. This would not go down very well in an earthly court, yet much less in the heavenly one.

Who was it who said 'Swear not at all?' *Ref.1.

It was the same One who said: 'For by thy words thou shalt be justified, and by thy words thou shalt be condemned.' *Ref.2.

There is a terrible price to pay for the 'For he's a jolly good fellow' image of lodge membership.

Curses on Freemasons

1. Lonely wives left at home, attacked in many cases by the spirits that the head of their home invoked at his lodge meetings.

We set a man free one night and he asked me to smash his badge for him. I replied that as it was his problem, and not mine, he should do it himself.

We prayed deliverance over him and he returned home, only to return a short time later in a very shocked state.

Apparently as he was renouncing his vows in our meeting, his wife was attacked by a spirit in her own home, that rendered her unconscious. We prayed for her and she was set free. She told us later that every time her husband went to a lodge meeting, she felt compelled to take a carving knife and go out and kill somebody.

2. Breakdown of marriage and family alienation. Children all out of control, showing no love, obedience or warmth within the family unit.
3. Sickness, strokes and death, miscarriages and female problems.
4. Sexual deviation.
5. Persistent financial trouble.
6. A great lack of true spiritual perception. A real battle to really enjoy the things of God.

Why all these curses, you ask?

Well, when your leader, or your federal head, a 33rd degree mason says in his official capacity:

'Lucifer is God';

what hope have you got? He spoke for you sir. (Full statement of Albert Pike pp96-97, Second Warning.)

What still continues to surprise me is the fact that many so-called 'Christian' leaders belong to the 'craft.'

A man called out in my public meeting one night, claiming that he was defending the craft. I answered:

'Witchcraft'

Some Church Leaders Involved.

Some Catholic priests. (Read 'In God's Name' by David Yallop.)

Some Anglican bishops and vicars.

Some Baptist leaders.

Some Salvation Army leaders. I visited a Salvation Army church with my wife one Sunday morning and the man who greeted us at the door, wore a masons badge. (Compass and Square.)

William Booth, the great founder of this Christian movement would revolve in his grave, if he knew all this had happened to his people.

Some Presbyterian elders and ministers.

Some Methodist preachers. etc, etc.

What hope have these churches got, I ask you, when the leaders go along in their ignorance with the key statement spoken by their great pontiff on the 14th July 1889.

'Lucifer is God.'

For any who are not yet convinced about the surreptitious nature of Freemasonry, please go to your local bookshop and buy 'The Brotherhood' by Stephen Knight.'

STATEMENT: Christianity and Masonry are opposites and are therefore incompatible, one with the other.

Any reader of this book who attends a church with any Freemason holding office, has a satanist in charge of their spiritual welfare. Please give your leader the ultimatum: 'Either you leave Freemasonry, or I leave your church.'

Question: Can these oaths and curses be broken and nullified?

Answer: Yes, but only through the Lord Jesus Christ.

'Christ hath redeemed us from the curse of the law, being made a curse for us, for it is written, cursed is everyone that hangeth on a tree.' *Ref.3.

Let us make it clear that the Freemasons' own writings damn

327

them. Most of these men do not have any logical reasoning ability left, once the demon spirit of the Entered Apprentice Degree is invited in with the appropriate witchcraft oath and symbolism. Proof, Proof, Proof.

From a recognized authority on Masonic doctrine entitled: 'Morals and Dogma of the Ancient and Accepted Scottish Rite of Freemasonry by the master Luciferian and occultist Albert Pike, Grand Commander from 1859—1891.' He held this top position for approximately 32 years and wrote down the rules.

Any reader of this book who is not a 33rd degree Freemason, please do not consider arguing. These are the rules. Either obey them or get out. We quote page numbers only from the 1966 edition.

1. Freemasonry hides its true teachings—you have been fooled.

Pp 104—105 'Masonry like all religions, all the Mysteries Hermeticism and Alchemy, CONCEALS its secrets from all except the Adepts, and Sages, or the Elect and uses false explanations and misinterpretations of its symbols to mislead those who deserve only to be misled, to conceal the Truth which it calls Light, fróm them, and to draw them away from it.

Truth is not for those who are unworthy or unable to receive it or would pervert it.' End quote.

Who is the Way to God?

Who is the Truth?

Who is the Life?

Who is the Light?

Jesus Christ the Lord. These characters proudly make their boast that anybody who is not in the upper echelon of their society i.e. 30th to 33rd degrees (Adepts, Sages, Elect) is fed LIES to keep him occupied.

Do you realise what that means sir? All the nights you locked yourself in your room, or sat up in bed repeating all that information to your wife from your little masonic book was an utter waste of time, for both you and your patient helper. It was a joke and the joke was on you.

2. Blue lodge men 1st degree, 2nd degree, 3rd degree. They start with you and waste your time.

P. 189—'The Blue Degrees are but the outer court or portico of the Temple. Part of the symbols are displayed there to the Initiate, but he is INTENTIONALLY MISLED BY FALSE INTERPRETATIONS. It is not intended that he shall understand them, but it is intended that he shall imagine he understands them.' (Emphasis added.)

Demonic Anger — A Feature
Does this make you mad? It should do.

By the way, 'ANGER' is a special quality in the Freemason's character — The masonic devil hates to be revealed or questioned. Challenge any mason and sit back with a smile as they fly off the handle.

Illustration: At a large public meeting, seating about three and a half thousand people in Australia in about the year 1987, we had made mention of the occult nature of Freemasonry during the course of the lecture.

The meeting closed and May and I sat chatting with friends in one of the front seats. An American man rushed up to us, face red, veins in neck extended and began to verbally attack me, using a very loud voice.

My wife and I felt quite relaxed, as this is part of our work to understand that on occasions such as this, we are not listening to a man of flesh and blood, but to a demonic spirit, using the man's vocal chords and by-passing his intellect.

Once you recognise a demon for what it is, and know that in the name of the Lord Jesus Christ, you have power over it, it leaves you feeling very calm, unemotional and in control. This man yelled on, as we sat quietly, smiled and waited.

'Behold I give unto you power to tread on serpents and scorpions and OVER ALL THE POWER OF THE ENEMY and NOTHING SHALL BY ANY MEANS HURT YOU.' *Ref.4. (Emphasis added.)

After a time of protest, with no apparent reaction from us, the man stopped, shook his head as if to clear it and then spoke logically for the first time.

'Oh, I am sorry, I shouldn't have spoken like that. I seem to have come unglued.'

Wives and families of masons, this will explain why Dad is such an uncontrollable mess at times. You pray for him, that God in His grace will set the poor fellow free from this satanic deception.

3. Freemasonry is Blasphemous.

With each witchcraft oath repeated, the candidate kisses the Volume of the Sacred Law e.g. Bible, thus sealing a witchcraft oath on the Holy Word of God.

Secondly, as the candidate draws to the conclusion of his vows in the Royal Arch Degree, he is asked,

'Brother Inspector, what are you?'

Listen to this and tremble. The poor misguided man, not in possession of his full faculties at the time, or he obviously would be petrified to carry on, takes the holy name of God as given to Moses on his lips and replies:

'I AM THAT I AM'.

May the Lord have mercy on their souls.

4. When and if a man reaches the 17th degree, which is entitled:'Knights of the East and West', he completes the initiation, revealing the Password:

'Jubulum' — significant in the Masonic links with the British, Jack the Ripper murders, (see video — Murder by Decree.) and the Sacred Word 'Abaddon'.

This latter word is also spoken of in the prophecies of Revelation as the King of Destruction. His name in the Greek equivalent is Apollyon.

Any readers who have attended my anti-occult meetings will recall hearing how, when casting this devil out of a young man, the devil bent him backwards so that his heels touched the back of his head. At the name of the Lord Jesus Christ, a terrible cry came from the young man's lips, which went across the room, right through the wall and way down the road.

AH — AAHH — H — H — H — H — h — h — h — h.

The masons have got a vicious one on their hands on this occasion. This individual is the king of the bottomless pit. So far, so bad. Lucifer joins Abaddon.

Read on, there's worse to come.

5. Can a Christian be a Mason?

Listen. 'No man can serve two masters, for either he will hate the one and love the other, or else he will hold to the one and despise the other....' *Ref.5.

There is your answer. Choose carefully.

A sign on a back road in Canada sums it up clearly.

'Choose your rut carefully. You'll be in it for the next 20 miles.'

(a) God and the Lord Jesus Christ. — End result — Heaven.

(b) Lucifer (Satan) and Abaddon (The Destroyer) — End result — Hell.

6. Freemasonry oaths elevate their system above the law of the country.

In the Royal Arch degree, the candidate swears to protect the 'brethren.' 'Murder and treason not excepted.'

This is simple language means that if you go to court against a mason, and a masonic judge in the upper degrees is presiding, you haven't got a show. Please see again these facts in 'The Brotherhood' by Stephen Knight.

It is interesting that just prior to 1990, the N.Z. Government passed a bill, seemingly out of the blue, to make 'treason' no longer punishable by death. I wonder how many masons are involved in the law system of this country; and why the government felt it necessary at this time in history, to pass such a bill.

E.C. countries, please notice this. Your governments will also commit treason and sell your individual countries out to international or World Government bodies when the time is right.

'Townsville Daily Bulletin', 28th January 1984. Quote:

'MP calls for probe into Freemasons KGB link. A conservative Member of Parliament called yesterday for a government enquiry into allegations that the Soviet Union used Freemasons to penetrate British Security Services at the highest level..'

Referring to Mr Stephen Knight's book, continue quote ..' great pressure was brought to bear on Prince Charles when he was in his twenties to follow family tradition and become one of Britain's 750,000 Freemasons......Though he is a member, Prince Philip has not been active in Freemasonry for 30 years, Mr Knight said and the Queen Mother 'a committed Bible-believing Christian', does not approve of the Masons...' End quote.

'Marlborough Express', 7th August 1984. Quote:

'An enquiry into allegations that a council corruption investigation and the career of a Scotland Yard Officer were unfairly influenced by Freemasonry is expected to get under way next week....' End Quote.

I have in my files a news cutting unfortunately with no date on it, about an inexplicable event which took place in a small New Zealand town.

In 1984, a woman was crossing a pedestrian crossing when she was struck by a car. The Ministry of Transport file on the case, later went missing.

Quote: 'In a report in 'The Press' yesterday, it was said by the pedestrian... that the Minister.... thought the file had been removed from the system to defeat the course of justice, and this was done with criminal intent.'

Now, in including this article in this chapter, I do not in any way link the Freemasons or any other group or individual with this case. I use it merely as an example of how easy it is to pervert the course of justice, by men who have taken what in their eyes, is an oath superior to any other allegiance they may have.

Roman Catholics and Freemasonry

Earlier on in this book, we quoted the Roman Catholics official stance on Freemasonry which has changed over the years.

In 1884 Pope Leo XIII said ....'The ultimate purpose of Freemasonry is the overthrow of the whole religious political and social order based on Christian institutions and the establishment of a new state of things, according to their own ideas and based in its principles and laws on pure Naturalism' (Catholic Encyclopedia Volume IX 1910.)

An Italian revolutionary general Garibaldi, joined the 33rd degree of the Scottish rite. Herewith, please read an extract from a secret létter of instructions which was sent to him at the time.

'Masonry being nothing else, but revolution in action, a permanent conspiracy with practical and religious despotism. No single degree reveals the whole truth, the veil is lifted by degrees which hide the truth from the eyes of the curious...' End Quote.

Origins of Masonry (It does not originate in Solomon's Temple)

(a) The Grand Lodge in England began about 1717. They brought in the first three degrees to the blue lodge at this time.

(b) Up until this point, they were in the main, tradesmen who met regularly with their secret signs and passwords.

(c) From 1717 onwards the Masons pretended to be associated with orders of warlike Knights, similar to the story of King Arthur and the Knights and the Round Table.

This was a far more exciting concept than the idea that it had been formed out of a stone-cutters guild.

N.B. It is for this reason that wherever we have been, every person who has the title 'SIR' is a Freemason. There may be some who are not, but I do not know who they are.

This shows the 'jobs for the boys' concept. You yourself can now investigate all 'sirs' and establish the veracity or otherwise of this claim.

Now with all this information, we are ready for a report from the churches on their attitude to Freemasonry.

'Challenge Weekly', 23rd October 1987, reported that the Church of England has endorsed a report produced by the General Synod, including some masons, that quotes:

'1. Freemasonry conflicts with the teaching of the Christian faith due to:

(a) Masonic rituals containing elements of worship.
(b) Freemasonry promotes a concept of salvation by works.
(c) That the name Masons give to God is blasphemous because it was an amalgam of pagan deities...' End Quote.

That applies to New Zealand.

Even in Great Britain the Church of England is getting into the act.

'Sydney Morning Herald', 15th July 1987. Quote

'Church leaders today voted by a big majority to back a report labelling Masonic rituals as 'blasphemy'.

The Church of England's General Synod, meeting in York, had been urged by one bishop not to conduct a witch-hunt or impose undue pressure on Christians who are Freemasons.

The Archbishop of York, ... called Freemasonry 'fairly harmless eccentricity' and said he was sorry churches had started getting solemn about it... ' End Quote.

What a statement by an Archbishop who should know better — sickening actually.

'The Bulletin Magazine' in Australia, 11th April 1989: Quote

'Are the Masons a menace? Are they just harmless old duffers making fools of themselves, or the secret power behind Australia's business, police and public service?...' End Quote.

A Sydney Rabbi who as a mason made a number of quotes in this article says:

Nothing to hide?

'The only thing that Masons will not reveal to non-Masons are particular modes of greeting and recognition of a fellow Mason. Apart from that I can hardly think of one thing in Masonry that one should keep from the public gaze ...' End Quote.

I really like this quote, as that is exactly what I am doing here, opening up the truth to the public gaze. Thank you sir.

Women Should Be Admitted

Finally, in these days of equality, 'Press', 6th May 1987. Quote: 'Rotary, 'must admit' women .....' End Quote.

This is the Supreme Court ruling in the USA.

I am waiting for a brave woman to insist on obtaining membership in the Masonic Lodge. These are days of equality aren't they? Where are the Women's Libbers — come on persons. Get into it. Another devil won't hurt you.

Next, we notice that according to David Yallop's book, 'In God's Name' a number of conspiratorial groups are named, which links:

The Roman Catholic Church — Vatican Bank

The Masonic Lodge — P2 of Italy.

The Mafia — who when they are murdered, all have Roman Catholic funerals, and while they are alive, have their profits laundered through the Vatican Bank.

In his book, Mr Yallop mentions three men who are named as international thieves.

i.e. Calvi — Murdered with Masonic ritual in Great Britain, or suicided.

Gelli — The P2 lodge master

Sindona — Extradited after the book was written and subsequently died mysteriously in an Italian jail.

For a long period since Yallop's book revealed the truth of all this, Archbishop Paul Marcinkus was afraid to come out of the Vatican and risk facing arrest by the Italian authorities; however he has subsequently passed away.

Remember the Roman Catholic law was originally against their members being Freemasons.

David Yallop pointed out that a new Common Law came in to force on November 27th 1983, which dropped the ruling that Freemasons are subjected to automatic excommunication.

Thus the Vatican masons are all safe and Lucio Gelli of the P2 Lodge can smile again.

What a dreadful web of corruption. How good it is to walk with the Lord.

'If we walk in the light as he is in the light, we have fellowship one with another and the blood of Jesus Christ his son cleanseth us from all sin.' *Ref.6.

What to Do

My humble advice to any reader who is linked in any way at all to this horrible system is:

1. Leave it.
2. Write a letter to the registrar saying: 'Please strike my name from the register. I no longer wish to have a masonic funeral.
3. Pray the sinners prayer at the end of this book.
4. Be delivered from Luciferianism (Satanism.) The prayer may be found in my book 'Second Warning' pp103-106. Burn and destroy all Masonic gear in your possession.

'The graven images of their gods, ye shall burn with fire. Thou shalt not desire the silver or gold that is on them, nor take it unto thee, lest thou be snared therein, for it is an abomination unto the Lord thy God.

Neither shalt thou bring an abomination into thy house lest thou be a cursed thing like it, but thou shalt utterly detest it and thou shalt utterly abhor it, for it is a cursed thing.' *Ref.7.

Information Vindicated

An ex 32nd degree mason friend of mind, now a Christian pastor in Malaysia, told me that everything I have been saying is correct. Now, as twice born believer in the Lord, he recommends that even the masonic Bible is polluted and should be burnt along with all the other gear.

They Must Be Warned

It is easy to assume that all the top men in the movement know all this, but the strange thing is that they don't.

Travelling through an overseas country with my wife some time ago, we had a stopover of fifteen minutes at a certain airport. I rang a pastor friend who told me a very interesting story.

Pastor...... 'I recently received a call on the phone from a top mason, who complained that my church had sponsored a series by Barry Smith, who during the course of his talks, made adverse statements about the lodge. These meetings were videoed and the videos were later distributed.'

The pastor then asked the top mason if he had seen the videos that he objected to. He replied that he hadn't, so it was agreed that the tape would be sent to him for his consideration. This was duly done.

I waited on the phone for the punch-line in this story. Apparently the top mason rang back again later, with the following statement, which delighted me immensely.

'I am convinced'.

What does this imply? It is the duty of every reader who has gained any knowledge on Freemasonry through either our books, or from any other source, to warn masons of the terrible spiritual danger they are in.

Some people say, 'I know how evil it is, yet I don't want to upset them.'

Imagine if I caught your son about to put a glass of poison to his lips and I tried to prevent him.' Before I can get to him, you stop me by saying:

'Please don't upset him. He thinks he is going to drink raspberry juice.'

'When I say unto the wicked, Thou shalt surely die, and thou givest him not warning, nor speakest to warn the wicked from his wicked way to save his life, the same wicked man shall die in his iniquity, but his blood will I require at thine hand.' *Ref.8.

Shouting and Raving to be Expected

I wish to also point out, that these men will probably shout and rave, yet you should remain calm at all times.

'Yet if thou warn the wicked and he turn not from his wickedness nor from his wicked way, he shall die in his iniquity, but thou hast delivered thy soul.' *Ref.9.

A Good Substitute Fellowship

To any ex-masons who feel lost and crave the fellowship of good men, I highly recommend a great Christian group to which I personally belong.

—Full Gospel Business Mens Fellowship International (F.G.B.M.F.I.)

Look in the telephone book in any major city and make contact.

To any man who claims to be a Christian and also a mason remember:

—Renounce your Christian faith OR

—Renounce Freemasonry.

Other Secret Groups

Question: What about the Oddfellows?

N.Z. 'Herald', 28th February 1980: Quote

'Ritual skulls keep their secrets—Three unidentified skulls repose in a musty basement of a hall in Helensville.... two small boys found the old skulls in the basement of the Oddfellows Hall... But Constable... was not happy.

The use of human relics in lodge initiation rites is 'just not on' he said. But the Auckland Deputy District Grandmaster elect of the Independent Order of Oddfellows disagrees. He said the skull was part of the initiation ceremony which dated back to the founding of the order in America in 1819.

'It's not witchcraft or anything like that' said Mr ...... All the lodges had a skull, usually only one, and there were about 100 lodges in the country.....While non-sectarian, the order followed the Bible and respected the moral of stories such as that told about the Good Samaritan ....' End Quote.

A Final Eyeopener

To any mason reading this section of my book, who wishes to debate the occult nature of this society;

(a) Pick up your 3rd degree Master Mason's certificate and notice the EYE of Horus (or Lucifer) and

(b) Look at Moses pictured standing on top of the left hand pillar.

Answer this please. Why is Moses pictured with horns on his head?

CHAPTER 50

The World Church System

Danger, Danger

The large room was packed out as I spoke about the link-up of religion with politics in these last day's prophetic lectures.

A man and his family suddenly arose and stormed out of the meeting. The audience soon heard him shouting from outside.

'Smith, when you come outside, I am going to knock your head off with a rock.'

At the conclusion of the meeting, we cautiously moved into our vehicle, and I told my family that it may be wiser the following evening if we all wore crash helmets.

On another occasion another dear man threatened me with crucifixion, should I return to that area.

By now, you, the reader, probably have an insatiable desire to travel with us, to meet such nice people.

Seriously now. Why does RELIGION evoke such an emotional response?

This chapter will answer the question without any emotion, so I invite you to read on.

Throughout much of this book, you will recall many references to the religious aspect in prophecy.

Where does it fit in with all this political and economic information? Where does it come from? Where do we find religion's origins? We shouldn't be afraid to find out the answer to this intriguing question, so I set myself to the task of answering it. In this chapter, we will deal with the end of all religion, Catholic, Protestant, Middle Eastern and Eastern, which will culminate in pure Satanism.

I have discovered that any person with a religious upbringing usually falls into one category or another.

(a) Satisfied and unable to think. (Ostrich—head in sand approach.)
(b) Satisfied and still able to think.
(c) Dissatisfied and not interested.
(d) Dissatisfied and looking for answers.

I address this chapter to groups (b) and (d).

338

A dear friend of mine, Max Rasmussen — now living in Apia Western Samoa, put it this way.

If there is a motor accident and there are bodies lying all over the road, wishing to assist, you stop at the scene and rush around lifting eyelids. When you see that some are completely lifeless, you leave them and look for those who are only injured.

Jesus said the same thing actually.

'Let the dead bury their dead.' *Ref.1.

A Brief History

We have discovered, hidden within the pages of the Holy Scriptures a history of the true and the false churches running side by side. Jesus referred to the two groups as the:

Wheat (True)   Tares (False)

The hidden code for this history lesson is uncovered in the book of Revelation with the seven church ages and also in the parables of Jesus found in the book of Matthew Chapter 13.

If we put them side by side, a clear picture emerges.

Revelation — Matthew

1. Ephesus — Parable of the Sower
2. Smyrna — Wheat and Tares (Weeds)
3. Pergamos — A Mustard Seed
4. Thyatira — Leaven (Yeast)
5. Sardis — A Buried Treasure
6. Philadelphia — A very beautiful Pearl
7. Laodicea — A Large Net

Outline

1. In the year 1986, my wife May and I stood in the streets of Jerusalem and I made a statement.

THE TRUE CHURCH STARTED HERE IN JERUSALEM.

'And when the day of Pentecost was fully come, they were all with one accord in one place.' *Ref.2.

Later on we read, after the gospel had been preached:

· 'Then they that gladly received his word were baptized, and the same day were added unto them about three thousand souls.' *Ref.3.

Now these people met in Jerusalem. This was the beginning of it all.

339

Note how and where they met.

a. 'And all that believed were together and had all things in common.

b. And they sold their possessions and goods and parted them to all men as every man had need.

c. And they continuing DAILY with one accord in the TEMPLE and from HOUSE TO HOUSE did eat their meat with gladness and singleness of heart,

d. Praising God and having favour with all the people. And the Lord added to the church DAILY such as should be saved.' (Emphasis added.)

My Question

Is your Christian fellowship anything like this today, or do you suspect things may have deteriorated?

A Valid Question

(i) **EPHESUS** THE FIRST CHURCH AGE. Started about 30 AD. The first church in Jerusalem corresponds with Ephesus in the secret code. They were the first faithful Christians who worked hard for the Lord.

'I know thy works and thy labour and thy patience and how thou canst not bear them which are evil.......' *Ref.5.

Notice the first church conducted beautiful spontaneous worship services.

'How is it brethren, when ye come together, every one of you hath a psalm, hath a doctrine, hath a tongue, hath a revelation. Let all things be done unto edifying.' *Ref.6.

You can detect the informality of it all. Genuine love for the Lord Jesus Christ drew them together.

It is imperative to understand that once they came to know Jesus in a very personal way, they met in several ways:

(a) The Temple — Obviously with all the dead religious form, the spiritual ones amongst them would not gain much at all, yet they continued there, much as some do in many churches today, not to learn, but to keep up contacts.

(b) House to house — The real fellowship and worship was gained in their informal house meetings, where they dealt with reality.

(c) There was no priest present. In fact the very concept of a man ruling over their spiritual life appalled them.

340

Nicolaitans

'But this thou hast, that thou hatest the deeds of the Nicolaitans which I also hate.' *Ref.7.

The word Nicolaitans comes from two words in Greek:

nikao—to conquer and

laos —the laity—the ordinary person.

It was and still is, a religious demon that takes over men and women who love high pulpits and platforms and all the priestly garb, which separates the priesthood from the ordinary people.

The early church hated it.

God hates it.

I also hate it, being a public speaker myself.

Jesus told them clearly not to elevate a man to this false position of authority and certainly not to call him 'FATHER', or even RABBI. Jesus certainly hit at man's religiosity.

'But be not ye called Rabbi, for one is your Master, even Christ, and all ye are BRETHREN.

And call no man your father, for one is your Father which is in heaven.' *Ref.8. (Emphasis added.)

Humility was the key in the early church.

'But he that is greatest among you shall be your servant.' *Ref.9.

(d) According to the Matthew 13 parable of Jesus, the early church Christians fed spiritually on the pure seed of the Word of God, which when planted in good soil (or a clean heart), not mixed with weeds (church tradition etc) brought forth a good crop.

The Root Determines the Fruit

'Ye shall know them by their fruits.' *Ref.10.

It is different today isn't it?

What is your church leader like?

—Does he smoke?

—Does he drink and mix with the boys?

—Does he swear and tell the odd dirty joke?

The fruit will tell you the root.

This early church continued on and spread from Jerusalem carrying its pure seed message everywhere.

Persecutions

These Christians upset the society of the day so much that a series of persecutions rocked its foundations, and drove them underground.

The persecutions were conducted mainly from ROME where the Roman Empire of the day had its capital.

The early Christians would take dangerous sea voyages across the Mediterranean to distant shores such as Italy, carrying the good seed of the pure gospel.

Imagine yourself arriving in the HEATHEN CAPITAL of the world, setting up a pure Christian home fellowship in secret, in opposition to the highly established religious Roman style worship which included

(a) High Priests and Emperor worship
(b) High dignitaries
(c) Statues to countless Roman gods.
(d) Altars
(e) Candles
(f) Religious vestments and garments for the leaders
(g) Superstitious doctrines e.g. telling the future by throwing the entrails of a goat and observing the angle of their landing.
(h) The worship in particular of the sun god.
(i) Magnificent buildings and religious temples.
(j) The High Priests acting like gods and the common people in abject fear and trembling of displeasing the hierarchy.

Is all this ringing a bell in your heart? Even as you read this, you are beginning to sense; 'Hey, this is true. I can see the little groups of Christians, faces glowing with heavenly joy, in the midst of all this heathen confusion.'

Roman Emperors

The main secular Roman persecutors were:

(a) Nero—64 AD—Probably executed Peter and Paul along with many others.
(b) Domitian—96 AD—Accused Christians of atheism as they refused to participate in Emperor worship.
(c) Trajan—98—117 AD—Called the church a secret society and an illegal religion. Look at that. The believers did nought but good for society, yet they suffered for it. Thus did their master, the Lord Jesus Christ before them.
(d) Hadrian—117-138 AD—Made martyrs out of quite a number.
(e) Antonius Pius—quite liked the Christians, but had to uphold the Roman law. Killed many including Polycarp.

343

There were others which led on to:

(f) Diocletion — For ten years under his reign, Christians were hunted in caves and dens, burned, tortured and thrown to wild beasts. An effort was being made to stamp out true Christianity. Even in Israel today, the Roman colosseums may still be viewed. My wife and I felt the horror by standing in the little cells that the early Christians huddled in, awaiting their encounter with the lions.

Catacombs — Beneath the streets of Rome, these galleries 8-10 feet wide and 4-6 feet tall extend for hundreds of miles. These areas were used for services, burials and refuge during these terrible first 25 years of history since the crucifixion of the Lord Jesus Christ.

Infiltration

(ii) **SMYRNA** — THE SECOND CHURCH AGE. Started about 100 A.D.

This second era shows us prophetically that a time of religious persecution was on the agenda. The true seed would shortly have to contend with the false weeds.

'Fear none of those things which thou shalt suffer, behold the devil shall cast some of you into prison that you may be tried ....' *Ref.11.

Shortly, the key word will be:

'Infiltration' — which leads to 'corruption'.

It is a strange phenomena in life that things always degenerate and never improve, unless outside artificial pressure is applied.

Illustration No. 1

You do not need to teach your children to do evil. You do not sit around the fire at night and say:

'Children, your mother and I will teach you swearing tonight, then on the other nights of the week, we will concentrate on such subjects as lying, stealing and murdering etc.'

No this is not necessary. You do however, have to teach good behaviour.

'Train up a child in the way he should go, and when he is old, he will not depart from it.' *Ref.12.

Illustration No. 2

A box of apples with one bad apple in it, will ultimately turn

344

all the apples bad. Never in all history has a box of good apples turned a bad apple good again.

Reality in Christianity
— Even so, within Christian fellowships.

A beautiful group of pure-hearted believers is quite simple to infiltrate and ultimately corrupt, owing to man's sinful frailty.

The code in Jesus second parable in Matthew 13 yields up its secret.

'The Kingdom of Heaven is likened unto a man which sowed good seed in his field:

But while men slept, his enemy came and sowed TARES among the WHEAT and went his way....' *Ref.13. (Emphasis added.)

Satan's Master Plan

Taking the real seed of the life changing gospel to HEATHEN ROME was a precarious step. It had to be done, yet, within 100 years of the Master giving his life to save us on the cross of Calvary, Satan (ex Lucifer) waited in the Roman wings, laughing up his sleeve.

He said, 'Here they come, the poor suckers. By the time I am finished with this Christianity, the people will not know up from down. With my ages of knowledge, I know that the best method for destroying something is to approach it, not from 'without' but from 'within."

Satan continues on with his thoughts.

'I must follow the system of 'gradual infiltration' with apparently superior ideas in running church life.

I'll start with 'leadership.' The Christian's strength at this moment of time lies in the ability to listen to God's Holy Spirit and thus they are impregnable.'

Sidling into a fellowship meeting one day, a pagan Roman made the suggestion that a leader should be appointed, which would make things easier all round, by taking the responsibility off the congregation, for the making of major decisions.

It sounded so right, a show of hands assisted the passing of the remit; — sometimes referred to as:

THE THIN EDGE OF THE WEDGE

Roman Bishops. A series of Roman Bishops were set in office from 67 AD — 154 AD.

Key thought — Believers 'led by the Holy Spirit continued on quietly from house to house and embraced no weeds of tradition, just the pure seed of God's Word, led and illumined by God's Holy Spirit.

[Please read this section again.]

Please note that although there were a series of Roman Bishops for 500 years from Christ,

THERE WERE NO POPES until the year 440 AD.

'What's that' you say?

THERE WERE NO POPES until the year 440 AD.

What about Peter being the first pope?

Two words cover this thought — 'Pure fiction.'

(a) There is no HISTORICAL evidence that he was even Bishop of Rome, never mind Pope of Rome.

(b) Not once in the Holy Scriptures did he ever claim any such position.

(c) The only thing that did apparently concern Peter on the leadership level, was that those coming after him would be involved in:

'Lording it over God's flock, rather than showing themselves examples.' *Ref.14.

Is Peter the Rock?

Now it is at this point that the wise 'hang in there,' and the ostriches say 'Enough — lead me to the sandpit.'

The message in the Gospel of Matthew, chapter 16 and verse 18 is a thoroughly good verse if read in context.

Read your own Bible from verse 13. Jesus is asking 'Who do people say that I am?'

Peter answers, 'Some say this and some say that, but I say: 'Thou art the Christ, the Son of the living God.' *Ref.15.

In verse 17, Jesus commends Peter for his answer and tells him that it was His Father's divine revelation that enabled him to get this correct.

Now, on to the 'crunch point.'

Verse 18. Jesus speaking to Peter recorded from the Greek language into our English Bibles.

By the way, our second daughter Rachel, is married to our son-in-law John, a lovely Greek born believer in the Lord Jesus Christ.' He has authenticated what I am about to write here.

'And I say also unto thee, thou art Peter (petros-pebble) and

346

upon this rock (petra-foundation stone, i.e. Peter's testimony that Jesus is Lord) will I build my church and the gates of hell shall not prevail against it.' *Ref.16. End quote. (Words in brackets added for clarity.)

The Greek language was not spoken by Jesus at this point. He spoke Aramaic, but the Greek translators never missed out on a minute point of difference in a shade of meaning. For this reason, their language is far more rich and full than English. The Greek translated into English should have made this 'vital, very important point' clear, but the translators failed us.

You question me at this point: 'Then the church was **not** built on Peter?'

Peter, Only a Foundation Member

Answer: 'Only partially. He was a foundation member along with the other apostles and prophets, but Jesus Christ the Lord is the key to the whole thing.

Proof, proof, I hear you cry. All right, here it is.

'Now then ye are no more strangers and foreigners but fellow citizens with the saints, and of the whole household of God.' *Ref.17.

This passage of course refers to twice-born believers in Christ, not your average religious go-to-church-regularly person.

'And are build upon the foundation of APOSTLES AND PROPHETS—JESUS CHRIST himself being the CHIEF CORNER STONE.' *Ref.18. (Words in capitals emphasised.)

Was Peter part of the foundation? — Yes, as an apostle, yet only a pebble.

Was James part of the foundation? — Yes, as an apostle, yet only a pebble.

Was John part of the foundation? — Yes, as an apostle, yet only a pebble.

Was Matthew part of the foundation? — Yes, as an apostle, yet only a pebble.

Was Philip part of the foundation? — Yes, as an apostle, yet only a pebble.

Was Bartholomew part of the foundation? — Yes, as an apostle, yet only a pebble.

Was Thomas part of the foundation? — Yes, as an apostle, yet only a pebble.

347

Was Simon the Canaanite part of the foundation? — Yes, as an apostle, yet only a pebble.

Was Andrew part of the foundation? — Yes, as an apostle, yet only a pebble.

Was James part of the foundation? — Yes, as an apostle, yet only a pebble.

Was Lebbeus part of the foundation? — Yes, as an apostle, yet only a pebble.

Was Judas Iscariot part of the foundation? — Yes, as an apostle, but he lost his position to Matthias.

Was Isaiah part of the foundation? — Yes, as a prophet.

Was Jeremiah part of the foundation? — Yes, as a prophet.

Was Ezekiel part of the foundation? — Yes, as a prophet.

Was Daniel part of the foundation? — Yes, as a prophet.

Listen, I'm going to stop the list here.

Many of you have never been told all this before. It is not your fault.

Peter was a likeable enough fellow, but like you and me, full of faults. God in his mercy allowed him to be a 'part' of the foundation only, but

PLEASE, PLEASE, if you wish to elevate someone, make it the CHIEF CORNER STONE — THE LORD JESUS CHRIST.

At this point, you throw up your hands in horror and say : 'It's not going to get worse is it?

Remember the bad apple? — Read on.

(iii) **PERGAMOS** — THE THIRD CHURCH AGE. Started about 154 AD.

Satan's infiltration really got under way at this point. The warning is given in unmistakable language.

'I know thy works, and where thou dwellest, even where Satan's seat is, and thou holdest fast to my name and hast not denied my faith....' *Ref.19.

At this point, God himself brings a clear word to the pure seed Christians, still meeting house to house, yet constantly under threat from the 'official' weed counterfeit run by none less than Satan — the master counterfeiter. The passage goes on to reveal God's anger.

'......I have a few things against thee, because thou hast there them that hold the doctrine of Balaam who TAUGHT Balak to cast a STUMBLINGBLOCK before the children of Israel to eat things sacrificed unto idols and to commit fornication.' *Ref.20. (Emphasis added.)

The two characteristics of this counterfeit weed system therefore are to do with:
1. Idolatry
2. Sexual sin.

The secret code found in the parables comes to our assistance once again.

'....The kingdom of heaven is like a grain of mustard seed which a man took and sowed in his field.

Which indeed is the least of all seeds, but when it is grown, it is the greatest among herbs and becometh a tree, so that the birds of the air come and lodge in the branches thereof.' *Ref.21.

In this chapter, no one church needs to be singled out for attention.

Religion is the name of the game

I was fascinated to learn some years ago, that the word religion itself comes from the basic root meaning:

TO BIND. In other words, turn religious and be bound up. Turn to God through Jesus Christ who is Lord and be set free.

'And ye shall know the truth and the truth shall make you free.' *Ref.22.

Buddha died looking for the truth, but Jesus said He was the truth.

Have you ever wondered where all the EXTRAS come from? The founder of Christianity had no extras at all, in fact when he wished to wash the single robe that he possessed, it is apparent that he would have to find a secluded beach on which to perform this task. Modesty would require this to be the case.

Now remember, this weed system started small, but like Fabian Socialism of today, gradualism led on to extra weeds being added to assist in the binding process of human souls.

Extras List (Unknown to the Pure Seed Christians)
1. Robes for religious duties. The Roman law officials wore very colourful garments and hats and it was suggested that the church hierarchy adopt this form of dress. This was not initially official practice but it soon caught on.
2. Incense long associated with various religious rites was unfortunately added by the enemy to the weed system, and helped remove the simplicity of Christian worship.
3. Candles, holy relics, scapulars, all helped confuse the main issues of the individual's personal relationship with the Lord.

4. The most subtle and satanic extra to be added was in direct rebellion against the stated will of God.

'Thou shalt not make unto thee ANY GRAVEN IMAGE, or any likeness of anything that is in heaven above, or that is in the earth beneath or that is in the water under the earth.

Thou shalt not BOW DOWN thyself to them, nor serve them, for I the Lord thy God am a jealous God....' *Ref.23. (Emphasis added.)

When any of the flock dared to question the presence of such statues to Jesus, Mary, Joseph and the saints, they were told by their leaders that these were 'aids to worship.'

In other words, their leaders were correct, and apparently God made a mistake with His specific command.

Danger in Images

Of course the people were not told the danger of statues and images. How could they possibly know that all religious statues and objects of veneration, including the CRUCIFIX, have demon SPIRITS in them and add not in blessing but in cursing the one who honours them.

No wonder God commanded His people to destroy them.

'The graven images of their gods, shall ye burn with fire... for it is an abomination to the Lord thy God.'

Notice the mustard seed started small, grew into a big tree and had birds resting in its branches.

These birds spoken of in this passage refer to terrible demonic religious oppression.

Referred to as Babylon by the prophet, this 'weed counterfeit church system' is referred to like this, in reference to its ultimate destruction.

'Babylon the great is fallen, is fallen and IS BECOME the habitation of devils and the hold of EVERY FOUL SPIRIT and a cage of EVERY UNCLEAN AND HATEFUL BIRD.' *Ref.25. (Emphasis added.)

I observed a sign on a wall of a shop which sums up the next chapter.

'As I sat musing one day, sad and lonely,

A voice came to me from the gloom,

Smile, cheer up and be happy,

Things could be worse!

So I smiled, did cheer up and was happy,

350

And behold things did get worse.

(iv) **THYATIRA** – THE FOURTH CHURCH AGE. Started about 300 AD.

From this period on, many of these EXTRAs became official weed church policy and were officially adopted.

Therefore from the 3rd century to the Reformation in the 16th Century, the openly EVIL time of this major religious deception began.

It was so gradual, people didn't notice the ROT SETTING IN.

Good News – note very well.

– From the first seed church, filled with genuine committed clean living believers, it was God's eternal plan that these dear persecuted folk would one day be gathered together and make up a BRIDE for His dear Son the Lord Jesus Christ.

The counterfeit weed group mixed fully in worldly affairs, finally moved to include:

'Politics' in with 'Religion'

At that point, God called it the Whore, or the Harlot or the Prostitute System.

Never let anyone ever say to you again, that the true church comes out of Rome. You know better now.

RECAP: In 1986, May and I stood in **Jerusalem**, where I said: 'The true church started here.'

In the same year we stood in the square outside St Peter's in **Rome**, where I said:

'The False church started here.'

There is no argument. We are dealing unemotionally with pure history at this point.

Regarding THYATIRA in our coded secret, we see a mention of the dominating 'prostitute' system rising up at this period of history.

'Notwithstanding I have a few things against thee, because thou sufferest that woman Jezebel which calleth herself a prophetess to teach, and to seduce my servants to commit fornication and to eat things sacrificed to idols.' *Ref.26.

'Behold I will cast her into a bed and them that commit adultery with her into great tribulation, except they repent of their deeds.' *Ref.27.

I have been absolutely shocked as I have read the historical record of this false weed system, built on 'extras' which have no relevance at all to the beautiful godly system founded by our Lord Jesus Christ.

Weed Prostitute group's EXTRAS made official. (These are approximate dates.)

320 AD	Wax candles 375 AD Veneration of angels and dead saints.
394 AD	The Mass as a daily celebration adopted.
431 AD	The worship of Mary and the term 'Mother of God' adopted.
500 AD	Priests dressing differently from the Laity (ordinary people). This began years before this, unofficially. of course.
593 AD	Gregory brings in the fake doctrine of Purgatory. There is no such place.
600 AD	The Latin language, for prayer and worship—not understood by many.
600 AD	Prayers directed to Mary.
610 AD	The title 'Pope' given to Bishop of Rome by a wicked emperor named Phocas.
709 AD	Kissing of the Pope's feet.
750 AD	Temporal power of the Popes began. Involvement in politics.
788 AD	Worship of images and relics. Idolatry official at this point. This had been unofficially going on for years, previous to this date.
850 AD	Holy Water with pinch of salt, blessed by priest.
890 AD	Veneration of St Joseph.
965 AD	The baptism of bells. Instituted by Pope John XIV.
995 AD	Canonization of dead saints, by Pope John XV. (The truth is every believer in Christ is a saint.)
998 AD	Fasting on Fridays.

11th Century—The Mass was gradually developed into a continuously enacted blasphemous sacrifice. The Scriptures clearly teach that Christ was offered ONCE FOR ALL. Hebrews 10:12.

1079	Pope Hildebrand, Bonniface the VII—The celibacy of the Priesthood. This is a doctrine of devils. I Tim. 4:1-3.
1090	The Rosary. Copied from Hindus and Muslim people.
1184	Inquisition of heretics.
1190	The sale of Indulgences—A licence to sin, on a pay

as you go basis. It was this evil that brought about the reformation.

1215	Transubstantiation — Turning the bread and wine supposedly into the literal body and blood of the Lord. Direct paganism.
1220	The adoration of the wafer (host). Pope Honorius gave the decree.
1229	Bible reading by ordinary people forbidden.
1287	The scapular introduced. Fetishism claiming this brown cloth with Mary's picture on, worn next to the skin will save one from evil.
1414	Communion cup forbidden to the ordinary people, which is in direct contradiction of Jesus' wish. He gave it to His own apostles to drink.

Remember 593 — Purgatory — Now again in 1439, it is proclaimed as a dogma of faith. What a damnable lie, and money making mechanism, playing on people's sorrow and fear for their dead loved ones.

$1000 cash reward is offered to any person by this author, who can find one verse in Holy Scripture about purgatory.

Sacraments Spoil Salvation

Paul spoke to a young believer Timothy, using these words regarding 'Salvation.'

'And that from a child thou hast known the holy scriptures which are able to make thee wise unto salvation through faith which is in Christ Jesus.' *Ref.28.

The seven sacraments of the weed prostitute system take the poor individual directly away from God's written and revealed method of salvation.

Hey, it is getting very serious at this stage, you will agree. Sacraments of the weed prostitute system.

(a) Baptism (wrongly administered to babies instead of believing older persons. First of all the child is exorcised with oil on its head and salt in its mouth to drive out demons.)

= Stage 1, away from the Holy Scriptures and faith in Christ Jesus.

(b) Confirmation — Links the child or adherent to the system.

= Stage 2, away from the Holy Scriptures and faith in Christ Jesus.

(c) Marriage — A thoroughly recommended practice, however

353

as a weed sacrament, binds the couple further to the system and leads them further away from the Holy Scriptures and faith in Christ Jesus.

(d) Mass and the Holy Eucharist — A blasphemous deception, where a weed prostitute priest pretends to change a man made wafer into the literal body of the Lord Jesus and the wine, into his blood.

Not only blasphemous, but also ridiculous. A mouse may then get at God and eat Him up after the service if the priest is not careful.

This major deception makes another god out of an element and a demon spirit of course can use any other god to act as a stepping stone for oppression.

The poor victim now moves a step further away from the Holy Scriptures and faith in Christ Jesus.

(e) Penance or Confession (which is commenced early in life) to a priest of the weed prostitute system, puts a tremendous physical strain on a man who is not permitted by the system to marry and thus fulfill his natural physical desires.

No wonder, the history of the system is filled with depravity and strange practices. It is not only unfair to the priest but leads the individual away from the Holy Scriptures and faith in Christ Jesus, not only to save but to also forgive.

Jesus is the High Priest — Go to Him only.

'My little children, these things write I unto you, that ye sin not. And if any man sin, we have an advocate with the Father, Jesus Christ the righteous.' *Ref.29.

This weed system leads away from the Holy Scriptures and faith in Christ Jesus.

(f) Holy Orders, only for men.

(g) Final Unction (Last rites). Here is a poor soul breathing his or her last gasp, and in comes you know who with his black book and religious artifacts.

Does he read the Holy Scriptures speaking of salvation through Christ to the dying person?

No — He continues on with his religious mumbo-jumbo set out for him by the weed prostitute system, and the unfortunate person misses out on Jesus for about the seventh time.

Christ's Work All in Vain

When I examined all the effort that our Lord Jesus Christ put in, to save us from our sins, set us apart as his own holy children, and give us assurance of everlasting life, I find it all very confusing. I believe the term used today is : CATCH 22.

As a preacher who holds large public rallies, I may feel obliged not to state all these 'facts' in the interests of:

LOVE – FELLOWSHIP and UNITY

and simply sit back and watch people go to hell, with no clear voice of warning.

People have reasoned with me about my two previous books, taking issue particularly with my observations on religious matters.

I am not a naturally vindictive person, like many I know, who go around bashing others. Ask my family.

Disunity?

On the other hand, when I do state these observations I am accused of bringing a spirit of disunity amongst the brethren.

I am not doing this as the two groups have absolutely nothing in common.

'Be ye not unequally yoked together with unbelievers, for what fellowship hath righteousness with unrighteousness, and what communion hath light with darkness, and what concord hath Christ with Belial, and what part hath he that believeth with an infidel. And what agreement hath the temple of God with idols, for ye are the temple of the living God..' *Ref.30.

The truth, I bring here, spoken in the spirit of love need not cause any distress.

Lancing a boil usually brings relief.

Only Ground for Unity

Weed prostitute people, listen.

Seed bride people, listen.

Our common ground is only the grace and mercy of God and His plan of salvation through the Lord Jesus Christ.

To those who's eyes have been opened as to the uselessness of the EXTRAS, this word comes with new power.

'Wherefore come out from among them, and be ye separate, saith the Lord and touch not the unclean thing and I will receive you.

And I will be a Father to you and ye shall be my sons and daughters saith the Lord Almighty.' *Ref.31.

355

The hidden code in Matthew Chapter 13, gives the appropriate parable at this 4th stage as being the leaven (or yeast.)

'....the Kingdom of heaven is like unto leaven which a woman took and hid in three measures of flour until the whole was leavened.' *Ref.32.

We have seen that through these terrible dark ages, the weed prostitute system usurped the place of the real true Christianity yet the real has always continued on, holding their gatherings large and small, and honouring the name of Christ who bought them with his precious blood.

Continue List of Extras

1508	The Ave Maria commenced and was completed by Pope Sixtus V at the end of the 16th Century.
1545	Council of Trent declared tradition as equal authority with the Bible. Actually, each destroys the other.
1546	Apochryphal Books added to the scriptures.
1560	The official creed of Pope Pius IV was imposed.
1854	The Immaculate Conception of the Virgin Mary proclaimed by Pope Pius IX in that year in spite of the fact that even Mary confessed to needing a Saviour. Luke 1:46-47.
1870	Pope Pius IX proclaimed Papal Infallibility.

This is dangerous ground to walk on. Any man trying this type of thing would do well to consider his personal meeting with the King of Kings, the real Judge.

STATEMENT: 75% OF THE RITES AND CEREMONIES OF THE WEED PROSTITUTE SYSTEM ARE OF PAGAN ORIGIN

I have in front of me at time of writing, a list of disgusting practices committed by the Popes in a period of history called: 'The Rule of the Harlots', which we will deal with later in the book.

All these dates are from 904 onwards (for any serious student of history). There was a full page on this subject in the Daily Mirror, Sydney Australia, dated 24th November 1986, under the headings:

'Intrigue — Immorality — Bickering — Marriages — Inquisition.'

I identified this article with a thought I read in a book entitled:

356

'Out of the Labyrinth' by L. H. Lehmann; where he points out that this weed prostitute system 'leaves you at death, not good enough for heaven, yet not bad enough for hell.'

Confusion Regarding Salvation

I think that sums it up. How many of its adherents or members can confidently say, 'I am saved now by the blood of Jesus? ☐
I have as a present possession, everlasting life? ☐
I don't need any EXTRAS? ☐
Christ has made me FREE? ☐
HALLELUJAH!
Please check the appropriate boxes.

(v) SARDIS — THE FIFTH CHURCH AGE. Started about 1483.

The corruption was unbelievable at this stage in history, yet there were still people of principle around both inside and outside this weed prostitute system.

Some Good Folk in Weed System

Our hero comes right from within the system which leads me to make my next STATEMENT:

NEVER LET THOSE 'OUTSIDE' THINK THAT ALL 'INSIDE' THE SYSTEM ARE CORRUPT

In actuality some of those dear ones inside this ultra-polluted organization have — more dedication, love and desire for the Lord, than those outside it.

I remember a speaker was once asked why it was that those who belonged to, or attended some of these orthodox religious groups, suddenly lit up with the fire of God, would become more dynamic than those who had been brought up in and had become familiar with seed bride teachings.

The answer was given:

A Key Thought

'If you have a measure of life, any more life given is not such a big deal. When you are in death and surrounded by death, any light and life at all presented to you is of momentous importance.'

Good News for Willing Teachable Believers

It is for this reason, I believe that in these last days, prophetically speaking, the Lord will pick many of those who previously had roots in this weed prostitute organisation, enlighten them, cleanse them, save them, replant their feet on the correct foundation— Christ, and use them in a very special and supernatural way.

I regret that it is sadly possible that those of us who have it apparently all together in the field of doctrine, sometimes lack in the field of reality, fire and love.

In the Sardis age we read:

'Thou hast a few names, even in Sardis who have not defiled their garments and they shall walk with me in white for they are worthy.' *Ref.33.

The man who found the buried treasure, in the coded history of Matthew 13 was none other than a monk in the weed prostitute religious system.

He watched things go from bad to worse and became so distraught within, it burned like a fire in his bones as he wept over the failures of the 'system' and sought out God's truth, just as some 'brave' readers of this book are doing now.

His name? MARTIN LUTHER 1483-1546

Luther saw the excesses all around him, and began to examine the system's beliefs.

He initially discovered 95 errors and nailed them to the church door at Wittenberg. A brave man indeed. We need more with parchments, hammers and nails in our day.

1. This man scourged and flogged himself, even inventing new ways of torture to bring him closer to God.
2. He dearly loved the weed prostitute system.
3. He visited the librarian who upon seeing his distress written all over his face asked him:

'And how are you Brother Martin?' He answered, pointing to his head. 'I know it all here.' Pointing to his mouth 'I can speak it all from here'. Pointing to his heart 'I have nothing here.'

Are you the reader feeling similar thoughts at this time?

Extras No Longer Necessary

4. One day in an act of penance, walking up some church steps on his knees, a burst of revelation suddenly hit him from the sacred scriptures:

'The just shall live by faith.' *Ref.34.

358

In the light of this verse, the REFORMATION started.

It was seen that the EXTRAS, (and there are many of them) were superfluous — no longer necessary.

Only Jesus and His work fully completed at Calvary had any real significance.

A Buried Treasure — Here is the secret code revealed once more.

'Again, the kingdom of heaven is like unto a treasure hid in a field, the which when a man hath found, he hideth and for the joy thereof, goeth and selleth all that he hath and buyeth that field.' *Ref.35.

Weed Group Hide Salvation

Martin Luther did exactly that. Knowing from experience the fact that the weed prostitute group HIDES the SIMPLE TRUE GOSPEL of SALVATION from its people, Luther set out to remedy the situation.

The simple gospel of salvation was on the way back. The seed bride group could now come out of hiding where they had been for centuries.

Stage 1. Like Lazarus, at Jesus command, they came back to life.

Stage 2. The EXTRAS now needed to be shed.

Luther gave up his:

(a) good name,

(b) his reputation,

(c) his position,

(d) his friends,

(e) his safety and security.

Why?

He had found a treasure, unknown to about 1 billion weed prostitute adherents, even today.

'For by grace are ye saved, through faith, and that not of yourselves, it is the gift of God. Not of works, lest any man should boast.' *Ref.36.

Notice at this point, that I as the author of this book, have not tried to persuade any person to leave the weed prostitute system.

God's word encourages people to do so, but I don't, as the warning is clear.

In pulling up the weeds, I may inadvertantly pull up some of the good seed people at the same time. All I do here, is present the history of the thing, and leave the rest to the Lord.

359

'The servants said unto him. Wilt thou then that we go and gather them up?

But he said, Nay, lest while ye gather up the tares, ye root also up the wheat with them.' *Ref.37.

Now in the closing days of this era, a great uniting ecumenical movement will bring many groups back under the umbrella of the weed prostitute system. They will unite. It is predicted that at this time an angel is involved in tying them up in bundles, thus preparing them for judgement.

'Let them both grow together until the harvest and at the time of the harvest, I will say to the reapers, Gather ye first together the tares and bind them in bundles to burn them, but gather the wheat into my barn.' *Ref.38.

Persecution really started at this point in history, from Luther onwards.

The weed prostitute system viciously attacked the seed bride wheat group, as is recorded in books such books as 'Fox's Book of Martyrs.'

Murdered

During a period of 1500 years, the Inquisition and other persecutions have been responsible for the deaths of:

68 million seed bride wheat believers, at the hands of the satanically inspired, weed prostitute false religious system (these figures are openly revealed in a book entitled 'The Martyrology' in the Vatican Library), and still some cry UNITY, UNITY at any cost.

Can I ignore the blood of 68 million beloved believers in Christ crying from the ground?

Do I seek revenge on their behalf? — NO.

'Dearly beloved, avenge not yourselves, but rather give place unto wrath, for it is written, 'Vengeance is mine, I will repay, saith the Lord.' *Ref.39.

Ridley & Latimer

Near the end of 1988, we went to visit my sister Jacqueline, and her husband Don and family near Oxford, England.

At that time, I fulfilled an early ambition. I stood on the cross in the middle of an Oxford Street, where two early Christian brothers of mine, gave their lives for Christ, at the hands of the weed prostitute system.

Date: Oxford England, 16th October, 1555.

These two men, Ridley and Latimer, refused to admit the blasphemy of the doctrine of transubstantiation (the bread and wine being turned into the literal body and blood of Christ.)

They were tied on either side of a stake and Latimer spoke first.

'Be of good comfort Master Ridley and play the man. We shall this day light such a candle, by God's grace, in England, as I trust shall never be put out.'

Ridley saw the flames rushing upwards and cried out 'Lord receive my spirit' and Latimer on the far side of the stake cried 'Oh Father of heaven, receive my soul.

The flames did their job well. Within seconds these two gracious men stood in the presence of the one who said:

'He who liveth and believeth in me shall never die.' *Ref.40.

Ridley however, suffered very badly before he died. The fire burned his lower portion before the upper torso, causing him to cry out:

'Let the fire come unto me – I cannot burn.'

Horrific is the key word. The weed prostitute group did this, and believe me, the Lord states that he has not forgotten.

The persecutions under this terrible weed group, was far far worse than anything secular Rome meted out to the early believers.

Religion Worse than Politics

This religious devil driving the prostitute weed system is described by the prophet as being 'drunken with the blood of the saints.'

How many? 68 million.

Others Picked Up the Spirit of Murder from Religion.

Later some so-called protestants, got involved in the murder syndrome killing some hundreds of persons who didn't see eye to eye with them.

Later, Calvin, Knox, John Wesley and others were used to restore some semblance of truth to the world on into the 18th century.

Bible reading became popular amongst the ordinary people.

Massive revival meetings were held and tens of thousands were saved and added to the family of God.

Luther's treasure, the Gospel of salvation did its work well. Christ took his rightful place again.

(vi) PHILADELPHIA – THE SIXTH CHURCH AGE.
Started about 1900.

In 1904, under a man called Evan Roberts, the Welsh revival broke out. People fell in the streets and fields under the power of God.

Even down in the bowels of the earth in the Welsh coal mines, men prayed and openly worshipped God.

In Azuza Street, Los Angeles, under the Spirit of God's influence, an old man named Seymour and his colleagues experienced a spiritual power explosion and miracles of God again began to take place.

'I know thy works: behold I have set before thee an open door, and no man can shut it, for thou hast a little strength and hast kept my word, and hast not denied my name.' *Ref.41.

People from all walks of life WHO WERE WILLING experienced this new burst of power.

Some seed bride people received it.

Some seed bride people rejected it, crying 'Not for today.'

Some weed prostitute people received it.

Some weed prostitute people did not receive it, crying 'It doesn't fit in with our established 'weed' dogma!'

The mystery code sums up this period in these words:

'Again, the kingdom of heaven is like unto a merchantman seeking goodly pearls.

Who, when he had found one pearl of great price, went and sold all that he had and bought it.' *Ref.42.

God's Power Returns Again

People who began to move in this supernatural realm with the Spirit of God were initially viewed with suspicion, and in many cases ostracised.

My personal testimony is that when we were living in the Pacific Island of Western Samoa, in the early 1960's, 3000 souls turned to Christ through a supernatural outpouring of God's power.

We wrote back to New Zealand rejoicing over these wonderful happenings, and received a reply saying:

'Be careful. It may be the devil.'

Wonderful. Satan apparently had become an evangelist for the Lord and was winning souls for Jesus.

The Charismatic Movement was raised up at this time, and the Pentecostals increased numerically.

362

(vii) LAODICEA THE SEVENTH CHURCH AGE. Started about 1970.

Things were humming along well. Charismatics and Pentecostals were all living on a high.

Souls were being saved by the thousands.

Bodies were being healed by the thousands.

Gifts of God's Holy Spirit were in evidence.

The key subject in many cases then moved from salvation — to power.

Gradually, David Wilkerson's warning came to pass.

We moved into a period of a Christless Pentecost.

Jesus made it clear that the work of God's Holy Spirit was to magnify and exalt the Lord Jesus Christ.

Number 3 exalts Number 2, who exalts Number 1, in the tri-unity.

'But when the comforter is come, whom I will send unto you from the Father, even the Spirit of truth which proceedeth from the Father, he shall testify of me.' *Ref.43.

And again,

'Howbeit, when he the Spirit of truth is come, he will guide you into all truth, FOR HE SHALL NOT SPEAK OF HIMSELF....' *Ref.44. (Emphasis added.)

The sad thing about this period is that the folk who called themselves believers in the truth, did the same things they had always done in their services, but little or nothing happened anymore.

Like Samson years before;

'And he wist not that the Lord was departed from him.' *Ref.45.

A description of this final church age, is spelled out for us in quite harsh, yet clear terms.

'I know thy works, that thou art neither hot nor cold,. I would thou wert hot or cold.

So then, because thou art LUKEWARM and neither cold nor hot, I will spew you out of my mouth.' *Ref.46. (Emphasis added.)

Have you ever been served up a lukewarm cup of tea or coffee? When your host turns the other way, you normally pull a face and utter a modern colloquialism:

'YUK'

This apparently is how the Lord feels about the Christian situation on earth right now at the end of the 1980's.

'Modern Christianity is', to quote the understatement of the year, 'not in very good shape.'

I laughed when an acquaintance of mine in New Mexico in the year 1988 spoke these words.

'The body of Christ is an emaciated invalid lying in bed with a 200 lb set of lips. It has developed out of all proportion, and it is hard to change.

Just because the lips are well-developed, it doesn't mean that what is coming out of them is necessarily right.'

This statement is harsh, yet partially true of some sectors, yet not all of the body of Christ.

A challenge to all who are concerned about the weaknesses in the work of the Lord, would involve a thorough reading of Isaiah Chapter 1, at this point, with emphasis on verses 18-20, showing again the great mercy of the Lord.

Three heresies have crept into sections of the seed bride group, which I will outline herewith.

No. 1 Heresy — Kingdom now

Taken to extremes, this teaching implies that the Christians are now doing the work, that we know, Biblically speaking, should be done by Jesus when He comes the second time.

Some of these folk even deny that He is coming a second time. How sad.

When Jesus said these words 'The Kingdom of God is within you', He was not lying. All born again Christians represent the kingdom of God on earth, but the true work of the kingdom will culminate at the second coming of our Lord Jesus Christ.

Reconstructionism

These people teach that the believers are going to move into politics and positions of responsibility to such a degree, that society in general will become subject to the laws of God and therefore, the second coming of our Lord Jesus Christ is almost irrelevant. I personally, find the latter part of this teaching dishonouring to the Word of God.

In saying this, I believe we still need to infiltrate society as 'salt'. Every town and sector needs fifth column infiltration.

You ask me 'Do you think Christians should get involved in politics, school committees etc, etc.?

Answer: 'Only if you are a super strong believer and feel genuinely called of God to do so, otherwise your Christian life will suffer.'

Hear the words of Paul.

'No man that warreth, entangleth himself with the affairs of this life, that he may please him hath chosen him to be a soldier.' *Ref. 47.

Imagine being in the army. The battalion is just moving into battle, and they ask where you are.

The answer is given, 'I'm sorry, Sergeant. He is not available at the moment. He is running a hamburger stall in the city.'

If you wish to get involved,
do it as Jesus did — be salty
do it was Paul did — be salty

We agree that 'Kingdom Now' taken in correct perspective applies only to the influence of born-again believers in the community.

The tunnel vision of some Christians implies that their particular church or belief is the only way.

We believe that Christians who are true followers of Jesus Christ will permeate their communities with the beautiful concept of living Christianity, bearing in mind at all times that it is the Lord Jesus Christ and His return that will bring the fullness of the Kingdom to this earth.

No. 2 Heresy — Hyper Faith. (Name it and claim it.)

This teaching was born of a genuine desire to see God move supernaturally once again.

Travelling through South East Asia and other parts of the world, my wife and I have met many folk who believe this doctrine and have gone to extremes with it. This has resulted in a loss of fellowship which was previously enjoyed with other believers.

Like the rest of us, these dear deceived people know that the Lord is not moving miraculously at this time and like us, they wish he would, but unlike us, they have latched onto a:

'Gnostic secret' that appears to assist God in working supernaturally, once again, even sometimes against his will.

It is a wink, wink, nod, nod situation. 'We 'know' something. It's a pity you haven't learned the secret yet.'

As one who has been out soul-winning for Christ for over 20 years, I watch the proponents of this gnostic (secret knowledge sect) continue on working for the Lord in their own way yet supposing all the time that they are working by

'Faith'

This gnostic secret however, is not true faith. It is a Satanic deception, which centres around the 'ego', or 'self'.

Springing from the New Age teachers, this thing has permeated sections of Christianity who should have known better.

Self realization
Self forgiveness
Self acceptance
Self worth
Self love
Success
Prosperity etc etc.

I do not read anywhere in the Scriptures, that either Jesus, Paul or any of the early Christians were into 'self' in any way whatsoever.

Which of these was it who said:

'It is no longer I that live, but Christ that liveth in me'? (Based on Galatians 2:20.)

Here is a statement by a missionary who regularly visits rich and poor countries. Whilst in an extremely poor area, he murmurs; 'Where are the faith teachers?'

That question really sums up what I am trying to say.

In truth, these dear brothers and sisters of ours, do not see any more souls saved or bodies healed, or miracles take place, than we do.

Sadly, when their 'faith prayers' do not succeed, in some cases, they blame the poor person who asked for their prayer as:

— Not having enough faith

— This leads to guilt and despair.

— This leads to pulling out of Christianity altogether.

It is a very dangerous doctrine indeed.

In saying all this, I recognise that many of the 'faith' churches are doing a tremendous job in the field of evangelism and I publicly state that this thrills me.

When the true revival hits the earth, we will all become one again because real things will happen to real people.

Heresy No. 3 — DON'T GO TO CHURCH

All over the country in New Zealand, and also around the

world, masses are pulling out of churches and spending their Sundays for themselves.

You ask them why and they say:

1. The church has nothing to offer me.
2. I don't get much fellowship there anyway.
3. The sermons are boring.
4. They sing too long.
5. I get more time with my family now.
6. I get my fellowship elsewhere.

Do you? Do you really? Come on—look me in the eye. God does not tell lies, nor give fruitless advice.

'Fellowship MUCH MORE as you see the day approaching' (Based on Hebrews 10:25.) i.e. the second-coming of Jesus. (Emphasis added.)

'Comfort one another with these words.' *Ref.48.

Which words? 'Christ is coming'. How can you do that if you don't fellowship?

My son Andy said to me, 'Dad, people criticize the church, but the Word of God says,

'Christ loved the church.' *Ref.49.

You ask me, 'Barry, do you attend church when you return home after your tiring missions?'

Answer 'Yes.'

Why? 'Because I am instructed 'Exhort one another daily, while it is called today, lest any of you be hardened through the DECEITFULNESS OF SIN.' *Ref.50. (Emphasis added.)

Traps for Young Church Dodgers

1. You say you have made alternative plans and fellowship in private homes.
   —Do you do this regularly and at least once on the Lord's day?
2. By speaking against the church, where do you send your new converts to Christ that you are continually out winning with all this spare time on your hands—to a fellowship?
3. Don't you feel a barrier when you meet one of your old friends who still attends a born again 'church?'
4. Do you realize that as far as the other Christians in your town or area are concerned, you may as well be dead'?

367

They never see you. Why, even the early Christians in the initial seed bride church still met in the 'temple' and then from house to house.

They knew the wisdom in keeping up 'contacts'.

You've been conned dear one.

(a) Take your Sunday mornings off, go on.

(b) Lie in bed. Think of us fellowshipping around Jesus all together as He commanded.

(c) Go to the beach in the afternoon. Don't bother honouring the Lord's day. It's all part of the same package of deception which leads to rebellion.

(d) Try and stop others going to church too. It will make you feel a great deal better.

By the way, you are also setting a lifelong and eternal pattern for your children and grand-children to follow. Are you happy with that?

I could never understand the following scriptures until recently.

'The love of many will wax cold.' *Ref.51.

'For there shall arise false christs, and false prophets, and shall show great signs and wonders insomuch that, if it were possible,
—they shall deceive the very elect.' *Ref.52.

'But evil men and seducers shall wax worse and worse, deceiving and being deceived.' *Ref.53.

If you are out of the fire, you are a lone brand, and will soon go out. You know that is what is happening to you now.

Your Bible is scarcely used,

The TV knob knows your fingers well,

You're on the skids if the truth were known.

'Let God be true and every man a liar.' *Ref.54.

The seventh church age thinks it is all right, but listen to God's over-view.

'Because thou sayest, I am rich and increased with goods and have need of nothing, and knoweth not that thou art

wretched

miserable

poor

blind and

naked.

I counsel thee to buy of me gold tried in the fire.' *Ref.55.

Listen, brother or sister in Christ. Ask the Lord for another chance.

Say Lord, let me go through the fire if necessary, but don't cast me away.

Now I have some really great news for genuine believers who come out from either camp, in a genuine search for reality.

(a) The seed bride or

(b) The weed prostitute

Time Running Out for the Weed Prostitute Group

First of all, let us make a STATEMENT: God does not intend to let the weed prostitute system continue on much longer. It has done more than enough damage.

If you talk to some of the members about the scandals in the system, they reply with their deluded minds working overtime:

'This shows you the supernatural protection afforded our group. It stands firm in spite of the many scandals.' — Remember to read David Yallop's book 'In God's Name'.

I have news for all these deceived ones, and it is all bad.

The Weed Prostitute is approaching high noon. It's destruction is not only assured, but predicted in very precise detail.

Church Union

This will continue to take place, as those who have any remaining links with or respect for the weed prostitute system, will ultimately 'go home to mother.'

Seed Bride Infiltrated

As we have already learnt, the genuine believers who have continued on meeting together and worshipping the Lord throughout the ages, are no longer being openly persecuted by the weed prostitute system.

This is a dangerous situation.

Come in to my parlour said the spider to the fly.

STATEMENT: Shortly, as the media is making clear, the groups who split away from the weed prostitute will link back again in union with her. — Remember the angel binds them together ready for burning; then comes the judgement of God.

.PROPHECY: 'And there came one of the angels which had the seven vials and talked with me, saying unto me.

Come hither and I will show unto thee the JUDGEMENT of the GREAT WHORE that sitteth upon many waters.' *Ref.56. (Emphasis added.)

369

INTERPRETATION: The waters in prophetic terms, refer to the nations of the earth.

STATEMENT: The whore, or prostitute is identified clearly.

PROPHECY: 'So he carried me away in the spirit into the wilderness and I saw a woman sit upon a scarlet coloured beast, full of names of blasphemy having seven heads and ten horns.' *Ref.57.

INTERPRETATION: The woman is the mother in charge of the weed prostitute group. In this scene, she is pictured riding a scarlet coloured beast. This is the new European Community leader, a political man influenced greatly by religion, (dominated may be a better word.)

PROPHECY: 'And the woman was arrayed in purple and scarlet coloured, decked with gold and precious stones and pearls, having a golden cup in her hand, full of abominations and filthiness of her fornication.' *Ref.58.

INTERPRETATION: The purple is the colour chosen for the Bishop of Rome. The scarlet coats trimmed with ermine are worn by the college of cardinals. The gold, precious stones and pearls speak of the immense wealth of the system, much of it given by the poor. The golden cup full of abominations reveals the systems' absolutely disgusting behaviour over the centuries, culminating in the death of one of their leaders who showing a rare display of morality, was about to unmask the Vatican Bank laundering fraud.

The filthiness of her fornication comes about through the twin evil practices of:

(a) The confessional

(b) The non-married status of the priests.

STATEMENT: The history of the seed prostitute system has been fairly cleverly covered up or played down, to this point in time.

Filth in the Weed System

During the period known as 'The rule of the Harlots' the following filth took place.

904-911 AD Sergius III had a mistress Marozia. She, her mother, Theodora and her sister filled the papal chair with their paramours and bastard sons; and turned the papal palace into a den of robbers.

This period is called also the 'Pornocracy'.

955-963   John XII, a grandson of Marozia was 'guilty of almost every crime, violated virgins and widows high and low, lived with his father's mistress, made the papal palace a brothel, was killed while in the act of adultery by the woman's enraged husband.'

984-985   Boniface VII murdered Pope John XIV and maintained himself on the blood-stained papal throne by a lavish distribution of stolen money. The Bishop of Orleans referring to John XII Leo VIII and Boniface VII called them 'monsters of guilt, reeking in blood and filth; Anti-Christ sitting in the temple of God.'

1033-1045   Benedict IX was made Pope as a boy of 12 years old through a money bargain with the powerful families that ruled Rome. Surpassed John XII in wickedness, committed murders and adulteries in broad daylight, robbed pilgrims on the graves of the martyrs, a hideous criminal, the people drove him out of Rome.'

1046-1047   Clement II was appointed Pope by Emperor Henry III of Germany, 'because no Roman clergyman could be found who was free of the pollution of simony and fornication....'

The same spirit prevails today, yet I do not wish to speak any more along these lines.

PROPHECY: 'And upon her forehead was a name written. BABYLON THE GREAT, THE MOTHER OF HARLOTS AND ABOMINATIONS OF THE EARTH.' *Ref.59.

INTERPRETATION: Notice the weed prostitute system is at this point referred to not as a 'woman' but a 'mother'. This means that she must have 'children.'

That is all who join together with her in the near future to form a:

SUPER-WORLD CHURCH including:

1. The weed prostitute mother system,
2. Approximately 5 major protestant groups,
3. Eastern religions,
*4. The church of satan,
5. The New Age Movement.

STATEMENT: This may not appear possible, but behind the scenes, all is being prepared.

371

PROPHECY: 'And I saw the woman drunken with the blood of the saints and with the blood of the martyrs of Jesus.' *Ref.60.

INTERPRETATION: We have read already of the countless souls who were sacrificed to this 'monster: or iniquity, the weed prostitute system.

It is stated that in the 30 years between 1540-1570, no fewer than 900,000 believers in Christ were put to death in a war of extermination.

The weed sought to destroy the seed.

Strange you will agree.

I can sit here writing all this and you can sit reading it and not feel anything.

Neither you nor I knew these people, yet they all had families and friends, they all felt pain, horror and fear when the so-called servants of God, dragged them from their homes to the torture dungeons.

Can't you hear their screams and piteous cries for help?

Have any of the holy and infallible leaders, bishops or even laymen in the weed prostitute system ever confessed to this or apologized for it?

NO!

Has God forgotten it?

NO!

Can we believers forget them and put their miseries out from our minds?

NO! NO! NO!

Can we forgive the perpetrators of these crimes?

By God's love and grace we can, but God will not.

Thus it is stated in the prophets.

Headquarters of Evil System Identified

To this point, you may be hoping desperately that we have given a wrong interpretation of all this.

Let us now see where the system is based.

PROPHECY: 'And here is the mind which hath wisdom, the seven heads are seven mountains on which the woman sits.' *Ref.61.

In this book of future events, we can't afford to go around making false and unsustainable claims, so let us now read the second part of this prophecy.

'And the woman which thou sawest, is that great city which reigneth over the kings of the earth.' *Ref.62.

INTERPRETATION: There are many cities in the world with seven mountains or hills; some of which are Tokyo, Japan — Bonn, West Germany (the hills here are away from the city) — Auckland, New Zealand — even Sydney, Australia; yet none of the aforementioned fits the conditions.

We are looking then, for a city which has:
(a) Seven mountains or hills
(b) A system which dominates many nations from that geographical area.

There is only one city, and the vast majority of students agree that it would naturally refer to the city of Rome. Within Rome however, is another State.

The Vatican State is religious, yet more importantly, very political.

End time prophecy makes it clear that these two will go together, hand in hand.

1. One World Government — controlled by a man named as Antichrist.
2. One World Religion — controlled by a man named as the False Prophet.

NOTES
1. Religion will dominate politics. i.e. The prostitute woman (world church) rides on the beast (E.C. Leader).
2. The E.C. and leader become tired of religious interference and destroy the religious system.

'And the ten horns which thou sawest upon the beast, these shall hate the whore, and shall make her desolate and naked, and shall eat her flesh, and burn her with fire.' *Ref.63.

3. You may ask why this must take place in this order.

'For God hath put in their hearts to fulfill his will and to agree and give their kingdom unto the beast until the words of God shall be fulfilled.' *Ref.64.

WHAT FURTHER PROOF DO WE NEED? LET'S NOT BE STUBBORN
4. The whole picture presented here therefore is not open for conjecture.

We have made clear statements herewith:

NO ANGER – NO MALICE – NO EMOTION – NO DOUBT

– and a CONFIDENCE in the veracity of God's Word.

At this point, it could well appear that I as an individual am against one group, and for another group.

That is not the point. I, as a committed Christian am:

FOR GOD and HIS PRECIOUS WORD.

Two groups outlined:

– Seed Bride group

– Weed Prostitute System

Within both of these groups, we have two more groups:

– The true and the false.

Some of the readers of this book say:

'I was brought up in the weed prostitute group since I was a child. In spite of the rottenness of the system, and this I have suspected for some time, my heart is genuinely towards God. Is there hope for me?'

Answer – 'Yes'.

Another says to me,

'I was raised in a seed bride group, without any of the 'EXTRAS' of religious trappings. My heart is towards God. Is there hope for me?'

Answer – 'Yes'

On the converse however, both of these groups have evil persons hiding in them.

God is no fool, and is impossible to deceive.

Scandals

All newspaper readers are familiar by this time with the scandals which appear from time to time, not from the weed prostitute group in particular, but from those who claim to be seed bride people.

'Then Peter opened his mouth and said, 'Of a truth I perceive that God is no respecter of persons.

But in every nation, he that feareth Him and worketh righteousness, is accepted with Him.' *Ref.65.

In other words – talk is cheap.

The Lord wishes to see some action and action He will have. At this point, you may ask, 'What are the Lord's revealed plans for the future?'

374

Future Plans — What to Do

1. To clean up his genuine people from within both the WEEDS and the SEEDS.

Rules: If you or I have been sinning:

(a) Stop it

(b) Confess it to the one mediator, the Lord Jesus Christ.

'If we confess our sins, he is faithful and just to forgive us our sins and to cleanse us from all unrighteousness.' *Ref.66.

(c) Replace that sin with something good.

(d) Most of all, make sure that we are not only born again but develop a daily intimate relationship with the Lord.

(e) Prepare for an 'uprooting' from your 'religious' surroundings to some form of fellowship that the Lord has planned for all His people in these last days.

Above all, don't rush around uprooting people from their fellowships. The Lord will speak gently, giving:

(a) A push from the old,

(b) A pull to the new.

Come out from among them

'And I heard another voice from heaven saying, 'Come out of her my people, that you be not partakers of her sins, and that ye receive not of her plagues.' *Ref.67.

In other words, it is important where you go to church. If you are in an evil system, you will collect the same rewards that they will receive.

If you are in a real genuine born again loving fellowship, you will reap the blessings thereof.

'For her sins have reached into heaven and God hath REMEMBERED her iniquities.' *Ref.68. (Emphasis added.)

Martyrs' Blood Cries Out

This tells us that the 68 million did not die in vain. They did not yield their life's blood for no purpose.

It has been said 'The blood of the martyrs is the seed of the church.'

A Martyr's Challenge

One of the young men in the group of five, who went to evangelise the Indians of South America left behind in a diary, many of his thoughts.

The whole group were massacred by the men they went to help. The missionaries' bodies were found floating in the river, faces down, with spears pushed into their bodies and pages from the New Testament pushed onto the spears.

Later, his diary was discovered and a passage read thus:

'A man is no fool who gives up that which he cannot keep, to gain that which he cannot lose.'

Good News for Fishermen

Years ago, on the shores of Galilee (and we have been there and stood on the spot,) the Master spoke these words.

'Follow me and I will make you fishers of men.' *Ref.69.

His words echo down through the ages to the decade leading on to Global 2000.

In the coded secrets, we now turn to number seven which corresponds to the final church age.

A Large Net

In these days, once the believers have either cleaned up their act, or conversely had their act cleaned up for them by the Lord, then there will be a final spiritual revival of God's power. The rotten pages of history will be expunged from the believers minds as they read with excitement.

'And I will RESTORE to you the years that the locust hath eaten, the cankerworm, the caterpillar and the palmerworm, my great army which I sent among you.' *Ref.70. (Emphasis added.)

That's strange. God confesses to sending these four lots of devourers amongst His people. Why?

Sorting Out Period

Answer:

— To sort out the real from the false

— the gold from the slag

— the seeds from the weeds.

'And it shall come to pass afterward, that I will pour out my Spirit on all flesh, and your sons and daughters shall prophesy, your old men shall dream dreams, your young men shall see visions,

And also upon the servants and upon the handmaids I will pour out my Spirit.' *Ref.74.

Every group and both genders of humanity will be involved.

Result: A great ingathering of souls for God the Father and His dear Son, the Lord Jesus Christ.

Does that please you? It does me.

To any who are angry and confused at this point, possibly even feeling 'trapped' remember the three stages:

3 Stages

SAD   — Because you don't know the Lord Jesus and His salvation.

MAD   — Because some Christian has spoken to you about the Lord.

GLAD   — When you finally submit and receive Christ.

'Again the kingdom of heaven is like unto a net that was cast into the sea and gathered of every kind.

Which, when it was full, they drew to the shore and sat down and gathered the good into vessels but cast the bad away.' *Ref.72.

Any person involved, as we are, in evangelism and soul winning for the Lord has,

(a) Many great thrills when you return to an area again and find people living strongly for the Lord.

(b) Some disappointments as you return and find some, in the minority of course, have returned to their old sinful ways.

'So shall be the end of the world: the angels shall come forth and sever the wicked from among the just,

And shall cast them into the furnace of fire, there shall be wailing and gnashing of teeth.' *Ref.73.

CHAPTER 51

God's Answer — A Spiritual Revival

Horrific isn't it?

This great religious deception as revealed in the preceding chapter, which makes people's lives a misery whilst they live on earth and afterwards (because it deprives those dear souls of God's magnificent salvation), leaves hell as their final destination.

'Why?' you ask.

Answer: Because God's law is clear. Somebody has to pay for our sin.

Either

a. Christ does

or

b. We do

because:

'The wages of sin is death but the gift of God is eternal life through Jesus Christ our Lord.' *Ref.1.

Please notice God is no fool. He refuses to be put down or defeated. He always provides His own ANTIDOTE.

'When the enemy comes in like a flood, the Spirit of the Lord will raise up a standard against him.' *Ref.2.

Prediction

I predict that from 1990 and onwards, first a trickle, then drops leading to a torrent of God's fullness and power will cover the earth.

'Be glad then ye children of Zion and rejoice in the Lord your God, for he hath given you the former rain moderately and he will cause to come down for you the rain, the former rain and the latter rain in the first month.' *Ref.3.

In the book of Acts chapters 1 and 2, we read of this happening in the early Seed-bride group = The former rain.

It is forecast to happen again = The former rain + The latter rain.

What To Expect

a. The World Government plans will be inexplicably disrupted.

378

b. EFTPOS will lead on to the 'mark of the beast' system, yet the Lord will provide supernaturally for His people.
'But my God shall supply all your need according to his riches in glory by Christ Jesus.' *Ref.4.
  c. The World Government advocates will 'tax' Christian groups until they operate in an underground fashion.
  d. Christians will either become thoroughly real with God, or throw in their faith.
  e. Christians living in sin will not be tolerated in the fellowship groups.
  f. The supernatural presence of God will invade fellowship meetings in tongues, interpretations, prophesies, dreams and visions. Healings will become normal and the non-believers will flock in, searching for answers.
  g. Multiplied thousands will be convicted by the Lord's Spirit. They will fall in the streets under God's power, and praise God on public transport.
  h. Thousands will be saved and join up with God's kingdom.
During the month of April 1962, my wife May and I along with other born-again believers experienced a foretaste of this revival in Apia, Western Samoa.
  1. About midnight, a boy shouted out that he could see the cross of Christ in the sky.
  2. Crowds of folk rushed outside to see this great phenomena.
  3. About 60 people fell down on the concrete, and others also fell as the night went on, some with babies in their arms, yet, because it was God's power, none were hurt.
  4. Many lay under God's annointing power from midnight until 8 a.m. with their arms raised up to heaven. (Challenge: You say it is not supernatural. You try lying on your back with your arms raised for eight hours, then write and tell me how you feel.)
  5. People sang in unison with the heavenly choirs.
  6. They spoke in unusual languages.
  7. They saw visions of heaven.
  8. We were told the names of villages to go and spread the gospel.
  9. Prophecies were powerful and given regularly.
  10. Result, over 3,000 souls were converted to Christ whilst we remained on the island and under the annointed preaching of Samoan evangelist Makisua Fatialofa and his wife Mau,

another 7,000 turned and received the Lord's graciously offered salvation.

11. Please let not any reader argue. You were not there. We were.

Simply read and learn. God's prophets do not lie.

It will happen again, but next time, on a world-wide basis. Are you ready for it?

CHAPTER 52

Don't Worry Believer

Fearful? No!

I am often asked by caring people as to whether all this knowledge and information bothers me in my personal life.

I confess that earlier on in the piece when I was beginning to share this message with people, some of the information used to cause me to lie awake at nights.

However, a portion of God's Word settled these qualms once and for all.

'And when these things begin to come to pass, then look up and lift up your heads for your redemption draweth nigh.' *Ref.1.

We have already established that the European Community is the final world power that will last for a very brief period of time, led by a charismatic Jewish-born, non-religious leader.

The prophets call this man by at least four titles:

Antichrist

Beast

Man of Sin

Son of Perdition

The later name was used to describe another man in Bible history i.e. Judas Iscariot.

Remember, the man dies, but the devil lives on. You cannot kill an evil spirit.

I predict therefore, that the man who will lead the E.C. will be the same man who brings about the Middle East Peace Treaty for a period of 7 years.

4 Stages

This great leader will appear to the world in 4 stages. The prophet portrays these stages as horses of differing colours. (See Rev.6.)

White horse — Antichrist brings peace.

Red horse — Antichrist — a powerful influence as Soviets invade Israel.

Black horse — Antichrist in the role of food distributor during a period of world famine.

Pale horse — Antichrist in full charge of the Mark of the Beast monetary system, involving the mark on the right hand or forehead.

Notice, a very interesting point, which is missed by most commentators.

This man will work extremely hard along with the E.C. nations to make this a world-wide system, but time will run out before he gets the EFTPOS extension up and running throughout the whole world.

A friend handed me a very revealing news cutting from the 'China Daily', 3rd April 1989. 'Chinese I.D.

Identification cards had been issued to 420 million Chinese, nearly two-fifths of China's population, by mid-march. By October 1, 500 million adult Chinese citizens will obtain identification cards and be required to use them in collecting cash, remittances, and postal materials, buying airplane tickets, marriage registration, and applying for business licenses....' End quote.

Apparently, the World Government advocates are after China, to include this nation in their plans.

Antichrist will Rule One Quarter of the World

I predict that this future world leader will have time to set up only one quarter of the earth's nations with this final demonic money 'mark'. The prophet makes it clear that these particular nations will move from a voluntary reception of the mark to a compulsory reception.

The penalty for non-compliance will be death, outlined in four ways.

Antichrist will be frustrated, yet will be unable to do any more.

Look at this description of the 4th (pale horse) stage.

'And I looked and behold a pale horse and his name that sat on him was Death, and Hell followed with him. And power was given unto them over THE FOURTH PART OF THE EARTH TO KILL—
 a. with sword
 b. and with hunger
 c. and with death
 d. and with the beast of the earth. *Ref.2.(Emphasis added.)

French Guillotine

The guillotine will be re-introduced, bearing in mind that France is a powerful member of the European Community.

Hunger of course will be the result of the impossibility of buying or selling unless one goes along with the system.

Death implies that during this period called Great Tribulation, rebels (so-called) will be hunted down and dispatched.

The days of Nero will be reintroduced and believers will be made sport of. We have actually viewed a colliseum and the little rooms that held the lions, the roofs worn smooth by the constant rubbing of the animals' coats, as they rushed through to destroy their victims.

Not only that, we have stood in the little cells where groups of early Christians huddled clinging on to each other as they prayed and committed themselves to the Lord that they were soon to meet.

Good News!

The moment the 7 year peace treaty is confirmed and signed in the Middle East, believers in Christ will know exactly where they are.

The first three and a half years (Beginning of Sorrows) the second three and a half years (Great Tribulation) i.e. a 7 year period.

Statement. The believing Christians are going to be caught up to be with the Lord on the eve of the second period of three and a half years. This period is called Great Tribulation.

Proof

Noah was rescued supernaturally BEFORE the day the flood commenced.

Lot was supernaturally rescued BEFORE the fire fell on Sodom and Gomorrah.

'Even thus shall it be in the day when the Son of man is revealed.' *Ref.3.

Meaning

Just as Noah was rescued and Lot was rescued, the twice born believers in the Lord Jesus Christ will be rescued on the eve of God's judgement.

This makes sense, as a king will always remove his ambassadors before declaring war on an enemy.

The miraculous catching away of this Christian group known as the bride of Christ will translate them into a spiritual dimension where they will meet God's Son who is spoken of on this occasion as the heavenly bridegroom.

Together, they will attend THE MARRIAGE SUPPER OF THE LAMB.

A Prophetic Description of this Translation

'For the Lord himself shall descend from heaven with a shout,
with the voice of the arch-angel
and with the trump of God
and the dead in Christ shall rise first.
Then we which are alive and remain
shall be caught up together with them in the clouds to meet the Lord in the air
and so shall we ever be with the Lord.
Wherefore, comfort one another with these words.' *Ref.4.

At this point of course, the world leader becomes extremely angry as his potential puppet slaves suddenly disappear.

To make sure no others escape his evil designs he now takes over food distribution during a time of world famine, and then makes the receiving of the new TRADING MARK compulsory.

Note

First three and a half years — the mark is voluntary.
Second three and a half years — the mark is compulsory.

The true believers are caught up to the Lord before it is compulsory.

Key

Do not miss out on God's revealed way of salvation. Turn to the back of this book for the prayer of salvation.

If you and I mean business with God, we are leaving this old scene, before the mark is made compulsory.

CHAPTER 53

Miraculous Provision Promised

As we have already learned — correct relationship with the Lord is the name of the game.

If, after reading the book to this point, you have turned to the back pages for the prayer of salvation, you will now enjoy reading how provision has been made for your future.

Rule

The economy of this world system is buying and selling.

The economy of God's kingdom is giving and receiving.

During our years of living in Western Samoa, a number of supernatural events took place, including the following.

One Sunday, I invited Pastor Makisua Fatialofa, with his wife Mau and the children, home for Sunday dinner.

When my wife May heard what I had done, she was very flustered as she told me that we had no money, or food.

I replied 'Never mind love. I have just finished reading a book describing the life of one George Mueller of Bristol, England. This man set up orphanages and collected the children from off the streets, fed, clothed and housed them.

Mr Mueller said 'For 50 years I have made my needs known to God, and He has never failed us. In fifty years, in answer to prayer alone, my children have never missed a meal.'

(To any non-believer reading this book, I say congratulations for staying with it. Now, extend your knowledge on matters spiritual and go and buy a book on Mueller's life from your nearest Christian bookstore.)

Back to my story. The Fatialofa family duly arrived and we seated ourselves around the table, which in turn was decorated with a table cloth, cutlery and a salt and pepper shaker.

I asked my friend Makisua to give thanks for the meal, advising him beforehand however, that there was nothing in the house to eat.

He gave thanks, with just the faintest hint of a smile about his lips. Having completed his prayer, and closing with the word 'Amen' — there it was — A KNOCK AT THE DOOR.

Racing for the door, I remember murmuring the words 'Just

like the book'. Upon opening it, there on the verandah lay a large cardboard box of steaming hot food. Chicken, pork, taro, bananas, coconut cream and onions, pisupo, chop suey — it was all there.

I didn't stop for one moment, I ran past the box and out on to the road endeavouring to waylay our mysterious benefactor. I looked right, left, up the road, down the road, behind the house. There was no dust, no sign of a car or a person.

I publicly state in my meetings 'I believe that we have been provided for by an angel.'

You reply 'I don't believe it' to which I say 'That doesn't faze me at all. We ate the food, you didn't.'

God's Promises
Do we have the promise of God for His provision?

'But my God shall supply all your need according to his riches in glory by Christ Jesus.' *Ref.1.

The 3 necessities are:
1. Food
2. Drink
3. Clothing

Years ago, the Master gave us this promise:

'Therefore, take no thought saying

What shall we eat? or

What shall we drink? or

Wherewithal shall we be clothed?

For after all these things do the Gentiles seek,

for your heavenly Father knoweth that ye have need of all these things.

But SEEK YE FIRST the kingdom of God and his righteousness,

and ALL THESE THINGS shall be added unto you.' *Ref.2. (Emphasis added.)

'All these things' equals food, drink, and clothing.

My family and I say 'Praise the Lord, it is true.'

For over 20 years, we are a living example that our God is alive, and is one who honours His promises.

If all this is new to you, please do not criticise; just seek first the kingdom of God and you will receive the Lord's divine attention also.

No church, no group, no individual has pledged support for us, but our God is miraculous. No public appeals; no hinting prayer letters; no business on the side.

The prayer of St Jerome applies here: 'Lord preserve us from any clergyman who is involved in business.'

In these last days therefore, we find 3 groups revealed:

a. This group will receive the mark on their bodies and go to hell forever.

b. This second group refuses the mark and are beheaded for their faith in Christ.

c. This third group gets a supernatural victory over the whole system.

'And I saw as it were, a sea of glass mingled with fire, and them that had gotten the VICTORY over the beast, and over his IMAGE, and over his MARK, and over the NUMBER OF HIS NAME, stand on the sea of glass, having the harps of God.

And they sing the song of Moses, the servant of God, and the song of the Lamb, saying,

Great and marvelous are thy works, Lord God Almighty, just and true are they ways, thou King of saints.' *Ref.3. (Emphasis added.)

I remember reading these prophecies some years ago, and my family asking me the meaning.

Herewith I tell you the reader this story of illustration.

Rule — God never moves until the last moment.

The Barry Smith family is camped alongside the Red Sea with the Children of Israel, having just moved out from Egypt where we were under the cruel rule of Pharoah.

Suddenly, a terrifying sound is heard, the earth trembles, and Pharoah's armies are sighted descending the hills that lead down to our encampment.

My family ask me what to do, so I hasten to Moses to enquire of him.

I knock on a tent pole and a weary voice says 'Come in'.

Moses at that stage assures me that he knows no more about the situation than I do, and advises me to return to my family tent with his words of assurance 'Don't call me, I'll call you.'

Time goes by. Pharoah and his army are upon us.

At one minute to twelve, Moses hears the voice of the Lord.

'Moses.'

'Yes, Lord.'

'Take your stick.'

'Yes, Lord.'

387

'Point it over the Red Sea.'

'Yes, Lord.'

Moses obeys, the Red Sea parts, and the Children of Israel, led by Barry Smith and family, cross to the other side on dry land.

Meanwhile, Pharoah spies the trail on dry land through the sea bed and cries 'For-wa-a-ard'.

They move out into the midst of the sea, and a voice from heaven cries 'Clo-o-ose' and all that remains is an Egyptian helmet, floating on top of the waters.

Barry Smith and family lead the Children of Israel in singing, dancing and rejoicing before the Lord.

Paraphrase

'I will sing unto the Lord, for he hath triumphed gloriously, the horse and rider thrown into the sea.' *Ref.4.

Just as God intervened miraculously on this occasion, believers may rest assured, that He will intervene miraculously once again in this our day.

We do not fear any of these things.

'For God hath NOT given us the spirit of FEAR but of POWER

and of LOVE

and of a SOUND MIND.' *Ref.5.

You may rejoice, resting in the knowledge that as the system increases in its binding influence, the Lord will tell us (at the correct time) what to do next.

By reading this book, you are now privy to some of the most highly secret knowledge on earth today.

Rejoice.

Before the flood, God warned Noah, who warned the people.

Before the fire on Sodom and Gomorrah, God warned Lot.

Before the coming of His Son from Heaven, God will warn the prophets who will warn the people.

'Surely the Lord God will do nothing but he revealeth his secret unto his servants the prophets.' *Ref.6.

Some years ago now, a man offered to make me a millionaire within a period of three months. All I had to do was to terrify my audience during my public meetings and then sell the DOOMSDAY (dehydrated) FOOD at the door at the conclusion of my meeting.

I must confess that sometimes men get stupid ideas in their heads, and it was probably for this reason that God said,

'It is not good for man to live alone.' *Ref.7.

I mentioned this man's plan to my wife, hoping for her approval before proceeding with the plan.

She smiled and said one sentence, which conveyed the impression to me that it was all over—'Barry, you know what the Bible teaches.'

'Quite right', I murmured, remembering once again the words of the Lord Jesus Christ—'Take no thought'. *Ref.8.

CHAPTER 54

A Supernatural Call

How did I get involved in all this? Me—a common school-teacher who stumbled on to a massive world wide plan to takeover and manipulate the life of every citizen of this planet.

The Rarotonga Adventure
Date: 7 September 1972.

The little plane winged its way across the Pacific Ocean en-route to Rarotonga, capital of the Cook Islands, via Fiji and the Samoa's.

On board this plane with me was a group of approximately ten Cook Island Christians who made up a magnificent singing group to accompany me on this lecture tour.

The night before we left, one of the ladies in the party, Bora Thompson, shared with us of three visions that she purported to have seen.

3 Visions

Vision no. 1—A window with a snake in it.

Vision no. 2—A second window also with a snake in it.

Vision no. 3—A window frame within which she saw a man flying in the sky with clouds where his legs should have been. He was sprinkling something liberally over the earth as he flew. A voice spoke twice saying—'The earth needs fertilizer. The earth needs fertilizer.'

Upon hearing this revelation, which did sound most unusual, I did not laugh as I knew that these sort of things were predicted to take place in a specific time in history.

'And it shall come to pass afterward, that I will pour out my spirit upon all flesh, and your sons and daughters shall prophesy, your old men shall dream dreams, your young men shall see visions.

And also upon the servants and upon the handmaids in those days will I pour out my spirit.' *Ref.1.

Each of these three visions was to be fulfilled within a period of 15 days, and I personally was going to receive divine instructions as to how to get this highly important message out to the world.

Vision no. 1 fulfillment

Arriving at the Rarotongan airport, I had my passport stamped and later in the day was requested to see the Chief Immigration Officer on the Island.

I was told by him, in no uncertain terms, that he was an atheist and had no time for my ilk whatsoever. What was more, I was told that if I attempted to hold any public meetings without a work permit (which he had the power to agree to or decline), I would be:

(a) Fined $50.00 (a great deal of money in 1972)
(b) Imprisoned
(c) Deported from the Island.

There it was. Snake no. 1 – Political.

We in the team immediately got into a huddle on the foreshore and prayed for help.

The deputy Premier spied us there and asked if he could help. After I had explained the situation, this man took me personally to visit the Chief Immigration Officer where the following conversation took place.

Deputy Premier – 'John.'

Immigration Officer – 'Yes sir.'

D.P. – 'Mr Smith has brought a team from N.Z. to preach the gospel on our Island.'

I.O. – 'Yes sir.'

D.P. – 'You will agree that the gospel is a good thing for our Island John.'

I.O. – 'Yes sir.'

D.P. – 'We are going to assist Mr Smith and his team aren't we John?'

I.O. – 'Yes sir.'

At that the Deputy Premier left me in the capable hands of my atheistic friend, who immediately gave me his clear word that we could continue on with our work unhindered, and with his FULL co-operation.

I felt sincerely sorry for this man.

Vision no. 2 fulfillment

We began our public meetings in the town centre of Avarua, speaking to the people about the Mark of the Beast System and related subjects.

Picking up a morning newspaper, we were astounded to read

391

a criticism of our meetings by one of the local church leaders.

He made it clear that we had no right to speak from the prophecies of Daniel or Revelation as nobody really understood these things.

Being one who delights in a challenge, I promptly sat down and put pen to paper.

The next day my answer was printed in the local newspaper and ran along these lines.

'Unless one was 'born again' of God's Holy Spirit, one wouldn't understand any of the Bible, including the books of Daniel and Revelation.' I went on to point out that the church, generally speaking, was 'sick' and needed an injection of life such as our team could give.

The response was not long in coming.

The next morning very early, I received a very abrupt message on the phone.

'Mr Smith, we wish to see you down at the church office at 9 a.m.' That was all. No please or thank you.

These men wielded great power and could have closed us down with a word.

At 9 a.m. Smith, the prisoner, stood on the mat, confronted by the head of the church and the missionary from New Zealand.

They dressed me down in no uncertain terms and told me that space had been reserved in the local paper for my apology. This I immediately agreed to as I had a clear word from God spoken to my spirit on the way to this meeting.

'... be ready always to give an answer to every man that asketh you a reason of the hope that is in you with MEEKNESS and FEAR.' *Ref.2.
(My emphasis added.)

In other words, 'don't try and be clever.'

This traumatic meeting came to an end, and as I left the room, I realised that the second vision had just been fulfilled. Snake no. 2 turned out to be — Religion.

Vision no. 3 — fulfillment

A few nights later, we were invited to speak in a meeting house around the coast in a village called Muri. (This is where the Heke Nui or Great Migration of the seven Maori canoes left from on the final stage of their journey from Raiatea to New Zealand.)

I finished my address and my interpreter indicated that I should ask an elderly village leader to close the gathering in prayer.

As he prayed, my interpreter became very excited. He said 'What do you think of that?' This man said these words in opening his prayer.

'Our Father in heaven. We thank you for sending these people from overseas to FERTILIZE our Island.' This man had gone against all etiquette and custom, in spite of the fact that he was a Government member, an elder in the church and a village leader; and used the forbidden word to Almighty God in prayer, the word 'manure'.

This whole trip was fraught with the supernatural intervention of God.

Another Vision

Soon after arriving on the island, we met a man who claimed that he had seen us all in a vision and that God had spoken to him about us.

Apparently, God had instructed this man to give us the use of his house, free of charge, during the time of our stay.

And a beautiful little place it turned out to be, nestled up in the Taku Va'ine valley amongst the banana and coconut trees.

My Call from the Lord

It was in that house, supernaturally provided by the Lord, that I received my supernatural call from the Lord on my future life's commission.

In that house at about 11 a.m. one morning, I was on my knees in my bedroom praying and weeping before the Lord. I prayed like this.

'Lord. I have served you in missionary work around the Islands of Polynesia for twelve years since 1960. I want to warn my fellow countrymen in New Zealand of all these things that are coming. Show me what to do, and how to do it.'

A Rhema

I waited quietly, then flicked the pages of my Living Bible open to a passage in Habakkuk 2:2&3. This appeared to leap off the page at me.

'And the Lord said unto me, write my answer on a billboard large and clear, so that anyone can read at a glance and rush to tell the others. But these things I plan won't happen right away.

Slowly, steadily, surely, the time approaches when the vision will be fulfilled. If it seems slow, do not despair, for these things will surely come to pass. Just be patient. They will not be overdue a single day.'

Paralyzed

As my eyes fell on these words, I was paralysed in the kneeling position. I couldn't get off my knees. I just stayed there crying and shaking under the power of God.

This continued on for some time and then I managed to stumble over to the bathroom, hoping that a cold shower might help.

Under the deluge of shower water, I shook and cried again as the finger of God Himself printed these words I had just read in my spirit.

We returned to New Zealand on the 19th September 1972, where I explained to my wife what had happened in the Cook Islands.

Sequel to the Story

It was now Christmas 1972, and my family and I were doing public meetings with a group called Open Air Campaigners in a Northland New Zealand town call Kawakawa.

My wife, May, reminded me of God's command. January the 1st was drawing near, and this was the date when the 6 member countries in the E.E.C. expected three further countries to join. Prophecy was rapidly turning into history. I had to move quickly.

I already knew that 'To obey is better than sacrifice.' *Ref.3.

We rushed down to the local Post Office, where I wrote down a number of events which would precede the second coming of the Lord and also 4 qualifications to prepare oneself for this event.

It was the end of December 1972, and the final newspaper for that year carried my article done in obedience to the Lord's revelation to me.

I well remember the excitement as I rushed down to the paper box with a friend David McBride. We ran back to the hall where our leader was giving us a final word for 1972 prior to his travelling south to Wellington.

We placed the six copies of the newspapers carrying my article, under our seats to be examined after the meeting.

Our leader Ken Rout rose to his feet oblivious of all that we had been up to and spoke these words.

'This morning, prior to my return to Wellington, I feel impressed of the Lord to read the following scriptures to you all. Let us turn to Habakkuk 2:2&3 and I wish to read it to you from the Living Bible.'

As he read these now familiar words, I began to get excited and May whispered to me 'Aren't these the verses the Lord showed you in Rarotonga?'

'**And the Lord said unto me, write my answer on a billboard large and clear so that anyone can read it at a glance and rush to tell the others. But these things I plan won't happen right away. Slowly, steadily, surely, the time approaches when the vision will be fulfilled. If it seems slow, do not despair, for these things will surely come to pass. Just be patient. They will not be overdue a single day.**'

Thus, my mission was to write down what I knew, and God, by His grace, gave me His confirmation exactly on the day when the article came out publicly. Naturally speaking, this was a statistical impossibility.

And some people wonder why I am so brimming with confidence in God and His Word.

Be Patient.

Along the way, folk have asked me when all these prophecies will be fulfilled. I simply quote 'if it seems slow, do not despair for these things will surely come to pass.'

As I pen these words, on the 21st October 1987 I have just been called away to the phone to answer a request for further meetings in Perth. We held four such public gatherings there earlier on this month, on the subject 'The World Monetary Crash and the New World Money System' and then of course on 'Black Tuesday' October 20th, Wall St, New York, presented us with the worst day in Stock Market history.

People are now ready to listen.

We are not talking nonsense.

We are talking reality.

Some have tried to argue.

My books are called 'Warning' not 'Argument'.

I have obeyed and written two previous books—Warning 1980 and Second Warning 1984.

Within the pages of this book, you are reading in very simple language, what is subtly happening to you and your supposed liberties.

It will also provide a sure answer to all your problems.

CHAPTER 55

Hell

No such place? Think again. Every city has its rubbish dump.

John Bunyan in his visions referred to earlier on in this book, had a glimpse of this dreadful place which he recorded in his book entitled 'Visions of Heaven and Hell'.

Quote—'Now, said my guardian angel, you are on the verge of hell, but do not fear the power of the destroyer, for my commission from the Imperial Throne secures you from all dangers.

Here, you may hear from devils and damned souls the cursed causes of their endless ruin.

The devils cannot hurt you, though they would, for they are bound by Him who has commissioned me.' End quote.

Scenes in Hell. Continue quote:
1. 'We observed two wretched souls tormented by a fiend who plunged them into liquid fire and brimstone while at the same time they accused and cursed each other.

'Cursed be your face that I ever set eyes on you. My misery is due to you. I can thank you for this. It was your clever persuasions that brought me here. You enticed me and ensnared me.

If you had set me a good example, I might now have been in heaven.

The other wretch answered, 'And I also can blame you. I was covetous, yet you were proud; and if I taught you covetousness, I learned pride and drunkenness from you. I taught you to cheat, but you taught me to lust, lie and scoff at goodness.' End quote.

From this sad discussion I learned that those who were companions upon earth in sin, will also be together in hell in punishment.

Although on earth they loved each other's company, they will hate each other in hell.

No wonder Jesus told the true story of the rich man in hades, to teach us the horrors of this very real place.

In this story, the two men spoken of were Lazarus, a beggar who obviously loved the Lord, and the rich man who had no interest in the things of God.

396

They both died.
1. The beggar went to Paradise.
2. The rich man went to Hades where he experienced the following emotions:
   (a) torment
   (b) thirst
   (c) memory
   (d) desire that his family would not also go to this place. He requested that Lazarus go and warn them. 'Then he said, I pray thee therefore father, that thou wouldst send him to my father's house. For I have five brethren, that he may testify unto them, lest they also come into this place of torment.' *Ref.1. End quote.

The request was refused, pointing out that the warnings were already written in the Scriptures.

Listen:

'If they hear not Moses and the prophets, neither will they be persuaded though one rose from the dead.'

Back to Bunyan's trip to Hell.
2. 'One I observed had flaming sulphur forced down her throat by a tormenting spirit.

When asked why he so obviously enjoyed his work, the fiend replied 'This is her just reward. When on earth, she had so much gold she could never be satisfied and never cared whom she ruined just so she could get her greedy hands on their wealth.
She was so miserable, she often went hungry and wore old ragged clothing rather than spend any of her massive wealth.
She wouldn't buy a house as she would be taxed if she did.
Gold was her god on earth, therefore I am filling her belly with it in hell.'
3. 'Not much further on, we observed a wretched soul lie on a bed of burning steel, almost choking with brimstone.

He cried out in anguish and desperation.

'Oh, what a wretch I am. Lost, forever, forever. Oh these terrible words, forever. Cursed for all eternity.

·What a fool I was to choose sin's short momentary pleasure in contrast with the pleasures of heaven.

How often I was warned. Why was I made with an immortal soul and yet be so careless as to not take care of it?'
4. Another lost soul speaks.

397

(a) 'In this dreadful place, I have lost the presence of the ever blessed God.

(b) Here we have lost the company of saints and angels and in their place, have nothing but tormenting devils.

(c) We have lost heaven too. The seat of blessedness.

(d) Not only that, to make our wretched state even worse, we have lost the hope of ever being in a better state. Things here are truly hopeless. A miserable person on earth has at least 'hope' left in reserve. It sadly is not so here. Well may our hearts break, since in this place we are both without hope or help.

(e) Our torments here are varying and all inclusive, afflicting each part of the body, tormenting also the soul which makes the whole thing unbearable.

(f) Another thing is, that our torment is so violent. The fire that burns us here is such that all the waters in the sea could never quench it.

(g) Also, another part of our misery is that it is ceaseless. It never stops.

(h) The company here adds to our troubles. Tormenting devils—shrieking souls—howling beings—dreadful oaths, is all our conversation. The torments of our fellow sufferers increases our pain also.

(i) This very place also increases our sufferings. It is an abstract of all MISERY—A PRISON—A DUNGEON —A BOTTOMLESS PIT—A LAKE OF FIRE AND BRIMSTONE—A FURNACE OF FIRE THAT BURNS TO ETERNITY.

(j) The cruelty of our tormentors also adds to our sufferings.

This being had just finished explaining all these dreadful things, when a tormenting devil spoke.

'Besides, you know you deserve all this. How often you received warning of this whilst you were living. When they told you of a hell you laughed. You were even so presumptuous to dare Almighty God to destroy you.

How often you have called on God to damn you. Do you now have the audacity to complain because he is answering your request.'

From what I had heard and seen to this point, it is now very clear to me that it is downright FOLLY and MADNESS to refuse offers of the Lord's grace, and to carry on working hand in hand with the destroyer.

5. Another cried out 'I was told by those I depended on, that if I cried out 'Lord have mercy on me' when I came to die, it would be enough to save me. But no, I left it too late, to my eternal sorrow.'

The devilish tormentor replied, 'You spent your days in pursuit of sin, wallowed in your filthiness and thought you would go to heaven when you died.

No, he that earnestly expects to go to heaven when he dies will walk in the ways of holiness and goodness while he lives.

If you had read the Scriptures, you would have known that 'WITHOUT HOLINESS, NO MAN SHALL SEE THE LORD.' *Ref.3.

Therefore, this is the sum of the matter, you were willing to live in sin as long as you could because you loved it so much. What impudence. God will not be mocked. You sowed, now you reap. You have no reason to complain now. It is too late.' End quote.

Extra note: Please understand that this passage does not imply that persons may not be saved on their death beds. It means that if they hear the gospel earlier, and postpone receiving the Lord's mercy through the Lord Jesus Christ, or when they are rebuked of the Lord, they refuse to change, they are mocking God, and will pay for the presumption.

Many will be in hell through 'inconsideration'.

Consider the destiny of your own souls.

Consider the destiny of the souls of your loved ones and friends and FLEE TO JESUS.

The year was 1954. I was a student at the old Bible Training Institute situated in Queen St, Auckland.

One lunch time, I was out on a stroll up the road when I met a former Bible class teacher named Selwyn Cunningham, in the street.

I will never forget his question which cropped up in the course of conversation.

Selwyn: 'Barry, why do people end up in hell?'

Self: 'Because of their sin against God.'

Selwyn: 'No. Not because of that, but because people bypass God's remedy for sin, that is the gift of salvation bought at the cross of calvary through the death of the Lord Jesus Christ.'

'And this is the condemnation, that light has come into the world, and men loved darkness rather than light, because their deeds were evil.' *Ref.4.

There is still room at the cross for you.

Turn to the back of the book for the sinner's prayer.

CHAPTER 56

Heaven

A boy in the United States entered a t.v. competition. The subject was entitled 'Why I like your programme the best.'

Naturally, he won with the following statement.

'I like your programme best because when it's finished, something better comes on.'

We believers are just like that. Really enjoying this life, yet always aware that the next one is far better.

A friend of ours, named Lou, and a beautiful believer in the Lord, had a great deal of trouble with his heart, which culminated in a massive operation.

He survived this surgery and was released once more to return to his job.

I well remember speaking at a large convention where this man was the song leader. He led the singing so vigorously that by the time he was finished, he was covered with a lather of sweat and was visibly stressed and shaking.

I said 'You know, if you carry on like this brother, you'll kill yourself; to which he replied 'It doesn't really bother me. I am ready to meet the Lord, so whether I live or die, I will continue to put in my best efforts with my song leading.'

Sure enough, a short time later, he was rushed up to the hospital where he 'died', yet was revived again.

To those who gathered around his bed, he spoke out very powerfully and said 'I've just been to heaven'. Heaven was his theme from then on. Visitors, doctors, nurses alike all heard one thing only.

HEAVEN!

The Christians of course prayed for his complete healing yet it became increasingly apparent that this was not to be.

He finally gathered family and friends around, gave them each a final word, and then asked the pastor of his church to ask the people to stop praying for him. He said 'They're holding me up. I want to go back to heaven.'

The believers stopped their prayers on his behalf and our dear friend returned to that wonderful place.

HEAVEN!

The sceptic who knows everything reads this chapter and laughingly tells his friends 'Nonsense. There is no such place. When you die, you die like a dog.'

I suggest that the only reason a person would wish to die like a dog is so that he can live like one.

A friend of ours vindicated the following story as being correct, as he was in the meeting when all this occurred. The event took place in Auckland, New Zealand.

During a Christian service, a man died. He was carried out to a back room where the believers sought the Lord for a miracle.

Sure enough, they felt after a time, that the man should be carried back into the service and propped up in a seat. This was duly done, and after a period of about two hours had elapsed, he came back to life again.

He spoke to those assembled there and said that he had just returned from a visit to heaven. He was then advised by some who were sceptical of his claim that he had probably been in a coma and had been hallucinating.

Here is the exciting part. He then informed his, by now very interested, listeners, that whilst in heaven, a young couple (known to most of the folk gathered that night) also arrived there. Upon hearing this, he was told that this could not be the case as at that time, they were on their honeymoon.

Listen. The very next day, the story he had told was confirmed, as it was revealed that the young honeymooners had been killed in a car smash at the very time this man was involved in his death-heaven experience.

To all non-believers, please don't bother trying to disprove either of these stories. We have masses of witnesses.

The fact is, you don't know enough about these matters.

Settle down, read and learn.

It is possible to be an expert in one field, yet be totally ignorant in another e.g. If I know nothing about computers, yet am highly skilled at growing roses, I should not harm my credibility by arguing with a computer expert on the mechanics of computerisation.

Key phrase. Let each person stick to their own field of expertise.

The author of one of the world's best selling books 'Pilgrim's Progress', not only saw into hell; he was also privileged to view heaven, and I am pleased to report that he left us a record of

402

that wonderful experience in his book 'Visions of Heaven and Hell'. His name was John Bunyan.

He continues: (I paraphrase this in simple English.)

'I was taken into the most glorious mansions of the redeemed and saw so much that human language cannot describe.

No wonder the Apostle John put it this way 'Now are we the sons of God, and it doth not yet appear what we shall be.' *Ref.1.

Even the Apostle Paul told us that he had been caught up into 'paradise' where he heard unspeakable things that it is not lawful for a man to utter. *Ref.2.

'But as it is written, eye hath not seen, nor ear heard, neither have entered into the heart of man, the things which God hath prepared for them that love him.' *Ref.3.

When I was first brought into this marvelous place, I saw hosts of bright messengers who welcomed me there with faces of pure joy and full satisfaction.

I saw also that perfect and unapproachable light, that assimilates all things into its own nature, for even the souls of the believers are transparent.

On the Throne of the glory of God, is seated the Almighty God.

Crowds of angels and believers sing continuously and worship Him who is seated on the throne.

HIS GLORIOUS PRESENCE MAKES HEAVEN WHAT IT IS

Rivers of pleasure continually flow from this throne bringing continuous happiness to heaven's millions of inhabitants.

There was no death there.

There was no sin there.

There was no sorrow there.

Only a tremendous freedom that made me want to stay on there forever. My messenger told me however, that after my visit, I must return to earth for a short season to fulfill the divine will.

Soon, we came face to face with Elijah. Although he had left earth hundreds of years before, I recognised him immediately.'

(Author's note: It is apparent that we will recognise people immediately upon reaching heaven's shores.)

·'Then shall we know, if we follow on to know the Lord....' *Ref.4.

Bunyan continues 'My messenger angel introduced me to Elijah as being one of the very privileged few to enter this place of divine light to learn of its glory and happiness.

403

This great prophet then asked me how it was that I had gained this great privilege, by which I understood that it was not general practice to let heavenly matters be understood by earthly beings.

Elijah went on to explain that although he did not die a death as other mortals did, but was taken alive into heaven in a whirlwind, the quality of life he was enjoying in heaven was so amazing as to be indescribable. 'Here', he said, 'our happiness is always new.'

(Author's note: Upon reading these lines, my mind went back to places like Disneyland in California, where millions of folk each year continue to haunt the place, always looking for a new thrill. The Disney people continually update their attractions, yet in spite of this, personal experience tells me that after the first visit, no matter what is served up, the thrill is GONE.

Old people there, vie with the young for rides on the amusement vehicles, yet it is all over in a moment and another 'kick' is sought for.

Heaven is not like that at all.

GOD'S PLEASURES WILL MAKE DISNEYLAND LOOK LIKE A BAD DREAM by way of contrast.

Elijah continues 'The great Three One gave permission for you to visit this place, to still any remaining doubts you may still have, and to strengthen your wavering faith.

The object of our happiness here is the Eternal God. As the divine perfections are infinite (never ending), nothing less than eternity can be sufficient to display their glory, which makes our happiness eternally admit also new additions, which also makes our knowledge of the Lord and His ways, also progressive.

The heart of man is so fine and curious in its structure that it can conceive almost anything that
was
is, or
is to come, in the world below.
Man can conceive
        the air being turned into crystal
        stones being turned into pearls
        grass becoming shining jewels
        every star advancing into a sun
and yet even these human conceptions fall far short of what the high eternal majesty has prepared for His faithful followers.

Tremendous Heavenly Benefits

1. First of all in heaven, the souls of the believers are freed forever from all that can make them miserable. The chief of these things of course is sin. On earth sin binds and leads them captive, often against their will. No wonder one cried out 'Who shall deliver me from the body of this death.' *Ref.5.

2. Next, in heaven, there is no occasion provided for any person to sin. Here the souls that were deformed and stained by sin on earth, are presented by the Lord Jesus to the Father 'without spot or wrinkle'. *Ref.6.

3. Here, we are freed from the effects of sin i.e. its punishments. Our joys here are 'positive' as well as 'negative'.

Although we enjoy the sight of God's presence here, we cannot explain it, as finite creatures can never explain infinite matters.

This doesn't really matter as it fills our souls with 'joy unspeakable and full of glory'. *Ref.7.

4. On earth, the believing Christian saints enjoy God and His blessings 'in measure'. Up here, it is all 'without measure'.

5. Below, the saints communion with God is many times broken off. Up here in heaven, it is uninterrupted enjoyment of God without intermission.

6. On earth, love is mixed with fear, and therefore, torment. Here our love for the Lord is greater than our love for ourselves, and fear is not present.

7. In heaven we can comprehend far more, because we are not limited by our senses.

8. Regarding the Trinity, the mysterious nature of it is unveiled to some degree.

From eternity, only God existed, yet not in solitude. The Godhead is not confused in unity, nor divided in number. There is a priority of order, yet no superiority in this Trinity.

They equally possess the same excellence and are equally the object of divine adoration.

On earth, all these mysteries appear to be unanswerable, yet in heaven, it is much clearer and fits into the heavenly scene in a very natural manner.

Bunyan noted, during the course of his heavenly visit, that some people there seemed to shine more than did others.

He was told the reason for this.

The more we see, the more we love, and love affects our souls

405

(minds, wills, emotions), and changes them, bringing these souls into a full relationship with the object of that love.

The object of this love is God, for GOD IS LOVE.

No person in heaven becomes jealous or angry when they see someone else's glory is greater than their own. The human vessels in heaven are of several sizes yet each is filled according to the capacity to receive.'

(Author's note: I hope you, the reader, can see as I can, how important it is to become loving and Godly in our behaviour whilst on this earth, as this will continue in heaven.)

One of the greatest possible joys in heaven is the sight of the LAMB OF GOD, the Lord Jesus Christ.

He is the one who trod the dusty roads of Palestine and finally was taken by wicked hands and crucified for us. He died in our place.

'The wages of sin is death.' *Ref.8.

Praise the Lord, we believers will catch our first glimpse of him shortly.

Watch for the 7 year peace treaty in the Middle East.

When we see Him for the first time, it will be in His real splendour, surrounded by angels and thoroughly changed believers.

In spite of all this power and glory, unlike earthly politicians who normally get carried away with their positions of grandeur, the Lord Jesus Christ remains kind, considerate and obliging in every way.

This will make heaven more like heaven to find Him reigning there, He who suffered so much for me on earth.

The happiness so evident in our Saviour, will add to our happiness, as He invites us to enter His joy.

Friends and relations will be also there. The last time you said goodbye to them was in sadness with feelings of loss. At this time, it will be all joy and undisturbed fellowship and friendship forever and ever. 'Unbelievable' cry some, yet in this heavenly dimension, it becomes the norm.

Here in heaven, we will understand all the mysteries that the great scholars, teachers and rabbis could not unravel. The Biblical texts that seemed to clash will harmonise at last.

Times of trial on earth, which in our eyes at the time seemed so unnecessary, will be revealed as an important part of the overall plan. These were only imposed as long as was considered necessary by our divine Lord and Master. He is not cruel in any way.

This ocean of happiness is bottomless and can never be exhausted.

In heaven, all worldly relations cease. There is no male or female as the Scriptures teach. All relationships are swallowed up in God.

Bunyan's guardian angel then appeared, with such brilliance as to dazzle him with brilliance.

The robe of glory worn by this being was simply a reflection of the Divine Majesty.

One last question remained.

What about these on earth who do not turn to Christ? Is there misery in heaven on their behalf?

The answer to this question was given thus; by one in heaven.

'Since I have left my earthly body behind, I have also left behind all fleshly relations. We are children of the Father here.

As for those I left behind on earth, I have committed them to God.

I shall be glad to see them as heirs of this vast inheritance, but if they continue on in league with the grand enemy of souls, and refuse the grace offered to them, and die in their sins, God will be glorified in His justice and in His glory, I shall still rejoice.'

Regarding earthly matters, the answer was given that the saints in heaven are not concerned too much with them, yet the angels are involved greatly in winning souls to Christ.

Listen to this passage on the duties of angels.

'Are they not all ministering spirits, sent forth to minister for them who shall be heirs of salvation.' *Ref.9.

To those readers who are not yet 'right with the Lord', the angels have been working overtime on you.

Have you ever wondered why you didn't die in that car smash, motor cycle accident, boating mishap, plane crash, medical incident or that operation, on the farm, at school, on your holiday, at home, in the war?

The angel was there to protect you.

Why?

Because you are an heir of salvation.

The Lord has His eyes on you. You know perfectly well, you should have died years ago.

My advice to you therefore, is 'Seek ye the Lord while He may be found'. *Ref.10.

Turn to the back of this book for the prayer of salvation.

In heaven therefore, the angels bring news to the redeemed of souls being saved on earth.

This adds to the excitement of this wonderful place.

Are you keen to get there? I am.

Illustration. A friend of mine in Australia took me out in his car one day.

Pointing to a giant concrete pillar that supported a main road overpass, he told me the following story.

'One day, feeling disillusioned in spite of my business success and supposed happiness in worldly terms, I determined to suicide on that pillar.

Driving down the motorway at high speed, I stood up in my car, my head on the roof lining and my foot on the gas pedal for greater pressure.

I pulled the wheel hard to the left and aimed for the pillar.

Try as I would, nothing would divert the car from its straight route.

Something was pulling the other side of the wheel.

I gave up, passed the pillar, after which the car was gently brought to a halt on the side of the road.

I bowed my head, thanked God for His mercy and asked the Lord Jesus Christ into my life to be my Saviour.'

Today that man is a Christian pastor.

My question to you is 'Who was pulling the other side of his steering wheel?

The story goes like this.

Two boys set out on a journey in the Alps, to visit an old man who lived in a cave.

Known for his very great wisdom, he was known as the Oracle, and had never been known to come out second best in a debate or an argument.

One of the boys carried a living sparrow behind his back, and they stood at the entrance to the Oracle's cave as he appeared.

The conversation went like this:

Oracle: 'Hello boys. Can I help you?'

Boy: 'Yes sir. We have heard of your wisdom. We have here a bird. Can you tell us whether the bird is alive or dead?'

The boys in their cunning had decided on the plan of action. Should the Oracle say it was alive, they would screw the bird's neck and kill it and then show it to the Oracle in a dead state. If, on the other hand, he replied that it was dead, they would release it and let it fly away, so all could see.

The Oracle thought silently for a moment, a flicker of a smile darted across his lips as he answered 'The choice, my dear boys, is up to you.'

THE CHOICE IS YOURS

The mother was startled to hear her small son cry out 'Mum, my hand is stuck in the vase.'

To her horror, she discovered that it was true. Not only was his hand stuck, but it was stuck in a most expensive vase, a family heirloom worth at the time about $50,000.00.

They tried everything — soapy water, vaseline, pulling and tugging, but to no avail.

Finally, the aid of the local policeman was enlisted, and this man took a very direct approach. Firmly grasping a hammer in his right hand, he said gruffly 'Please look the other way Madam.'

She cried as she heard the shattering of the porcelain, recovered herself for a moment, then burst into tears once more.

Reason: She saw her little boy triumphantly hold up his fist with the words 'Well, at least I didn't drop my five cent piece.'

Are you, Sir or Madam, prepared to give up the glories of an eternity of joy and satisfaction in the presence of Almighty God and the Lord Jesus Christ, for your five cents worth of worldly fun, praise from your earth-bound acquaintances, fear of other's comments should you submit to God, ambitions to climb higher in this world?

'For what shall it profit a man if he gain the whole world and lose his own soul?' *Ref.11.

CHAPTER 57

Calvary

Situated directly behind the Arab bus station in Jerusalem is an oddly shaped hill.

The Pilgrim Hotel nearby was to be the resting place for our tour party in November 1988. Looking out from our bedroom each morning, we could see this place, merely a matter of yards away.

THE PLACE WHERE GOD PUT ON A HUMAN BODY in the form of the LORD JESUS CHRIST, and allowed His created beings to nail Him, the CREATOR to a rough wooden CROSS.

The Jewish prophet said that at a certain time in history, God would send a Saviour to earth. This was prophesied over 700 years before it actually occurred, and happen, it did.

'Behold the Lord himself shall give you a sign. Behold a virgin shall conceive and bear a son, and shall call his name Immanuel.' *Ref.1.

The hill has 3 main caves shaped like the sockets in a skull; two for the eyes and one for the mouth.

'And when they were come unto a place called Golgotha, that is to say, a place of a skull.....and they crucified him....' *Ref.2.

Sad—even as I write, tears come to my eyes. Why did they do this? What made them do it? Why didn't He put a stop to it?

However, the point is, had He not gone through with it all, I would still be lost in my sins and hell-bound. You also would be lost in your sins and hell-bound with no hope of reprieve.

Why?

Because 'For the wages of sin is death, but the gift of God is eternal life through Jesus Christ our Lord.' *Ref.3.

Remember the old Sunday school hymn, 'There was a green hill far away, without a city wall.'

1. The hill is not green, it is brown and dusty.
2. It is situated outside the wall of old Jerusalem and nearby is a garden.

'Now in the place where he was crucified, there was a garden, and in the garden a new sepulchre, wherein was never yet man laid.' *Ref.4.

3. The Lord Jesus Christ was obviously not crucified on top of this skull shaped hill, but just alongside the road. The Romans used to crucify their victims alongside roads as films such as 'Spartacus' reveal very clearly.

'And they that passed by him reviled him, wagging their heads...' *Ref.5.

4. The weed prostitute group of course has its own location for their Calvary, right inside the old city. They have built a huge edifice over it, and year by year, hundreds and thousands of deceived 'pilgrims' follow a false path, the supposed stations of the cross to this edifice; with a man acting the part of Jesus, carrying his cross.

During 1986, May and I set foot inside this building for the first and last times. We saw people rush in to kiss the floor at this false Calvary.

THE DEMONIC PRESENCE HERE WAS HORRIFIC

Any future tourists who accompany us on our tours will need to visit this place without our company.

Contrast the real Calvary and the beautiful PEACE of the garden tomb where they buried our Lord.

Listen—He rose again on the third day.

Jesus is alive. Jesus is alive, I say!

1. The debt for sin has been settled.
2. His precious blood was the cost.
3. An angry God has been appeased.
4. Justice has been seen to have been done.
5. It cost the Lord His very life's blood.
6. Salvation is now offered as a free gift.
7. It will cost you your selfishness.
   It will cost you your sinful life.
   It will cost you your pride.
   It will cost you your fear of man.
8. It is a free gift now to any one who will receive it.
9. It is a fully completed package deal. Christ has done the job fully to get us saved, converted, born-again, and to prepare us for a new life in the spirit.
10. It must be accepted and received by the sinner without reservation.

Say it with me:

'For God so loved the world that He gave His only begotten

son that whosoever believeth in Him should not perish but have everlasting life.' *Ref.6.

God was so gracious in providing this lovely salvation for us, that it will take eternity to explain the magnitude of His grace and love.

'That in the ages to come, he might show the exceeding riches of his grace in his kindness toward us through Christ Jesus.' *Ref.7.

Imagine missing out on this gift.

Imagine catching a glimpse of heaven, whilst stumbling unwillingly down the dark tunnel leading to hell.

Imagine the remorse, the grief, the self pity, the self recrimination, only to hear the dreadful cry 'TOO LATE'.

In my mind's eye unfortunately, I can see a foolish person reading this, and then attempting to make light of it just to prove 'You can't scare me.'

Years ago in Europe, a little gypsy boy and his mother set out in their horse-drawn caravan for a destination a few miles away.

The night was extremely dark with the rain pouring down, the thunder rolling and the lightning flashing.

They came to the banks of a broad fast flowing river. The horse seemed to sense that something was amiss, yet they urged him on.

Sure enough, the bridge was gone and horse, caravan and its occupants were tossed into the billowing torrent.

The boy managed to grasp on to one of the bridge pillars and held on tightly whilst scanning the waters for a sign of his mother. He soon spied her, arms flailing under her black knitted shawl, struggling desperately to reach the shore.

With a voice full of desperation, he cried out 'Mother, here I am. Catch hold of my hand.'

She saw him, yet continued her futile struggle for self-preservation, missing his outstretched hand by a matter of inches.

The current carried her swiftly away to her death, as the boy lapsed into unconsciousness.

He was picked up later by the searchers, attended to and put into the psychiatric ward of the local hospital.

Until the day of his death many years later, people would pass his padded room, observe him huddled in a far corner, crying the same sad words over and over:

'MOTHER, I TRIED TO SAVE YOU BUT YOU
WOULDN'T LET ME.'

To you, the reader of this factual book, I beg, may you never hear the SAVIOUR say similar words as these to you:
'I TRIED TO SAVE YOU BUT YOU WOULDN'T LET ME.'

There is still room at the foot of the cross for you.

Turn to the sinner's prayer at the back of this book.

In 20 years of travelling and speaking, it has been my privilege to have had ample opportunity to read the life stories of other servants of the Lord.

My favourite has to be a preacher of the 1900's era called Billy Sunday from the United States.

Billy was an ex-baseball player who was converted to Christ later in life, and laid down his baseball bat to pick up a Bible.

One story stands out, and shows the truth that '....none of us liveth to himself, and no man dieth to himself.' *Ref.8.

We all affect others and take them with us to heaven or to hell.

Billy Sunday arrived in a small U.S. town to hold a crusade.

Together with a handful of helpers, the Billy Sunday Tabernacle was erected on a prominent street corner, and amazed the local people with the simplicity of its construction.

One nail held each board on to the wall so that in case of fire, the congregation could burst right through to safety.

The local ministers held a meeting to introduce Mr Sunday, and to meet initially in a spirit of unity.

At this meeting, it was suggested that he should go and visit the local mill manager as the town was based around the mill. The idea was, that should the manager commit himself to the Lord, it would certainly have a ripple effect amongst the staff and their relatives.

Seeing the wisdom in this form of reasoning, he set out for the mill and soon observed a sign which read 'Manager'.

He knocked and was invited in, and noticed that the manager was pouring a drink from his well-stocked liquor cabinet.

The conversation was very businesslike.

B.S.: 'Good morning. My name is Billy Sunday. I have come to invite you to give your life to God.'

The manager turned, opened the door, flung his glass of whiskey into the bushes and turned back with tears shining in his eyes.

B.S.: 'I take it then sir, to mean that you will accept my invitation and attend my meetings at the tabernacle down on the corner.'

413

Manager: 'No, I won't. As far as I am concerned, the church is full of hypocrites.'

B.S.: 'So is hell. Therefore, if you do not wish to go there and be with them forever, why not come to church and be with them for only a short time.'

He went on, 'If you went home today and your dog bit you on the leg, would you kick your wife?'

Manager: 'No, I would kick the dog.'

B.S.: 'Then, please stop kicking God because of the hypocrites. Will you attend my meetings?'

The reasoning finally broke through.

The manager reached out and shook hands with Billy Sunday and said 'I will'.

That night, the building was packed out. There was standing room only.

Billy took the platform and as he spoke his eyes moved backwards and forwards scanning the crowd, looking for the mill manager.

Sure enough, there he was right in the back of the tabernacle listening with very great interest, so as not to miss a word.

When Billy drew his message to a close, as was his custom, he invited people to come forward to shake his hand, thus signifying that they were making a public commitment of their lives to the Lord Jesus Christ.

'Whosoever therefore shall confess me before men, him also will I confess also before my Father which is in heaven.

But whosoever therefore shall deny me before men, his will I also deny before my Father which is in heaven.' *Ref.9.

In simple English, the Lord is saying here:

'If you stand publicly for me and confess me openly before men, I will stand publicly for you and confess you openly before my Father at the judgement.'

Question: Will you require the services of a lawyer at the judgement?

Better make a public stand for the Lord down here.

Meanwhile back to the story. The mill manager was so keen he could not contain himself any longer, nor wait for the crowd to move.

He ran along the back of the seats, arriving in first place at the front. He grasped Billy Sunday's hand in a firm grasp, affirming with his lips at the same time that he was receiving Jesus Christ as his Saviour and Lord.

414

The man left the meeting thoroughly saved, and within the space of one full week, through his powerful testimony and his changed life, 60 workers in his mill also turned their lives over to the Lord.

a. The author of this book together with his family, are committed believers in the Lord.

How about you?

b. We also are doing our best to lead others to the Lord.

How about you?

c. We read the Bible and pray regularly as a family as we realise that time is running out on this old earth.

How about you?

d. We are working at putting the Lord and others first in our lives, as this brings real satisfaction.

How about you?

It is quite a revolution isn't it?

You say, is all this possible in my life?

Yes!!

Is it difficult to get into this new pattern of living?

No!!

Why?

Because there are tens of thousands of persons making this choice for the Lord even as you read.

Soon, there will break out the largest spiritual revival that the earth has ever witnessed.

It happened in Los Angeles in the early 1900's.

It happened in Wales in 1904.

It will happen in your country soon.

The prophets did not lie.

'And it shall come to pass afterwards that I will pour out my spirit upon all flesh...' *Ref.10.

If you sincerely wish to be part of this final earthly movement of the Spirit of God, you'll need to join His family.

It needs to be a new birth experience.

INVITATION

It was a dark and foggy night in the streets of London.

A bobby on his beat came across a little ragged waif, huddled and crying under a street lamp.

He helped him to his feet and questioned him.

Policeman: 'What's your name son?'

Boy:	'Sammy, sir.'
Policeman:	'What's your father's name?'
Boy:	'Dad.'
Policeman:	'And what about your mother?'
Boy:	'Mum, sir.'
Policeman:	'That's no good. Do you know where you live.'

The boy thought for a moment, a large tear cutting a track down his dirty cheek.

Boy:	'No-o-o-o sir. Oh, wait a moment. There is a great big white cross at the end of our street.

IF YOU CAN LEAD ME TO THE CROSS, I WILL FIND MY WAY HOME FROM THERE.'

With the following information and prayer of salvation, I will lead you, the reader, to the Cross.

The Lord Jesus Christ will lead you home from there. Are you ready?

Remember, the price of blood has already been offered and in the words of Scripture:

'For God so loved the world *(your name).............. that He gave His only begotten Son (Jesus) that whosoever *(your name)............. believeth in Him (Jesus) should not perish (or go to hell) but have (not wait for, hope or think about) everlasting life.' John 3:16. (Words in brackets added for meaning.) *Put your name here.

It is as clear as that.

The Bible teaches that there are three steps, plus one, to possess this life from God.

Find a quiet place.

Kneel down, or get into an attitude of prayer.

(Sit if necessary.)

Start praying. Here are the three steps:

1. Repent of your sin. Turn to Jesus.
2. Believe that He died for you.
3. Receive Him – Invite Him into your heart. Plus –
4. Tell someone what you have done.

If you find that you do not know how to pray, here is the prayer of Salvation.

PART ONE:

(Say out loud) 'Lord Jesus Christ, I come to you now, because I am a sinner.

Today, Lord Jesus, I repent of my sin, I turn away from my sin, and I turn to you.'

PART TWO:

'I believe, dear Lord, that you died for me *(your name)................ I thank you Lord, because your blood covers all my sins. No one else can save me, only Jesus.'

PART THREE:

'Right now, I open the door of my heart (put your hand to your chest and open outwards). Come into my heart Lord Jesus. Wash me. Cleanse me, and make me your child. I receive you now by faith.

Help me to live for you every day until you come again.

I close the door (use your hand again, bring it back towards your chest) and Jesus is inside.

I thank you Lord Jesus, because today, by faith, I have received you and you have received me.

Amen.'

HERE IS THE PROMISE:

'To as many (anybody) as received Him (Jesus), to them gave He power to become the Sons of God.' John 1:12. (Emphasis added.)

Your choice this day gives you that power, and right, to call yourself a Son of God—Praise Him now in your own words.

Please fill in the certificate on the back page and then:

1. Copy it out again into the front page of your Bible.
2. Send another copy to me immediately so that I can send you further assistance.
3. Go and tell someone what you have done.

'That if thou shalt confess with thy MOUTH, the Lord Jesus, and shalt believe in thine HEART that God has raised Him from the dead, thou shalt be saved.' Romans 10:9. (Emphasis added.)

That which is in your heart, must come out of your mouth.

This is your starting point.

Now: Steps to help you continue on for Christ.

1. Pray daily.

417

2. Read your Bible daily. Start in John's Gospel, because it speaks about salvation and everlasting life.
3. Witness, or tell others about Christ.
4. Link up with a Bible-based Christian group or Church.
(I may be able to help you here as I have friends in many different groups and denominations.)

WELCOME TO THE FAMILY OF GOD. I look forward to meeting you up there.

Your friend,
Barry Smith.

Some helpful Steps:
1. Go to your Christian bookshop and learn about the spiritual revival that is coming soon. Buy the little booklet 'He Will Tell You Things To Come' or write to 'Derek Prince Ministries', P.O. Box 2029, CHRISTCHURCH, NEW ZEALAND. Ph: 664 443.
2. Get involved with a lively born-again loving Christian group.
3. Be baptised by immersion.
4. Seek for and receive the baptism in the Holy Spirit, and stay filled with the Lord's love, daily.
5. Become a witness for the Lord. Don't be afraid. If you are not accepted by one, prayerfully seek out another person.
6. Learn the sinner's prayer off by heart and use it to help others.
7. Find a Christian friend of like mind and read the Scriptures aloud one to the other and discuss them.

As boys my friend David Garratt and I used to read the Bible aloud one to the other. Today, we are both serving the Lord.

'Faith cometh by hearing and hearing by the Word of God.'
*Ref.11.

In order that you may never forget this great day, I include here a copy of your New Birth Certificate.

418

At................ on ....
        (Time)   (Date)

I.......................................
        (Name)

received the Lord Jesus Christ as my own Saviour.
I thank Him.

Signed:......................

At................ on ....
        (Time)   (Date)

I.......................................
        (Name)

received the Lord Jesus Christ as my own Saviour.
I thank Him.

Signed:......................

At................ on ....
        (Time)   (Date)

I.......................................
        (Name)

received the Lord Jesus Christ as my own Saviour.
I thank Him.

Signed:......................

Answer to puzzle in Chapter 13 — There were 6 'F's.

REFERENCES

Chapter 3   Ref.1. — Prov. 22:7

Chapter 4   Ref.1. — Gen. 11:6-9
             Ref.2. — Deut. 29:29
             Ref.3. — 2 Thess. 2:6-7
             Ref.4. — Dan. 9:27
             Ref.5. — Rev 20:15
             Ref.6. — Rev 17:8

Chapter 5   Ref.1. — Ps. 61:2
             Ref.2. — Acts 1:8b
             Ref.3. — Dan. 12:10b
             Ref.4. — Deut. 33:27a
             Ref.5. — Heb. 13:8
             Ref.6. — Prov. 22:7

Chapter 6   Ref.1. — Jas. 5:4

Chapter 7   Ref.1. — Gen.12:3a

Chapter 8   Ref.1. — Amos 4:12b

Chapter 9   Ref.1. — 2 Tim. 1:7
             Ref.2. — 2 Cor. 5:10
             Ref.3. — Jn. 14:6
             Ref.4. — Jn. 1:12
             Ref.5. — Isai. 55:6-7

Chapter 11   Ref.1. — Ps. 2:1-3
             Ref.2. — Ps. 2:4

Chapter 14   Ref.1. — Isai. 57:20-21
             Ref.2. — Isai. 53:6a

Chapter 15   Ref.1. — Lk. 21:5-6
             Ref.2. — Lk. 21:27
             Ref.3. — Lk. 21:28
             Ref.4. — Rev. 1:9b
             Ref.5. — Rev. 13:1a

Chapter 17   Ref.1. — Gen. 1:11

Chapter 18   Ref.1. — 2 Cor. 5:10?

Chapter 37   Ref.1.—Gal. 3:13
                 Ref.2.—Dan. 8:25
                 Ref.3.—Dan. 11:21b
                 Ref.4.—Dan. 9:27a
                 Ref.5.—Isai. 14:12a
                 Ref.6.—2 Cor. 4:3&4a
                 Ref.7.—2 Cor. 4:4b
                 Ref.8.—Rev. 18:15&18
                 Ref.9.—Rev. 6:5-6
                 Ref.10.—Rev. 6:7-8
                 Ref.11.—Isai. 59:19b
                 Ref.12.—Jer. 17:9a
                 Ref.13.—1 Thess 5:3

Chapter 38   Ref.1.—Gen. 11:6b&8a
                 Ref.2.—2 Cor. 5:17

Chapter 39   Ref.1.—Dan. 7:24,20,8

Chapter 40   Ref.1.—Dan. 2:42
                 Ref.2.—Hab. 2:42
                 Ref.3.—Hab. 2:7
                 Ref.4.—Rev. 17:12
                 Ref.5.—Rev. 17:13
                 Ref.6.—Dan. 2:43
                 Ref.7.—Rev. 17:17
                 Ref.8.—Dan. 11:36a
                 Ref.9.—Rev. 17:14
                 Ref.10.—Rev. 19:20
                 Ref.11.—Rev. 17:10b
                 Ref.12.—Dan. 2:45b

Chapter 41   Ref.1.—Prov. 22:
                 Ref.2.—Deut. 21:18-21
                 Ref.3.—Prov. 20:27
                 Ref.4.—Josh. 24:15 partial
                 Ref.5.—Jer. 17:9
                 Ref.6.—Prov. 22:15
                 Ref.7.—Prov. 22:6
                 Ref.8.—Prov. 13:24
                 Ref.9.—Prov. 19:18
                 Ref.10.—Prov. 23:13-14
                 Ref.11.—Prov. 29:15
                 Ref.12.—Gal. 2:20—a song based on this verse

Chapter 42	Ref.1.—Prov. 22:28
	Ref.2.—Matt. 18:7
	Ref.3.—Hos. 8:7a
Chapter 43	Ref.1.—II Pet. 3:8b
	Ref.2.—1 Jn. 5:12a
	Ref.3.—Jn. 1:9
	Ref.4.—Rom.6:23a
	Ref.5.—Matt. 10:28
	Ref.6.—Jude 6
	Ref.7.—Ps 85:10
	Ref.8.—Rom.10:13
	Ref.9.—II Tim. 3:7
	Ref.10.—1 Pet. 3:7
	Ref.11.—Gen. 1:26a
	Ref.12.—Gen. 2:18
Chapter 45	Ref.1.—Mk. 16:16-17a
	Ref.2.—Eph. 6:12
	Ref.3.—II Thess. 2:8
	Ref.4.—Rev. 16:13-14
	Ref.5.—Deut. 18:20
	Ref.6.—Deut. 18:21-22
	Ref.7.—Deut. 29:29a
	Ref.8.—Rev. 12:12b
	Ref.9.—Mk 16:17a
	Ref.10.—Matt. 24:24
Chapter 46	Ref.1.—Prov. 14:12
	Ref.2.—Prov. 23:7a
	Ref.3.—Phil. 4:8
	Ref.4.—Eph. 4:15
	Ref.5.—Matt. 24:23
	Ref.6.—1 Thess. 4:16a
	Ref.7.—Prov. 23:2
	Ref.8.—Rev. 6:5
	Ref.9.—Rev. 6:6a
	Ref.10.—Prov. 29:25a
	Ref.11.—Isai. 51:12 portion
	Ref.12.—Prov. 5:22
	Ref.13.—Ps. 40:2-3
	Ref.14.—Jn. 14:6
	Ref.15.—Isai. 5:20
	Ref.16.—II Thess. 2:10b-11a
	Ref.17.—Ezek.18:25
	Ref.18.—II Thess. 2:12

423

Chapter 47   Ref.1. — Prov. 14:12
              Ref.2. — Acts. 4:10a & 12
              Ref.3. — Gen. 3:5
              Ref.4. — Jn. 1:29
              Ref.5. — Lk. 17:26

Chapter 48   Ref.1. — Gen. 28:15
              Ref.2. — Deut. 30:3
              Ref.3. — Isai. 31:5
              Ref.4. — Isai. 66:8
              Ref.5. — Ps. 83:1
              Ref.6. — Ps. 73:2
              Ref.7. — Ps. 73:13-14
              Ref.8. — Ps. 73:17
              Ref.9. — Ps. 73:18
              Ref.10. — Isai. 43:6
              Ref.11. — Zech. 12:3
              Ref.12. — Isai. 27:13
              Ref.13. — Zeph. 3:10
              Ref.14. — Matt. 11:28
              Ref.15. — Rom. 11:25b
              Ref.16. — Zech. 13:6
              Ref.17. — Jn 1:11-12
              Ref.18. — Jn 1:13

Chapter 49   Ref.1. — Matt. 5:34
              Ref.2. — Matt. 12:37
              Ref.3. — Gal. 3:13
              Ref.4. — Lk. 10:19
              Ref.5. — Matt. 26:24a
              Ref.6. — 1 Jn 1:7
              Ref.7. — Deut. 7:25-26
              Ref.8. — Ezek. 3:18
              Ref.9. — Ezek. 3:19

Chapter 50   Ref.1. — Matt. 8:22b
              Ref.2. — Acts 2:1
              Ref.3. — Acts 2:41
              Ref.4. — Acts 2:44-47
              Ref.5. — Rev. 2:2a
              Ref.6. — 1 Cor. 14:26
              Ref.7. — Rev. 2:6
              Ref.8. — Matt. 23:8-9
              Ref.9. — Matt. 23:11
              Ref.10. — Matt. 7:16a

Ref.11. — Rev. 2:10a
Ref.12. — Prov. 22:6
Ref.13. — Matt. 13:24
Ref.14. — 1 Pet. 5:3
Ref.15. — Matt. 16:16
Ref.16. — Matt. 16:18
Ref.17. — Eph. 2:19
Ref.18. — Eph. 2:20
Ref.19. — Rev. 2:13a
Ref.20. — Rev.2:14
Ref.21. — Matt. 13:31-32
Ref.22. — Jn. 8:32
Ref.23. — Ex. 20:4&5
Ref.24. — Deut. 7:25
Ref.25. — Rev. 18:2
Ref.26. — Rev. 2:20
Ref.27. — Rev. 2:22
Ref.28. — II Tim. 3:15
Ref.29. — 1 Jn. 2:1
Ref.30. — II Cor. 6:14
Ref.31. — II Cor. 6:17-18
Ref.32. — Matt. 13:33
Ref.33. — Rev. 4:4
Ref.34. — Rom. 1:17b
Ref.35. — Matt. 13:44
Ref.36. — Eph. 2:8-9
Ref.37. — Matt. 13:28-29
Ref.38. — Matt. 13:30
Ref.39. — Rom. 12:19
Ref.40. — Jn 11:26a
Ref.41. — Rev. 3:8
Ref.42. — Matt. 13:45-46
Ref.43. — Jn. 15:26
Ref.44. — Jn. 16:13a
Ref.45. — Judg. 16:20b
Ref.46. — Rev. 3:15-16
Ref.47. — II Tim. 2:4
Ref.48. — 1 Thess. 4:18
Ref.49. — Eph. 5:25
Ref.50. — Heb. 3:13
Ref.51 — Matt. 24:12
Ref.52. — Matt.24:24
Ref.53. — II Tim. 3:13
Ref.54. — Rom. 3:4
Ref.55. — Rev. 3:17&18a

Ref.3. — Heb. 12:14 paraphrase
Ref.4. — John 3:19

Chapter 56   Ref.1. — 1 Jn. 3:1-2 paraphrase
Ref.2. — II Cor. 12:4
Ref.3. — 1 Cor. 2:9
Ref.4. — Hos. 6:3
Ref.5. — Rom. 7:24b
Ref.6. — Eph. 5:27 middle
Ref.7. — 1 Pet. 1:8b
Ref.8. — Rom. 6:23a
Ref.9. — Heb. 1:14
Ref.10. — Isai. 55:6a
Ref.11. — Mk. 8:36

Chapter 57   Ref.1. — Isai. 7:14
Ref.2. — Matt. 27:33&35a
Ref.3. — Rom. 6:23
Ref.4. — Jn. 19:41
Ref.5. — Matt. 27:39
Ref.6. — Jn 3:16
Ref.7. — Eph. 2:7
Ref.8. — Rom. 14:7
Ref.9. — Matt. 10:32-33
Ref.10. — Joel 2:28a
Ref.11. — Rom. 10:17

Printed in the United States of America by:

Solid Rock Books, Inc.
979 Young Street, Suite E
Woodburn, Oregon 97071
Phone: (503) 981-0705
FAX: (503) 981-4742

A FREE catalog of other books, audio tapes and video tapes
is available upon your request.